A
GLOBAL
AGENDA

Issues Before
the 47th
General Assembly
of the
United Nations

A GLOBAL AGENDA

Issues Before the 47th General Assembly of the United Nations

An annual publication of the United Nations Association of the United States of America

John Tessitore and Susan Woolfson, Editors

University Press of America
Lanham • New York • London

Published by
University Press of America,®Inc.
4720 Boston Way
Lanham, Maryland 20706

3 Henrietta Street
London WC2E 8LU England

ISSN: 1057-1213
ISBN 1-880632-01-2 (cloth : alk. paper)
ISBN 1-880632-00-4 (paper : alk. paper)

Cover by Scott Rattray

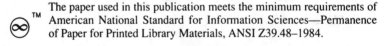

Contents

Contributors

José E. Alvarez (Legal Issues) is an Associate Professor of Law at George Washington University's National Law Center, where he teaches international law and international organizations.

Michael R. Chambers (Cambodia) is a Ph.D. candidate in the Department of Political Science and a member of the East Asian Institute at Columbia University.

Ivo H. Daalder (Arms Control), Director of Research at the Center for International Studies at the University of Maryland, is the author most recently of *The Nature and Practice of Flexible Response: NATO Strategy and Nuclear Forces since 1967* (1991) and *Arms Control in the Post-Cold War Era: The Need for a Cooperative Approach* (1992).

Russell M. Dallen, Jr. (Introduction to Making and Keeping the Peace; Other Colonial and Sovereignty Issues), Senior Fellow in Policy Studies at UNA-USA, holds degrees in law and international law from Columbia, Nottingham, and Oxford universities.

Leonard Doyle (Refugees) is the United Nations and New York correspondent for *The Independent* (London).

Josef Federman (International Space Year; Other Social Issues: Aging), a UNA-USA Communications Intern, studies at the Middle East Institute of Columbia University's School of International and Public Affairs.

Felice D. Gaer (The "USSR" and East and Central Europe; Human Rights) is Executive Director of European Programs at UNA-USA, and from 1982 to 1991 served as Executive Director of the International League for Human Rights.

Katrin C. Herrling (Other Social Issues: Crime), a UNA-USA Communications Intern, is a student of the European Business Programme, pursuing her studies at Kingston upon Hull, England, and Münster, Germany.

Charles Higginson (Law of the Sea) is Executive Director of the Washington-based Council on Ocean Law.

Jennifer L. Hobbs (Health; Other Social Issues: Shelter and the Homeless), a UNA-USA Communications Intern, recently completed a master's degree in international affairs at Columbia University, with a speciality in Russian Studies and in human rights.

Wendy Hsieh (Other Social Issues: Disabled Persons; The Status of Women), a UNA-USA Communications Intern, is specializing in international policy analysis and management at Columbia University's School of International and Public Affairs.

Christopher C. Joyner (Antarctica) is Professor of Political Science and a member of the Elliott School of International Affairs at George Washington University.

Craig Lasher (Population) is a senior policy analyst and legislative assistant at the Population Crisis Committee, a private nonprofit organization that works to expand the availability of voluntary family planning services worldwide.

Anthony Mango (Finance and Administration) worked for the U.N. Secretariat from 1960 to 1987. Between 1970 and 1983 he headed the secretariat of the Advisory Committee on Administrative and Budgetary Questions, and in 1983–87 he served as Secretary to the U.N. Pension Board. Since his retirement he has done consultancy work for the United Nations.

Martin M. McLaughlin (Food and Agriculture) is a consultant on food and development policy.

Jennifer Metzger (Environment and Sustainable Development) is UNA-USA's Public Affairs Coordinator and environment columnist of the Association's newsletter, *The InterDependent*.

George H. Mitchell, Jr. (Economics and Development) is Assistant Professor of Political Science at Tufts University and the Fletcher School of Law and Diplomacy.

W. Ofuatey-Kodjoe (Africa), Professor of Political Science at Queens

College and at the City University of New York (CUNY) Graduate Center, directs the CUNY Seminar on Contemporary Africa and the fellowship program of the University's Ralph Bunche Institute.

Edmund Piasecki (Central America; Cyprus; Information) is a former UNA-USA Research Associate currently working on multilateral issues in Washington, D.C.

Sterett Pope (The Middle East and the Persian Gulf) writes regularly on the Middle East for a number of publications.

Trevor Rowe (Afghanistan) is United Nations correspondent for *The Washington Post*.

John Tessitore (Co-Editor) is Director of Communications at UNA-USA.

Susan Woolfson (Co-Editor) is Managing Editor of Communications at UNA-USA.

Anastasia Xenias (Drug Abuse, Production, and Trafficking; Other Social Issues: Children and Youth), a UNA-USA Communications Intern, is specializing in international political economy and Western Europe at Columbia University's School of International and Public Affairs.

Preface

Reporting from U.N. Headquarters one January a few years back, the U.N. correspondent of *The New York Times* informed his readers that "From September to December every year, the United Nations stages its annual extravaganza at Turtle Bay. . . . But now the United Nations' finest hour is over. Hibernation has begun. The committee rooms are empty, the lounges deserted. . . . Like Gen. Guy Sternwood in Raymond Chandler's famous novel, United Nations headquarters is preparing to sleep the Big Sleep. . . ."

Although the reporter was indulging in a bit of hyperbole, no one would have argued his point, writing as he was in 1988. At the time, few if any U.N. observers saw that the geopolitical reformation just under way would soon transform the United Nations from an organization that looked asleep each January to one that quite literally never sleeps.

In 1992, covering the activities of the United Nations is a full-time, year-round job. Since the hectic days preceding the Gulf War, the Security Council has had an agenda of unprecedented size—and scope. This is one result of a new willingness by some states to enlarge the Security Council's traditional view of what constitutes a threat to peace and security, including such factors as human rights, mass movements of people, internecine warfare, and even the environment. Ironically, this new thinking—promoted largely by the West and resisted generally by developing nations, which are wary of all big-power maneuvers—has created a new sort of division at the United Nations, taking the place of the old East-West divide.

As the issues put before the Security Council have become more complex, U.N. peacekeeping missions have increased in number and kind. In war-ravaged Cambodia, Secretariat professionals, bolstered by U.N. peacekeepers and an international police force, are actually supervising the work of national ministries while a coalition of former warring factions attempts to govern the country as citizens prepare for elections. In Yugoslavia, peacekeepers and observers are struggling to implement the next step in conflict resolution following months of intensive negotiation under the leadership of U.N. Special Envoy Cyrus Vance. And in

Somalia, the scene of brutal and chaotic intratribal warfare, the U.N. is struggling to provide relief to a population that continues to suffer almost unimaginable hardship. To this, one adds the many ongoing missions in southern Lebanon, on the Golan Heights, between Iran and Iraq, on Cyprus, and more.

It is not by chance that the U.S. media and, in turn, the American public, are far more aware of U.N. activity than was the case in 1988. Today we cannot open our daily paper or turn on radio or TV without hearing news of the United Nations—a recognition of the crucial role that the world body has come to play in U.S. policy-making. But perhaps more notable than the *amount* of copy is the *nature* of the reporting. While we have long come to expect coverage of the world's hotspots, no one in 1988 would have dreamed that a national magazine would devote major space to a discussion of administrative reform at the United Nations itself (*Time*). Nor would one have anticipated a 15-minute examination of the election of a U.N. Secretary-General on a major evening news show (MacNeil/Lehrer). In short, the media have moved beyond the obvious story—beyond "sound bites" and perfunctory coverage of troops in the field—and they are taking a close look at how the U.N. system works, what it can and cannot do, what changes might be made, and—so very important—how it affects the lives of American citizens.

We at the United Nations Association, who have worked in these areas for many years, can only smile.

It is always our pleasure to acknowledge here the many men and women who have made this series possible. To our contributors, identified in the preceding pages, we extend our deep gratitude for a mighty load of work performed under less than ideal conditions—and for very little material reward. Obviously, it is their professional commitment that gives life to *A Global Agenda*.

Working with our authors are the gracious U.N. employees who aid them in their quest for information and documentation, and who offer constructive criticism of the texts to help us avoid embarrassing sins of omission and commission. To these international civil servants, so numerous that they must remain nameless, go our very real thanks.

And finally, it is always especially satisfying to express our appreciation to the cadre of communications interns who, as volunteers, devote so many working hours to the researching and development of this text. Tirelessly assisting authors, digging deep for elusive documents, tracking down precise dates, solving the mystery of contradictory information—even drafting shorter sections—these wonderful young people are an inspiration and a delight. And so our thanks go to Josef Federman, Daniel Grossman, Katrin Herrling, Jennifer Hobbs, Wendy Hsieh, David

Jensen, Fiona Middleweek, Matthew Rosenwasser, and Anastasia Xenias. With such a generation now coming into its own, the world has much to be hopeful about.

John Tessitore
Susan Woolfson

New York, 1992

I
Making and Keeping the Peace

Never before has it seemed that the United Nations was so popular with its member States. Never before have its services been requested with such frequency, not only its traditional role of peacekeeping and peacemaking, but in a new role, that of giving assistance to democratic institutions in the countries of the third world. And never before have the expenses incurred by our Organization in the service of peace been so great. Finally, never before have our funds been so low.

—Secretary-General Boutros Boutros-Ghali

Nineteen ninety-two was an exciting year for the United Nations, and 1993 promises to be yet another. After years of neglect the world body is decidedly back in vogue—and in the media. The 23-nation peace-enforcing operation in Iraq and Kuwait helped to give the Organization an aura of success and relevance. The 46th General Assembly saw the launching of large-scale peacekeeping missions in Iraq, Kuwait, Yugoslavia, Western Sahara, and Cambodia. A new Secretary-General, Boutros Boutros-Ghali of Egypt, took office as of the beginning of the year, giving the Organization a new face. And on January 31 the heads of the 15 Security Council nations met for an historic Summit, at which time they mandated the new Secretary-General to produce a far-reaching report by July 1 with recommendations for strengthening U.N. peacemaking, peacekeeping, and preventive diplomacy.

One of the first actions taken by the new Secretary-General was to **restructure the Secretariat**—eliminating 14 senior posts and concentrating the decision-making process in seven key departments. The actions of the new Secretary-General during his first six months in office indicate that although there has been a great deal of discussion in recent years about amending the U.N. Charter, member states can have a stronger Organization by implementing the collective security provisions of the existing Charter and by making creative use of Charter provisions.

An area that may eventually require **Charter revision** was highlighted at the Security Council Summit. There Japan—currently a non-permanent Council member—used its opportunity to press for a reform issue dear to its heart: permanent Japanese **membership in the Security Council.** "It is important to consider thoroughly ways to adjust the Security Council's functions, composition and other aspects so as to make it more reflective of the realities of the new era," said Japanese Prime Minister Kiichi Miyazawa. "This is a process in which Japan is prepared to take an active part" [S/PV.3046].

Japan currently pays 12.45 percent of the regular U.N. budget, second only to the United States, which pays 25 percent. And in June 1992 the upper house of the Japanese Diet approved a long-debated and highly controversial bill that allows up to 2,000 Japanese soldiers to join the troops of other nations in U.N. peacekeeping operations abroad, though in noncombative capacities only. Opposed by Social Democrats and Communists, who believe it contradicts Japan's pacifist constitution, the bill won the support of a growing number of Japanese who believe their country should assume a greater political role in global affairs [*The Economist*, 6/13–19/92].

Anticipating some changes to the composition of the Security Council in the not too distant future, the United Nations Association of the USA has suggested the creation of a **third category of Council membership,** to consist of **four reserved seats**—one for each of the world's major regions. The two largest states in each region would alternate in filling the region's "semipermanent" seat. Currently those regional powers appear to be Egypt and Nigeria in Africa; Brazil and Mexico in the Americas; India and Japan in Asia; and Germany and Italy in Europe. It seems possible that such a "reserved alternation" could be informally incorporated into the existing rotational system. Because the remaining U.N. member states may not agree to a dimunition of their opportunity for nonpermanent membership (currently there are ten nonpermanent seats, with five nations chosen each year for a two-year term), Council membership may have to be expanded by four, to 19 [Edward C. Luck and Toby Trister Gati, "Whose Collective Security?" *The Washington Quarterly*, Spring 1992].

The demand for U.N. peacekeeping operations has increased dramatically in recent years. Prior to 1988 the United Nations launched 13 peacekeeping operations; since that time it has established an equal number. And, as conflicts between and among ethnic groups pose an increasing threat to international peace and security, it is clear that the Organization will be called on to do even more. In 1992 the United Nations began to deploy peacekeepers and other staff in Cambodia and Yugoslavia, the second and third largest operations in its history. From January to June 1992 the number of **U.N. peacekeepers deployed in the field quadrupled,** from 11,500 to 44,000. While it is too early to evaluate some of the operations, the scorecard appeared mixed at mid-year.

In **El Salvador,** the United Nations has been extremely successful, negotiating a peace accord, which was signed in Mexico on January 15, 1992. In the wake of its success, the U.N. Observer Mission in El Salvador (ONUSAL) received an enlarged mandate to help rehabilitate the country and train a new police force.

Launched on February 28, 1992, the U.N. operation in **Cambodia** is the most ambitious yet, with the U.N. Transitional Authority in Cambodia (UNTAC) supervising the day-to-day administration of the country, helping to repatriate over 360,000 refugees, and preparing for elections in the spring of 1993.

In **Somalia,** where bloody civil war has plagued the country for the past two years, the United Nations established the U.N. operation in Somalia (UNOSOM) in April 1992. In May, UNOSOM was able to bring about a cease-fire, and U.N.-chartered ships were able to bring food into Mogadishu. The Secretary-General has appointed a Special Representative, Mohammed Sahnoun, former Deputy Secretary-General of the Organization of African Unity, to work toward a solution to the conflict.

In **Yugoslavia** the United Nations has been less successful. There the Organization decided upon a division of labor: The European Community (EC) would handle the political problems, and the United Nations would deal only with peacekeeping, in this instance the U.N. Protection Force (UNPROFOR). Unfortunately, the EC and the United Nations were long unable to negotiate a lasting cease-fire, though at mid-year there was some hope that a new cease-fire might hold and that relief flights would be allowed to land at the airport in Sarajevo.

In **Afghanistan** the United Nations worked for many months to prepare a peace plan, but in April 1992 a military coup ousted President Mohammed Najibullah and, with him, the U.N. peace plan. In **Western Sahara,** where the Polisario have fought a long war of independence against Morocco, the United Nations met with similar difficulty. The U.N. Mission for the Referendum in Western Sahara (MINURSO) failed to hold a referendum at the beginning of 1992 on the future of the territory. In a bid to reactivate the stalled peace process, Secretary-General Boutros-Ghali appointed a new Special Representative, Yaqub Khan, former Minister of Foreign Affairs of Pakistan. Khan is hopeful that elections can take place in 1993. Finally, in the dispute between **Armenia and Azerbaijan** over the **Nagorno-Karabakh** enclave, the United Nations and the Conference on Security and Cooperation in Europe (CSCE) remained unsuccessful at mid-year in resolving that violent conflict.

Of course all of this activity costs money—a lot of money—and that is hampering the effectiveness of many operations. In 1987 the U.N. member states were asked to pay $233 million for peacekeeping. In 1991 that figure was $421 million. In 1992 members will pay about $2.7 billion. One of the Organization's biggest problems continues to be finances. Many operations were delayed because of funding shortages. Others were hampered in the field, with U.N. peacekeepers having to beg for housing from the very governments with which they were trying to be tough. During the first five months of 1992, unpaid assessments for the regular budget and for peacekeeping more than doubled, from $816.6 million to $1,898.7 million.

The U.N.'s financial difficulties have been exacerbated by the increased number of peacekeeping operations as well as by **delays in member states' payments**—particularly by the major contributors—for these operations and for the regular budget. Throughout 1992 short-term loans between and among certain peacekeeping operations were necessary to cover the daily operational requirements of other peacekeeping accounts. As of June 1, 1992, only 14 member states had fully paid their assessments for both the regular budget and peacekeeping operations. These nations were Austria, Bhutan, Botswana, Canada, Denmark, Finland, Ghana, Liechtenstein, Malaysia, Namibia, the Netherlands, New Zealand, and Sweden.

1. The "USSR" and East and Central Europe

When the 46th General Assembly began, the post-Communist states of East and Central Europe brought their problems onto the U.N. agenda with a flourish. For the world body's first 45 years, it did not address Europe's problems because of cold war rivalries. The peaceful transitions in East and Central Europe in late 1989 brought a congratulatory euphoria to the 45th Assembly's General Debate in 1990. But by late 1991 the 46th Assembly was presented with a more complex situation: Ebullience was expressed over the failure of the coup in the USSR, yet a sense of trepidation and uncertainty was evident because of the direction events had turned in Yugoslavia, where a full-blown ethnic/national civil war had been in progress since June of that year. Furthermore, the economic needs of the East and Central European states were by then recognized as much greater than initially thought, and the Eastern bloc states were now increasingly viewed as competitors with the Third World for development assistance and investment—no small concern for an organization already polarized by North-South conflicts.

Yugoslavia

No U.N. initiative to resolve a conflict has highlighted as many problems of the "new world order" as has the situation in the former Yugoslavia.

When the 47th General Assembly convenes in September 1992, the heads of state and foreign ministers will undoubtedly still be faced with this situation and the perplexing challenges it has posed to the world body.

The United Nations undertook action on Yugoslavia in support of efforts by the European Community to reach a negotiated political settlement of the conflict. The United Nations proposed a division of labor between the two organizations, agreeing only much later—and with considerable doubt whether the proper conditions prevailed—to conduct a peacekeeping operation in Croatia. This operation, more than any other, has revealed the limits of the U.N. concept of peacekeeping. Two U.N. Secretaries-General and their staffs have made it clear throughout—and particularly by April and May when the Bosnian situation was in turmoil—that peacekeeping must be based on a political agreement among all parties to maintain a genuine cease-fire. U.N. peacekeeping, they explained, is not "peace-enforcement," in which a heavily armed U.N. military force quells an insurrection and unblocks roads, airports, and communications routes, etc. Such an operation, they went on to say, requires far more personnel, equipment, and expense than is associated with peacekeeping, and would probably entail substantial loss of life. Chagrined by the critical public reaction when Secretary-General Boutros Boutros-Ghali called for a pull-out of peacekeeping troops from Bosnia in May 1992 because of unsafe conditions, the Security Council called on him to do more [S/Res/752] and later adopted sweeping sanctions against Serbia, suggesting that the Council might yet undertake enforcement measures needed to establish a "security zone" at Sarajevo airport and to assure that humanitarian assistance gets through to those needing emergency help [S/Res/757].

Initially, in September 1991, the Yugoslav civil war was an internal conflict. Still, European nations argued that it posed a threat to regional peace and security as evidenced by a significant refugee flow into neighboring countries, overflights of some of those countries, and, most significantly, the belief that, if unchecked, the conflict would spread to neighboring states. The 12 nations of the European Community, like the post-Communist states of East and Central Europe, told the 46th General Assembly that unless the "authoritative voice" of the Security Council was sounded, and a mandatory arms embargo was imposed, this conflict and others like it would envelop the region. France's Foreign Minister put it simply: "The conflagration is building and threatens to spread. Time is running out" [A/46/PV.6].

Days after the 46th Assembly convened, the Security Council took action on the civil war at a meeting attended by foreign ministers (September 25, 1991). Its **first-ever resolution** [S/Res/713] **imposing Chapter VII sanctions (an arms embargo) in Europe** was controversial because it identified the three-month-old civil war as a **threat to inter-**

national peace and security, thereby making it an appropriate subject of the Security Council's concern under Article 2(7) of the U.N. Charter. At that session, eight governments spoke about the decision to take action, with U.S. Secretary of State James Baker making the strongest speech in support of such action. Several members, among them Yemen, Zaire, and Romania, expressed doubts over the Council's "interference in internal affairs" in Yugoslavia. Others, including China, Cuba, and India, are reported to have expressed their doubts in private consultations. But all supported the resolution—adopted unanimously—once it had been requested in writing by the Foreign Minister of Yugoslavia, who addressed the Council at length.

Resolution 713 set out a role for the United Nations in "full support" of the "collective efforts for peace and dialogue in Yugoslavia" undertaken under the auspices of the European Community, which had been engaged in a number of efforts to monitor and mediate the conflict, and "with the support of . . . the Conference on Cooperation and Security in Europe." Yugoslavia was not a member of the EC, but it was a member of the Conference on Security and Cooperation in Europe (CSCE). The resolution referred, in its preambular paragraphs, to Chapter VIII of the U.N. Charter, which specifies cooperation with regional organizations.

In addition to the mandatory arms embargo, the resolution appealed for the peaceful settlement of disputes and urged parties to honor recent cease-fire agreements and to negotiate through the EC-sponsored Conference on Yugoslavia. These themes were to be repeated in subsequent resolutions. Beginning what was to be a lengthy and delicate process of U.N. involvement, Resolution 713 "invited" the Secretary-General "to offer his assistance without delay" and to report back.

After meeting with foreign ministers and making a public "appeal" to all parties on October 2, Secretary-General Javier Pérez de Cuéllar announced the appointment of **Cyrus R. Vance,** former U.S. Secretary of State, as his **Personal Envoy on Yugoslavia.** Vance set out on October 11, 1991, for the first of what would turn out to be seven missions to Yugoslavia by May 1992. Over the next eight months the extraordinary efforts of Vance and his associates were to lead the United Nations to broker the only cease-fire in Croatia that seemed to hold, and to develop a plan, which they later implemented, to deploy an unusually large peacekeeping operation—consisting of some 14,000 persons—in the ethnically mixed but Serb-dominated Croatian territories of Eastern and Western Slavonia and Krajina, which were named "U.N. Protected Areas." That force, the **U.N. Protection Force (UNPROFOR),** was assigned to oversee maintenance of a cease-fire, the demilitarization of the conflict areas, and an easing of ethnic tensions by assuring equitable law enforcement in areas where armed conflict raged. Although its focus was always the problematic territories in Croatia, it was decided to put the headquarters of UNPROFOR in Bosnia-Herzegovina in a largely symbolic effort to forestall conflict in the ethnically diverse republic. Later, UNPROFOR itself became a target in Bosnia-Herzegovina, where the pattern of violence seemed to be a replay of the aggression that had previously rocked Croatia.

By the time the Security Council adopted far-reaching economic and other sanctions on May 30, 1992 [S/Res/757]—its ninth substantive resolution on the Yugoslav conflict (not counting three resolutions on admission of Slovenia, Croatia, and Bosnia-Herzegovina to the U.N.)—the situation had changed considerably. With the U.N. peacekeeping force nearly fully deployed, the Croatian situation seemed at an uneasy calm, but Bosnia-Herzegovina had spiraled out of control following international recognition of the republic in spring 1992.

Whereas there had been no public debate at the Security Council on the resolutions adopted since the September meeting, with **Resolution 757** imposing sanctions every member of the Council spoke publicly, explaining its vote. Since September the principal site of armed conflict had changed from Croatia to Bosnia-Herzegovina, and many nations (China, Hungary, Japan, and India) commented on the fact that the situation had deteriorated greatly in only a few weeks. Furthermore, technically, for the United Nations **the conflict was no longer an internal one** that "threatened" the peace of the region. By May it was indisputably considered an international conflict: The former Yugoslav republics of **Slovenia, Croatia,** and **Bosnia-Herzegovina** had been recognized as **independent states** by the international community and **admitted to the United Nations** in late May.

As Venezuela reminded its colleagues in the strongest affirmation of this new situation by a Security Council member, "Yugoslavia is no longer in the midst of a civil war. . . . Belgrade is today waging war against other states, sovereign members of our organization." Zimbabwe, while recognizing this change, expressed its annoyance with the United Nations, reminding the Council members that they had originally explained that any recognition of the former Yugoslav republics as independent entities would occur only in the context of an overall political settlement—and that the Secretary-General had himself warned in December that premature recognition was dangerous. The world body, Zimbabwe charged, was now facing the consequences of its premature recognition.

The conflict, however, was still seen as a dangerous threat to the other countries in the region—all the more so since the USSR had dissolved in the midst of the Yugoslav crisis, giving rise to a dozen new states already enveloped in ethnic disputes, some of which had led to armed conflict. Speaking at the May 30 meeting, Belgium warned that

Yugoslavia demonstrated "the path that should not be followed"; the Russian Federation (facing its own problems) called it a "real threat to the countries of the region" and to international peace and security; and the United States cited its "grave challenge" to the principles of the U.N. Charter itself.

Few could forget that World War I began in Sarajevo, the capital of Bosnia-Herzegovina, and that as Yugoslavia dissolved, neighboring states such as Greece and Albania had already entered into substantial disputes over the disposition of its once-united lands. For its part, **Hungary,** a member of the Security Council, which is concerned about the 400,000 Hungarians in the Vojvodina province of Serbia, had complained bitterly not only of overflights and a massive refugee flow across its borders but also of the poor treatment of the Hungarians in Vojvodina. With fierce attacks on Muslims in Bosnia-Herzegovina, and the potentially explosive situation in the Albanian-dominated Kosovo region of Serbia, concern over possible Turkish and Albanian involvement heightened.

The fact that the Yugoslav conflict is so heavily based on ethnic and national animosity makes it particularly troublesome for the region—a complex quilt of ethnic, linguistic, national, and religious minorities, where borders have repeatedly changed over the centuries. And while several countries have expressed concern about the need to protect the human rights of all minorities, and UNPROFOR's concept paper addresses this matter, it has not been a major focus of diplomatic or Security Council attention.

In contrast, the **humanitarian crisis** resulting from the Yugoslav conflict became a major focus of U.N. concern in May. Not mentioned at all in the September resolution, the topic was first addressed in the Secretary-General's reports following each of the Vance missions. Initially, the United Nations reported that in addition to over 40,000 refugees in neighboring countries, more than 900,000 persons were internally displaced from the conflict in Croatia [S/23836, 4/24/92]. By May 12 the Secretary-General stated that over 520,000 persons had been displaced in Bosnia-Herzegovina (12 percent of the republic's population); at the end of the month, he reported that displacements continued "on a massive scale." The Secretary-General confirmed that in Bosnia-Herzegovina these were often forcible deportations in which displaced persons had to sign documents stating that their departures were voluntary. He explained this situation candidly in his report of May 26: "For some of the parties the infliction of hardship on civilians is actually a war aim, as it leads to the desired movements of populations from certain areas. Therefore there appears to be a predisposition to use force to obstruct relief supplies" [S/24000, 5/26/92, para. 18]. He also explained that civilians trapped in the besieged cities were targets of both irregular forces and the **Yugoslav National Army (JNA).** Humanitarian aid shipments were commandeered, and relief workers harassed and killed.

Like other wars, Yugoslavia's horrific conflict has wrought a severe toll on the civilian population. In breach of humanitarian laws of war, human rights standards, and common decency, civilian targets (including such cultural treasures as the resort city of Dubrovnik and the mosques and historical buildings of Bosnia-Herzegovina) have been systematically bombed by the combatants. Amnesty International reports on the torture of prisoners taken by Serb, Croat, and Federal Army troops, as well as on the practice of summary and arbitrary executions. The International Committee of the Red Cross, which has brokered the release of thousands of prisoners, has been trying to facilitate joint efforts to bring humanitarian aid to the hundreds of thousands of the internally displaced. At the end of May the Secretary-General estimated that 300,000 to 400,000 people were in need of emergency relief [ibid., para 7.]. The U.N. High Commissioner for Refugees along with UNICEF and the World Health Organization (WHO) have taken part in efforts to bring relief to the civilian victims of this conflict.

In their discussion of sanctions, numerous members of the Security Council referred to the humanitarian situation. Venezuela singled it out as the "basic" reason for its vote in favor of sanctions, India stressed its concern and noted it had insisted that food and medical aid be exempted from any trade sanctions imposed, Hungary called the situation "catastrophic," while the United States termed it "of nightmare proportions." Even China, which abstained on the sanctions vote, mentioned its concern over the humanitarian situation, and Austria threatened that if the airport was not opened and aid delivered, "further measures" would be required.

Although the United Nations initially placed blame on all sides, citing Croatian incursions in parts of Bosnia, by May [S/23900, 5/12/92] the Secretary-General stated that all international observers had identified the principal aggressor as ethnically Serbian Bosnians. Serbs launched heavily armed operations to expel non-Serbs—particularly Muslims—from their homes, killing and bombarding civilians in efforts to create "ethnically cleansed" Serbian areas, which, it was believed, Serbia sought to annex. Again, speaking at the May 30 Council meeting, the United States called this "brutal aggression," India described itself as "horrified," and Morocco—speaking on behalf of the Islamic Conference—termed it "genocide" and "crimes and practices unprecedented except, perhaps, in the Dark Ages" [S/PV.3082, 5/30/92].

Resolution 757 noted the complexity of the Yugoslav situation and stated that "all parties bear some responsibility for the situation"; but it condemned the authorities in the "Federal Republic of Yugoslavia (Serbia and Montenegro)" for failing to comply with Resolution 752 of May 15, which demanded that all parties cease fighting and all outside interference in Bosnia and Herzegovina stop. In the debate, member states noted that the "authorities" in Belgrade bore the primary responsibility and were, in fact, the aggressor. Some states, including Britain and France, agreed with India that "no one among the adversaries is beyond reproach." At the same time, some of them also declared that, as Hungary put it, "we all know very well which party bears the overwhelming responsibility." The United States, as in September 1991, was the most critical of Serbia's role, speaking of its "aggression" against Bosnia and of "repression" in Serbia. But Sir David Hannay, the British Ambassador, was the most explicit. After noting that responsibility for the Yugoslav situation is "shared among many," he declared: ". . . there is really no doubt at all where the principal responsibility now lies: with the authorities, civil and military, in Belgrade. . . . It is simply no good suggesting that they have nothing to do with the events . . . in Bosnia and Herzegovina. Multiple rocket launchers are not found in Serbian peasants' barns. They are provided from the supplies of the Yugoslav National Army. They are munitioned from their supplies. . . . They are fuelled; they are paid for. . . . If the authorities in Belgrade really wanted us to believe their protestations of innocence, I doubt if they would be bombarding Dubrovnik today. They must think we are very stupid people indeed."

Summing up the Yugoslav experience at a May 18, 1992, Washington, D.C., press conference, Secretary-General Boutros Boutros-Ghali said the U.N.'s Yugoslav operation, on balance, was "not a success." In a subsequent report to the Security Council on the feasibility of protecting international humanitarian aid programs in Bosnia-Herzegovina [S/24000, 5/26/92], he proposed either (a) protection through respect for agreements, particularly new agreements on the provision of humanitarian relief like those agreed to in other conflict situations in the world, or (b) armed protection. As to the first, he noted the "lamentable" performance of the parties in Bosnia-Herzegovina in honoring their agreements. As to the second, he reminded the members of how "extremely difficult and expensive" such operations can be, and noted that any hostile or coercive action in Bosnia-Herzegovina might undermine cooperation of the parties with UNPROFOR in Croatia. Telling the Council it is for them to decide whether they wish to deploy troops, he nonetheless expressed his view that "a more promising course would be to make a determined effort to persuade the warring parties to conclude and honour agreements permitting the unimpeded delivery of relief supplies to all suffering civilians . . ." [para. 23].

The Security Council members, in imposing sanctions a few days later, persevered in their search for measures that might turn the operation into a success, but they left open options for unspecified stronger action. Like many in the media in the United States and abroad, they reflected publicly on the lessons learned from the efforts of the United Nations. Morocco, Cape Verde, and Venezuela chastised the world body for waiting too long to act, urging that such mistakes be avoided in the future. Yet China and Zimbabwe, which both abstained on the sanctions resolution, called for a longer delay—a warning period before sanctions were imposed (a view shared by India). Zimbabwe noted that it was time for the Council to go beyond peacekeeping and humanitarian operations, and for the Secretary-General to undertake peacemaking "actively." Looking ahead, Russia proposed that an international commission be set up to punish those responsible for "slaughtering civilians" and called for other decisive actions, including asking the Security Council to work out a set of criteria so that the Secretary-General can automatically trigger Council consideration of sanctions against those responsible for such bloodshed.

Commentators have reflected upon the comparative **role of the United States and the European Community** in addressing the conflict. Some have blamed U.S. disinterest in the early stages, whereas others have noted that it was only U.S. leadership that finally spurred the Council to action on wide-ranging sanctions. The European Community, which had sent—and then removed—an observer mission to the region, which had convened the unsuccessful Conference on Yugoslavia, and which had led the way toward early recognition of the former Yugoslav republics, seemed to many to be ineffective, albeit active. Still others have blamed the "atavism" and cynicism of **Serbian President Slobodan Milosevic,** who reportedly used the breathing space provided by UNPROFOR troops to redeploy and equip Serbs in Bosnia as part of his effort to create a "greater Serbia."

By June 8 relentless bombardment of Sarajevo had reached a fever pitch, and Bosnian President Alija Izetbegovic appealed to President George Bush for unilateral U.S. bombardment of Serbian gun positions in the hills overlooking the city [*The New York Times*, 6/9/92]. The U.N. Security Council met that day to respond to a new plan by the Secretary-General for reopening the Sarajevo airport for the delivery of humanitarian supplies. The Secretary-General, citing his responsibilities in Security Council Resolution 757, reported that on June 5, in "a significant breakthrough," an agreement had been reached among the parties and that he recommended a four-phase U.N. operation to implement the reopening of the airport. Initially, 60 military observers would supervise the withdrawal of anti-aircraft weapons, and—assuming the pact held—the United Nations would later dispatch a 1,000-person infantry battalion to ensure the immediate security of the airport. This would be followed by relief workers and civilian personnel whose job would be to help deliver goods and run the airport and, finally, by the actual opening of the airport for "humanitarian and official flights" [S/24075, 6/6/92].

The Security Council took a first step toward addressing the situation in Sarajevo when it endorsed this plan in a cautionary resolution—Resolution 758—on June 8. According to the resolution, the cease-fire observers could go forth promptly, if the Secretary-General wished, but it required the Secretary-General to return to the Council for the authorization to deploy the infantry battalion envisioned in phase two—and only after "an effective and durable cease-fire" was in place. By June 29 the Secretary-General was able to report formally to the Security Council on the "considerable progress" toward U.N. control of the airport: "Though an absolute cease-fire has not yet been achieved . . . UNPROFOR must seize the opportunity" [SG/SM/4773]. Shortly thereafter the Security Council authorized **a Canadian battalion** to secure the airport [S/Res/761], which was to receive initially some six to seven humanitarian flights daily. Meanwhile, the carnage away from the airport continued.

On June 30 the Secretary-General asked the Security Council to turn its attention to the increasingly unstable situation just outside the U.N. peacekeeping zone in Croatia. Resolution 762 established a new mechanism—a joint commission of UNPROFOR and Croatian authorities—to oversee restoration of Croatian authority in these troubled areas, referred to as "pink zones." In calling for this new action, the Secretary-General raised the prospect of the collapse of the whole U.N. plan in the region.

More than anything, the Yugoslav operation to date has revealed both the reluctance of the Western powers to use force to intervene in a turbulent, ethnically complex internal conflict and the limited role that traditional U.N. peacekeeping can play. The Secretariat, for its part, was so acutely aware of these limits, the cost-cutting pressures that delayed the operation, and the lack of agreement among the former Yugoslav parties to the conflict, that it drew public attention to these matters and called for withdrawal. Yet *The Washington Post* warned that "half-measures may turn out to be pathetic footnotes to the greatest collapse of common purpose in Europe since World War II" [5/29/92], and *The New York Times* stated that "U.N. peacekeepers have become a cover for Western inaction" [5/21/92].

It remains to be seen what further directions the Yugoslav operation will take. It may also serve as a basis for continuing to explore ways to make the United Nations more effective in addressing, and perhaps resolving, situations of ethnic or other internal conflict in post-Communist Europe and worldwide.

Security Council and Other U.N. Resolutions Concerning Yugoslavia
Security Council Resolution 713 (9/25/91):
Imposes mandatory arms embargo; appeals for peaceful settlement of

disputes; urges parties to honor recent cease-fire agreements; expresses full support for negotiations through the European Community-sponsored Conference on Yugoslavia; "invites" Secretary-General "to offer his assistance without delay" and to report back.

Security Council Resolution 721 (11/27/91):
Expresses hope that the Secretary-General can present early recommendations, including possible establishment of peacekeeping operation; endorses statement of Personal Envoy Cyrus Vance that peacekeeping cannot be envisaged without all parties first complying with the November 23, 1991, Geneva agreement calling for Croatia to lift its blockade of Yugoslavia National Army (JNA) barracks, and for JNA to leave Croatia.

Security Council Resolution 724 (12/15/91):
Approves Secretary-General's report containing concept paper for peacekeeping; declares that conditions for peacekeeping do not yet exist; endorses plan for small preparatory group, including military personnel, to prepare peacekeeping operation; sets up committee to review compliance with arms embargo and recommend measures to respond to violations.

Security Council Resolution 727 (1/8/92):
Welcomes the signing, under the auspices of the Secretary-General's Personal Envoy, of an Implementing Accord on January 2, concerning the modalities for implementing the unconditional cease-fire agreed to by the parties on November 23, 1991, in Geneva. Endorses the Secretary-General's recommendations to send advance group of 50 military liaison officers to promote maintenance of cease-fire.

Security Council Resolution 740 (2/7/92):
Increases advance team to 75 persons; urges expedited preparation for peacekeeping operation so that it can be deployed immediately following the Security Council decision; expresses concern that the U.N. plan is not fully accepted by all parties; urges cooperation with the Conference on Yugoslavia and compliance with the U.N.'s arms embargo.

Security Council Resolution 743 (2/21/92):
Establishes U.N. Protection Force (UNPROFOR) peacekeeping operation, recalling that it is an "interim arrangement to create the conditions of peace and security required for the negotiation of an overall settlement" of the Yugoslav crisis; urges earliest possible deployment; wants an operational budget that maximizes the portion that Yugoslav parties to the conflict pay; calls the Secretary-General to report back on the

operation within two months; urges efforts to ensure the safety of U.N. and EC personnel.

General Assembly Resolution 46/233 (3/19/92):
Appropriates $250 million for initial expenses of UNPROFOR.

Security Council Resolution 749 (4/7/92):
Calls for "earliest possible full deployment" of peacekeepers; approves the Secretary-General's plan for full deployment of UNPROFOR by mid-May 1992; urges parties and others to maximize contributions to help secure the most efficient and cost-effective operation possible; calls for full freedom of aerial movement of the force, and cooperation with the EC in achieving cease-fires and a negotiated solution to the conflict.

Statement by President of the Security Council (4/10/92):
Expresses alarm over rapid deterioration of situation in Bosnia-Herzegovina; reiterates Res. 749 appeal for end to fighting; asks Secretary-General to send Special Envoy to the region.

Statement by President of the Security Council (4/24/92):
Notes the deterioration in the situation in Bosnia-Herzegovina and demands all interference from outside cease; welcomes EC and Secretary-General efforts to obtain respect for April 12 cease-fire; notes decision to "accelerate" deployment in Bosnia-Herzegovina of 100 military observers from UNPROFOR; publicly condemns the use of force in Bosnia-Herzegovina; condemns all breaches of the cease-fire; urges three communities in Bosnia-Herzegovina to participate actively and constructively in EC talks on constitutional arrangements for Bosnia-Herzegovina; calls on parties to facilitate humanitarian assistance.

Security Council Resolution 752 (5/15/92):
Demands an end to all fighting, respect for cease-fire, and cooperation with EC in seeking negotiated settlement; demands that all interference from outside Bosnia-Herzegovina stop; demands respect for the territorial integrity of Bosnia-Herzegovina; demands that all parties cooperate with UNPROFOR and the EC Monitoring Mission and respect their safety; notes the urgent need for humanitarian aid and asks the Secretary-General to consider how he will provide protection for its delivery; demands that all regular and irregular forces in Bosnia-Herzegovina be disarmed and disbanded; asks the Secretary-General to consider how to disarm forces in Bosnia-Herzegovina and to consider the feasibility of a peacekeeping mission to Bosnia-Herzegovina; calls for an end to forcible expulsions and other attempts to change ethnic composition in former

Yugoslavia; notes that the full deployment of UNPROFOR is now achieved in Eastern Slavonia and requests their full deployment elsewhere.

Security Council Resolution 753 (5/18/92):
Recommends admission of Croatia to the United Nations.

Security Council Resolution 754 (5/18/92):
Recommends admission of Slovenia to the United Nations.

Security Council Resolution 755 (5/20/92):
Recommends admission of Bosnia-Herzegovina to the United Nations.

General Assembly Resolution 46/236 (5/22/92):
Admits Slovenia to the United Nations.

General Assembly Resolution 46/237 (5/22/92):
Admits Bosnia-Herzegovina to the United Nations.

General Assembly Resolution 46/238 (5/22/92):
Admits Croatia to the United Nations.

Security Council Resolution 757 (5/30/92):
Notes that all parties bear some responsibility for conflict; reaffirms support of EC negotiating efforts; deplores that "demands" on Resolution 752 have not been complied with; demands that any elements of Croatian Army in Bosnia-Herzegovina comply with Resolution 752; condemns the failure of authorities of Serbia and Montenegro and JNA to meet Resolution 752; decides that states shall adopt wide-ranging sanctions against the Federal Republic of Yugoslavia (Serbia and Montenegro), which include economic sanctions against trade in all but food and medicine for humanitarian purposes, an end to air transport unless specifically approved, reduced diplomatic staff in Yugoslavia, prohibition on "sporting contacts," and cultural, scientific, and other exchanges; demands that all parties create immediately "the necessary conditions for the unimpeded delivery of humanitarian supplies to Sarajevo and other destinations . . . including the establishment of a security zone encompassing Sarajevo and its airport. . . ."

Security Council Resolution 758 (6/8/92):
Noting the June 5 agreement among the parties to reopen Sarajevo airport for humanitarian purposes, enlarges the mandate and strength of UNPROFOR to take full operational responsibility for functioning and security of airport as recommended by the Secretary-General; authorizes the Secretary-General to deploy, when he judges it appropriate, 50

military observers, personnel, and equipment to Sarajevo to supervise the withdrawal of anti-aircraft weapons and heavy weapons to create security for reopening airport; requests the Secretary-General, once "an effective and durable cease-fire" is in place, to return for additional Security Council authorization before deploying an UNPROFOR infantry battalion to "ensure . . . immediate security of the airport"; strongly condemns all parties responsible for cease-fire violations; demands that all parties and others concerned create the necessary conditions—including compliance with the cease-fire agreement—for the unimpeded delivery of humanitarian supplies; demands that all parties and others concerned cooperate fully with UNPROFOR and international humanitarian agencies, taking all necessary steps to ensure the safety of their personnel.

The USSR Dissolves

The collapse of communism in the USSR following the failed coup in August 1991 also brought the dissolution of the multinational state known as the Union of Soviet Socialist Republics.

The Baltic States; Ukraine and Belarus

Among the first orders of business before the 46th General Assembly in September 1991 was the admission of **new U.N. members**—including the three Baltic states: **Estonia, Latvia, and Lithuania.** Their universal recognition as independent states began when Russian President Boris Yeltsin, the hero of the resistance to the attempted takeover, acknowledged the independence of the Baltic states only three days after the coup failed. The international community quickly followed his lead, forcing even the USSR to accept the new situation.

Following admission to the General Assembly, each Baltic state reminded the Assembly that its independence was smothered when the USSR illegally annexed the states under the infamous Molotov-Ribbentrop Pact of 1939. From their very first statements as U.N. members the Baltics have repeatedly demonstrated that their top priority in the world body is the **withdrawal of the troops of the occupying power—the Soviet Union.** In the months since then, they have issued letters to the Security Council, made speeches, and reiterated the centrality of this issue, hoping that First or Third World states would back their claims. Instead they have found that the USSR, and later the Russian Federation, has been able to block any substantive discussion of the topic in the Security Council. When asked to report along with all other U.N. members on measures to assure that no arms are transferred to Libya, Latvia, for example, pointed out that it could not provide such assurances since former Soviet troops were still on its territory and that it could not inspect the bases.

The Baltic states have gone so far as to raise the important question of whether the troops stationed in the Baltic republics are in fact under Russian control or are a dangerous military force unto itself. In a combined letter to the Security Council, the three countries charged that the troops in the Baltics undertake maneuvers (called harmful to the environment) without informing anyone in the Baltic governments, and also engage in such illegal activities as selling weapons and property and clearing forests [S/23756, 4/25/92].

In the discussions of self-determination in the Third Committee of the 46th General Assembly in 1991, many countries welcomed the Baltics, recalling their struggle for self-rule. By and large, these were states that had been silent on this issue during the years of Soviet occupation. The Netherlands, speaking on behalf of the European Community, welcomed the Baltic states to their "rightful place among nations" and asked that they pursue an open and constructive negotiation with the Soviet Union to settle outstanding issues between them [A/46/C.3/SR.3]. Egypt, Chile, Japan, Nigeria, Uruguay, Syria, and Tunisia all used the Baltic context to call the international community to action in other cases involving the right to self-determination. Statements by the Soviet Union reflected its acceptance of the changes within its own country brought about by the recent declarations of independence and national sovereignty by the majority of its republics. But the USSR also called attention to the accompanying strife between nationalities [A/46/C.3/SR.5].

Unless an agreed timetable for withdrawal is worked out with the Russian Federation before the 47th General Assembly, it is likely that the Baltic states will again focus their efforts on this issue at the Assembly, where they should be able to garner verbal support from the Third World. At the 1992 Conference on Security and Cooperation in Europe (CSCE) in Helsinki, the Baltic republics crossed swords with the Russian Federation (and some nongovernmental human rights groups) concerning Baltic citizenship laws aimed at assuring that the representatives of the "occupying power" do not automatically become citizens. Charges of discrimination (and even racism) have been leveled against the Baltics because of their treatment of the Russian-speaking populations in each country. It can be expected that this situation, and the status of minorities throughout the region, may be raised by the Russian Federation at the 47th General Assembly.

Ukraine and Belarus, which had been members since the world body's inception, began to demonstrate a much more independent position during the 46th General Assembly—even before the USSR dissolved entirely. This was most noticeable in the General Assembly's First

Committee (political and security issues), where Ukraine tended to take positions different from the USSR, particularly on nuclear questions.

From the USSR to Russia at the United Nations

All eyes were on Russia as the fall of 1991 progressed and the **Commonwealth of Independent States (CIS)** replaced the USSR. But few outside the United Nations ever realized the sleight of hand with which the Russian Federation—without any debate or vote—slipped into the Security Council and took over the USSR's permanent seat in that powerful body. On December 24, President Boris Yeltsin of Russia sent a letter to the United Nations stating that Russia, as the "continuing state" of the former USSR, would occupy the seat formerly held by the Soviet Union. The precedent he was following was that of "British India." With its independence from the British Commonwealth in 1947, India retained the U.N. membership of the former British India on the grounds that it was the continuing state. Pakistan, which split from British India, became a new member of the United Nations. The other ex-Soviet republics acted similarly, and all but Georgia had become new members of the world body by spring 1992.

Russia took this step in late December, when the General Assembly had already completed its work. In this way, with quiet encouragement from the United States and other permanent members, Russia was able to take over the Council slot without anyone raising the controversial issue of Security Council reform or enlargement. Yeltsin's letter went unchallenged and, in effect, was accorded the status of a legal instrument. There have been reports that China raised questions about the transition, but it chose not to obstruct it. After all, although the U.N. Charter states that the "Republic of China" is a permanent member, the world body long ago gave that seat to the "People's Republic of China" without worrying about the technical language of the Charter [Gertrude Samuels, "Russia Slips into the Soviet Seat," *The New Leader*, 2/10–24/92]. The change from the USSR to Russia was accomplished during the same month that Yuli Vorontsov, the Soviet Ambassador, was President of the Security Council. Russia asked him to stay on as its permanent representative.

Russian leaders have stressed their intention to use their privileged position to continue to place a high premium on the strengthening of the world body—expanding and strengthening the policy approach of the USSR's diplomats in the last few years. On January 27, 1992, Boris Yeltsin wrote to Secretary-General Boutros Boutros-Ghali stating that "The most important task facing [Russia] is the definition of its role in the maintenance and strengthening of international peace and security." Specifically citing the "special responsibility conferred on Russia by its status of permanent member of the Security Council," Yeltsin said that for Russia to perform "its unique historic mission" it needed stability within the former USSR and "constructive cooperation" with others to strengthen international security. And writing in the spring 1992 issue of *Foreign Affairs,* Russia's Foreign Minister, Andrei Kozyrev, stated that "Russia . . . intends to promote in every possible way the strengthening of the United Nations as an instrument to harmonize national, regional, and global interests."

The **Security Council Summit** of January 31, 1992, which was attended by 13 heads of state and two foreign ministers, served to formalize the international acceptance of Russia in the Council seat. Immediately after Yeltsin's speech, British Prime Minister John Major, sitting as President of the Council, stated: "I know the Council would wish me to welcome Russia as a permanent member of our Council. You are very welcome indeed" [S/PV. 3046, 1/31/92, p. 48]. Yeltsin thanked the world community for its support and for understanding that, as he put it, the future of the entire planet depends on the success of the reforms in Russia [ibid., p. 43]. Stressing the importance of human rights, he called upon the Security Council to underscore its responsibility to protect them. Noting the special role of the United Nations even in "the ice age of confrontation," he stressed the particular value placed on "the peace-making experience of the U.N." and averred that "the new Russian diplomacy will contribute in every possible way to the final settlement of conflicts in various regions of the world that have been unblocked with the assistance of the U.N. We are ready to become more fully engaged in these efforts." Stating that Russia would now participate in peacekeeping operations and contribute to their support, he endorsed the French proposal for a "special rapid response mechanism . . . to ensure peace and stability" [ibid., p. 47]. He promised that in the Security Council, Russia would be "a firm and steadfast champion of freedom, democracy, and humanism" and do all it can to achieve the goal of making current trends irreversible [ibid., p. 48].

The new flexibility of the **Russian Federation** has been seen in a number of areas, notably in its policy regarding **U.N. peacekeeping.** At a press conference immediately following the Summit, Yeltsin stated for the first time that Russia would welcome peacekeepers to help restore tranquility to the inflamed Nagorno-Karabakh region of former Soviet Azerbaijan. And, in keeping with Yeltsin's pledge to participate, Russia sent an infantry battalion to participate in UNPROFOR, the U.N.'s Yugoslav peacekeeping effort. The Russian Federation has spoken in support of the Cambodian peacekeeping operation, the largest in the Organization's history, noting that its success depends upon the commitment of the parties on the ground to peace and to the protection of human rights.

Both Yeltsin at the Security Council Summit in New York and

Kozyrev at the Conference on Disarmament in Geneva have stressed that the major difference in security matters today is that Russia regards its relationship with the United States and the West as one of partners, not adversaries. As a result, Russia's leaders have underscored the need to proceed to dismantle nuclear weapons, and to reassure Western countries that they are serious and responsible about this intention and that, despite the dissolution of the USSR, its nuclear force will not fall into unfriendly hands. (For example, Kozyrev told the Conference on Disarmament in February 1992 of Russia's proposal to separate launchers and warheads so they could not be fired without weeks' or months' notice; he also spoke of developing strong new laws on export controls.)

As elsewhere, however, the **economic and social** side of this equation loomed large among Russia's concerns. Yeltsin's message to the Conference on Disarmament was to remind the other states that the cold war had left behind mountains of weapons, huge armies, and defense-oriented industries employing millions of workers, and that Western cooperation was needed to cope with the economic and social needs of these people and to launch major initiatives to convert these industries [U.N. press release DCF/131, 2/13/92].

On the other hand, the Russian Foreign Minister, citing the need for a chemical weapons elimination treaty as a top priority, stated that Russia now faced extremely difficult problems involving the **destruction of its chemical weapons.** It has the technology to handle the problem, but democracy poses a new challenge: The main problem now facing Russia is to secure the consent of the population and local authorities in building appropriate facilities for chemical weapon destruction and waste disposal. Kozyrev appealed for Western help and international cooperation in resolving these matters. In view of the severe environmental degradation in the USSR, and the strength of popular organizations that have sprung up pressing for environmental safeguards and protections throughout the country, this will be a great challenge for the new government (see below for more on environment, Chernobyl, and aid).

Another new policy is Russia's strong **advocacy of implementation measures in U.N. human rights forums.** While a trend had been developing in this direction for several years, the USSR rarely took action on country-specific proposals, and tended to address the strengthening of legal instruments, or human rights treaties, rather than of ad hoc implementation mechanisms. Now, Russia sent a leading former dissident, Sergei Kovalev, Chair of the Russian Parliament's Human Rights Committee, to head its delegation to the Commission on Human Rights, and appointed as his deputy another former dissident and legal expert, Vyacheslav Bakhmin. Foreign Minister Kozyrev was sent to make a speech before the Commission in Geneva in which he praised international "interference" by human rights advocates, citing Amnesty International by name, and in which he called for ways to perpetuate the efforts of the U.N. Centre for Human Rights and of legal experts throughout the world to assess the conformity of past and new Russian laws with international human rights obligations. Exhibiting the kind of candor that distinguishes Russia from the USSR most vividly, Kozyrev said Russia still had to radically change past practices that led to human rights violations. Progress still needed to be made in his country regarding abuses affecting treatment of prisoners, soldiers, the disabled, the poor, and refugees from areas of interethnic conflict.

Reiterating the formula adopted at the September 1991 CSCE meetings in Moscow, Yeltsin told the Summit that human rights and freedoms "are not an internal matter of states" [U.N. press release 3046, p. 46]. The Russian Federation had been among the strongest advocates of the CSCE's new human rights monitoring procedure, which calls for mandatory observers to be sent when human rights violations are alleged.

At the 1992 session of the Commission on Human Rights, the Russian Federation became a vocal advocate of an Austrian proposal to establish a new emergency mechanism to permit the Commission on Human Rights to dispatch investigators to human rights crises when they occur, and of a U.S. initiative to assign an expert to monitor free elections—before and after they occur—as a means of strengthening democracy and preventing conflicts. Russia even called for a reexamination of the entire human rights agenda, which had grown increasingly polluted (diluted) with topics the USSR had championed years earlier as a way to decrease the U.N.'s emphasis on civil and political rights violations.

In many areas, however, Russia's positions mirror or only advance slightly beyond those of reformist Soviet delegations. This is noticeable, for example, in its emphasis on legally binding norms and legalization in various areas, its positions in the Special Committee on the Charter of the United Nations and on the Strengthening of the Role of the Organization (an ad hoc committee of the General Assembly), its call for U.N. Secretariat reform, etc. In these areas the Russian Federation's activism seems based on a view of a more effective world body, able to prevent conflict even if it means getting involved where few wanted an international organization active before, not excluding "internal matters."

In 1992 the Russian delegation has advocated that the United Nations pay greater attention to **humanitarian intervention** and institutionalize means of early warning of crisis situations, and it has emphasized that, as Sergei Ordzhonikidze told the Special Committee on the Charter, the "international community should work to resolve internal conflicts and should support democratic solutions to internal problems." It has called for regional organizations to take coordinated steps to strengthen human rights and the rights of minorities—a subject the USSR had argued it had resolved, but which has emerged as one of the great threats to the stability of the entire former Soviet bloc.

An indicator of the new Russian role at the United Nations comes in the appointment of **Vladidmir Petrovsky** as **Under-Secretary-General for Political Affairs.** Petrovsky, the former Deputy Foreign Minister of the USSR, is prominently associated with the USSR's initiatives to strengthen the United Nations during the period of *perestroika.* Russia's ability to propose new ideas and ways to strengthen the Organization seem unlimited, but they are at odds with the hard economic realities of a struggling power as it faces huge assessments to pay for the work of the world organization. Despite its good intentions, Russia has become second to the United States as the top debtor to the world organization, owing $138 million as of mid-May 1992 [U.N. press release SG/SM/4752, 5/18/92, p. 12]. Whereas the Baltic states and even Belarus have asked to have their assessments reviewed, seeking reductions, Russia, as a permanent member of the Security Council, has been more discreet. However, this will be an issue to watch during the 47th General Assembly.

Thus, it is perhaps not surprising that among the dramatic changes regarding Russia and the republics has been the attentiveness of each new state to **U.N. development programs and agencies** that can assist in economic reconstruction. In the past the USSR had been classified as a donor nation by the U.N. Development Programme (UNDP) and UNICEF. But in 1992 all the new states of the former Soviet Union except Tadzhikistan and Georgia (the latter, which had been in turmoil and where an elected government had been ousted early in 1992, was not a U.N. member as of June 1992) had requested and been given "recipient status" with UNDP. In May, Russia also asked for and received this status. Missions from UNICEF, WHO, the World Food Programme, and other agencies have evaluated the situation in the former Soviet Union and have begun planning their own efforts to assist in the economic transition in progress. As noted above, these programs, traditionally focused on the needs of the developing countries, are experiencing some tension over whether funds and human resources can or should be devoted to Russia and any of the other countries in transition. The outcome of this process for all the former Soviet states will no doubt be the subject of ongoing efforts at the 47th General Assembly and beyond.

The New States of the Former Soviet Union

Although the states of the former Soviet Union were admitted promptly to the Conference on Security and Cooperation in Europe (CSCE) in January, the United Nations took a bit longer to decide upon when and how to admit the republics. At the Security Council Summit, Boris Yeltsin stated that Russia supported the earliest possible admission of all the new republics to the world body. The Security Council considered the applications submitted by the various countries in February, and made its own positive recommendations, which were acted upon at the reconvened session of the 46th General Assembly on March 2, 1992. There, eight former Soviet republics were admitted into the world body [A/46/PV.82, 3/2/92].

Upon admission, representatives of each of the new member states assured the Assembly that they would abide by the solemn commitments and principles of the U.N. Charter, including the peaceful settlement of disputes and the nonuse of force. Several speakers lectured the former republics about the importance of these principles and commitments, with the main focus being turned to the armed conflict in the ethnic **Armenian enclave of Nagorno-Karabakh**, located within the borders of Azerbaijan—a long-standing source of conflict between Armenia and Azerbaijan, which has been in an acute phase since 1988. In the most formal presentation, Portugal, on behalf of the European Community, set forth all the prior references, by the President of the Security Council and through the CSCE, to the commitment to nonuse of force in settling disputes. Each of the five regional groups active in the world body greeted the new members, with the Latin American, East European, and West European groups also referring specifically to the obligation to settle disputes peacefully. The United States spoke specifically about the need for Armenia and Azerbaijan to cooperate with the mediation efforts launched by the Russian Federation's Foreign Minister, and the agreement of February 20 for the establishment of a cease-fire in Nagorno-Karabakh, the lifting of blockades in the region (Azerbaijan had long blockaded Armenia, and was not permitting humanitarian aid to reach Nagorno-Karabakh), and the return of "hostages," i.e., prisoners and civilians captured by each side to the conflict [ibid., p. 26].

Both Armenia and Azerbaijan referred to the conflict, in moderated tones, with Armenia reminding the Assembly that it supported the right of nations to self-determination, and Azerbaijan declaring its mourning over the very recent and brutal massacre of civilians in the Azeri town of Khojali—a town near the region's main airport from which multiple rocket launchers had fired daily upon the civilians in the enclave's capital city, Stepanakert. Earlier, when the Security Council had recommended admission of Azerbaijan, it had drawn special attention to Azerbaijan's obligation to settle disputes peacefully and, by implication, to end harassment and bombardment of Nagorno-Karabakh's Armenians.

Perhaps the most distinctive address of the welcoming session came from the departing Ukrainian Ambassador, who spoke on behalf of his country, Belarus, and the Russian Federation. He agreed with the numerous speakers who emphasized each country's obligation to peaceful dispute resolution, but pointed out that the United Nations has a reciprocal obligation, in their view, to use its peacemaking capacity "to promote a settlement of the conflicts and disputes which unfortunately still cast a shadow over certain new Members . . ." [ibid., p.61]. He then set forth a formula for ending the conflict—including an immediate cease-fire and full-scale talks that would include the participation of *all* interested parties (read: including the Armenian population of Nagorno-Karabakh, which had held a referendum and declared its independence from Azerbaijan not long after the Azeri leaders declared they would end the enclave's special administrative status—one of several events that local Armenians saw as a threat to their very existence). In tones reminiscent of Boris Yeltsin's January 31 press conference, the three republics now formally and specifically supported "the possibility of involving the peacemaking mechanisms of the United Nations. . . ."

Nagorno-Karabakh

Thus began a new phase of U.N. concern with ending the armed conflict in one of the former Soviet Union's hottest "hot spots"—Nagorno-Karabakh. Various appeals had been made by Armenia and nongovernmental organizations in prior years, particularly in 1991 when Soviet forces joined with Azerbaijani units in an attempt to forcibly deport Armenians from the region, and when random arrests and escalation of the armed conflict grew. But they remained unacknowledged and unanswered as long as the USSR existed—and opposed "interference" in what was still its internal affair. Once the two republics were admitted to the United Nations as independent member states, the dispute was viewed by the world body as an international one. By this time, however, the military conflict had grown dramatically.

With the demise of the USSR came the departure of Soviet troops, and vast arms supplies and equipment were turned over to local groups. Local Armenian "self-defense forces" seemed outnumbered and in danger—until the massacre of Azerbaijanis in the town of Khojali in late February 1992 and a distinct turn in military fortunes in favor of Armenians. Azerbaijan (as well as Turkey and Iran) began to urge the United Nations to take action, and on March 6, following the Secretary-General's meeting with the Azeri Foreign Minister in New York, the spokesman for Mr. Boutros-Ghali issued a statement in which he expressed deep concern at the continuing fighting and many deaths, and again called for a peaceful settlement of the dispute [U.N. press release SG/SM/ 4711, RFE/975, 3/6/92]. In the days following, some other delegations, including Ukraine, made public statements of concern about the conflict reaching a "critical point" and about the need for an immediate cease-fire. Soon thereafter, and quite unexpectedly, the Secretary-General announced that former U.S. Secretary of State **Cyrus Vance** would undertake a **fact-finding mission** to Nagorno-Karabakh. Vance's much publicized effort coincided with a similar endeavor by the Conference on Security and Cooperation in Europe. After his return, informal consultations in the Security Council led to agreement that the CSCE would take the lead in peacemaking—holding a peace conference and serving to provide third-party mediation—and that the United Nations would provide humanitarian assistance and other technical advice to the CSCE as requested.

While the CSCE was developing its plans for a peace conference and for dispatching a 100-person monitoring mission (akin to a peacekeeping force), the conflict grew in scope. Armenian self-defense forces from Nagorno-Karabakh achieved additional military victories, and by May 10—even as CSCE mediators tried unsuccessfully to enter the region—they took over Shusha, the last Azeri town in the region. Azerbaijan appealed to the Security Council to consider the "flagrant violation of Azerbaijan's sovereignty and territorial integrity" when Shusha was occupied and destroyed, and to restrain Armenia and prevent further escalation of the conflict [S/23894, 5/10/92]. On May 11, Armenia requested an emergency meeting of the Council to discuss the escalation of the conflict, the continuing blockade of Armenia, and—its greatest worry—the threat of potential outside intervention in the region. (Turkey had been dropping hints that it might intervene.) Armenia specifically asked the Council to dispatch peacekeeping forces to "the Nagorno-Karabakh Republic" and to take other measures. Referring to the frequent cease-fire agreements between Armenia and Azerbaijan and their almost instant violation, Armenia pointed out the lack of confidence of the local Armenian population in the enclave, and expressed the view that an international peacekeeping force was essential to provide the local inhabitants with the confidence that a permanent peace process and respect for their human rights would be assured [S/23896, 5/11/92].

Finally, on May 12, 1992, the Security Council did meet—for a total of four minutes. The President read out a rather general statement that had been agreed to in prior consultations. In it, Council members expressed their deep concern over the situation, commended and supported efforts taken by the CSCE and others, and welcomed the urgent dispatch by the Secretary-General of a fact-finding mission to the region, aimed at finding ways to assist efforts to reach a peaceful settlement. The mission team was also to contain experts to examine specific ways the international community could provide "prompt humanitarian assistance"—which reportedly had not yet been pursued despite the recommendations of the earlier Vance mission. The Council called on all parties to take all steps to end the violence. It recalled the statements about peaceful settlement of disputes made when the countries in question joined the world organization [S/23904, 5/12/92]. Shortly thereafter, Azerbaijan reported that Armenian forces had forged a humanitarian corridor from Armenia to Nagorno-Karabakh through the town of Lachin, calling this open "military aggression," in gross violation of Charter commitments. Threatening to escalate the conflict further, Azerbaijan warned that it "has sufficient force and the means to implement appropriate measures" [S/23926, 5/14/92]. As armed exchanges began in another region altogether—on the border of Armenia and the autonomous republic of Nakhichevan (part of Azerbaijan but sharing no common border with it), tension escalated. Efforts at the CSCE to obtain condemnation of Armenia failed when Armenia refused to agree to a text that deplored its actions; however, the **North Atlantic Assembly** adopted a critical statement. The Azerbaijanis circulated all of these in New York [S/24053, 6/2/92]. The United Nations, with its fact-finding mission then in the Nagorno-Karabakh region, was silent at this time.

During this period the internal political situation in Azerbaijan was in turmoil. Starting with the February massacre in Khojali, events in Nagorno-Karabakh seemed to have a decisive impact on ousting the former Communist President of Azerbaijan, Ayaz Mutalibov, and bringing member of the Azerbaijani Popular Front into positions of power. Matters became so confused that one day elections were on and the next day they were off, with Mutalibov restored to the presidential office. Thereafter, he was ousted again and the elections were rescheduled. During this time the United Nations continued to defer to the CSCE to take the lead role by convening an emergency session of its long-awaited Conference on Nagorno-Karabakh, which began on June 1. Meanwhile, on June 7 the opposition Azerbaijan Popular Front leader Abulfez Elchibey was elected president in the country's first free and contested election. It remains to be seen whether the approach of leaving the peacemaking to a regional organization without experience in such matters will prove successful. The U.N.'s own fact-finding mission has expressed doubt, arguing that the U.N. is better equipped at lower cost to mediate the conflict. For its part, the United Nations appeared to move very slowly and cautiously, without making its reports public or even taking on the humanitarian responsibilities it had promised to shoulder until June.

Throughout all this tension, other armed conflicts in the former Soviet Union—most significantly in the Trans-Dniester region in Moldova and in South Ossetia in Georgia—continued to rage. The Nagorno-Karabakh crisis was seen as a possible herald of other, similar conflicts throughout the troubled region, and some pressed for the United Nations to address it appropriately. Observers suggested that a U.N. overcommitment in Cambodia and Yugoslavia and its efforts in Somalia had now led it to be very cautious about taking on responsibilities for Nagorno-Karabakh. While the new Secretary-General's wings were somewhat clipped in this conflict—as well as others that might arise in the region—by the reluctance of the United States and other major donor countries to provide adequate financial support for peacekeeping operations, it was also related to the Secretary-General's deliberate decision to let regional organizations handle the *peacemaking* whenever possible, leaving the United Nations to take on technical *peacekeeping* or humanitarian actions only.

U.N. Aid to the Former Soviet Republics

The collapse of the USSR and the serious deterioration of social and economic conditions in the former Soviet republics led the United States to convene a conference, in January 1992 in Washington, to coordinate, accelerate, and expand international assistance to the newly independent states. The United Nations and six other international organizations were invited to participate, alongside 47 countries from the developed and developing worlds. The crisis, the United States pointed out, affected close to 300 million people in lands occupying a sixth of the world landmass, and was a global emergency requiring a global response. Critical emergency needs (food, health and medical supplies, shelter, and energy) were needed immediately. But so was technical assistance to meet the challenge of the transitions to market economies.

The United Nations participated in the conference, emphasizing its ability to act both in an emergency capacity and in assisting in the long-term transition/developmental process. Uncharacteristically, the U.N. system as a whole presented a combined paper, bringing together and highlighting the capacities of its many departments and specialized agencies. As expected, the major donors entrusted macroeconomic reform initiatives to the leadership of the International Monetary Fund and the World Bank. The Organization for Economic Cooperation and Development was assigned the task of coordinating policy advice and technical assistance, reversing the Group of Seven's earlier decision to entrust the Commission of the European Community with coordination of aid assistance by the 24 industrialized countries. NATO was designated the lead agency for logistics, transportation, and distribution.

Only in the area of medical assistance were U.N. agencies, specifically WHO and UNICEF, called on to play major roles. WHO was designated a possible clearing house for the collection, updating, and assessment of information on needs and medical aid programs, and for sharing information on any diversion of medical aid. UNICEF was recognized for its traditional role in emergency medical work. As for technical assistance programs in the new republics, U.N. officials felt that their abilities in this area would surely come into play, but for the moment most donor nations emphasized their own bilateral channels and agencies. The developing countries that were present at the conference did little to encourage the United Nations; on the contrary, they were fearful of exposing the U.N. system to the risk of seeing its resources diverted from the South to the East.

(Poland, Hungary, and Czechoslovakia proposed a form of "triangular trade" in which the West would buy goods from them and donate them to the former Soviet states, thus helping the economies of both areas. They also offered to make available their own experiences and lessons learned in the difficult transition to market economies.)

After the conference, U.N. agencies undertook a series of needs assessment missions and programs in the medical and other areas. The enormous needs of the new republics became apparent and were detailed in reports by UNICEF, UNDP, and other agencies during the spring months. As a result, in April 1992, Secretary-General Boutros-Ghali concluded that it would be useful to establish six interim U.N. offices in the former Soviet states that were now members of the world organization. These were to be organized jointly by **UNDP** and the **U.N. Department of Public Information,** and would serve as a means for a consolidated U.N presence that could provide a variety of services: short-term emergency assistance, specialized international knowledge and information about aid programs, and human development. However, the UNDP Governing Council, meeting in May and taken aback by the Secretary-General's unilateral move, authorized the UNDP to open only a "limited number of temporary and/or regional offices," to give priority to those countries with the lowest per capita gross national products and highest indicative planning figures (IPF), and to report back for further directions [UNDP Gov. Council decisions, 1992/29, 1992/43].

For the first time, UNICEF's Governing Board agreed to take up the subject of assistance to East and Central Europe and the former Soviet states as a separate agenda item at its June 1992 meeting. Because of worries about diversion, UNICEF (like UNDP) emphasized that financial resources for its aid activities to the region would come from new sources.

Chernobyl and Environmental Issues

In 1990 the United Nations began a program of assistance to three Soviet republics in response to their call for help in the aftermath of the Chernobyl nuclear accident. Only a few of Russia's many ecological disasters are well known in the West, and the Chernobyl accident is by far the most prominent. But in places as diverse as Semipalatinsk in Kazakhstan, Chelyabinsk in Russia, and the Aral Sea between Kazakhstan and Uzbekistan, the effects of the USSR's unconstrained policy of

nuclear testing and **wanton environmental degradation** have become the very real focus of outrage by local residents who are plagued with epidemic levels of disease and cancer, and who are facing severely polluted air, water, and ground. As a result of joint Belarus, Ukraine, and Russian efforts, the United Nations continues to emphasize the importance of international cooperation in the cleanup of the Chernobyl nuclear accident, and to help them develop and find financial and technical support for programs to address and mitigate the consequences of the disaster. Working together under the coordination of the Director-General of the **U.N. Office in Vienna,** some 15 U.N. organizations and agencies established an **Inter-Agency Task Force** and developed a plan for funding and carrying out activities that would help alleviate the effects of the accident and help the populations most affected. In September 1991 a pledging conference was held at U.N. Headquarters for the **United Nations Trust Fund for Chernobyl**—the first of its kind for the former Soviet republics. Although initial pledges fell far short of the $125 million goal, subsequent commitments have brought the Trust Fund closer to that sum. Despite the dissolution of the USSR, the three republics remain committed to the joint plan. A wide variety of U.N. agencies have already been working on programs to address the disaster, and the 46th General Assembly has expressed appreciation for the help so far and has asked U.N. agencies and others to continue to help [A/46/150]. It also asks the Secretary-General to submit a report to the 47th General Assembly, at which the topic will be further discussed.

The **Earth Summit in Rio,** and the whole UNCED process, has revealed considerable tension and even competitiveness between the G-77 developing countries and the former Eastern-bloc countries, particularly Russia and Poland. Throughout the negotiating process, Russia repeatedly attempted to broaden language that referred to "developing countries" to include "countries with economies in transition" or even all "recipient" countries. The developing countries steadfastly resisted this, with the result not only of **heightened East-South tensions** but also of achieving the impossible: Controversies over UNCED led the former Eastern group at the U.N. to convene, with *all* former bloc members participating, to discuss substantive questions *as a bloc.* Similar East-South tensions have also been apparent in a wide variety of U.N. development agencies, with developing countries opposed to assistance to the economies in transition because they are concerned that the already small donor funding is being diverted to help the former Eastern-bloc countries. While some of this may come to a head, or find a temporary resolution at the Rio meeting, these tensions are sure to reemerge throughout the 47th General Assembly Session.

East and Central Europe

The historic changes and challenges facing East and Central Europe since the transformation to democratic regimes in late 1989 have been plainly visible at the United Nations. New leaders and, in many cases, new diplomats have come to the world body both to call upon it to help in the enormously complex transitions they are experiencing and to offer their support in strengthening the Organization itself. As comparatively small states struggling to emerge from the limits placed on them by the polarization of the cold war, the East and Central European countries have looked to the West and to multilateral institutions—beginning with the European Community and the global economic institutions—for support and guidance. The leaders seem to recognize that many of the most difficult problems facing the region—ethnic strife based on resurgent nationalism, the consequences of past policies of environmental degradation, growing streams of refugees and migrants, and, of course, the transition to market economies—can be most effectively addressed through multilateral institutions, whether regional or global.

Characteristically, when the heads of state and foreign ministers of the East and Central European states came to the 46th General Assembly in the fall of 1991, they expressed concern about the enormous transition before them. A year later, in the face of increasing hardships and the dashed expectations of their citizenry, they are searching to preserve and reinforce support for economic transition. The opening speeches at the General Assembly are an opportunity both to show the people back home that their leaders are pressing local concerns in world bodies and to demonstrate the seriousness of those concerns to other world leaders. The 46th General Assembly saw its share of both tendencies in the speeches of the East and Central European leaders.

Hungary's Prime Minister, Joszef Antall, reminded the world body that it was 35 years since Hungarians had "cried out to the U.N. for help"—and had been ignored, with the exception of a few delegations and individuals, whom he praised. Only now, with the complete exit of former Soviet troops, has Hungary regained its sovereignty. Similarly, Czechoslovakia's Foreign Minister, Jiri Dienstbier, pointed out that the United Nations had failed to rally to Czechoslovakia's side after the infamous 1968 Warsaw Pact invasion. The Organization, he argued, belatedly and imperfectly reflects world developments rather than standing "in the forefront."

With such raps on the knuckles of the world body behind them, these and other East European leaders turned to the issues that now marked them as different from those governing in the Communist period. In addition to stressing their own economic needs, they emphasized their preeminent commitment to and support for international human rights standards and practices and measures taken to adhere to binding legal instruments in this area; their enthusiastic support for democracy, and for the changes in the USSR following the failed coup attempt; their participation in and support for Desert Storm actions against Iraq (even if to their financial detriment), and their affirmation of the correctness of such U.N. actions to forestall and reverse aggression; their concern about the Yugoslav situation and the importance of U.N. preventive diplomacy in this and other conflicts throughout the ethnically diverse and troubled region; and their involvement in building and joining European and global multilateral institutions, including the multilateral banks and the European security organizations, particularly the CSCE. Following tradition, many of them also addressed a variety of the current issues before the Assembly—with the added touch of support for repeal of the infamous "Zionism is racism" resolution [A/Res/3379 (XXX)], as well as their support for genuine achievements to safeguard the environment through the UNCED conference, and more.

Czechoslovak Foreign Minister Dienstbier announced that in this, his second appearance before the General Assembly, he was abandoning the tradition of commenting on the agenda in favor of broader concerns. He sketched out a vision of the United Nations as a truly universal organization, one that needed to bridge the chasm between North and South, and to solve such global problems as environment, energy, population, migration, crime, terrorism, drugs, and disease. Arms production must be converted into production that actually benefits the environment, and the defense of human rights must be a prime objective. Echoing the Moscow CSCE Conference on the Human Dimension, Dienstbier cautioned the world body that no one could any longer argue that sovereignty, or "non-interference in internal affairs," was an excuse to permit mass violations of human rights. He called for U.N. reform— of the General Debate, of institutions and structures—and ridiculed the practice whereby heads of state and foreign ministers present their opening speeches in the General Debate to virtually empty halls, followed by no debate whatsoever.

Thoughtful as his speech was, it clearly reflected the frustration felt by the former dissidents of Communist Eastern Europe arriving—after some 40-odd years—at the United Nations only to find its public debates and procedures so structured that the critical problems facing their countries seemed to be hardly noticed. The former East European-bloc states will need to expend considerable diplomatic effort and creativity in order to make their voices and positions—and their problems—heard by the world body. Dienstbier has appealed to the world community to do more—as in his opening comment to the Helsinki meeting of the CSCE, at which he served as chairman in 1992. Feeling the mounting uncertainty and impatience with the transitions in East and Central Europe that were pulling his fellow Czechs and Slovaks to the polls to reject his own party, Dienstbier told the CSCE foreign ministers: "I might be dramatizing the situation too much, but I do not think that any member state of the CSCE has been reacting to the precipitous events in an adequate manner."

The U.N. Response to the Needs of the Economies in Transition

The United Nations has responded to the needs of the countries in transition in East and Central Europe in characteristically diverse—and rather modest—ways. The developed countries of the West have, by and large, expressed their support for, and enthusiasm about assisting with, the changes under way among the new "Eastern" group members. U.N. technical agencies have expanded their programs in the region, but have been constrained from doing much more by a **combination of financial pressure from the West and political pressure from the South.** In 1991 the significance of the changes was deemed so great that the first-ever ministerial-level discussion at the U.N. Economic and Social Council (ESOSOC) was devoted to the impact of the changes in East-West relations on the growth of the world economy (particularly of the developing countries) and on international economic cooperation. Numerous other economic bodies analyzed and discussed these changes in advance of the ECOSOC session.

This sudden attention to a part of the world previously best known in the United Nations for its rigidity and routine support for Soviet positions produced its own backlash: Developing countries saw support for the East and Central European countries as competing with their own needs within the U.N. system. As a result, they laid down a marker in one operational development body after another: Assistance to the Eastern group countries must not come from a diversion of resources already directed to the developing countries; it must come from **"additional" sources.** Only after this protective position had been clearly articulated, backed politically by the Third World, and agreed to by donor nations were the developing countries ready to address the question of what was happening in the East. To make matters worse, this debate occurred in the context of a particularly poor economic situation, with global output falling for the first time since 1945, European and North American economies failing to recover as had been forecast, and world trade falling for the third year in a row. These constraints did little to encourage the East and Central European states, which saw their own output falling by a full 25 percent over a two-year period, with 1991 worse than 1990.

ECOSOC's special discussion produced no official declarations or conclusions, but its chairman summarized the findings of the debate by noting that governments felt the improvement in East-West relations represented a positive development globally, and that the South would benefit from it in the long term although there might be some short-term negative effects, notably the weakening of trade links. Furthermore, it was generally acknowledged that structural reform in the East would be longer and more complex than originally thought, and its social costs might produce some political backlash in the form of authoritarian opposition or outward migration. The **collapse of intra-Eastern trade** posed a problem. Diversion of official development assistance might occur, but its avoidance was to be stressed; any new financial inputs to the East must be additional. Using tax incentives to stimulate investment was viewed as a good idea, but only if investors in the South receive the same encouragement on the same terms. The same was true for the debt burden. The chairman also noted the viewpoint that it is important for the East to develop trade links with the South because it may set a pattern of financial flows for the future.

This debate continued at the 46th General Assembly, and while there was some controversy over definitions (What constitutes "diversion"? Official Development Assistance only? All investments? All commercial transactions?) the Assembly called on the Secretariat to monitor and report again on these matters at the 47th Assembly [A/Res/46/202].

As described above in the section on Chernobyl and the environment, efforts of the "Eastern group"—still consisting of the East and Central European countries and Russia and the successor states to the former Soviet Union—to be included as recipients of U.N. **environmental projects** have not been received sympathetically by the developing countries. Here, as elsewhere, developing countries fear the diversion of already insufficient resources and are unwilling to make compromises that might hurt their own chances of receiving assistance.

The same situation applies in the main in **UNICEF:** After a bitter debate, the 1991 Governing Council reached the conclusion that while UNICEF was a universal organization that could not completely ignore East and Central Europe, it could not spend any more than its regular budget for analysis and activity in the region (about $1 million). Anything else would have to be additional. Thus, although in 1991 UNICEF sent emergency missions to assess the conditions of Romanian orphans said to have become infected with the AIDS virus, it stood by during much of the Yugoslav conflict, and was able to help in the much-publicized evacuation of women and children from Dubrovnik when the city was under bombardment only after it received a special grant for this purpose from the European Community. In 1992, UNICEF heard vigorous pleas from the Eastern countries—including Russia—for a more flexible and better-funded role regarding the turmoil in the Eastern part of Europe. A separate agenda item on this matter for UNICEF's June

1992 Executive Board meeting was agreed upon after much debate and controversy.

In mid-1992 the **Economic Commission for Europe (ECE),** assessing the economic situation and its significance for the region, reported to the July 1992 session of ECOSOC that the situation in the eastern part of Europe not only warrants continued attention but that its social and political conditions could engender undesirable consequences.

> It has proved fairly easy to break up the old structures but extremely difficult to build the new. . . . A growing fear is that the increasing economic strains will lead to disillusion and impatience, both with the idea of a market economy and with the democratic process. If Western Governments wish to reduce these growing risks, a much greater commitment to the success of the reform process will be needed on their part [E/1992/45, 5/6/92, *Summary of the Economic Survey of Europe in 1991– 1992*].

The ECE secretariat has proposed a broader approach to coordination, one that benefits from the "great many useful lessons . . . from the way in which Marshall [Plan] Aid for Western Europe was organized." A clearly defined framework, the ECE argues, such as the creation of a "second European recovery programme," in which the commitment of Western governments to the ultimate success of the transition process would be more explicit, could cushion the transitions so that the "inevitable mistakes could occur without damaging confidence" [ibid.]. Otherwise, they warn, "growing introspection" and attention to domestic economic and social problems in the Western countries will only be disturbed by a major crisis—and hasty decisions. Whether or not ECOSOC will recommend U.N. measures to respond to these challenges, the 47th General Assembly will surely hear these concerns voiced again in its Second Committee, which discusses economic and development questions. In 1991 the East and Central European states were comparatively quiet in the Second Committee—except in the debate regarding the agencies that do direct development work and implementation, such as UNDP, UNICEF, and the U.N. Industrial Development Organization (UNIDO). Then, virtually every country in the region spoke about the importance of these programs globally and about the need to make them work more actively or fully "on the national level" and in their own countries in particular.

Minority Conflict and Preventive Diplomacy

The armed conflicts that have raged in Yugoslavia, Moldova, and Nagorno-Karabakh are all rooted in **internal and minority-related communal rivalry.** As several Security Council members have noted, such ethnic strife threatens to grow into a general conflagration in the region unless international measures bring the existing fighting to an end; and some observers have drawn ominous parallels between the weak Western response to this situation and that of the period leading to the Spanish Civil War and the Munich agreement. In this context, increasing attention has been directed at the need to address "root causes" of the conflicts, including questions of human rights, discrimination against women, and economic deprivation.

The statement issued by the **Security Council Summit in January 1992** [S/2500] called on the Secretary-General to prepare recommendations to strengthen the U.N.'s capacity for "preventive diplomacy, . . . peace-making, and peace-keeping." Indeed, all the Western and European members of the Council (but not Russia) referred to preventive diplomacy in their Summit speeches, with British Prime Minister John Major explaining that this means "action to avert—or at least contain—crises . . . before tension becomes conflict" [S/PV. 3046]. Hungary's Foreign Minister—the only representative of that troubled region sitting on the Security Council—was impassioned on the subject. He stated that U.N. peacekeeping should not be "merely to confine conflicts and to preserve the *status quos*, but . . . contributing creatively to removing hotbeds of crisis by upholding democratic values and enforcing respect for human rights" [ibid.]. Hungary has been the most vocal country in the region on the need to affirm and enforce minority rights in the region and world-wide. Because a third of all Hungarians live outside the country's borders, this has become a major priority of Hungary's foreign policy.

For years the United Nations had ignored the subject of **minority rights and protections,** emphasizing instead the need to develop universal human rights standards and protections, but the 47th General Assembly will be asked to adopt a declaration on minority rights—the result of a 25-year effort at the U.N. Commission on Human Rights. It is, as the Russian Federation's representative noted, a "minimum" proclamation of standards and rights. In contrast, the CSCE has adopted stronger standards and is actively considering a Dutch initiative, which has broad support, to establish a High Commissioner for Minorities to enforce these rights and engage in preventive consultations. When the CSCE opened in March 1992, 15 foreign ministers spoke about the need to establish measures to address minority questions, including seven from the East (five of which are new state members of the CSCE).

Ukraine led the 46th General Assembly to call for the Commission on Human Rights to speed up its completion of a draft declaration on the rights of national, linguistic, or ethnic minorities. This was the first resolution addressing this subject adopted by the Assembly, and the draft convention would be the first major instrument on this subject adopted by the United Nations. In view of the ethnic and national conflict in the region, and the problems of the many minorities, this subject is particularly important to all the states of the region.

Former Yugoslavia: Human Rights Concerns

In addition to the activity of the U.N. Security Council on Yugoslavia, the situation in the country (or *countries*) was a focus of attention in some of the human rights bodies of the United Nations. In the General Assembly and elsewhere, Hungary has been particularly vocal in calling attention to the human rights and humanitarian problems posed by the war, noting the 50,000 refugees of all nationalities who had fled to Hungary, as well as mentioning discriminatory and abusive actions against the sizable Hungarian minority in Yugoslavia's Vojvodina province.

Much of the Third Committee's discussions on human rights violations in Eastern Europe focused on the crisis in Yugoslavia. The European Community [A/46/C.3/SR.44], Norway [SR.45], Austria [SR.47], Sweden [SR.48], Czechoslovakia [SR.48], Canada [SR.50], Hungary [SR.51], Albania [SR.51], and Ukraine [SR.52] all made special mention of the Yugoslav situation. Albania, the most strident, stated that ethnic Albanians in Yugoslavia's Kosovo province were the most repressed people in Europe. Yugoslavia [SR.53] replied that it was understandable that it had been mentioned so often in the debate, but that it was taking action to reestablish order, in cooperation with the international community. However, Yugoslavia also charged that the attitude shown by Albania only exacerbated interethnic friction in Yugoslavia and was a reflection of Albania's own thinly disguised territorial aspirations. After it defended its treatment of ethnic Albanians, charges were exchanged again.

It is worth noting that the distinguished and authoritative expert treaty supervisory body, the **Human Rights Committee,** on November 4, 1991, called upon Yugoslavia to report to it in a **special procedure** that it had only recently adopted to consider human rights in crisis situations. After that review, in April 1992, the Committee specifically noted that "difficulties had arisen in . . . Kosovo" and expressed its concern over the deterioration in the situation of minorities, especially the Albanians and Hungarians. Throughout the country, the Committee stated, violent interethnic conflict had led to "widespread violations of most of the rights safeguarded" by the **International Covenant on Civil and Political Rights.** The Committee expressed "its gravest concern" over the atrocities committed, and cited "the many cases of summary or arbitrary executions, forced or involuntary disappearances, torture, rape, and pillage committed by members of the Federal Army" and paramilitary groups, noting that the Yugoslav government had failed to punish the guilty and prevent any recurrence of such acts—giving rise to an atmosphere of impunity.

Refugees

As noted by Mrs. Sodako Ogata, the **High Commissioner for Refugees (UNHCR)**, refugee concerns have gained increasing significance in Eastern Europe as many of the region's countries evolve from a source of refugees into a sanctuary for them [A/46/C.3/SR.34]. For this reason, many of these countries have become more involved in the work of UNHCR. In 1991 Czechoslovakia, Hungary, Romania, and Poland acceded to the **U.N. Convention relating to the Status of Refugees.** UNHCR's role in Eastern Europe has also become more complicated as the causes of refugee problems in many countries have shifted from political persecution and repression to economic hardship. Accordingly, UNHCR has responded flexibly by facilitating the provision of economic, humanitarian, and legal assistance in those areas. Of course, events in Yugoslavia have been of particular concern to the High Commissioner.

Although it recognized the invaluable role of the United Nations and UNHCR at the global level, Czechoslovakia argued that the creation of **an all-European mechanism to deal with migration** should be given priority. But other Eastern European states placed primary emphasis on the work of UNHCR. This emphasis by such countries as Poland [SR.37] and Hungary [SR.36] can be explained by the growing flow of refugees into and through these countries in recent years. In addition, it is no doubt linked to the fact that the European countries, and particularly the European Community, have made it known that the Association Agreements with the Community are to be linked (unofficially) to the conclusion of agreements with the UNHCR on the refugee conventions. Moreover, they reportedly demanded that specific measures be adopted in each country to stem the westward flow of East and Central European migrants. Accordingly, during the General Assembly debate both countries related that the increased number of refugees had stretched the limits of their ability to provide the necessary protection and assistance to those refugees, and that the help of UNHCR was invaluable. Notably, UNHCR opened an **office in Warsaw** in 1992.

At the other end of the spectrum, countries such as Albania and Romania [SR.36] are facing a very different refugee problem. As Albania's government (then still led by reform Communists) told the Assembly, the hordes of Albanian nationals leaving that country should be considered economic immigrants rather than political refugees and their problems solved on that basis. In this regard, Albania placed emphasis on concluding international agreements on legal migration for temporary employment and on the need for foreign investment.

2. The Middle East and the Persian Gulf

The Gulf War and Its Aftermath

Following the end of the Gulf War in March 1991 and the **Security Council's passage of Resolution 687** in April 1991, the Council faced the daunting task of restoring peace to the Persian Gulf and demilitarizing Iraq. "The mother of all resolutions," as 687 was soon dubbed, set forth the Council's unconditional terms for peace with Iraq: The resolution demanded that Iraq recognize its border with Kuwait as demarcated before the war, and that it pay reparations for damages resulting from its occupation of Kuwait and its conduct of the war. Resolution 687 also established a demilitarized zone along the Iraq-Kuwait border to be patrolled by U.N. peacekeeping forces. Finally, 687 mandated the partial demilitarization of Iraq and the destruction of Iraqi weapons of mass destruction (WMD) under U.N. direction and surveillance, including Baghdad's nuclear, chemical, and biological weapons capabilities. Further, the Council maintained the complete trade embargo it had imposed on Baghdad in August 1990 under **Resolution 661** [see *A Global Agenda: Issues/ 46*] pending full Iraqi compliance with Resolution 687.

The "mother of all resolutions" imposed new and demanding responsibilities on the United Nations and the Council itself, including the supervision and monitoring of Iraqi demilitarization, and it set a significant precedent in expanding the Council's powers, under Chapter VII of the U.N. Charter, to intervene in the internal affairs of nation states, raising new questions and debate regarding the limits of national sovereignty. Submitting to the "unjust terms" of 687 under indignant protest, Iraq has continued to contest and obstruct U.N. prerogatives and actions, especially with regard to the investigation and destruction of Iraq's nuclear and ballistic systems. Baghdad's stubborn resistance and its defiance of numerous U.N. directives has repeatedly earned the censure and fury of the Security Council, which, under the leadership of Secretary-General Javier Pérez de Cuéllar, has extended its powers to enforce, and not merely direct, Iraqi compliance.

During the spring and summer of 1991 the issue of U.N. sanctions and their suspension by the Security Council provoked lively debate at the United Nations. The devastation of Iraqi society, and the stubborn refusal of Hussein's regime to cooperate with the United Nations' implementation and monitoring of Resolution 687, presented the Council with a dilemma: To lift sanctions would be to reward the defiant Iraqi dictator, to maintain them would punish his people beyond endurance. The **damage Iraq had sustained** during the Gulf War was staggering. The U.S. Defense Department estimated that up to 100,000 Iraqi soldiers may have died during hostilities, and experts have further estimated that between 5,000 and 15,000 civilians died during the war, and that up to 86,000 more perished in the four months following the cease-fire due to disease, malnutrition, and civil war [*The New York Times*, 6/5,22/91].

Systematically targeting Iraq's infrastructure, the Allies had effectively "bombed Iraq back to the Stone Age," as one U.N. observer noted shortly after the cease-fire. Despite the U.S. Defense Department's insistence that Allied precision bombing had spared civilian lives, only 7 percent of bombs dropped by the Allies were "smart"; the rest were conventional ordnance, which wreaked devastating "collateral damage," in Pentagon parlance, on the Iraqi people. An international team of health experts visiting Iraq in November 1991 concluded that 900,000 Iraqi children were malnourished, and 100,000 were on the brink of starvation. Sixty percent of Iraqi households had no water, and two-thirds of those that did received contaminated water. Prices in the country had jumped 20-fold in the last year [*Middle East International*, 1/24/92].

In August 1991 the Council passed **Resolution 706,** allowing Iraq to sell $1.6 billion of oil, 30 percent of which would go to reparations and costs borne by the United Nations for activities in the region. The Allies were concerned that the remaining proceeds serve the humanitarian needs of the Iraqi people and not the political purposes of their leader. In September the Council addressed this problem with the passage of **Resolution 712,** which endorsed a plan the Secretary-General had submitted to establish monitoring and accounting mechanisms to supervise the sale and use of the Iraqi oil revenues. (The Council also rejected a proposal by the Secretary-General to raise the one-time sale to $2.5 billion.) But Iraq rejected these measures and protested both 706 and 712 as intolerable infringements on its sovereignty [*The Boston Globe*, 8/16/91]. As late as April 1992 the oil remained unsold, following a fruitless round of negotiations in New York.

U.N. attempts to monitor and direct Iraq's postwar demilitarization also met with systematic resistance in Baghdad. Invoking a familiar and traditional view of international law, Iraq decried the Security Council's demilitarization demands as arrogant and illegal, and then tried to frustrate nearly every U.N. directive. A pattern soon emerged whereby Iraq protested each succeeding U.N. directive, obstructed and often harassed the U.N. mission sent to monitor Iraq's compliance, and, finally, under threat of ruinous punitive measures, capitulated to U.N. demands on or after deadline. This "cat-and-mouse game" may have earned Saddam Hussein the admiration of some Arab nationalists, but only at the cost of infuriating many members of the Security Council and provoking the chamber to expand its demands and prerogatives.

In July 1991 the **International Atomic Energy Agency** (IAEA) condemned Iraq for concealing its nuclear arms industry, the first such censure of a signatory to the Non-Proliferation Treaty. In September the

Agency dispatched a mission to monitor the dismantling of Iraq's nuclear armaments facilities and stockpiles, but at the end of the month Iraq detained 44 U.N. inspectors, led by American David Kay, confiscated documents they had taken from Iraqi facilities, and accused them of spying for the U.S. Central Intelligence Agency. Four days later Baghdad released the inspectors, who carried away nearly 5,000 pages of documentation relating to Iraqi nuclear weapons. During a second IAEA mission to Iraq in January 1992, Baghdad admitted that it had acquired from several German firms the components for up to 10,000 gas centrifuges used to produce enriched uranium. **IAEA chief inspector Maurizio Fabrizzi** later confirmed that Iraq had accounted for all nuclear-related equipment purchased in Germany, according to German authorities [*The New York Times*, 9/14/91].

In October 1991 a U.N. team of ballistic-missile experts flew to Baghdad to supervise the destruction of Iraq's remaining SCUD missiles. Baghdad insisted they use Iraqi helicopters, but the U.N. envoys toured 28 sites in Iraq in new German helicopters supplied for this purpose. In the course of its inspections the team discovered a 350-mm "supergun" and components for a larger 1,000-mile-range cannon. Baghdad had long denied the existence of both weapons.

In early October the Secretary-General submitted to the Security Council a 32-page report proposing sweeping new measures "to insure Iraq does not again acquire weapons of mass destruction [WMD]." The report recommended the establishment of a U.N. Special Commission on Iraqi Disarmament to supervise ongoing monitoring procedures, thereby fulfilling the third stage of the assessment-destruction-monitoring process mandated by Resolution 687. The United Nations would now monitor civilian as well as military facilities, under the provisions of 687, and Iraqi noncompliance would be subject to Security Council action under Chapter VII of the U.N. Charter [*The Christian Science Monitor*, 8/6, 19/91].

In February 1992 the Security Council strongly condemned Iraq's failure to comply with a U.N. deadline to allow inspectors to begin destroying equipment used to produce long-range missiles. The Council also "deplored and condemned" Iraq's failure to disclose information concerning its WMD capability. **Rolf Ekeus, head of the U.N. Special Commission,** then visiting Baghdad with a 14-member ballistic missile inspection team, declared Iraq "in material breach" of Resolution 687, and ordered his team to leave the country [*The New York Times*, 2/29/92].

Iraq called the Council's statement "hasty. . . [and] full of falsehoods and slanders." Iraqi Foreign Minister Tarik Aziz, addressing the Council in early March, demanded that it respect Iraq's sovereignty, and protested that the U.N. monitoring commission had acquired far too much power, especially since Iraq had destroyed all the weapons systems relevant to

Resolution 687. Many members of the Council were outraged. French delegate Jean Bernard Mérimée spoke for the consensus among permanent Council members when he called Aziz's speech an "unacceptable" challenge to the basic monitoring mechanism mandated by 687 [*The Christian Science Monitor*, 3/13/92]. But the Iraqi Foreign Minister's protests echoed the views of many Arab and Third World members, who felt that the Security Council had become dominated by the world's one remaining superpower, and had arrogated cruel and unusual new powers to oppress independent states who legitimately defied U.S. hegemony.

A week following the speech, President Saddam Hussein dropped Iraqi objections to the U.N.-directed destruction of Iraqi ballistic equipment and released new information about Baghdad's WMD stockpiles. Meanwhile **U.N. inspector Derek Boothby**, on mission in Baghdad, called Iraqi cooperation "businesslike," but noted that "a credibility gap" concerning Iraq's SCUD arsenal remained [*Middle East International*, 3/20/92].

In late March the IAEA ordered the destruction of the al-Athir industrial complex southeast of Baghdad, which it said was the site of ongoing nuclear research and production. Iraq denied the charge, but Hussein approved the U.N. destruction of al-Athir in early April, one day before the deadline set by the Security Council. By mid-April, Demetrios Perricos, head of the U.N. wrecking crew, reported that 90 percent of al-Athir had been destroyed. "The Iraqis have lost their credibility," Perricos added. "I believe only what I see" [ibid., 4/17/92].

The Arab-Israeli Conflict and the Occupied Territories

Forty years after the establishment of the state of Israel, the Arab-Israeli conflict persists. The conflict subsumes a multitude of complex local, national, and regional disputes, but at its core lies the Palestine Question. During the 1980s various U.S. peace plans and inter-Arab initiatives failed to bridge the enormous differences separating Israel from the Palestine Liberation Organization (PLO), two parties that had long refused to recognize or even address each other. But in December 1987 this diplomatic stalemate was shaken by a massive and sustained Palestinian uprising, or *intifadah,* in the Occupied Territories, forcing Israelis to confront Palestinian demands for self-determination, and pushing the Palestine National Council (PNC)—the PLO's parliament in exile—to recognize Israel formally. But since then Israel's government has declined to reciprocate, refusing to recognize Palestinian claims to self-determination or the legitimacy of the PLO.

In October 1991, after months of intense diplomacy, **U.S. Secretary of State James Baker** made history by convening in Madrid the first-ever direct negotiations between all parties to the conflict. In the next five months four rounds of Arab-Israeli talks in Washington showed little progress: At each stage the parties confirmed their commitment to continue the talks, but without agreeing on what they would discuss. Each round became entangled in a thicket of procedural issues, leaving questions of negotiating principles and agenda unaddressed.

The United Nations has remained at the margins of the search for peace in the Middle East. Over the past 20 years the General Assembly has relentlessly reviled Israel for its occupation of the West Bank and the Gaza Strip, territories it has claimed since the Six-Day War of 1967. Israel has ignored the actions of the General Assembly, protesting the body's strong pro-Arab bias. The United States has attempted during this period to broker an elusive "peace process" on largely Israeli terms. Under the Reagan administration, a series of desultory U.S. initiatives foundered on Israel's refusal to talk to the PLO, even after the organization recognized Israel at Algiers in 1988. (The Algiers Declaration did result in the renewal of a U.S.-PLO dialogue that Washington had suspended in 1974. Washington resuspended contacts with the organization in June 1989, citing the PLO's failure to condemn an aborted amphibious raid on Israel by a radical Palestinian faction.)

The Bush administration launched its first Middle East peace initiative in 1989. Promoting negotiations between Israel and a non-PLO Palestinian delegation, Secretary of State Baker made five trips to the region in as many months in early 1990, but his efforts came to nought as Israel stiffened its conditions for talks and its requirements for Palestinian interlocutors.

Secretary Baker's largely procedural approach—and his pose of disinterested honest broker—could not prevail in an atmosphere of chronic crisis, further polarized by **expanding Israeli settlements in the Territories** and a new wave of **Jewish emigration from the Soviet Union** to Israel. Spurred by a new Soviet policy of unlimited emigration (and also by changes in U.S. immigration law, which sharply curtailed immigration quotas for Soviet Jews), several hundred thousand Soviet Jews arrived in Israel, and up to a million more were expected, sparking panic and protest among Palestinians throughout the Arab world.

The Arab-Israeli peace process, as elusive as ever, was eclipsed by Iraq's invasion of Kuwait on August 2, 1990. When Iraqi President Saddam Hussein offered to withdraw from Kuwait if Israel withdrew from the Arab lands it had occupied in 1967, his "linkage" between the Gulf crisis and the Arab-Israeli conflict was rejected out of hand by Washington and its Arab allies. But following the decisive and stunning victory of U.S.-led allied armies over Iraq in March 1991, U.S. diplomats returned to the Arab-Israeli dispute with new hopes. They saw the Gulf War as the kind of sea change, like the October War of 1973, that might recast the dynamics of the Arab-Israeli conflict and its long moribund peace process.

Certainly the war had changed much in the region, but not necessarily for the better where the Arab-Israeli conflict was concerned. On the one hand the survival of the Riyadh-Cairo-Damascus axis, the heart of the anti-Iraq regional alliance that the United States had successfully promoted, suggested that Saudi Arabia, Egypt, and Syria might cooperate on negotiations with Israel. Further, the Gulf crisis and the allies' triumphant reconquest of Kuwait devastated the prestige and effectiveness of the PLO, which had taken Saddam Hussein's "linkage" to heart and supported him during the war, making the organization, and the Palestinians as a whole, even more desperate to deal. The war had also further crippled Arab solidarity. Recriminations between Gulf Arabs and Palestinians were particularly bitter, and the latter now found themselves isolated within the Arab camp as a whole. Saudi Arabia cut its financial support to the PLO, rechanneling its assistance to the Territories through the more radical Islamic group Hamas. Several Gulf countries expelled Palestinian residents during the Gulf hostilities, and the liberation of Kuwait and the restoration of its monarchy led to reprisals by "resistance" vigilantes that left at least 30 Palestinians dead and many more tortured and detained, according to the human rights group Middle East Watch [*The New York Times*, 4/10/91]. Further, the restored Kuwaiti government refused to readmit hundreds of thousands of Palestinian residents who had fled the emirate during the hostilities, as had the monarchy itself. Moreover, the Israelis, who had seen the Arabs' largest army decimated in the war and watched Palestinians cheer Iraqi SCUD missile attacks on Tel Aviv, seemed less amenable than ever to making concessions on the Palestine Question.

From August 1990 through April 1991 the Gulf crisis naturally preoccupied the Security Council, although the Council did pass several resolutions critical of Israel during this time. In late March 1991, Secretary Baker launched a new Middle East peace initiative. After eight months of global diplomacy, including six trips to the region and talks in Europe and the Soviet Union, Baker achieved what had eluded his predecessors for over 20 years: face-to-face negotiations between Arabs and Israelis. In mid-October 1991, Baker and Soviet Foreign Minister Boris Pankin announced in Jerusalem that a preliminary round of Arab negotiations—to include representatives of Israel, Syria, and Lebanon as well as a joint Jordanian-Palestinian delegation—would open in Madrid at the end of the month. The Secretary of State did this by solving the two principal disputes that had frustrated the peace process for so long: the overarching structure of the conference and the nature of Palestinian representation. For all his persistence and ingenuity, Baker succeeded not so much by forging new compromises between Arabs and Israelis as by delivering Arab concessions to an Israeli government determined to discuss peace only on its own terms. Throughout this process the Israeli government struck a pose of defiance: It inaugurated new settlements on the West Bank, two of which were announced to coincide with two of Baker's trips to the Jewish state, and it lobbied the U.S. Congress for extraordinary financial assistance against the express wishes of President Bush. Israel sought $10 billion in loan guarantees from the United States, which would allow it to borrow at a lower interest rate to finance the immigration of Soviet Jews. But Israel refused to freeze new settlement activity in the Occupied Territories, the U.S. condition for granting the loan guarantees [ibid., 9/13/91].

Arab-Israeli differences on the structure of an "international peace conference" date from the 1970s. The Arabs had long insisted on a U.N.-sponsored conference attended by all the parties to the conflict and chaired by the five permanent members of the Security Council. This formula, first framed by the Brezhnev-Carter Communiqué of 1978, would achieve a "just, lasting, and comprehensive" peace in the region, which all parties would negotiate together. Israel rejected the notion of U.N. sponsorship, protesting the pro-Arab bias of both the General Assembly and the Security Council. Israel also insisted on a series of separate and independent bilateral negotiations between concerned parties, on the model of the 1978 Camp David talks between Israel and Egypt.

In 1990 Secretary Baker had promoted a compromise formula: The United Nations would nominally sponsor a multilateral umbrella conference chaired by the United States and the Soviet Union, which would quickly adjourn to a series of bilateral negotiations. Baker made some progress, but his formula, essentially the Israeli position with multilateral trimmings, proved acceptable to no one. The Secretary pushed the same formula in 1991, and this time he succeeded by making additional procedural concessions to Israel and securing the support of all the Arab parties. During a tour of the region in July 1991, Baker secured the support of Syria, Lebanon, Jordan, and finally Israel for a conference sponsored by the United States and the Soviet Union and attended by U.N. and EC observers. This "international" umbrella conference would adjourn to separate bilateral negotiations and would have no authority over their proceedings.

There remained the thorny question of Palestinian participation. Israel has consistently refused to negotiate with the PLO, which it has long viewed as a fundamentally illegitimate "terrorist" organization operating beyond the bounds of international law. Therefore no PLO officials could attend peace talks, and Israel further insisted that neither could Palestinians residing in East Jerusalem or outside the Occupied Territories. Nor would Israel permit Palestinians it deemed acceptable to form a separate delegation during the talks. The formula Baker proposed in July 1991 secured all these Israeli demands. The PLO was excluded from negotiations, though they attended and advised; and Israel effectively won the right to veto by name all Palestinian delegates, who together would form half of a joint Palestinian-Jordanian delegation. For their part, the PLO and the Palestinian leadership in the Territories agreed to these terms in mid-October.

The Madrid Conference opened on October 30 and adjourned on November 3 to bilateral talks, which concluded on November 8 without any agreement on the date, venue, or agenda of the next round of bilateral talks. At the invitation of the United States, a second round of talks began in Washington on December 4, with the Israeli delegation arriving five days later in protest. The actual negotiations lasted four days and bogged down amid Israeli demands that the United States play no role in separate bilateral negotiations, which should be conducted in separate cities, and that all talks be moved to the Middle East or Europe. Israel had established two new settlements in the West Bank since the onset of the Madrid process [ibid., 12/16/91].

Delayed for a week by the late arrival of Arab delegations protesting Israeli deportations in the Territories, bilateral talks resumed in Washington on January 13, 1992. This third phase lasted three days and scored one procedural success: Israel agreed to a de facto two-track mechanism whereby Palestinians and Jordanians would effectively negotiate with Israel separately while nominally part of the same joint delegation. Compromised by Israel's detention of one Palestinian negotiator and its refusal to allow four others to exit the Occupied Territories through Jordan, a fourth round of bilateral talks in Washington adjourned on March 4 without setting a date or venue for the next round. Arab diplomats expressed growing frustration over the absence of any progress on questions of substance. A fifth round of bilateral talks was scheduled in Washington on April 27, but little progress was expected pending Israeli elections in June.

Meanwhile, a second multilateral round of talks was held in Moscow on January 28, 1992. Eleven Arab states attended, along with delegations from the United States, Russia, the European Community, Canada, Japan, and Turkey. Syria and Jordan refused to attend, protesting Israel's refusal to allow Palestinians to choose their own representatives. The Palestinians did send a delegation to Moscow, but decided not to attend the conference's plenary sessions. The Moscow talks adjourned after three days and issued in New York a boilerplate statement reaffirming its support for Security Council Resolutions 242 and 338.

Four years of open rebellion in the Occupied Territories, together with the PNC declaration in Algiers, have very much changed the terms of the Palestine Question, but have done little to bring Israel closer to compromise. In Israel the *intifadah* has shattered the illusion that peaceful coexistence between Arabs and Israelis under the present occupation is still possible. The uprising has vindicated many moderates, both Israeli and Palestinian, who have long felt that peace must be made before Israel's de facto annexation of the Occupied Territories becomes irreversible. But the *intifadah* has not arrested the rightward movement of Israeli politics; indeed, in the short run, it strengthened this trend. The Likud government formed by Yitzhak Shamir in early 1990 proved the most militant in Israeli history. An Israeli Housing Ministry report shows that in 1991, Israel built 65 percent more housing units in the Territories than in any previous year [*Middle East International, 2/7/92*]. Following Israeli elections in June 1992 and Yitzhak Rabin's formation of a new Labor government—the first in 15 years—many in and out of Israel expressed the hope that Israel might now approach the peace process in a greater spirit of cooperation and compromise.

In 1991, Israel loosened the army's "rules of engagement" in the Occupied Territories, making it easier for Israeli soldiers to fire upon Palestinians, and also allowed Jewish settlers to police the Territories in "civil guard" units for the first time. Between December 1987 and December 1991, over 1,000 Palestinians have been killed in the Territories by Israeli security forces, and some 14,000 were being held in detention camps and prisons [*The New York Times, 2/2/92, 2/4/92*; UNRWA annual report 1990–91]. And in January 1992, days before talks were scheduled to resume in Washington, Israel deported 12 prominent Palestinians from the Territories in reprisal for the killing of a Jewish settler in the Gaza Strip [*Middle East International, 1/10/92*]. On January 6 the **Security Council** voted unanimously to condemn the deportations in accordance with the Geneva Convention of 1949 [S/Res/726]. This was the sixth time the United States chose not to veto a Security Council resolution condemning the practice, which had resulted in the deportation of 66 Palestinians since the start of the *intifadah* [*The New York Times, 1/7/92*].

The 46th Session of the General Assembly passed a number of resolutions condemning Israel's occupation of the West Bank and the Gaza Strip. The Assembly's resolution on "The Situation in the Middle East" [A/Res/45/54] repeated the body's conviction that "the question of Palestine is at the core of the conflict" and that a just solution to the Arab-Israeli conflict must include the PLO. The resolution demanded "the total and unconditional withdrawal by Israel from all the Palestinian and other Arab lands occupied since 1967, including Jerusalem." It also reaffirmed its call to convene an international peace conference under the auspices of the United Nations.

Following the Algiers Declaration of 1987, the General Assembly acknowledged the proclamation of the State of Palestine and changed the name of the PLO's U.N. mission to the Palestine Observer Mission

[A/Res/43/177]. Forty-four countries voted against the resolution, including Israel, the United States, and the entire NATO bloc.

In December 1991 the 46th Session of the **General Assembly repealed its Resolution 3379,** a 1975 resolution that labeled Zionism a form of racism. One hundred eleven nations voted to repeal 3379 (Arab nations among them), 25 voted against, and 13 abstained. It was only the second time in the history of the United Nations that the General Assembly voted to rescind a resolution [*The New York Times,* 12/17/91]. Following the historic vote, Israeli Foreign Minister David Levy declared that "They have cleaned the stain from the U.N."; and White House spokesman Marlin Fitzwater said Israeli President Shamir had told President Bush in a phone call that "the Jewish people are grateful for the President's leadership" in repealing the resolution [*The InterDependent* 18, no. 1, (1–2/92)].

The 47th Session of the General Assembly will again address these issues, and will likely consider additional resolutions condemning Israel's occupation of Arab lands.

Lebanon

Persistent sectarian strife and public disorder have kept Lebanon in a state of virtual anarchy since the outbreak of the Lebanese civil war in 1975. But in the last two years the government of **Lebanese President Elias Hrawi,** assisted by the Syrian army and Arab mediation efforts, has made significant progress in extending the rule of the central government and restoring order to Lebanon. Hrawi's success remains preliminary and tenuous, and further momentum toward the reintegration of Lebanon will depend on the wishes of outside powers, principally Syria and Israel, and most of all on the will of the country's many fractious militias to sacrifice their hard-won positions of influence for an elusive greater good.

The power vacuum created by the civil war led to the occupation of large parts of the country by Syria, which invaded in 1976 at the behest of beleaguered Christian forces. Syrian occupation saved the Christians from defeat and ruin, but only dampened the ferocity of intra-Lebanese strife. The situation was further complicated by Israel's invasion of Lebanon in 1982. In 1985, Israel's withdrawal from southern Lebanon to a six-mile-wide **"security zone"** north of the Israeli border raised new hopes that Lebanese internal disputes might be peacefully resolved; but without a functioning central government or a national consensus on how to restore one, Lebanon's many private armies continued their bloody turf battles.

Throughout the 1980s, Lebanon wrestled with the growing threat of partition into two separate Christian and Muslim ministates. This trend toward partition was decisively checked in November 1989 when Lebanese legislators, together with Arab heads of state, wrote a new Lebanese constitution, offering more power to Muslim groups while retaining equal status for the Christians. The **Taif Agreement,** which was rejected by several Christian leaders, also mandated a phased withdrawal of Syrian forces from most areas of the country.

Elected in November 1989 by a rump Lebanese parliament, President Elias Hrawi set about securing support for the new Lebanese constitution among Lebanon's many Christian and Muslim militias. In October 1990, Hrawi announced his **"Greater Beirut" plan,** which called for the disarming of militias in and around the capital by mid-November and the reestablishment of Lebanese sovereignty over this area. The next step in the Taif process called for the dissolution of all militias throughout the country, the full restoration of Lebanese internal sovereignty, and the full implementation of the reformed National Charter. To the astonishment of many, the Greater Beirut plan was achieved in mid-December 1990, when Samir Geagea withdrew his Lebanese Forces militia from the capital to his Christian enclave north of the city, two weeks over deadline.

President Hrawi's push for territorial integration scored another historic victory in July 1991, when the Lebanese army, supported by Syrian units, disarmed the large Palestinian enclave in and around Sidon. Over 60 died in Sidon alone, and some 6,000 Palestinian fighters surrendered, signaling the end of Palestinian autonomy in southern Lebanon [*Middle East International,* 7/12/91].

The complete disarmament and dissolution of all Lebanese militias remains a distant goal. The country's many militias have wandered in the killing fields of Lebanon for so long that they have developed instincts and interests that leave little room for more abstract notions of national sovereignty and well-being. Since the signing of the Taif Agreement in September 1989, Syria, which has occupied large parts of Lebanon for almost 15 years with up to 40,000 troops, has firmly supported the initiatives of the Lebanese army to reclaim military control of Lebanon. Further extension of the Taif process in southern Lebanon will be difficult: The entrenchment of Israeli troops and the **South Lebanese Army (SLA)** in Israel's "security zone" north of the Lebanese-Israeli border, and the presence of the equally determined Shiite Hizbollah north of Israel's "security zone," may act to preserve southern Lebanon as a bloody skirmishing zone for years to come.

Violence in the south has abated over the last five years, but shows no sign of resolution. During this period the fiercest fighting has been the "war of the camps" of 1985–87, when the Shiite Amal, supported by elements of the Syrian and Lebanese armies, repeatedly stormed three Palestinian refugee camps in Beirut and southern Lebanon, bringing Palestinian settlements to the brink of starvation and epidemic by February 1987, at which time Amal lifted its siege and allowed shipments of food and emergency supplies into the Palestinian camps [*Time*, 2/23/87]. More recently, brutal battles between the Shiite Amal and the Palestinians, and also the Hizbollah, have underscored Amal's fierce determination to control southern Lebanon. In June of 1990, an inter-Shiite battle, pitting Amal against the Hizbollah, but also involving PLO fighters, claimed almost 200 lives in two weeks in a contest to control the southern district of Iqlim al-Tuffah [*Middle East International*, 8/2/90].

Meanwhile, fighting along Israel's "security zone" continues. The Hizbollah, whose power and influence grew initially in the wake of the Israeli invasion, has repeatedly fired rockets on settlements in northern Israel and attacked Israeli and SLA positions in southern Lebanon, prompting retaliation in force by Israeli warplanes. Various PLO factions have continued to stage raids across the border, although Yasser Arafat's Fatah group suspended raids into Israel after the U.S. and the PLO began a short-lived dialogue in December 1988 [*The Economist*, 3/4/89]. The PLO's defeat in Sidon by Lebanese forces in July 1991 has greatly reduced the PLO presence in the area, but Israeli raids against both PLO and Hizbollah positions continue.

At the end of 1991, as Arab-Israeli peace talks began in Madrid and Washington, Israel stepped up its attacks across its "security zone" into Lebanon proper. In late October, Israeli forces and elements of the South Lebanon Army launched an eight-day combined ground and air offensive into the Nabatiye area, attacking Hizbollah bases and Shiite villages. In January 1992, Israel bombed the headquarters of a radical PLO faction ten miles south of Beirut, killing ten including three PLO fighters. The following month Israel raided southern Lebanon and assassinated Hizbollah leader Abbas Musawi along with his wife and children [*Middle East International*, 3/6/92].

The mandate of the **United Nations Interim Force in Lebanon (UNIFIL)**, which was sent to restore Lebanese sovereignty in southern Lebanon in 1978 after an Israeli incursion, has been thwarted by Israel's refusal to evacuate its "security zone," and also by the harassment of local militias, including the Israeli-backed South Lebanon Army. UNIFIL has also had to contend with the violence of the Hizbollah, which has not been appeased by Israel's withdrawal from most of southern Lebanon in 1985 and remains committed to the "liberation" of Jerusalem and the destruction of Israel.

Another war between Syria and Israel in Lebanon is unlikely. In April 1986, allegations that Syria was behind a failed attempt to blow up an Israeli airliner spurred rumors of a new war, but tensions between Syria and Israel quickly subsided. Israel's withdrawal to its security zone in southern Lebanon in 1985 has eased friction between the two countries, restoring Lebanon as a buffer zone separating the Syrian and Israeli armies. At present, Israel, Syria, and the Shiite Amal all have an interest in checking the growth of PLO and Hizbollah influence in southern Lebanon. Both insurgent groups threaten to upset the delicate strategic balance that Israel and Syria have struck.

UNIFIL, which has nearly 6,000 troops in southern Lebanon, continues to play its peacekeeping role, although its U.N. mandate proscribes the use of force to stop guerrilla attacks or Israeli countermeasures. Since the establishment of UNIFIL, 156 members of the force have died, 60 as a result of hostile fire and bomb or mine explosions. During the last six months of 1988, 5 UNIFIL soldiers lost their lives in accidents and 17 were wounded, 10 of those from hostile fire or explosions. A UNIFIL soldier was killed in November 1991 when Israel bombarded Shiite villages in southern Lebanon [*The New York Times*, 11/16/91].

Libya and Terrorism

In the opening months of 1992 the Security Council passed a series of resolutions enjoining Libya to surrender two Libyan citizens to be tried in foreign courts for charges relating to the **downing of two civilian airliners**—Pan Am Flight 103, which exploded over Lockerbie, Scotland, in December 1988, killing all 280 passengers, and a Union des Transports Aériens (UTA) DC-10 airliner that exploded over Niger in September 1989. The Security Council resolutions, which ordered the government of a soverign state to surrender its nationals to stand trial in the courts of other states and imposed sanctions for failure to comply, was unprecedented. From the perspective of established international law, these resolutions were more than controversial, and fueled fears among Arab and Third World countries that the Security Council had become a rubber stamp for U.S.-inspired intervention against sovereign states.

In October 1991 a French magistrate issued warrants for the arrest of two Libyan secret servicemen, charging them with the bombing of the UTA airliner over Niger. The following month the United States and the United Kingdom accused Libya of masterminding the Lockerbie bombing, and announced plans to extradite two more Libyan nationals. Critics assailed both sets of charges as motivated more by politics than by justice. The Lockerbie charges seemed especially suspect as they ignored a large body of evidence suggesting that Ahmed Jibril's Popular Front for the Liberation of Palestine had manufactured in Syria the bomb that destroyed Pan Am Flight 103, with assistance from both Damascus and Teheran.

Nevertheless, in January 1992 the Security Council passed **Resolution 731**, urging Libya to "cooperate fully in establishing responsibility for the terrorist acts" by effectively extraditing six Libyan nationals to stand trial and give evidence in foreign courts of law. Libya refused, but it later offered to cooperate with an inquiry into the cases pending at the World Court in The Hague. But in March, the Security Council passed **Resolution 748,** imposing sanctions on Tripoli should it fail to comply with Resolution 731. Ten Council members voted for the resolution; China, Cape Verde, Morocco, India, and Zimbabwe abstained. Resolution 748 cut all commercial, diplomatic, and transport links to Libya; the Council ordered all U.N. member states to report to the Council by May 15 on compliance, and mandated a review by the Council of ongoing measure every 120 days.

In the wake of the voting, rioting swept embassy row in Tripoli, and the Venezuelan mission was badly damaged. In the weeks following Resolution 748, its sanctions were put into effect, and they were observed by Libya's Arab neighbors [*Middle East International*, 5/1/92].

UNRWA

The United Nations Relief and Works Agency for Palestine Refugees in the Near East (UNRWA) was created in 1949 to provide humanitarian support for some 700,000 Palestinian refugees. Today the agency extends a wide range of welfare services to some 2.5 million eligible Palestinian refugees in the Middle East, about a third of whom live in refugee camps. It provides education to 350,000 Palestinian students in Jordan, Lebanon, Syria, and the Occupied Territories. UNRWA also supplies shelter materials, emergency medical supplies, and food relief for more than 108,000 Palestinians it classes as "special hardship cases."

UNRWA's regular operations for 1992 were budgeted at $277 million. In December 1991, 37 countries pledged $149 million for this purpose, with the largest pledges coming from the United States and Sweden at $63.5 and $23.7 million, respectively [*UNRWA News*, 12/11/91]. The greatest challenge UNRWA now faces is how best to use its severely limited resources to serve its large and quite needy constituency.

As in past years, the anarchy and violence of Lebanon have imperiled both UNRWA clients and personnel, making the agency's work extremely difficult and dangerous. Since June 1982, 26 UNRWA workers have been killed in Lebanon, out of a total staff of 2,300. In February 1988 two UNRWA employees were kidnapped near Saida in southern Lebanon, allegedly by supporters of PLO renegade Abu Nidal [*The New York Times*, 2/6/88]. The agency played a vital role in getting emergency food and medical supplies into the Palestinian refugee camps that the Shiite Amal has besieged at various times since May 1985. Since the start of the Palestinian uprising in December 1987, UNRWA has reported extreme difficulties in meeting emergency demands for food, water, and medical care in the refugee camps of Gaza [U.N. press release DH/85/88]. Since the start of the Palestinian uprising in December 1987, seven UNRWA staffers have been killed by unidentified assailants as alleged Israeli collaborators, and 64 have been held in administrative detention by Israeli military authorities. In January 1992, Israeli authorities deported an UNRWA employee, along with 11 other Palestinians, from the West Bank [*UNRWA News*, 4/30/91, 1/8/92; UNRWA annual report 1990–91]. The agency has repeatedly protested what it views as Israeli harassment of its personnel in the Territories. Israel has responded that the arrests and detentions are justified on grounds of national security.

3. Africa

The General Assembly has two main items on its "Africa agenda" for 1992: It will be monitoring the apparent dismantling of apartheid in South Africa, examining the prospects not only for the country's future but also for improved relations between the Republic and its neighbors; and it will be discussing reports by the Secretary-General on the various armed conflicts that are contributing to the deterioration of the continent's economies. In the case of drought- and civil war-ridden Somalia, where the situation in the capital is so chaotic that both U.N. and nongovernmental relief missions have been at a virtual halt, the Security Council has been asked to consider using peacekeeping forces to protect the Organization's own aid workers. Africa's economic crisis was given extended consideration at the 46th Session, which adopted a New African Agenda for African Development. The first report on the implementation of that document is not due until the 48th Session in 1993, but current events and other factors suggest the likelihood of preliminary discussions at the 47th.

Apartheid

Events in South Africa since the summer of 1991 have convinced the majority of U.N. member states that **the end of apartheid may be in sight.** On September 14, 1991, South Africa President F. W. de Klerk, African National Congress President Nelson Mandela, and other political leaders signed a Peace Accord and pledged an end to civil violence. On October 25, at a conference of the Patriotic/United Front, the call went out for an all-party conference to take up the matter of a Constituent Assembly. On December 20, responding to this call, the representatives of 19 parties—among them, the South African government, the African National Congress (ANC), the Inkatha Freedom Party, and the Bophu-thatswana government—joined in a remarkable **Convention for a Democratic South Africa (CODESA).** At its conclusion all but the last two gave their "solemn commitment" to strive for a free and open society, based on democratic values, where the dignity, worth, and rights of every South African are protected by law; and to set in motion the process of drawing up a new constitution. This **constitution,** the 17 agreed, would establish a united, democratic, nonracial, and nonsexist state with sovereign authority over the whole of its territory. Furthermore, it would ensure the separation of powers among branches of government, with appropriate checks and balances; lay the foundation for a multiparty democracy (with an electoral system based on proportional representation and calling for regular elections and universal adult suffrage on a common voters' roll); and acknowledge the diversity of languages, cultures, and religions of the people of South Africa. Finally, all civil and human rights and liberties would be protected by an entrenched and justiciable Bill of Rights.

CODESA set up five working groups to prepare for a plenary meeting in March of 1992. These groups were to deal with political participation and the role of the international community; constitutional principles and the constitution-making body and process; arrangements for a transition to multiracial democratic rule; the future of the four nominally independent republics (Bophuthatswana, Ciskei, Transkei, and Venda); and the time frame for implementing decisions.

The prospects for negotiations were given a boost by the March 18 **referendum,** which was called by President de Klerk to challenge the Conservative party's assertion that most whites were against anti-apartheid reforms (and which brought initial objections from such groups as the ANC about whites-only balloting). In the referendum, which saw an 85 percent turnout, whites voted 2-to-1 in favor of dismantling apartheid, and de Klerk announced, "Today we have closed the book on apartheid." Now the negotiations between the government and the ANC began in earnest [*The Christian Science Monitor,* 4/30/92].

In negotiating South Africa's constitutional future, a particular sticking point has been the **arrangements for a transition to multiracial democratic rule.** On the eve of the May plenary, the CODESA working groups were divided over the percentage of votes required for acceptance of a constitutional provision. The government and Inkatha were holding out for a high figure, the ANC—expected to win more votes in a free election for a constitution-making body—for a significantly lower one [*The New York Times,* 5/15/92]. In the event, notes the *Financial Times,* the convention failed to clear this "most important hurdle. . . . Codesa ended in deadlock. The working groups were suspended, and the management committee—comprising senior members of all main parties—was charged with finding a way out of the most serious hold-up in the negotiating process since Mr. Nelson Mandela's release in February 1990" [6/5/92].

The government's actions to dismantle apartheid have already done much to end the hostility that has characterized the U.N.-South Africa relationship since 1952, when the General Assembly established the U.N. Commission on the Racial Situation in South Africa. Especially since 1960 and the Sharpeville massacre, the General Assembly has issued a stream of resolutions condemning apartheid and recommending drastic action against South Africa, and it followed these up with an **International Convention on the Suppression and Punishment of the Crime of Apartheid** and a **Decade of Action to Combat Racism and Racial Discrimination** as well. South Africa, defiant throughout much of this period, more recently attempted to deflect some of the attacks by introducing measures it claimed were reforms; but when the Republic introduced a state of emergency in 1985, banning many opponents of apartheid or detaining them without trial, the General Assembly stepped up its anti-apartheid activities, renewed its request that the Security Council impose economic sanctions and an oil embargo on South Africa, and continued to condemn Pretoria's actions to destablize neighboring states.

In December 1989 the Assembly met for its 16th Special Session, dedicated to the question of apartheid, and issued a **"Declaration on Apartheid and Its Destructive Consequences in Southern Africa"** [A/Res/S-16/1]. The declaration called attention to "a conjuncture of circumstances" that "could create the possibility of ending apartheid through negotiations" and indicated the steps the present government could take to supply "clear evidence of profound and irreversible changes" in South Africa: Release all political prisoners and detainees unconditionally, lift the bans and restrictions on all organizations and persons, remove all troops from the townships, and end the state of emergency and all political trials and executions. The 45th General Assembly resolved to keep all existing sanctions against South Africa in place until the telling evidence was received, and requested a report from the Secretary-General at the next session.

By the time the 46th Assembly convened in 1991 there had been some dramatic evidence of progress toward change in the Republic. The **46th Session** welcomed the signing of the National Peace Accord, the preparations for CODESA, and the government's measures to repeal the major apartheid laws, while urging the government to release the remaining political prisoners and remove all other repressive and discriminatory legislation. Despite the less than complete evidence it had demanded, the Assembly called for the restoration of international sporting, scientific, academic, and cultural ties with South Africa but once again requested the Secretary-General to report on the situation in South Africa at the next Assembly session [A/Res/46/79]. It was now that many countries began moving to normalize their relations with the Republic.

A number of situations continue to pose problems for the transition from apartheid to democratic rule in South Africa—important among them the **persisting animosity between the Zulu-based Inkatha Freedom Party and the ANC,** which has led to factional violence in Natal province and in the black townships around Johannesburg. This violence not only threatens instability but has given rise to charges by the ANC that government security forces are promoting it, effectively casting doubt on the government's credibility. The massacre of 40 persons in Boipatong, with alleged South African police complicity, in June 1992 led the ANC to withdraw from the CODESA negotiations on the 23rd of the month. To restore some of his credibility, President de Klerk took the unprecedented step of calling for international investigation of township violence and the alleged police misconduct. Sure to be another source of problems for a "new" South Africa is the apparent determination of right-wing white groups to secede from South Africa and establish an autonomous Afrikaner-Boer nation within a Boerstaat, or farmer state.

The 46th General Assembly expressed the belief that domestic developments in South Africa, and particularly the Peace Accord, were strengthening the **prospects for peace in the entire southern Africa region** [A/Res/46/160]. Over two decades, South Africa's strategy for survival has been marked by destabilizing efforts in neighboring states, Mozambique and Angola in particular, where such efforts have included not only direct military attack but support for the Mozambique National Resistance (RENAMO) in the one case and for the forces of the National Union for the Total Independence of Angola (UNITA) in the other. In 1984, Mozambique agreed to expel the ANC from its territory as a condition for withdrawal of South African support for RENAMO (the Nkomati Accords), and Angola signed a similar document (the Lusaka Accords), but South Africa did not cease its actions against these and other **Frontline states.** By 1987 the devastating effects of war and movement toward an understanding between Moscow and Washington had put the governments of Mozambique and Angola in a mood to negotiate with their enemies and attempt a reconciliation. With regard to **Angola,** aggressive diplomacy by the United States produced the New York Agreement of 1988, which arranged for the withdrawal of Cuban troops over 30 months (in company with Pretoria's acceptance of Security Council Resolution 435 of 1978 calling for an independent Namibia) and inaugurated peace talks between the Angola government and UNITA.

The U.N. Security Council, lending support to this agreement, established the **U.N. Angola Verification Mission (UNAVEM),** which oversaw the departure of the last Cuban by May 1991. U.S. and Soviet mediation efforts beginning in September 1990 resulted in a peace settlement of Angola's 16-year civil war on May 1, 1991; and not many days after the Cuban departure, the Council agreed to enlarge and prolong the mandate of UNAVEM, now **UNAVEM II**, to include the monitoring of presidential and legislative elections. (Yet to be settled are the more than 750,000 refugees and internally displaced people that the war had produced. The World Food Programme is providing food aid under the second phase of a Special Relief Programme for Angola.) The U.N. Secretary-General's report on Angola dated October 31, 1991, noted that UNAVEM II had been successfully deployed and would remain at its post until the conclusion of general elections on November 30, 1992 [S/23191].

The conflict in **Mozambique** too appears to be winding down, buttressed by Protocols on Electoral Principles signed by Mozambique and RENAMO on March 12, 1992 [*Mozambique Update, 4/30/92*]. At the direction of the 46th Assembly, the 47th will be considering such matters as cooperation between the U.N. system and all the Frontline states [A/Res/46/160] as well as special economic and humanitarian aid for both Angola [A/Res/46/142] and Namibia [A/Res/46/204]—over whose transition to independence another U.N. force presided not long ago.

The African Economic Crisis

Africa's economic crisis seems not only persistent but permanent—and of catastrophic proportions. As the New York-based, nongovernmental North South Round Table concluded in 1991:

> Africa as a continent has become increasingly marginalized. Its share of the world economy had fallen to under 2% by 1985; its terms of trade have fallen by 40% since 1980 while its indebtedness to the rest of the world has risen to some $280 billion. Perhaps worst of all, serious poverty has risen while incomes per head in Sub-Saharan Africa have fallen by 20% over the decade. According to World Bank projections, Africa is the one continent in which the number of poor is still projected to increase over the next decade by an additional 85 million by the year 2000, over a period when the number of poor elsewhere in the developing world is anticipated to fall by 385 million [*The Challenge of Africa in the 1990s*, p. 1].

Forced to depend on an international political economy that continues to reduce the terms of trade for the continent's export commodities, the states of Africa have been severely limited in their capacity to acquire sufficient resources for development. This problem is exacerbated by the internal policies of most African states, whose attempts to control prices and exchange rates and to subsidize some sectors of the economy have contributed to the generally dismal economic performance.

In 1980 the OAU adopted a blueprint for African development, **the Lagos Plan of Action for the Economic Development of Africa, 1980–2000 (LPA)**, which was based on the idea that the *main* obstacle to

African development is the continent's position of dependency in the international political economy and that the way out is through a strategy of collective self-reliance and regional integration. The plan's priorities were to achieve self-sufficiency in food production, eliminate illiteracy, develop indigenous manpower, and integrate development with African socio-cultural values. A year later the World Bank issued its own blueprint, **Accelerated Development in Sub-Saharan Africa: An Agenda for Action (AD)**, in which it argued that although external factors do play a role in Africa's economic crisis, the main causes are domestic policy deficiencies. The AD's prescription for economic recovery included eradicating overvalued currency rates, giving priority to agricultural development; improving economic management; and liberalizing the continent's economies. The LPA and the AD were often considered opposing tendencies in the search for appropriate strategies for African economic recovery, but some observers believe that the AD can be viewed as a short-term recovery plan that is essential to achieving the longer-term objectives of the LPA [see W. Ofuatey-Kodjoe in C. Murphy and R. Tooze, *The New International Political Economy* (Boulder, Colo., 1991), pp. 184–86]. Many African countries followed the prescription of the World Bank but to little avail.

The 13th Special Session of the General Assembly in May 1986 was a recognition of the seriousness of the situation; and out of this realization came the **U.N. Programme of Action for African Economic Recovery and Development 1986–1990 (UNPAAERD)**, which made specific policy recommendations for the African governments and established the levels of capital assistance to be provided by the international community. A midterm review of UNPAAERD in 1988 [A/43/664] and a report by the Secretary-General to the General Assembly in the same year [A/43/500] indicated that the goals of the action program were not being met and that this was largely due to insufficient external financing and protectionist policies of the industrialized countries.

By the end of 1987, over 35 African countries had embarked on **International Monetary Fund (IMF)-mandated structural adjustment programs (SAPs)**—a package that included currency devaluation, reduction of government deficits, and privatization of government industrial and agricultural enterprises. While most observers agree that the African countries are in need of internal policy reforms, the SAPs prompted sharp debate. In a series of studies—"Adjustment Lending: An Evaluation of Ten Years of Experience" and "Sub-Saharan Africa: From Crisis to Sustainable Growth"—the World Bank defended the SAPs on the grounds that countries pursuing SAPs were showing better signs of economic recovery than were others. The U.N.'s **Economic Commission for Africa (ECA)** rebutted this finding in its "Statistics and Policies: ECA Preliminary Observations on the World Bank Report 'Africa's Adjustment and Growth in the 1980s' " [Addis Ababa: ECA, 1989]. Following this review, the ECA developed its own **"African Alternative Framework to Structural Adjustment Programmes for Socio-Economic Recovery and Transformation" (AAF-SAP)**, which called on African governments "to move beyond the narrow preoccupation with short-term adjustment to embrace a range of far-reaching policy reforms that seek to transform the very structures of their economies" [Addis Ababa: ECA, 6/6/89]. The Secretary-General's Interagency Task Force on African Recovery, meeting in Arusha, Tanzania, in February 1990, adopted an **"African Charter"** that stressed the benefits of popular participation in the continent's economic recovery and recommended measures by governments, the United Nations, and donor agencies to encourage such participation. The 45th General Assembly adopted this charter and set up a committee of the whole to conduct a final review of UNPAAERD [A/Res/45/178].

In 1991, at its 46th Session, the Assembly considered and adopted the conclusion of that review committee: "None of the goals of the United Nations Programme of Action were fully realized" [A/46/41]. UNPAAERD's failure, said the report, was largely due to a lack of resources, which was due in turn to insufficient aid, to the disastrous decline in commodity prices, and to the huge debt incurred by most African countries. Since the 1980s, in fact, aid flows to Africa have stagnated in real terms. In 1990, official development assistance for Africa from all sources amounted to $15.9 billion, about the same as in the previous year. (Aid from the Soviet Union and Eastern Europe, some $510 million in 1985, had tumbled to zero that year; and Arab donations, $960 million in 1980, totaled only $96 million.) Nor does Africa's aid future seem much brighter. The Development Assistance Committee of the OECD has noted that, given other demands on its resources—in Eastern Europe, for example—increases in aid to Africa "may remain rather modest" [quoted in *Africa Recovery* 5, no. 4 (12/91), p. 8]. There are predictions too that the International Monetary Fund will not be a major source of external financing; and commercial bank lending, as well as direct foreign investment, are expected to be minuscule.

Since Africa derives 70 percent of its **export earnings** from raw materials, it is more seriously affected than others by the downturn in commodity prices. Of the 16 commodities of foreign exchange relevance in Africa, all but four (cocoa, rubber, tea, and tobacco) are facing sharp price falls over the next ten years; and by 2005, say some estimates, real prices will be at less than 60 percent of 1980 levels [*Africa Recovery* 6, no. 1 (4/92), p. 8]. The problem of low earnings is worsened by Africa's heavy indebtedness and its debt-servicing problems. In 1991 the total debt of sub-Saharan Africa stood at $175.8 billion, with an average debt service-exports ratio of 20.5 percent and a debt-export ratio of 340.8 percent

[*Africa Recovery* 5, no. 4 (12/91), p. 41]. Given this combination of indebtedness, reduced prospects for aid, and falling commodity prices, sub-Saharan Africa will face an acute finance gap throughout the 1990s—an estimated average of $3–$4 billion per year even if, against all likelihood, aid and net private foreign investment were to double during this period.

On the basis of the review of UNPAAERD, the 46th General Assembly adopted a **"New Agenda for the Development of Africa in the 1990s"** based on the idea that "Africa's development is primarily the responsibility of Africans." In this document, "the international community accepts the principle of shared responsibility [for the debacle] and full partnership with Africa and therefore commits itself to giving full and tangible support to the African efforts" [A/Res/46/151]. The objective of the "New Agenda" is to achieve an average real growth rate in gross national product of about 6 percent a year through the decade, paying special attention to such goals as increased life expectancy, lower rates of child and maternal mortality, and improved health, water, sanitation, basic education, and shelter [*Africa Recovery* 5, no. 4 (12/91)].

The international community committed itself to finding a solution to the African debt crisis. This would include further cancellation or reduction of ODA debt and debt service, and the encouragement of write-offs of private commercial debts (employing such techniques as debt-equity swaps, debt buy-backs, and debt-for-poverty alleviation). The international community also pledged to work toward the attainment of the U.N. target of allocating 0.7 percent of the GNP to ODA; and to improve the scope and operation of such compensatory finance schemes as the European Community's STABEX and SYSMIN stabilization funds, the IMF's Compensatory and Contingency Financing Facility, and the Swiss Compensatory Financing Programme, with a view to increasing and stabilizing the export earnings of African countries [ibid.; see also A/Res/46/151].

On the agenda of the African countries, which have committed themselves to sustainable development at all levels of socioeconomic activity, are such items as democratization, the creation of an environment suitable to the adoption of rational population policies, agricultural and rural development, and the development of effective regional and subregional economic cooperation and integration. In Resolution 151, the 46th General Assembly pledged to monitor the implementation of this New Agenda, to begin with a report by the Secretary-General to the 48th General Assembly, followed by a midterm review in 1996, and a final review and assessment in 2000. During two of the intervening years, 1995 and 1998, the Economic and Social Council will monitor the implementation process.

Internal Conflicts

Exacerbating Africa's economic woes in the post-cold war era is an epidemic of violent internal conflicts, and no region of the continent is immune. For a variety of reasons—including lack of leverage with the various parties, little direct interest in the outcome of their battles, and commitments elsewhere—the five permanent members of the U.N. Security Council have stood back from the fray, while various other U.N. bodies continue to administer to the hundreds of thousands of refugees now huddled in neighboring countries. The countries of refuge are invariably in economic straits, and may also be in the throes of civil war themselves.

A 4,000-man peacekeeping force deployed by the Economic Community of West African States has failed to stop the fighting in **Liberia**, which began in early 1990 and soon saw the rise of competing factions—as well as the swelling of Africa's refugee rolls, when an estimated half of Liberia's population fled their homes for other countries or other areas. In that same year, an intensification of the fighting in the 30-year war between **Ethiopia and Eritrea** led to an influx of refugees in neighboring **Somalia** and, in January 1991, to the collapse of the Somalian government. Somalia, released from 21 years of harsh rule, had no time to celebrate, however. Already suffering from the drought plaguing the entire Horn of Africa, it was soon visited by a new plague—a war between two clans of its former leader's own tribe—and now Somalis began fleeing to adjoining states in great number. Those who remained in the capital city were relentlessly shelled by opposing militias; and so dangerous was the situation in Mogadishu by the end of 1991 that all foreign embassy and nearly all U.N. personnel were pulled out, and even the International Red Cross halted its food deliveries [*The InterDependent*, Spring 1992]. With no discernible purpose to the fighting and anarchy the only rule, peacemaking efforts by the Organization of African Unity were frustrated repeatedly in 1991; and even when U.N. Secretary-General Boutros Boutros-Ghali brought representatives of the warring factions and the regional organizations together in New York and negotiated a cease-fire that was signed on February 14, it was months before there was any evidence that the fighting was winding down or that the U.N. could begin delivering aid. In light of these less-than-promising developments, the Security Council on March 17 supported the Secretary-General's decision to dispatch a technical team to Somalia to work out the modalities of a cease-fire and to develop a plan—and the mechanisms—for ensuring the delivery of humanitarian aid [S/Res/746]. In April the Council voted to establish a **small U.N. operation in Somalia (UNOSOM)** to monitor the cease-fire in Mogadishu; and it called on the international community to support the implementation of the **"90-day**

Plan of Action for Emergency Humanitarian Assistance to Somalia"
[S/Res/751].

On May 13, speaking at the National Press Club in Washington,
D.C., the Secretary-General was able to announce that "a week ago, for
the first time in many months, a United Nations-chartered ship carrying
5,000 tons of food was allowed to dock in Mogadishu" [text reproduced in U.N.
press release SG/SM/4752, 5/18/92]. But as Mogadishu was showing signs of
improvement, there were indications that other areas were disintegrating
further "in terms of the number of factions and depth of divisions
between them," as one diplomat characterized the situation [*The Christian
Science Monitor*, 5/19/92].

In **Sudan,** drought, famine, and a civil war between the Arab-
Muslim north and the black-African south have continued to generate
hunger and refugee flights—and so too, more recently, the Islamic-
military regime's policy of herding Khartoum's squatters into desert
camps at gunpoint [*The New York Times*, 6/3/92] and its sweeping program of
Islamicization. With the overthrow of the Mengistu government in
Ethiopia in May 1991, the rebel forces in the Sudanese Peoples Liberation
Army lost the mainstay of their support, and within a year the Sudanese
armed forces, aided by Iranian military advisors and deliveries of Chinese
weapons, had taken the field [ibid., 5/26/92]. Further ensuring victory, the
government had placed a ban on all shipments of aid to the south [ibid., 6/
8/92]. By spring 1992, when an estimated 7.2 million people in Sudan were
said to require emergency food aid [ibid.], the World Food Programme
and the U.N. Children's Fund had been forced to withdraw their
personnel, and the United Nations had suspended Operation Lifeline
Sudan, under whose auspices it had been feeding these hungry millions
[ibid., 4/15/92].

At its 45th Session in 1990, the General Assembly requested the
Secretary-General to coordinate the work of the U.N. system—and
mobilize financial, technical, and material assistance—for the rehabilitation and reconstruction of Liberia [A/Res/45/232]. During the 46th Session
the Assembly passed similar resolutions on Somalia [A/Res/46/167] and Sudan
[A/Res/46/178], as well as on **Chad** [A/Res/46/171] and **Djibouti** [A/Res/46/175]. At
the time these resolutions were passed, the **immediate survival of an
estimated 23.9 million people in the Horn** was already in serious
question [*The Economist*, 11/9/91].

4. Central America

The Peace Agreement signed January 16, 1992, by the Government of El
Salvador and the Frente Farabundo Martí para la Liberación Nacional
(FMLN) brought to a close one of Central America's longest and

bloodiest civil wars. Over 75,000 Salvadorans, mostly civilians, had lost their lives in the 12-year struggle between the U.S.-backed government forces and the five leftist rebel groups comprising the FMLN. The Agreement likewise marked the end of 24 months of intense U.N. intermediation between the warring sides in its first major diplomatic effort in the region. Under the accord, the United Nations will remain engaged in Salvadoran domestic affairs until the elections in 1994, verifying the compliance of both sides with the cease-fire provisions and a complicated set of political and economic reforms.

An uneasy peace had come to Nicaragua in 1990, prompted by U.N.-monitored elections in April, but the world body has been able to contribute only marginally to the long and difficult process of reconstruction since then. Continued civil strife and renewed fighting by rebel forces, which had been disarmed by U.N. peacekeepers following the elections, aggravate the serious and only slowly improving economic situation. The region's longest-running and least visible civil conflict continued to wrack Guatemala, but talks between the government and rebel leaders, with the participation of a U.N. observer, produced the first agreement on negotiating a political settlement since the outbreak of hostilities in 1954. A year into the negotiations, little progress had been made in actually ending the war, which has already claimed 100,000 lives and left 40,000 missing.

El Salvador

Progress toward a comprehensive peace settlement in El Salvador had been slow and sporadic since the initiation of direct talks between the government and rebel leaders in April 1990. By the following spring there seemed little reason to believe that negotiations could, in fact, be brought to a successful conclusion by year's end. Only two accords had been signed by the opposing sides up to that point—the **Agreement on Human Rights (San José Agreement)** of July 1990 and the **Mexico City Agreements** of April 1991—and neither addressed the key questions of army reform and the timing of a permanent cease-fire. In the absence of flexibility on those issues at the negotiating table, the situation in the field deteriorated, with government forces attempting once again to regain control over rebel-held territory.

Twelve months of shuttle diplomacy by the **Secretary-General's Special Representative to the talks, Alvaro de Soto,** and many weeks of face-to-face meetings between government and rebel representatives had not substantially changed the position of either side regarding acceptable cease-fire conditions. The government continued to insist on an immediate cessation of hostilities, the demobilization of rebel forces, and the return of land seized by displaced peasants. The FMLN offered only a temporary cease-fire—an "armed peace"—pending the end of government repression of its political activities, the implementation of radical economic and social reforms, and sharp reductions in the size and political power of the armed forces [*The Economist*, 5/25/91].

U.N. officials had hoped that the entry into force of the verifications provisions contained in the San José Agreement on human rights would have a positive effect on the peace process as a whole. On July 26, 1991, the 101 members of the **U.N. Observer Mission in El Salvador (ONU-SAL)** opened the two-month preparatory phase of the verification process, establishing offices around the country; gathering background information from relevant government officials and nongovernmental organizations; and visiting resettled, repatriated, and displaced persons as well as populations living in conflict zones. The observers also began to receive reports of alleged abuses, which were turned over to competent judicial authorities pending the mission's assumption of its full investigatory powers on October 1 [A/45/1055-S/23037].

While aimed primarily at improving the deplorable human rights conditions in the country (it is the first observer mission mandated to oversee compliance with a substantive accord rather than a cease-fire or an election), ONUSAL was also clearly intended to increase the confidence of both sides in the peace process and accelerate negotiations toward a cease-fire. At both sides' request, the mission had been established and deployed before a cessation of hostilities could be arranged—another first in the history of U.N. peacekeeping operations [*The New York Times*, 8/14/91]—and the Secretary-General had suggested that the initial contingent of human rights monitors could be quickly augmented with military observers or troops to verify or enforce a negotiated peace [S/22494].

With this agenda in mind, the Secretary-General's Special Representative set about to expand upon the constitutional reforms contained in the Mexico City Agreements, particularly those referring to greater civilian control over the military. But three rounds of talks on army reform and technical aspects of a cease-fire held between late May and mid-August 1991 failed to produce additional written agreements (none were necessarily expected, the United Nations claimed) [U.N. press release, CA/45, 6/24/91] and no further negotiations were scheduled.

Conditions and Guarantees

It had become clear that the original framework for negotiations agreed upon at the commencement of direct talks would have to be modified. The Geneva Agreement had stipulated a two-phase approach to a comprehensive settlement, encompassing initial talks on a cease-fire to be followed by separate negotiations on "conditions and guarantees" for the "reintegration" of former guerrillas into Salvadoran society. But the government's decision to renew offensive military operations, the army's demonstrated disregard for civilian authority, and the history of human rights abuses against the political opposition convinced the FMLN to demand guarantees up front.

In addition to the armed-peace idea, which would allow continued recruitment and military maneuvers by the rebels, the FMLN cease-fire proposals ranged from the complete demilitarization of the country to the "fusion" of the FMLN with the army or, at the very least, the incorporation of a significant number of guerrillas into the national armed forces. All of these proposals were judged unacceptable by a government already criticized from the right for having given away too much with too little in return. After the breakdown of the talks in August, **Salvadoran President Alfredo Cristiani** publicly rejected any rebel participation in the military as a "total impracticality" and argued that the rebels' best security guarantee involved the conversion of the FMLN into an unarmed political party [*The New York Times*, 8/26/91].

Alarmed that the three-month impasse could endanger the gains made in the peace process to date, the United States and the then Soviet Union offered their services to the Secretary-General and requested that he once again become personally involved in the negotiations [S/22963]. (Pérez de Cuéllar had participated in negotiating the Geneva Agreement and had interceded on several subsequent occasions in the process.) Announcing his willingness to play a more active role, the Secretary-General in turn requested both Washington and Moscow to respond to "a number of concrete ideas" he had previously discussed with them aimed at "cutting the Gordian knot" impeding progress on a cease-fire [S/22947]. These ideas evidently included supplying conditions and guarantees to the rebels other than those already rejected by the government.

Rebel leaders would later report that the United States in particular played a "key, positive role," beginning at this time, "in making a negotiated settlement possible" [*The Christian Science Monitor*, 1/6/92].

Having received satisfactory and confidential replies from U.S. and Soviet sources, the Secretary-General issued invitations to the Salvadoran government and the FMLN during the last week of August requesting that the parties meet with him separately at U.N. Headquarters for a new round of talks beginning September 16. In anticipation of a successful outcome to the negotiations, de Soto was reportedly formulating a "compressed agenda" of issues that would have to be settled once a cease-fire agreement had been reached [*The New York Times*, 9/3/91].

With international pressure increasing for a quick settlement, government and rebel leaders alike were unprecedentedly forthcoming in their public statements, and attempted to show flexibility and reasonableness in the face of purported intransigence and extremism from the other side. President Cristiani announced his government's willingness to cut the armed forces, separate the paramilitary police units from the army, and create an independent civilian police force [*The Economist*, 9/14/91]. The guerrillas emphasized their intention to transform part of their military force into a peaceful political movement. They also confirmed publicly for the first time specific proposals for reforms in the military, including the "purification" of the army through removal of suspected human rights violators, recruitment of individuals with "diverse political views" in the armed forces and the police, and revisions in the national security and defense doctrines [*The New York Times*, 9/3/91].

The New York Agreement

The Secretary-General "received encouraging reactions to his ideas," according to a spokesman, which were presented separately to President Cristiani and the five rebel leaders in New York on September 17 [ibid., 9/20/91]. Over the next four days Cristiani again rejected proposals for including FMLN fighters in the military as well as a rebel offer for a "one-year truce" if the talks made substantial progress; but after intensive negotiations on September 22–23, the El Salvadoran President announced to the General Assembly that the "main roadblocks" to a settlement had been lifted [ibid., 9/24/91]. Through a spokesman, the Secretary-General would say only that the "gap appears to be closing" but that "roadblocks still remain" [U.N. press release CA/50, 9/23/91].

Press reports, unconfirmed by U.N. officials, described Pérez de Cuéllar's plan as providing for substantial rebel participation in a new civilian police force—created to replace the current military-controlled police—but excluding the integration of guerrillas into the army. Some broad-based "political mechanism" was also reportedly being considered, which would oversee the implementation of reform, especially of the armed forces. Equal representation for the government, the rebels, and other groups was contemplated for this body [*The New York Times*, 9/23/91]. Another marathon session of talks on September 23–24 was necessary to consider the 25 amendments offered by the government to the original proposals, according to rebel sources. Cristiani was also said to be holding out for a broader agreement dealing with rebel demands for purification and reduction of the armed forces before leaving New York [ibid., 9/25/91].

On September 25 the Secretary-General announced to the press that with the signing of a "broad agreement on conditions and guarantees for the reintegration into society of members of the FMLN, . . . the Gordian knot has been untied." Follow-up negotiations on the remaining "substantive matters" and a "brief, dynamic cease-fire" were to commence

October 12 [U.N. press release CA/51, 9/25/91]. Seventeen months into the U.N.-brokered talks, a final accord was in sight.

The New York Agreement [A/46/502-S/23802] called for the establishment of a **"National Commission for the Consolidation of the Peace"**—to be known by its Spanish acronym **COPAZ**—which corresponded to the political mechanism mentioned in earlier press reports. Consisting of two representatives each from the government and the FMLN and one from every political party in the Legislative Assembly, COPAZ was to oversee the implementation of all political agreements reached between the opposing sides. Actual implementation would be left to the government and the FMLN themselves. Functioning by majority vote, COPAZ institutionalized rebel demands for civilian monitoring of and participation in the process of negotiated reform, particularly regarding the armed forces, without incorporating the FMLN into the army. The Archbishop of San Salvador and a delegate from ONUSAL were named as observers to the process.

Further agreement was reached in principle on purifying and reducing the armed forces, as well as on revising national military doctrine and training. Purification was to be handled by an ad hoc committee, with the participation of two nonvoting army officers. The negotiators also sketched out an agenda for the establishment of the National Civil Police originally provided for in the Mexico City Agreements, and stipulated that organization of the new force should not await the conclusion of a cease-fire or other political agreements. Applications from former FMLN members were to be considered on a nondiscriminatory basis. Regarding economic and social reform, private landholdings above 245 hectares would be used to meet the needs of peasants and landless farmers, and the occupation of land by rebel families and their sympathizers in guerrilla-controlled regions of the country would continue without government interference, pending a legal solution to the problem of landownership.

Government and rebel negotiators signed a second accord in New York approving the "Compressed Negotiations" [A/46/502/Add.1-S/23082/Add. 1], an agenda for further talks aimed at finalizing agreement on items already the subject of agreements in principle. "Compression" referred to the simultaneous rather than sequential pursuit of agreements on a cease-fire and the conditions and guarantees sought by the rebel factions. This meant that all issues considered in the compressed negotiations were to be settled before the imposition of the short and dynamic cease-fire alluded to by the Secretary-General. The government and the rebels had compromised on their respective demands for an immediate cessation of hostilities and an armed peace of indeterminate duration. In addition to the armed forces—including the security forces, the intelligence service, and paramilitary units—agenda items included the judicial and electoral systems, cease-fire conditions, verification by the United Nations, and a timetable for implementation of the comprehensive peace accord.

"International guarantees" of continued support for the peace process called for in the New York Agreement were provided by the **Security Council** and the **Group of Four Friends of the Secretary-General—Colombia, Mexico, Spain,** and **Venezuela**—on September 30. In **Resolution 714,** the Security Council explicitly endorsed the Agreement, "express[ed] its readiness to support the implementation of a settlement," and "urg[ed] both sides to exercise maximum and continuing restraint, particularly with respect to the civilian population." The Group of Four, which had actively participated in the U.N.-brokered talks and hosted direct negotiations, likewise expressed its "deep satisfaction" at the progress achieved to date, called on the Secretary-General to remain personally involved, and underscored the need for close cooperation between the opposing sides and among the country's "institutions, political parties, and social forces" [A/46/515-S/23101].

Toward a Cease-Fire

Follow-up negotiations were not even under way before rightists on the government side and many rank-and-file members of the guerrilla movement expressed their dissatisfaction with the deals struck by their respective leaders in New York and their continued distrust of their military and political foes. The army was reportedly disturbed by the timing of the accords (that same week a jury had convicted two officers of the 1989 slayings of six Jesuit priests, their cook, and her daughter) and the existence of secret written understandings with the rebels guaranteeing guerrilla participation in the new national police force. The rebels pointed to the recent government offensive against a guerrilla stronghold just north of the capital; the acquittal in the Jesuit case of seven other accused soldiers, some of whom had confessed to carrying out the actual killings; and the failure of the government even to bring charges against senior officers believed to have authorized the massacre. It was far from certain, in the view of some rebel fighters, that the army would continue to cooperate with the courts, either in the sentencing of the two convicted officers or in the promulgation of the judicial reforms contemplated in a comprehensive peace agreement [*The New York Times,* 10/4/91; *The Economist,* 10/5/91].

Direct talks convened as scheduled on October 12 in Mexico City and recessed after ten days of "cordial and constructive" negotiations. The United Nations reported "significant progress" in discussions of military reform and the initiation of exploratory talks on the "conceptual character" of cease-fire arrangements [U.N. press release CA/53, 10/23/91]. Negotiations resumed November 3 without incident. But continued maneuvering by both sides for strategic advantage in the field prompted the

Secretary-General to remind negotiators five days later that arrangements for a cease-fire were to be based on the situation on the ground as of April 4, 1990—the date of the Geneva Agreement. Continued fighting could not retroactively alter that situation, he pointed out, and territory won or lost since the Agreement was meaningless in determining mutually acceptable conditions for a cessation of hostilities [U.N. press release CA/54, 11/8/91].

Pérez de Cuéllar's personal appeal for restraint bore fruit on November 14, when the FMLN announced that it would unilaterally cease all offensive operations at midnight, November 16 [U.N. press release CA/55, 11/14/91]. The government promised "corresponding measures," and only minor skirmishes were reported over the next week [*The New York Times*, 11/20/91]. On November 21 the government announced an immediate ban on all aerial and heavy artillery bombardment of guerrilla positions, prompted by rebel delays in reconvening the peace talks in protest over continued government incursions deep within rebel-held territory. As a result, the level of fighting and combat-related deaths dropped dramatically throughout the country [ibid., 11/22/91].

Negotiations in Mexico were now at their most critical stage if they were indeed to constitute the final round of talks and lead to a comprehensive peace agreement by the end of the year. The major players began to exert gentle but steady pressure publicly and privately on both the government and the FMLN to accelerate the negotiations.

The United States and the Soviet Union, in a joint statement of December 2, reiterated their intention to provide all possible support to the parties in reaching agreement on outstanding substantive issues and a cease-fire. They urged the implementation of initial measures aimed at national reconciliation within the month and emphasized their belief that a U.N.-supervised cease-fire was urgently required to consolidate gains made in the peace process and to put a definitive end to the conflict [A/46/766-S/23278]. Briefing representatives of the Group of Four on December 6 regarding progress achieved to date, Pérez de Cuéllar said "the moment is fast approaching . . . when negotiations should move to New York," where he could personally intervene in the final phase of the talks if necessary. Arrangements for verification of the cease-fire were also set to begin with the participation of Marrack Goulding, Under-Secretary-General for peacekeeping [U.N. press release CA/56, 12/6/91].

As further impetus to the peace process and the transition to national reconciliation, the Secretary-General announced on December 10 the appointment of the three members of the **Commission on the Truth,** charged under the Mexico City Agreements with investigating serious acts of violence committed in El Salvador since 1980 and reporting publicly thereon [U.N. press release CA/57, 12/10/91]. Regarding the current human rights situation in the country, ONUSAL had released its first substantive report the month before, announcing that it had received just over 1,000 complaints of alleged violations of the San José Agreement since the inception of the mission's mandate. The observer mission had begun to investigate many of these and made specific recommendations to the Secretary-General regarding ways in which both the government and the rebels could improve their observance of the San José Agreement. ONUSAL emphasized that past human rights violations fell outside its mandate, except in cases where new evidence is uncovered, prosecutions are still under way, or past abuses form part of a systematic practice of human rights violations that have continued into the present [A/46/658-A/ 23222].

Talks ended in Mexico on December 10 with major disagreements still unresolved. The government rejected the main rebel demand for guarantees on guerrilla participation in a new civilian police force as representation by quota, and the two sides were still far apart on a scheme to redistribute land to peasants and rebel sympathizers, plans for cutting the armed forces, and legal protections on the rights of former guerrillas to organize politically. Both sides had nevertheless agreed to further meetings with the Secretary-General in New York, beginning December 16 [*The New York Times*, 12/11/91].

The New York Act

Four days into the talks the Secretary-General announced for the first time his keen personal desire to set the negotiations "on an irreversible course to conclusion" before the expiration of his term of office on December 31. To do so, he called for an end to "public debate"—and presumably leaks to the press—on the issues at hand by all representatives of the parties and the negotiators themselves. Final negotiations were conducted in absolute secrecy [Statement by the Secretary-General, 12/19/91].

In the **New York Act** [A/46/863-S/23504], signed at midnight on Pérez de Cuéllar's last day in office, December 31, the government of El Salvador and the FMLN announced the conclusion of "definitive agreements," which completed talks on all substantive items contained in the Compressed Negotiations. A cease-fire agreement was also announced, governing all technical and military aspects relating to the separation of the warring parties in the field and the dismantling of the FMLN's military structure. When implemented, the Act would mark the end of the Salvadoran armed conflict. Under the terms of the agreement, the **official cessation of hostilities** would take effect **February 1, 1992,** and would conclude, according to a strict timetable for the implementation of the cease-fire and all substantive accords signed since the San José Agreement, on October 31, 1992. Another provision stipulated that the timetable was to be worked out at subsequent talks, scheduled to begin January 5. Both sides further agreed to respect the informal truce then in effect and announced their intention to sign the final peace agreement in Mexico City on January 16.

The **New York Act II** of January 13, 1992 [A/46/863-S/23504], set the timetable for the implementation of all the accords comprising the comprehensive settlement, and the new Secretary-General, Boutros Boutros-Ghali, began readying the United Nations to undertake the monitoring and verification tasks assigned to it under the agreement. On January 14, the Security Council approved the Secretary-General's request to enlarge the mandate of ONUSAL to cover the verification of the cease-fire and the monitoring of public order pending the establishment of the National Civil Police. **Resolution 729** authorized the establishment of one military and one police division in ONUSAL, consisting of 372 and 631 observers, respectively, and 95 civilian staff, and extended the mission's mandate through October 31, 1992.

In **Resolution 730,** adopted coincidentally with the signing of the final agreements in Mexico City, the Security Council terminated the mandate of the **U.N. Observer Group in Central America (ONUCA),** deployed since November 1989 to monitor compliance with the Esquipulas II Agreements (a peace plan ratified in August 1987 by Costa Rica, El Salvador, Guatemala, Honduras, and Nicaragua), in order to allow the Secretary-General to transfer some of its personnel and equipment to ONUSAL before the February 1 Salvadoran cease-fire. Stationed along the borders and in the capitals of the five states of the region, ONUCA's 132 military observers were to verify that aid to irregular forces and insurrectionist movements had been terminated and that the territory of one state was not used for attacks on another state. Costa Rica and Honduras expressed "unease and concern," according to the Secretary-General, when informed of the decision, but the Council agreed that the needs in El Salvador must take precedence. Also figuring in the termination of ONUCA were the mounting costs of maintaining an ever-increasing number of peacekeeping operations in the field, and the growing belief that such operations should be established to carry out a specific task for a specific period and then be disbanded [S/23421].

The Peace Agreement

At the signing ceremony the Secretary-General called the Peace Agreement [A/46/864-A/23501] "the crowning achievement of a long and arduous journey" and said it constituted "a revolution achieved by negotiation" [U.N. press release CA/61, 1/16/92]. Totaling more than 90 pages, the agreement contained nine separate accords, addressing the full range of political, economic, and social ills that had prompted the resort to arms 12 years before. The accords varied widely in length and complexity, with consensus on the most controversial subjects spelled out in painstaking detail. Only nine paragraphs were needed to cover judicial and electoral reform and the U.N.'s verification authority, subjects of previous agreement. Provisions pertaining to economic and social questions, the political participation of the FMLN, and the timetable for implementation ran to 18 pages, with the bulk of the agreement taken up by the three accords governing military reform, the establishment of the National Civilian Police, and the cessation of armed conflict.

Those latter provisions commited both sides to phased reductions in their forces under international supervision. Immediately following the cease-fire, ONUSAL would oversee the separation of government and rebel forces and verify that each had reported to some 150 designated sites around the country within a week's time. By early March the forces were to be further concentrated, with soldiers assembling at 62 locations and rebels at 15 others. ONUSAL was then to verify the inventories of all arms and ammunition held by both sides and to store all rebel arms—save personal weapons—pending their destruction by the rebels themselves in early October. Between March and October the rebels were gradually to leave the secure areas to return to civilian life, surrendering their weapons as they did so.

All combat units of the 6,800-person guerrilla forces would be dismantled by October 31, along with three-and-a-half of the five elite counterinsurgency battalions of the army. The remaining battalions would be dissolved by November 30, and the entire army cut by about half—to approximately 30,000 members—within two years. Early action would be taken against the military-led public security forces, numbering some 17,000 personnel. The National Guard and the Treasury Police were to be subsumed into the army by March, the National Intelligence Department dissolved by June, and the paramilitary civil defense forces disbanded by July. The National Police would be closely monitored by ONUSAL and gradually phased out over the two years required to recruit, train, and deploy the new National Civil Police.

The numerous substantive and procedural reforms on military as well as nonmilitary matters contained in the accords were to be given the force of law through approval by the Legislative Assembly. The reform process would begin with the adoption of a preliminary bill formalizing COPAZ, the oversight body of the entire process. Its ten members—two from the government (including one army officer), two from the FMLN, and one each from the political parties represented in the Legislative Assembly—were sworn in by President Cristiani on the first day of the formal cease-fire. COPAZ was to submit draft legislation to the Assembly converting treaty provisions into statutes, establishing new governmental entities where necessary, and approving appointments of officials and staff. The actual implementation of the reforms would be left to the various institutions to be set up under the different accords.

Regarding the armed forces, an ad hoc commission would undertake purification; the Truth Commission would decide how best to end the impunity of army officers before civilian courts; and appropriate legislation would be proposed and adopted on suspending conscription. A National Public Security Academy would be set up to train the new police force. Judicial reforms included the establishment of a National Council of the Judiciary to guarantee the independence of courts of law from political parties and the state, and the appointment of a National Counsel for the Defense of Human Rights, i.e., an attorney general with specialized investigatory powers. A Special Commission would study and approve draft amendments to the electoral code.

Among economic and social questions, the problem of landownership within conflict zones would be handled by another special commission empowered to settle disputes between current holders and rightful owners. A Forum for Economic and Social Consultation would work out broad agreements on promoting equitable economic and social development, and the government would cooperate with the FMLN in drafting a National Reconstruction Plan. Finally, to ensure the political participation of the FMLN, the civil and political rights of former guerrillas would be recognized through legislation or "other measures," political prisoners would be freed, and full guarantees and security extended to returning exiles. The FMLN would also be legalized as a political party.

Despite the comprehensiveness of the accords, serious problems with their design and implementation were immediately evident. Regarding security arrangements, the army would remain twice as large after the mandated cuts as it was before the outbreak of the war in 1980, raising questions as to whether its power and influence would really be reduced as intended. The possibility of continued human rights abuses might be further increased by the two-year delay in completely eliminating the old army-led police force, called the "Achilles' heel" of the entire agreement. On economic and social questions, implementation of the national reconstruction plan would make the country heavily dependent on foreign assistance. The government and the rebels would also have to reach basic agreement on the content of the plan to attract external funding in the amounts required: The costs of reconstruction had been estimated at $1.8 billion. This could prove difficult, since the government was not obligated under the peace agreement to accept changes in the plan that might be recommended by the opposition [The Christian Science Monitor, 2/3/92].

The accords also require formal approval of reform legislation by the Legislative Assembly, stipulations that might stall full implementation of the overall agreement if political campaigning in advance of the 1994 elections heats up. Because it both holds the presidency and constitutes the majority party in the legislature, the **Nationalist Republican Alliance (ARENA)** party could conceivably block reforms were moderates like Cristiani replaced by members of the vocal right-wing faction. Analysts say concerns that the February 20 death of radical right leader and ARENA founder **Roberto d'Aubuisson** might set off a power struggle within the party and turn the government against the peace process should be balanced by the party's need to field a candidate who can win against a coalition of leftists contesting free elections for the first time. Cristiani is prohibited by law from succeeding himself in office [ibid., 2/24/92].

Such political concerns were said to have figured prominently in the mutual decision to amend the agreement within a week of its signing by adopting a limited amnesty for all government and guerrilla forces. COPAZ announced preliminary agreement on amnesty terms on January 23, and the legislature approved it the same day. Under the Law of National Conciliation, intended to encourage the swift return of rebel leaders from exile and the full participation of all combatants in the cease-fire arrangements, soldiers or rebels convicted of serious or violent crimes in jury trials (as in the Jesuit case), those committing such offenses between December 31 and the signing of the peace accords, and anyone implicated in politically motivated killings of noncombatants and other human rights abuses by the Truth Commission were excluded from pardon [*The New York Times*, 1/24/92]. Critics charged that the amnesty, though ostensibly limited, was general in effect, pertaining not only to acts of war but also war crimes and crimes against humanity, and thus would prevent the prosecution of human rights abuses on both sides. This was so, they argued, because the small size and brief mandate (six months) of the Truth Commission would make the identification and investigation of all alleged violations of human rights and other high crimes a virtual impossibility. Guerrilla leaders, army officers, and others who might have been removed from political contention by such allegations were effectively freed by the amnesty to pursue public office [*The Christian Science Monitor*, 2/7/92].

On the day following announcement of the amnesty, a Salvadoran judge handed down 30-year sentences against the two army officers convicted in the 1989 Jesuit killings. (Two other officers, though acquitted by the jury, were sentenced to three years each, as was another officer not tried by jury.) The government had vigorously sought pardons for the men, which could be forthcoming. Six months after the Truth Commission recesses, the Legislative Assembly can vote to reconsider the case and lift the sentences, either by pardoning the officers or by applying the limited amnesty to them [*The New York Times*, 1/25/92].

Reconstruction and Reform

The government wasted no time in getting the National Reconstruction Program off the ground or in appealing for political support among the country's rural poor in the former combat zones near the Honduran border. President Cristiani announced a $14.3 million first phase of the program February 2, targeting the needs of 800,000 people in 106 communities hardest hit by the war [ibid., 2/3/92]. FMLN leaders immediately complained that they had not been consulted on the plan as stipulated in the peace agreement. Discussions with the former rebels began February 14 under the mediation of the **U.N. Development Programme (UNDP)** [*The Christian Science Monitor*, 2/21/92]. UNDP is also charged under the accords with administering a national reconstruction fund, advising the government on ways to mobilize external support, assisting in the development of projects and programs likely to attract such support, and facilitating the involvement of bilateral and multilateral development agencies. In the field, UNDP is to provide technical assistance and help avoid overlap between activities supported by the national plan and those already being pursued by NGOs at the local and regional level.

The government will probably be able to finance short-term reconstruction—aimed at providing electricity, water, roads, and schools in the war-ravaged sections of the country—through small-scale public works projects. In addition to their relatively modest cost, these projects would supply immediate work to thousands of returning soldiers and guerrillas. The **U.S. Agency for International Development (USAID)** plans to spend about $30 million to support such projects in 1992. But major repairs to the infrastructure—large-scale road building, replacement of bridges, and expansion of the electrical grid—will require multilateral development assistance. The **InterAmerican Development Bank** has reportedly pledged some $150 million, and the **World Bank** prepared to announce its contribution to the reconstruction effort in March [ibid., 3/21/92].

Money problems have also plagued the implementation of the security arrangements under the cease-fire accord. The United Nations is seeking an additional $2 million to allow ONUSAL to house and feed rebels reporting for demobilization and several million more in training funds for the new police force [*The New York Times*, 2/2/92, 2/11/92]. In an unprecedented move, UNDP agreed to "support" the training, apparently by donating staff to the effort, but planned to appeal to the international community to cover the estimated $6 million cost [U.N. press release CA/62, 1/20/92]. As of early February, U.N. officials were arranging a special collection among the permanent members of the Security Council for the Salvadoran police academy, due to be established May 1.

The most troubling issue to be dealt with in the reconstruction period may well be reform of the land-tenure system. The right wing of President Cristiani's National Republican Alliance party is opposed to surrendering individual landowning rights to the peasant-run cooperatives set up in territories occupied by the rebels since the outbreak of the war. Conservatives further charge that many of the cooperatives are unprofitable and endanger the production of major export commodities, such as coffee. Despite these criticisms, the peace agreement obligates the government to propose ways in which rebel families and their sympathizers can become owners of the lands they occupy. One proposal is the establishment of a "land bank," which would offer rightful owners either cash payments or lands elsewhere in the country [*The New York Times*, 2/2/92, 2/11/92].

The problem is compounded by the occupation of land never under rebel control or in disputed areas, situations not clearly covered in the accords. In addition, were landowners to turn down government compensation in cash or in kind, peasants would be subject to removal from their cooperatives by the armed forces under international supervision—a potentially explosive situation and one that would involve a highly controversial use of impartial peacekeeping forces [*The Christian Science Monitor*, 2/14/92]. The United Nations is already in danger of being drawn more deeply into the dispute by a March 4 request from the Honduran government for the deployment of U.N. observers along the Salvadoran-Honduran border. The appeal came in the wake of allegations by Honduran military intelligence that Salvadoran rebels had occupied lands in border areas long in dispute between the two governments [*The New York Times*, 3/5/92]. Having recently withdrawn ONUCA from the region, the United Nations is unlikely to grant the request.

A variety of problems relating to the implementation of the peace agreement, including how to interpret certain key provisions, were discussed in three days of talks between the government and the FMLN, under the mediation of U.N. Under-Secretary-General Marrack Goulding [U.N. press release CA/63, 3/16/92]. The discussions, which ended on March 14, seemed to produce practical solutions acceptable to both sides, but the Secretary-General concluded in his report of May 26 that "serious delays in implementing various provisions of the agreements" remained an ongoing problem that "undermined each side's confidence in the other's good faith" [S/23999].

While the initial separation of forces had been completed on schedule (February 6), the Secretary-General expressed particular concern about the failure of both sides to further concentrate their forces at the 77 agreed-upon locations by the March 2 deadline. In an effort to preserve the overall timetable governing the implementation of all nine peace accords, Goulding had persuaded government and rebel leaders later that month to accelerate the movement of their forces to the designated sites. The rebels had submitted a revised schedule for their demobilization to ONUSAL before Goulding's departure, and the government pledged similar action. By the end of May, however, Salvadoran army personnel continued to occupy one disputed location, and some 8 percent of FMLN forces remained outside the 15 safe zones identified in the peace agreement.

According to the Secretary-General's report, the technical and financial problems involved in housing and feeding the thousands of soldiers and rebels reporting for demobilization were responsible for some of the delays in concentrating the opposing forces, at least initially. The government's refusal to withdraw army personnel from certain military installations on national security grounds also contributed to the problem. But the Secretary-General cited attempts to maintain the Treasury Police and the National Guard as public security forces as the major impediment to the full and timely implementation of the cease-fire accord. Goulding had won assurances that former police and guard personnel transferred to the army would not be used in the enforcement of public order and would be subject to the restrictions and reductions spelled out in the accords. Nevertheless, as of late May 1992 some 3,500 of them remained in their original barracks and outside the concentration points.

The transfer of large numbers of personnel from these two public security bodies to the National Police and army—and the "conversion," rather than outright elimination, of the Treasury Police and the National Guard into Military Police and the Frontier Guard, respectively—further complicated the issue. ONUSAL has sought clarification of the government's intention in establishing the new forces, as well as the purpose of legislation—approved by the Legislative Assembly on April 23—that did not clearly abolish existing treasury and guard units. ONUSAL has also asked for information on the security personnel transferred to the National Police, which would allow close monitoring of their activities.

Responding to the lack of government cooperation, the FMLN has continued to delay the concentration of its own forces. Rebel leaders have also refused to allay U.N. concerns that the FMLN retains clandestine caches of arms and ammunition over and above the weaponry inventoried and verified by ONUSAL.

On a related matter, Goulding had reported progress in establishment of the National Civil Police, an apparent reference to finding suitable headquarters for the National Public Security Academy. The Secretary-General stated in May, however, that the premises were not expected to become available until early July—well beyond the May 1 deadline for recruitment to begin. The refusal of the government to place a suitably large facility at the disposal of the Academy in a timely manner, the Secretary-General pointed out, would mean that class sizes would be reduced and the eventual deployment of the civil police further delayed. Also as of late May, COPAZ had not yet acted on the draft laws establishing the Academy and the civil police as legal entities; and the appointment of a Director General, scheduled for March 2, was still pending. Citing these delays, as well as others relating to progress on land reform and on the legalization of the FMLN as a political party, the rebels failed to meet the May 1 deadline for the return of 20 percent of their forces from the safe zones to civilian life.

As of mid-year the understandings reached during March talks concerning the interpretation of land-reform provisions were holding up well. To encourage a solution to the problem of land-ownership in former conflict zones, Goulding had suggested that government and rebel delegations to the special commission that was set up to handle the issue begin their work by verifying the land inventory submitted by the FMLN under the accords. He had further suggested that both sides cooperate with ONUSAL in arriving at a mutually acceptable interpretation of the provisions in dispute. In his final suggestion, Goulding sought to improve the atmosphere for negotiations by inviting the rebels to "do everything possible" to prevent further expropriation of land and inviting the government to make comparable efforts in ending dispossessions.

The implementation of other economic and social provisions has gone less smoothly, according to the Secretary-General. The Forum for Economic and Social Consultation, set to convene May 11, was postponed; and uneven progress in restoring public administration in the former conflict zones (i.e., the return of all elected mayors and judges) prevented the national reconstruction plan from becoming fully operational. Programs to promote the reintegration of soldiers and rebels into civilian life also remain to be established, but the FMLN has begun to organize itself as a political party pending official legalization. The approval by COPAZ of the law establishing the Office of the National Council for the Defense of Human Rights and the Legislative Assembly and appointment of a Counsel may help accelerate the concentration of rebel forces in the field and their reintegration into society.

In concluding his report, the Secretary-General alluded to ongoing meetings between government and FMLN leaders to establish a new timetable for implementing the accords and for recovering time lost in the numerous delays to date. Both sides expressed to him their belief that this could be done by the next reporting period.

Guatemala

Lacking the intense U.N. involvement and ongoing international pressure that made the Salvadoran accords possible, peace talks in Guatemala have made little progress since opening in April 1990. Plagued by many of the same socioeconomic inequalities and political excesses as El Salvador, Guatemala is considered an even tougher challenge for international mediators, owing to the extreme brutality of the military and the inability of the small and poorly organized resistance to force major concessions from the government. After signing the **Agreement on a General Agenda** in Mexico City on April 26 [A/45/1009-S/22573], the government of **President Jorge Serrano** and representatives of the four rebel groups comprising the **Guatemalan Revolutionary National Unity** movement (known by its Spanish acronym URNG) held seven more rounds of talks through February 1992 but failed to reach a consensus on even the first point of the 11-item agenda. At the insistence of both sides, the participation of the **Secretary-General's Special Representative** to the talks, **Francesc Vendrell**, has been limited to that of Observer.

Only the second civilian to hold the presidency since the army relinquished direct control over the government in 1986, Serrano came to office in January 1990 promising "total peace" and an end to political and human rights abuses by the military. However, politically motivated killings of civilians had actually increased since the initiation of direct talks—from 304 reported cases in 1990 [*The Economist, 7/20/91*] to 321 for the first half of 1991 [*The Christian Science Monitor, 7/26/91*]—and the government's peace plan, announced at the outset of the negotiations, was immediately criticized as offering little more than an amnesty for the rebels in return for their surrender. Estimated to number only 1,500 to 2,000, the guerrillas face a half-million-man paramilitary force loosely organized into "civil patrols" and a 45,000-member army. The U.S. Department of State has alleged that the patrols and the army-led security forces operate "with almost total impunity" and are responsible for most of the kidnappings, torture, summary executions, and "disappearances" meted out to human rights activists, trade unionists, leftist politicians, and members of the indigenous Indian population considered sympathetic to the rebels [*The Economist, 7/20/91*].

After the third round of negotiations in July 1991, agreement on a pact of reforms addressing the first half of the first agenda item on "democratization" seemed likely. Monsignor Rodolfo Quezada Toruno, President of the National Reconciliation Commission (CNR) and Conciliator to the talks, said he hoped to see a joint declaration on strengthening democratic processes in the country [*Financial Times, 7/26/91*], and President Serrano expressed his readiness to make the legislative and constitutional changes necessary to implement it [*The Christian Science Monitor, 7/26/91*]. The Queretaro Agreement was signed July 25, and negotiators agreed to take up the second half of the first item, **human rights**, at the fourth round of talks in September. At that time, the President predicted an end to the war in six to eight months.

By the end of the fifth round in October, however, talks were deadlocked, and Serrano refused to continue direct negotiations until the two sides adopted a more conciliatory stance. Monsignor Quezada and U.N. Observer Vendrell shuttled back and forth between government officials and rebel negotiators, reportedly seeking major concessions to close the gap. The disagreement stemmed from rebel demands for international human rights monitoring in Guatemala and government compensation to victims of past abuses. Before signing any cease-fire or peace agreement, the guerrilla leaders insisted on the establishment of a truth commission, operating under U.N. auspices, to investigate human rights violations and the implementation of measures to prevent such occurences in the future [*The Christian Science Monitor*, 11/26/91]. The government rejected U.N. involvement as unconstitutional and unnecessary. The office of human rights ombudsman had been created under Serrano's precedessor and was widely regarded as objective and "relatively fearless" [*The New York Times*, 12/10/91]. The government would consider guarantees to the rebels only within the context of a final peace accord. It specifically refused the guerrilla demand to disband the civil patrols—called the eyes and ears of the army in the countryside—in advance of a complete cessation of hostilities.

With the civil war winding down in El Salvador and the success of his presidency dependent on the resumption of peace talks, Serrano's position appeared to soften somewhat by late December. As a substitute for the truth commission, which was completely unacceptable to the army, he offered to discuss the establishment of a "mechanism for pardon and reconciliation" and said that the government was prepared to offer compensation "in the form of aid to entire communities, not individuals." Past abuses would be handled through the dissemination of existing U.N. human rights reports, while the ombudsman was already empowered to prevent abuses in the future. Serrano also claimed that recently implemented judicial reforms allowed the courts to investigate and prosecute human rights abusers, and said that the government and the rebels were nearing a "partial agreement" on human rights [ibid.].

Continued pressure from the United States for the resolution of notorious cases of abuse against U.S. citizens was also beginning to bring results. Seven enlisted men were charged by a military tribunal with the June 1990 kidnapping and murder of Michael DeVine, a proprietor of a guesthouse in the Guatemalan countryside. (Three officers were questioned by the tribunal but released.) The Bush administration had cut off its relatively small ($2.9 million) military aid program to Guatemala over the incident in December 1990, and Congress later approved a joint resolution conditioning further economic aid on the resolution of it and similar cases [ibid., 12/13/91]. The case of Diana Ortiz, an Ursuline order nun, may now also go forward, despite her controversial two-and-a-half-year delay in testifying to allegations of kidnapping, torture, and sexual abuse at the hands of security forces in November 1989 [*The Washington Post,* 4/8/92]. The fate of a freelance journalist who disappeared in 1985 may be close to resolution, as the family of Nicholas Blake believes it has located his remains as well as those of Griffen Davis, an amateur photographer seen with Blake shortly before his disappearance. The family agreed to pay a reward for information in the case and not to pursue charges against the members of a civilian patrol thought to have carried out the killings [*The New York Times,* 3/25/92].

The United States has been unable to exercise the leverage against Guatemala it has used against other South and Central American countries, due in part to the refusal of the Guatemalan military since 1977 to accept overt military aid tied to human rights concerns. The Bush administration has, however, continued to supply security assistance called "Economic Support Funds," which, critics charge, could be cut off pending army concessions in the peace talks [*The Christian Science Monitor,* 1/10/92].

In a significant human rights decision not involving U.S. citizens, an army lieutenant and a sergeant were convicted by a military court and sentenced to 16 and 4 years, respectively, for the December 1990 massacre of 13 in the village of Santiago Atitlan. While the verdicts represented a rare prosecution of army personnel, the massacre itself led to the withdrawal of the army garrison from the town and demands from a number of other small communities for similar action. Observers noted that further evacuations could weaken the army's control over the administration of local governments and create a grassroots trend toward greater civilian authority over the military, but plans to strengthen the remaining garrisons were already under way [*The New York Times,* 2/12/92; *The Christian Science Monitor,* 3/11/92].

Some progress was reported on human rights questions when the talks between the government and rebels resumed in mid-December 1991, but President Serrano's prediction of a partial accord failed to materialize by the conclusion of the eighth round of negotiations in late February 1992. Disagreement focused on three points: The government shifted its position somewhat to accept a truth commission in principle, but continued to oppose giving any such body prosecutorial powers over individuals or institutions; rebel calls for greater governmental observance of international agreements governing the treatment of prisoners and civilians also reportedly went unheeded; and the government reiterated its refusal to dismantle the civil defense patrols until hostilities had ceased, and only in cases where involuntary participation or abusive behavior could be proved [*The New York Times,* 2/27/92]. On March 2 a civilian court sentenced a former patrol member to death for the murder of a civilian in 1991, the first time such a conviction and sentence have been handed down in the Guatemalan courts. The sentence is under appeal and if upheld will mark the first legal execution in the country since the transition to civilian rule [*The Christian Science Monitor*, 3/11/92].

That same month the government reached agreement with Mexico on the safe return of the **44,000 Guatemalan refugees** who fled to that country after violent counterinsurgency campaigns in the early 1980s. Plans to repatriate 10,000 refugees a year with the support of the **U.N. High Commissioner for Refugees (UNHCR)** and international donors are pending further talks in May; and Guatemala has already launched a $66 million resettlement project, with $40 million expected to come from foreign donors. Although the 775 Guatemalans who left Mexico for home during the first three months of 1992 is twice the number that left during all of 1991, anywhere from 40 to 90 percent of the refugees may choose to remain behind [ibid., 4/16/92].

The resettlement of populations uprooted by the armed conflict is the seventh of the ten agenda items not yet addressed as peace negotiations inch forward. Organizations representing the majority native population have demanded inclusion in the talks when negotiators consider the third item on identity and rights of indigenous peoples, but their participation is considered unlikely [ibid., 11/26/91]. Without such support from national groups and the active involvement of the international community through the United Nations, replicating the broad agreements reached in the Salvadoran negotiations will be an extremely slow and difficult process. The list of the other eight outstanding items hints at the difficulties that lie ahead: strengthening civilian authority and the role of the army in a democratic society; constitutional and electoral system reform; socioeconomic considerations; the agrarian situation; bases for bringing the URNG into the political life of the country; arrangements for the final cease-fire; timetable for the implementation, fulfillment, and verification of agreements; and signing of the agreement on a firm and lasting peace and demobilization of the military.

Nicaragua

Action by the Security Council in monitoring the election of **President Violeta Chamorro** and demobilizing the contra rebels in 1990 gave way to more involvement by the General Assembly, the U.N. Development Programme (UNDP), and the **U.N. Economic Commission for Latin America and the Caribbean (ECLAC)** in rebuilding Nicaragua during 1991 and 1992. The General Assembly welcomed the signing of phase II of the National Conciliation Agreement on Economic and Social Matters on August 15, 1991 [A/Res/46/109A], which addressed the controversial issues of property rights and privatization; but ECLAC noted that after eight years of civil war, 61 percent of the Nicaraguan population lived in extreme poverty. The country had become the second poorest in the hemisphere, after Haiti. With emergency relief from the Organization of American States (OAS) and the U.N. High Commissioner for Refugees (UNHCR) winding down for the 100,000 people displaced by the conflict, UNDP got a $2 million revolving credit program under way to allow small farmers to invest in equipment and supplies, and began administering a $25 million program aimed at rebuilding infrastructure like schools, hospitals, and homes [*World Development*, 9/91].

Such efforts do little, however, to address major structural deficiencies in the economy, including a $10.8 billion foreign debt, 13,500 percent annual inflation, and more than 50 percent unemployment. Nor could they address divisive political problems like land redistribution. Civil unrest broke out in June, July, September, and November of 1991 over attempts by anti-Sandinista deputies in the National Assembly to overturn radical property laws adopted in the final days of Sandinista rule. Designed to prevent the eviction of all those receiving land or property titles under the former regime—including rural families, urban squatters, and other beneficiaries of agrarian reform—the laws also protected Sandinista party officials given property for personal or political gain [*South*, 9/91]. The legislature approved repeal of the property laws in June, but President Chamorro vetoed the action rather than risk alienating the Sandinista National Liberation Front (FSLN)—still the largest political party in the country—in advance of the 1996 elections. The troubles were compounded by the apparent unwillingness of the army and police, which remain under the control of Sandinista loyalists, to reassert control and arrest those responsible for the wave of bombings, seizures of anti-Sandinista radio stations, and occupations of public buildings [*The Economist*, 6/29/91].

National security was further endangered by the decision of several hundred former contras, beginning in April 1991, to take up arms against the army and Sandinista sympathizers. Largely confined to the northwest section of the country, these "recontras" launched relatively few operations against government forces during the year, and violence against the civilian population was still relatively rare; but efforts to disarm them were a governmental priority [*The New York Times*, 9/12/91]. The ability of the resistance to rearm despite having surrendered some 18,000 weapons to U.N. peacekeepers in 1990 indicated that military hardware was still readily available (ONUCA reported no confirmed evidence of external assistance, however [S/23173]), and fears of full-scale warfare reemerged.

The economic picture improved somewhat after currency devaluation in March reduced inflation to 80 percent per month for 1991 and the government began to divest itself of state-run companies. The United States forgave Nicaragua's $260 million debt to Washington in September [*The New York Times*, 9/26/91] and disbursed $430 million in aid between Chamorro's inauguration and the end of 1991. The World Bank and the

International Development Bank supplied another $1.2 billion [*The Christian Science Monitor*, 3/24/92]. The government also announced a $278 million public works and housing program in November. While unemployment remained high through 1991, small businesses began to spring up, many opened by demobilized soldiers and laid-off government workers with severance pay received from the government. Cash and consumer goods supplied by returning exiles also fueled growth, and the outlines of a capitalist free-market economy began to take shape.

Political instability grew despite the economic upturn, as extremist elements on both the left and the right voiced increased dissatisfaction with the government's policy of national reconciliation. Aggravated by continuing labor unrest, the situation had reached crisis proportions by late 1991, forcing President Chamorro and former President and FSLN leader Daniel Ortega to abandon the close working relationship that had existed between them since Ortega's electoral defeat. To deal with the growing polarization, Chamorro called for a national dialogue on the labor problems, as well as discussions on a right-wing proposal to establish a municipal police corps in the capital Managua independent of Sandinista control. Attending the dialogue for the first time would be the now fiercely anti-Sandinista National Opposition Union (UNO) party, which had originally elected Chamorro and now sought in particular to override her veto of the property-return bill [ibid., 11/26/91].

The perception of disarray within the FSLN and discontent with the autocratic leadership style of Daniel Ortega was reinforced by the surprising success of his brother, Defense Minister Humberto, in wooing U.S. military and diplomatic support for his efforts to downsize and "professionalize" the Nicaraguan army. The rise of a reformist wing in the party rejecting violence and supporting the government's economic adjustment plan presented further challenges to a leadership floundering for an effective political message [ibid., 2/25/92].

For its part, the government faced an increasingly volatile situation in rural sections of the country, where former Sandinista army soldiers began rearming themselves and engaging in violent clashes with ex-contra forces. Protesting the government's failure to provide jobs, houses, and land to demobilized military personnel, about 400 soldiers and 1,000 Sandinista sympathizers seized control over the northern city of Ocotal on March 5, 1992. They relinquished the city after a week of negotiations and surrendered their weapons for small cash payments and promises of land and housing [*The New York Times*, 3/16/92].

The payments were part of a government-sponsored program, reportedly costing some $3.5 million, aimed at disarming all Sandinista and contra irregulars under the supervision of the OAS. Beginning their work in January, special disarmament brigades—made up of soldiers, police officers, and former contras—had collected about 17,000 weapons by

March, with a little more than half from recontra forces [ibid., 3/16/92]. But the effectiveness of the program in providing genuine disarmament and bringing peace to the countryside has been questioned. The poor condition of many of the arms turned in for payment led to speculation that both sides were holding on to their best weaponry. Citizens were in effect encouraged to find and sell weapons. Moreover, the likelihood increased that more towns would be taken over for profit [*The Christian Science Monitor*, 3/24/92].

The economy continued to rebound in 1992, assisted by an inflation rate below 1 percent per month and foreign aid estimated at $741 million. But recovery is expected to be slow and painful, as external assistance is increasingly diverted to El Salvador and Central and Eastern Europe, and foreign investment, especially in the job-producing industrial and agricultural sectors, awaits a resolution of the current political troubles. The government must now decide whether to ease the suffering of the population by building a safety net of basic social legislation or introduce even more radical austerity measures to attract capital before development assistance dries up.

5. Cambodia

The signing in Paris of the **"Agreement on a Comprehensive Political Settlement of the Cambodia Conflict"** on October 23, 1991, set the stage for the most complex and ambitious peacekeeping operation in the history of the United Nations. The U.N. Transitional Authority in Cambodia (UNTAC) has been established by the Security Council to supervise the cease-fire in the country's civil war; to organize and conduct the free and fair election of a constituent assembly that will decide Cambodia's form of government; and to launch the country's rehabilitation and reconstruction. But UNTAC's mandate only suggests the job at hand. So great has been the devastation that a virtual rebuilding of the country is required. The success of that long and complex effort will not be assured once a new, democratically elected government takes office—in 1993, if all goes according to plan. As a result, the U.N. system will be asked to play a considerable role in Cambodia's development well into the future. Such involvement will require the financial and political leadership of important U.N. member states.

What is seen as of greatest importance at present, not only to Cambodia but to shaping the U.N.'s role in the new world order, are UNTAC's attempts to keep the peace among the parties to the latest phase of the Cambodian civil war. This phase was inaugurated by the **Vietnamese invasion** in December 1978 to unseat the brutal **Khmer Rouge regime led by Pol Pot.** The invasion and subsequent Vietnamese operations in Cambodia had the backing of Vietnam's patron, the **Soviet Union.**

When the Vietnamese installed **Heng Samrin** and **Hun Sen** as the leaders of a new government in Phnom Penh just ten days into 1979, the Khmer Rouge fled to Cambodia's border with **Thailand.** Although near the brink of extinction, the group regained its health under a new Sino-Thai alliance. In February 1979, **China** attempted to "teach Vietnam a lesson" through a limited invasion of northern Vietnam. After withdrawing its troops, Beijing began its effort to "bleed Vietnam white" by applying military pressure on the northern border while aiding (with Thailand's assistance) Khmer Rouge attacks on Vietnam's troops and on the troops of the **People's Republic of Kampuchea (PRK),** as Cambodia was now designated.

UNTAC Calendar

October 23, 1991	Signing of the Agreement on a Comprehensive Political Settlement of the Cambodian Conflict, establishing the mandate of the U.N. Transitional Authority in Cambodia (UNTAC).
November 9, 1991	U.N. Advance Mission in Cambodia (UNAMIC) begins deployment.
March 15, 1992	UNTAC begins deployment.
March 30–December 31, 1992	Repatriation of refugees in Thai border camps.
June 13–October 1, 1992	Cantonment of all military forces and demobilization of 70% of these troops.
October 1–December 31, 1992	Voter registration.
Late April/Early May 1993	Elections for Constituent Assembly.
May through July 1993	Drafting of Cambodian Constitution.
August 1, 1993 (approx.)	Constituent Assembly ratifies Constitution and transforms itself into a Legislative Assembly. UNTAC mandate ends.

By 1982, China and the members of the **Association of Southeast Asian Nations (ASEAN)** had entered into a coalition to isolate Hanoi and its puppet regime at the United Nations and in other international forums. To unify the resistance movement and gain a degree of international acceptance for the Khmer Rouge, ASEAN and China (with encouragement from the **United States**) formed the **Coalition Government of Democratic Kampuchea (CGDK)**, made up of the Khmer Rouge of Pol Pot and two noncommunist resistance groups: the National United Front for an Independent, Neutral, Peaceful, and Cooperative Cambodia (FUNCINPEC) of Prince Norodom Sihanouk; and the Khmer People's National Liberation Front (KPNLF) of Son Sann, a former Sihanouk prime minister. Prince Sihanouk served as the Coalition's titular head, and for years the United States was a prime supporter politically, as well as a supplier of nonmilitary aid to the two noncommunist factions.

No real progress was made toward a political solution of the Cambodian conflict until Mikhail Gorbachev took the reins of government in the Soviet Union in 1985. The press of domestic economic problems led the Kremlin not only to seek improved relations with neighbors and old adversaries but also to terminate its massive aid to Hanoi, which had been helping to sustain Vietnam's military operations in Cambodia. Improved relations among the Soviets, Chinese, and Americans reduced tensions among these major sponsors of the four Cambodian factions, and the suspension of Soviet aid to Vietnam forced Hanoi to withdraw from Cambodia and seek a modus vivendi with China. The reduction of tensions also gave an impetus to **multilateral efforts at spurring a Cambodian settlement.** Meeting through their U.N. missions in New York in January 1989, the **five permanent members of the U.N. Security Council (the Perm Five)**—Britian, China, France, the Soviet Union, and the United States—sought to develop a Council resolution that could provide the basis for a comprehensive peace process. When these discussions proved slow-paced, France called for a conference of all interested parties in Paris. This **Paris Conference on Cambodia (PCC)**, cochaired by France and Indonesia, met the following August but was suspended at the end of the month when the four Cambodian factions failed to reach any sort of agreement on the basic issue of power-sharing, whether in a transitional arrangement or in a future coalition government. Other stumbling blocks included the composition of the international control mechanism, the organization of the cease-fire, and the use of the word "genocide" in the final documents [see *Issues Before the 45th General Assembly of the United Nations*, p. 52]. (In the course of the August session, the conference had dispatched a survey mission to Cambodia under the Chief of Staff of the U.N. Truce and Supervision Organization, which reported back on the major logistical problems a peacekeeping operation would face in the country.)

In October 1989, U.S. Secretary of State James Baker called upon the Perm Five to resume work among themselves on the framework for a political settlement that could be presented to the Cambodians, and in January 1990 the five began a series of meetings in New York and Paris that resulted in the draft text of November 26, 1990, and, nearly a year later (with some modifications by the Cambodians), in the comprehensive agreement signed in Paris. While the Perm Five worked on the framework for the agreement, a second series of meetings was held among the Cambodian factions to obtain their acceptance of the Perm Five plan and reach agreement on its details. Several of these meetings were hosted by Indonesia (the Jakarta Informal Meetings of July 1988 and February 1989 were the first to bring together the four factions) and by Thailand—neighboring states with an interest in bringing peace to the region. Australia was another important actor, developing the peace plan (based on an idea of U.S. Congressman Stephen Solarz) that evolved into the current agreement; and so too Japan, which hosted a meeting in Tokyo at which the Hun Sen government (which changed its name from PRK to **State of Cambodia [SOC]** in 1989) and the two noncommunist factions agreed to the creation of a Supreme National Council (SNC) during the transition period.

The **U.N.'s involvement in Cambodia's peace process** dates back much further than the initiation of the Perm Five talks. In 1982, well before the cold war showed signs of receding, then-Secretary-General Javier Pérez de Cuéllar drew on the U.N. executive's reputation for neutrality to launch a good offices mission in Cambodia, mainly through his Special Representative for Humanitarian Affairs in Southeast Asia, Rafeeuddin Ahmed. The same reputation for neutrality will aid the efforts of the new Secretary-General, Boutros Boutros-Ghali, and his **Special Representative Yasushi Akashi,** named as **head of UNTAC** on January 9, 1992. U.N. Headquarters itself played a significant role in the affair—as one of the few places in which two major actors, the United States and China, could regularly interact after the Tiananmen Square massacre of June 4, 1989. For many years more, of course, the U.N. General Assembly has been the locus of efforts by ASEAN to isolate politically and diplomatically the Vietnamese-installed regime in Phnom Penh; recognition of the CGDK's possession of Cambodia's U.N. seat was a major symbol of the international community's rejection of the Vietnamese occupation. And because the United Nations is seen not only as neutral but also as the embodiment of the will of the "international community," it is perhaps the only organization that can implement so delicate and far-reaching a mission and give the new Cambodian government the international legitimacy it will require.

The Paris Agreement

The role envisioned for the **U.N. Transitional Authority in Cambodia** in securing Cambodia's future is set out in Annex 1 of the Agreement of October 23, 1991, signed by the participants in the Paris peace conference. Secretary-General Boutros-Ghali followed up with a **report to the Security Council on the U.N. plan and budget** [S/23613, 2/19/92; S/23613/Add.1, 2/26/92] for carrying out that role. The Council gave its approval on February 28, and UNTAC began deploying personnel on March 15.

The Agreement called for the U.N. to assume its "transitional authority" at the signing of the Agreement in October 1991 and to relinquish it upon the formation of a new Cambodian government three months after elections. These elections have been scheduled for no later than early May 1993, and if all has gone according to plan, UNTAC would terminate on or around July 31. The operation, initially budgeted at $1.9 billion, is widely expected to cost as much as $3 billion. Additional sums for refugee resettlement and rehabilitation are to be supplied by voluntary contributions rather than by peacekeeping assessments [*The New York Times*, "Week in Review," 3/1/92]. The plan calls for 15,873 peacekeeping troops, 3,600 police, and 2,432 civilian administrators and electoral officials. (The **U.N. Advance Mission in Cambodia [UNAMIC]**—which arrived in November 1991 to help the Cambodians maintain their cease-fire, establish mine-awareness and mine-clearing programs, and prepare for the deployment of UNTAC—eventually deployed 1,380 peacekeeping personnel [ibid.] at a cost of $33.6 million [S/23613/Add.1, 2/26/92]. As simply the advance team, sent to establish a U.N. presence during the preparations for UNTAC, UNAMIC was absorbed into UNTAC on March 15; its costs are part of the UNTAC budget.) U.N. personnel will be augmented by 4,000 locally recruited staff during voter registration and by 56,000 locals during the voting itself, as well as by an estimated 7,000 locally recruited support staff and 2,500 interpreters for all UNTAC components [ibid.].

During the transition period, says the Paris Agreement, the **Supreme National Council (SNC)**, composed of all four factions, will be "the unique legitimate body and source of authority" for all of Cambodia and will represent the country's "sovereignty, independence and unity" [Article 3]. It is the SNC that "delegates to the United Nations *all powers necessary* to ensure the implementation of this Agreement" [Article 6, emphasis added]. Annex 1 makes that U.N. mandate more explicit: UNTAC will have "the powers necessary to ensure the implementation of this Agreement, including those relating to the organization and conduct of free and fair elections and the relevant aspects of the administration of Cambodia." It also provides a mechanism for overcoming deadlock or obstructionism in the SNC: **Prince Sihanouk** can make decisions in the absence of group consensus; and should he be incapacitated for any reason, that **decision-making authority** falls to the Special Representative of the Secretary-General [Section A]. The only condition placed on decisions by the SNC or Prince Sihanouk is that they be consistent with the Agreement, and the Special Representative is authorized to make that determination.

Prince Sihanouk is given this special role in the SNC because he is Chairman of the Council—a position initially viewed as providing a tie-breaker between the six representatives of the Phnom Penh government and the six representatives of the former CGDK. The Prince himself was chosen for the job since he appeared to be the most likely political figure around whom the Cambodian people would rally, having served as king, prime minister, and then head of state between 1941 and his overthrow in 1970.

Annex 1 of the Paris Agreement also grants the Special Representative and UNTAC the power to place U.N. personnel "in administrative agencies, bodies and offices of all the Cambodian Parties," and asks UNTAC to supervise the civil police forces of all parties [Section B, paras. 4 and 5]. It was evident from the Secretary-General's report to the Security Council in February that he intended UNTAC to make full use of its powers and authority. To that end, he requested all the Cambodian factions to provide "full freedom of movement and communications" to U.N. troops [S/23613, 2/29/92, para. 81]. In the Secretary-General's discussion of the four factions' civil police components, he reaffirmed that the Agreement assigns to UNTAC the "supervision of all law enforcement and judicial processes," and he demonstrated a resolve to shape these police units to fit UNTAC's needs and not the factions' by noting, for example, that the Khmer Rouge will have to reduce their police force by 4,000 men [ibid., paras. 102 and 120]. Further asserting UNTAC's authority, the Secretary-General reaffirmed the understanding of Annex 4 that refugees "must return to their homeland voluntarily" and "to the place of their choice" [ibid., para. 133]. It also became clear that UNTAC is to be deployed throughout the country and will reach into provinces, districts, and villages as is necessary to implement its mandate.

UNTAC on the Ground

UNTAC's mandate has seven components, relating to: human rights, elections, military affairs (the cease-fire, demobilization, and remaining Vietnamese forces), civil administration, civil police, refugees, and reconstruction—although the degree of UNTAC involvement varies among (and sometimes even within) these components. For example, the United Nations will have full control over the election process and over the **demobilization of 70 percent of each faction's military forces** but only a coordinating role in the rehabilitation effort. (Although the Agreement encourages full demobilization by the time of the elections [Annex 2, Article V, para. 2], and the Secretary-General has also urged full demobilization, the fears of Hun Sen and the SOC that the Khmer Rouge might hide some guerrillas and thus gain a military advantage were carried into the settlement, resulting in the 70 percent figure.)

To carry out its responsibilities for **civil administration**—the mandate gives UNTAC **"direct control"** over all Cambodian agencies, bodies, and offices in the fields of foreign affairs, national defense, finance, public security, and information—the U.N. plan calls for a staff of 834 (including the headquarters personnel who oversee the entire operation). Although the Secretary-General interpreted "direct control" to mean that "the United Nations alone . . . has the responsibility for determining what will be necessary in these fields," he also intends to rely on codes of conduct and guidelines for management [S/23613, 2/19/92, paras. 94, 95], indicating that he envisions UNTAC not as the administrative bureaucracy but as the monitor and supervisor of existing Cambodian operations from positions at national and provincial centers. The monitoring process below the provincial level will rely heavily on a complaints-and-investigation mechanism.

Flexibility will be UNTAC's guiding principle. It can, when required, become more directly involved in the governing process and issue binding directives. And it can single out any administrative areas for closer supervision beyond the five specified. Education, communications, and health are suggested candidates. Given constraints on financial and human resources, however, UNTAC is forced to be as economical as possible.

It is not civil administration, however, but **peacekeeping** that worries many observers—based on the fear that the Khmer Rouge, the strongest of the rebel forces, will successfully hide troops and arms from UNTAC and launch a military coup at some point in the electoral process. Related to this is a lack of faith on the part of some that U.N. peacekeepers will enter the regions controlled by the Khmer Rouge, where troops and arms would be hidden. But in fact the Secretary-General's deployment plan calls for the **stationing of U.N. troops** at the 95 regroupment and 52 cantonment centers throughout the country that will be used in the demobilization process, as well as at 24 fixed sites along all of Cambodia's land and sea borders and at the four main airports (to verify the permanent withdrawal of "foreign" [read: Vietnamese] troops); and troops will also staff the **mobile supervision and monitoring teams.** The U.N. peacekeepers' presence in Khmer Rouge territory was vividly demonstrated in February, when the Khmer Rouge attacked the head of UNAMIC [*The New York Times*, 1/27/92].

Annex 2 of the Paris Agreement supplies a number of mechanisms that effectively limit the rewards of **withholding arms and troops** from the official demobilization process: It provides for the destruction of any arms caches uncovered, for the demobilization of troops in excess of those on the lists presented to UNTAC, and for UNTAC's investigation of violations of the Agreement, whether as a result of allegations or on its own initiative. (Observers have noted that the opportunities for cheating by any of the four parties would be checked further if U.N. member states were to offer information gathered by their own intelligence communities.)

UNTAC's military component is integral to all the other components—from the mine-clearing that will ensure the safety of returning refugees (and everyone else) to the cantonment and demobilization of military forces that (with the police component) will ensure public safety and create an environment conducive to conducting free and fair elections. For this reason, **cantonment and demobilization** must be concluded before voter registration begins. The majority of UNTAC's military forces were deployed by June 13 (two weeks behind the original target date), allowing UNTAC to commence the regroupment, cantonment, and demobilization of the Cambodian factions' armies. The demobilization of 70 percent of these forces would be completed by September 30, with voter registration to begin in October [S/23613, Annex II, 2/19/92].

Elections for the 120-seat Constituent Assembly to design and ratify the constitution of a new Cambodia and then transform itself into a Legislative Assembly will be held in early May 1993. The number of seats for each province is to be based on the province's share of the national population, and each province's seats will be allocated "in accordance with a system of proportional representation on the basis of lists of candidates put forward by political parties" [Paris Agreement, Annex 3; and S/23613, 2/19/92, Section B]. The details of the electoral process are left to the electoral law that UNTAC will develop; a draft was presented by Special Representative Akashi to the SNC on April 1, 1992 [U.N. press release CAM/ 134, 4/1/92]. UNTAC has been charged with organizing all aspects of the elections and, as its initial contribution, began a massive civic education and training program in April 1992. In theory, at least, virtually the entire electoral process will be computerized—requiring software, hardware, and printers that can process both Khmer script and romanized Khmer.

Because of Cambodia's "special history," **human rights** is a top priority of UNTAC, but provision is made for only a modest staff at headquarters and no one devoted exclusively to human rights concerns at the provincial level or below. The reason, according to the Secretary-General's initiating report, is that *all* UNTAC staff will "be charged with carrying out human rights functions as an integral part of their primary duties" [para. 21]. Further, all UNTAC staff receive special human rights training and materials, and the **civic education and training program** is providing human rights training to the Cambodians themselves. UNTAC's supervision of the civil administration will enable it to monitor the human rights situation, as will the complaints-and-investigation mechanism. Moreover, all four factions signed the documents, dated April 20, 1992, by which the SNC acceded to the **International Covenants on Civil and Political Rights and on Economic, Social, and Cultural Rights.** This commits (if it does not guarantee) the Cambodian leaders to respect the human rights and fundamental freedoms of all Cambodians—and adds to the pressure on them to comply fully with the Paris Agreement [U.N. press release SG/SM/4733, CAM 143, HR/3640, 4/20/92].

Nation-Building

The documents related to the comprehensive settlement do not offer many details about the political, social, and economic **reconstruction of Cambodia,** but that was not their purpose. Such details are left to the Constituent Assembly, which will be elected in spring 1993, and to the government that assumes office after the constitution has been accepted. The Agreement focuses instead on the sort of short-term rehabilitation efforts and foundation-building that are a prerequisite to those initial elections.

The first step in rebuilding Cambodia is the **repatriation of the refugees in border camps.** This operation, although run by the **U.N. High Commissioner for Refugees (UNHCR),** will be facilitated by UNTAC and carried out under the overall authority of the Special Representative. The police, civil administration, military, and human rights components of UNTAC were designed with the repatriation process in mind.

On March 30, 1992, the first convoy of refugees returned from Thailand under this $116 million repatriation program that is scheduled to last nine months [S/23613, para. 137]—a date coinciding with the end of voter registration in December. Ninety percent of the 370,000 refugees had expressed their desire to return to Cambodia under U.N. auspices, but by the end of April the program had returned only 5,763, far short of the nearly 10,000 per week required for meeting the formal schedule [Secretary-General's Progress Report, S/23870, 5/1/92].. Sergio Vieira de Mello, the UNHCR official in charge of the repatriation effort, cites logistical problems, the condition of Cambodian roads after more than two decades of war, and the slowness of mine clearance; and he noted that, with the start of the monsoon season in June, the program would be forced to halt for several months [*The New York Times*, 4/12/92]. A further complication is the fact that the vast majority of the refugees have asked to be resettled in **western Cambodia** and more than half of them (57 percent) in Battam-

bang province alone [S/23613, para. 139]. These locations provide the repatriated Cambodians with the quickest escape route to Thailand should the
comprehensive settlement collapse—and some of the best farmland in
Cambodia. But the concentration of so many returnees in these western
provinces is causing a conflict between the U.N. offer of five acres to
each returning family and the actual supply of arable and mine-free land.
This land shortage also threatens to delay the repatriation process.

Among the other problems facing the repatriation operation are an
epidemic of a form of malaria that appears resistant to the usual medical
treatment [U.N. press release H/2777, 3/17/92], the logistics of supplying all returnees with a resettlement package (housing materials, household and
farming items) and with food over a period of 12 months—and, as ever,
the question of funding. In mid-March 1992 the United States announced
a contribution of $15 million to UNHCR and Japan a contribution of
$27 million, raising their contributions to $20 million and $35 million,
respectively [*Far Eastern Economic Review*, 4/2/92]. By May 25, reported a UNHCR
spokesman, appeals for funds to aid the Cambodian refugee repatriation
and resettlement explicitly had netted the agency $26.4 million—almost
a third of UNHCR's $84.3 million share of the operation.

Related to the repatriation effort is the launching of the **repair of
Cambodia's infrastructure.** The Declaration on the Rehabilitation and
Reconstruction of Cambodia, one of the documents of the Paris Agreement, foresees the physical rebuilding of the country as a two-phase
process: a short-term phase concurrent with the transitional period,
under UNTAC supervision; and a medium and long-term phase that will
be in the hands of the new government. Paragraph 10 of the Declaration
says that phase one must pay "particular attention" to "food security,
health, housing, training, education, the transportation network and the
restoration of Cambodia's existing basic infrastructure and public utilities." The Secretary-General's appointee to the post of **Coordinator of
the Rehabilitation Programme,** Berndt Bernander, will lead this effort
and attempt to ensure that the infrastructural requirements of both the
repatriation program and of UNTAC's broader operation will be met
[U.N. press release CAM/127, 3/17/92].

As part of the rehabilitation process, UNTAC will be providing a
reintegration training program to the demobilized soldiers of the
various armies [S/23613, 2/19/92, para. 154] to complement the civic education
component offered to all citizens. On the soldiers' curriculum are small-
scale production, small-scale enterprise development, basic finance and
marketing, and the development of such skills as vehicle maintenance,
carpentry, and food processing. Thus, while the transition period does
not begin the actual reconstruction of the country, it is intended to lay
the groundwork for a democratic and essentially capitalist Cambodia of
the future.

Financial and Political Requirements

UNTAC is not only the most ambitious peacekeeping operation in U.N. history but also the most expensive. And it comes at a time when the Organization's largest contributors are being asked to underwrite several other peacekeeping operations, when many are being asked to contribute toward the reconstruction of Eastern Europe and the former Soviet Union, and when most are feeling the pinch of economic and other problems at home. The United States already owes $112 million for previous U.N. peacekeeping operations [*The New York Times*, 5/9/92]; and Russia, $127 million in arrears for previous operations, is not expected to pay its 11 percent share (it inherited the Soviet seat and thus the Soviet share) of the Cambodian operation [ibid., "Week in Review," 3/1/92; ibid., 3/6/92]. Visiting Cambodia a month after UNTAC began deployment, Secretary-General Boutros-Ghali said that $560 million of these assessments had to be deposited in the U.N. account soon or the operation would be placed at risk [U.N. press release SG/T/1726, 4/21/92].

Based on the **formula used to finance such operations,** each of the Perm Five pays a slightly higher percentage of the costs than it pays for the U.N. budget in general. Thus the United States, which pays 25 percent of the U.N. budget, is assessed at about 30 percent of the costs of UNTAC, while Japan and Germany—industrial powers that are not among the Security Council's Perm Five—pay about 12 and 8 percent, respectively; and the entire European Community (which includes Perm Five members France and Britain) pays an assessment roughly equal to the U.S. assessment [*Far Eastern Economic Review*, 2/27/92; *The New York Times*, 3/6/92]. It is Washington's belief that **Japan,** the world's second-ranking economic power and a force in the region, should contribute more to peacekeeping than it is currently assessed, and when Special Representative Akashi, a native of Japan, stopped off in Toyko en route to Cambodia last March, he told Foreign Minister Michio Watanabe that he expects Japan to contribute $1 billion—a third of the expected final cost of UNTAC [*The New York Times*, 3/12/92]. Tokyo had been planning to play a leading role in the coordination and funding of Cambodian reconstruction efforts, and in mid-March it not only increased its donation to the repatriation program but pledged to exceed its assessments for the costs of the peacekeeping operation [interview with State Department official involved in Japan affairs, 3/16/92]. The expectations of increased Japanese financing for U.N. operations in Cambodia fuel the debate over an increased Japanese role in U.N. decision-making. As for the United States, by early July it had paid in full its $10.2 million assessment for UNAMIC and $112.3 million toward the $244.8 million it already owes for UNTAC. (The U.S. assessment for the entire 18-month operation is $577 million; by June 2 the United States had sent bills for two installments.)

UNTAC, to be successful, must also be able to draw on a fund of **political will,** on the part of the Perm Five and the other participants in the Paris peace conference. Such political pressure, say observers, is sure to help strengthen the will to cooperate of the four Cambodian factions, which, after all, relied extensively on their external patrons over the years, and U.N. officials are quick to point out that it was only the will of the international community to move the process forward that prevented the collapse of the U.N. peacekeeping operation in Namibia on its very first day. In the Cambodia case, any of the factions could violate the Paris Agreement, although it is the Khmer Rouge who have been so charged.

Not only is pressure from the international community necessary to prevent the Cambodian parties from breaking their agreements, it also seems necessary to keep the Supreme National Council actively involved in governing the country during the transition period. In the face of a severe budget problem, the Phnom Penh government has cut back spending on health, education, and transportation, effectively surrendering these important areas to UNTAC [*The New York Times*, 4/17/92]. More important, many of the SNC members left the country for days at a time in April—weeks at a time in the case of Prince Sihanouk—and sometimes not a single Cambodian decision-maker remained in Phnom Penh. Special Representative Akashi, stating that the United Nations would leave Cambodia one day, warned the Cambodians not to become too dependent on foreigners to run the country [*The New York Times*, 4/18/92].

So far the United Nations and the international community have indicated their commitment to pursue the Cambodia settlement. The real problems have been within Cambodia. Because the UNTAC timetable was designed to bring elections as quickly and economically as possible in the Cambodian context, significant delays will increase the costs of the operation—raising additional problems of funding (and also, it is feared, increasing the ability of the Khmer Rouge to convince or coerce rural populations to vote for their candidates when election time rolls around). The importance of a strong U.N. presence to the success of the Cambodian settlement became clear in the months following the Agreement. By the time UNTAC began deploying its personnel in mid-March 1992, corruption was rampant in the Phnom Penh government, there was fighting between Khmer Rouge and Phnom Penh forces in several provinces, banditry was on the increase, dissidents were being intimidated (in one instance, a senior government official critical of his colleagues was assassinated [*Far Eastern Economic Review*, 2/27/92]), and protection rackets using new deployments of mines to terrorize the population were spreading rapidly [ibid., 2/20/92].

The Paris Agreement provides **mechanisms to resolve these and other problems,** and Special Representative Akashi has begun using them since UNTAC's deployment. The provision for decision-making by Sihanouk if the SNC is deadlocked or by the U.N. Special Representative if Sihanouk has been incapacitated is one means of dealing with potential problems. The Agreement also provides mechanisms that anticipate serious violations of the settlement. In the event of a violation or threat of violation, Article 29 instructs the co-chairs of the PCC to "immediately undertake appropriate consultations" with their fellow members (noting that this is "without prejudice to the prerogatives of the Security Council"). Article 5 of the companion Agreement Concerning the Sovereignty, Independence, Territorial Integrity and Inviolability, Neutrality and National Unity of Cambodia also provides that the parties will immediately consult among themselves and pursue the steps necessary to correct the violation peacefully—everything from requesting the assistance of the PCC co-chairs to referring the matter to the U.N. Security Council, invoking Article 33 on the peaceful settlement of disputes, or (in the case of human rights violations) to the "competent organs of the United Nations." These mechanisms provide for a flexible response, in keeping with the seriousness of the threat.

Still, it is not clear what leverage any of these mechanisms might have on Pol Pot and the Khmer Rouge, who claim to have embraced democracy and the free market but whose acceptance of the Agreement appears marginal at best. UNAMIC charged the Khmer Rouge with **violations of the cease-fire** when they shot at a clearly marked U.N. helicopter on a reconnaissance mission on February 26, and again when they refused to allow U.N. observers into areas under Khmer Rouge control [*The New York Times*, 3/5/92]. In the same late winter–early spring period there were Khmer Rouge attacks in central and northern provinces designed to expand their territorial control [*Far Eastern Economic Review*, 4/9/92, 4/23/92; *The Washington Post*, 3/16/92; *The New York Times*, 3/14/92]. And days before the start of the repatriation operation, the Khmer Rouge launched an intimidation campaign in two of their refugee camps, using the detention of two civilian camp leaders and the murder of two other people to convince refugees to resettle in areas under Khmer Rouge control [*The New York Times*, 3/26/92]. This prompted Mr. Akashi to pressure the members of the SNC to reaffirm the right of all refugees to choose for themselves a final destination in Cambodia [U.N. Daily Highlights, DH/1113, 4/3/92] and, a few days later, to condemn the Khmer Rouge outright for failing to cooperate fully with the United Nations. He threatened to take the issue to the Security Council if they did not mend their ways [*Far Eastern Economic Review*, 4/23/92]. The Khmer Rouge's refusal to comply with the Paris Agreement continued into July as they registered still more cease-fire violations, denied UNTAC full access to and freedom of movement within areas under their control, and (most threatening of all) refused to join the other three parties in the cantonment and demobilization of troops called for in the second phase of the settlement [Special Report of the Secretary-General, S/24090, 6/12/92; *The New York Times*, 7/3/92]. It remains to be seen whether Khmer Rouge behavior—or the Paris Agreement—will be altered so that UNTAC can proceed with its mission.

Elections and the "New" Cambodia

During his visit to Cambodia in April, Secretary-General Boutros-Ghali reaffirmed his commitment to the formal election timetable [U.N. press release SG/SM/4732, CAM/142, 4/21/92]—elections that the Agreement views as achieving the goal of political self-determination for the Cambodian people. The Cambodians are now being schooled for those elections and the birth (if the drafters of the new constitution adhere to the principles outlined in Annex 5) of a Western-style liberal, pluralist democracy with "periodic and genuine" elections. To this end, Special Representative Akashi submitted a draft electoral law to the SNC on April 1 [U.N. press release CAM/134, 4/1/92]. There are still a number of uncertainties about the post-election period, however.

UNTAC is charged with holding "free and fair" elections in a neutral political environment, and most analysts assume that under such conditions the Khmer Rouge would win only a small number of the 120 seats in the Constituent Assembly. It is unclear how much influence the Pol Pot group would then have in **drafting the new constitution,** since there is not yet an agreement on the procedures to follow in drafting that document. Annex 5 of the Paris Agreement stipulates that the constitution is to be adopted by a two-thirds majority of the Constituent Assembly, but, again, says nothing about the voting on individual provisions. It is also left to the Constituent Assembly and its new constitution to devise the means of **choosing a head of state or head of government** in the future. Since the constitution-drafting period is technically part of the transition period, the SNC and UNTAC will continue to play their executive role in Cambodia throughout it. Far from certain, however, is the reaction of the Khmer Rouge or any of the other groups to a poor showing in the elections, and a continued U.N. presence might be required to guarantee the installation of the new government by the end of July 1993.

Most of the other decisions involved in the state-building process (such as **designing the institutional structure** of the new government) are also left to the Constituent Assembly. The only governmental body called for by the Agreement in addition to the Legislative Assembly is an independent judiciary [Annex 5, para. 5]. The Agreement does go on to say, however, that Cambodia will be a liberal, pluralistic democracy not only politically but (by calling for constitutional guarantees of political, civil, and human rights) socially as well [ibid., para. 2].

Most of the decisions on economic reconstruction will also be left to the new government, again in the name of Cambodian self-determination. The only concrete provisions of the Declaration on the Rehabilitation and Reconstruction of Cambodia are the suggestions to rely on entrepreneurship and market forces and to create an **International Committee on the Reconstruction of Cambodia (ICORC)** to coordinate bilateral and multilateral aid [paras. 12 and 13]. The United Nations and its agencies are expected to work closely with ICORC. A "donors meeting" was held June 20–22 to begin coordinating the aid expected to flow into the country in 1993. Some $880 million was pledged at the meeting [*The New York Times*, 6/23/92].

Because the Cambodian effort to rebuild the country's political and economic institutions will require international assistance and guidance and the agencies and programs of the United Nations will be called upon for these efforts, the world body and SNC have already begun discussing the possibility of a **residual UNTAC presence** after the formation of the new government. It is the new government that would have to make the formal request, which must be accepted by the U.N. Security Council.

An important—and difficult—decision for the Constituent Assembly and the new government will be the handling of **past human rights abuses,** particularly those of the Khmer Rouge. Aware that a tribunal under the Genocide Convention might ensnare more political leaders than would serve the cause of national reconciliation, the new government might choose to seek the permanent exile of Pol Pot and his chief aides instead.

6. Afghanistan

Since the 1988 signing of the Geneva Accords, the United Nations has actively attempted to secure peace and national reconciliation in Afghanistan. But its efforts were overtaken by events when on April 16, 1992, Afghan **President Mohammed Najibullah** stepped down and fled into hiding. The United Nations suddenly found itself sidelined without a substantive role, as contending factions fought for control of Kabul and the surrounding countryside.

Only two weeks earlier **U.N. special envoy Benon Sevan** had expressed optimism at the possibility of a political settlement when he announced that Najibullah and most of the rebel factions had agreed to an accelerated peace plan that would transfer power to an interim government in Kabul by May or sooner. But Sevan soon found himself groping for a role after Najibullah fled to a U.N. compound in Kabul and competing factions rushed to fill the power vacuum left by his sudden departure. As fighting engulfed the country, Secretary-General Boutros

Boutros-Ghali publicly declared to reporters on May 18 that the United Nations's efforts "have not been successful" [SG/SM/4752].

The hostilities subsided significantly after an agreement brokered by Saudi Arabia was reached between the two major Muslim guerrilla factions on May 25. Apart from a cease-fire, the two sides committed themselves to hold elections within six months. However, sporadic fighting continued as the two groups and other factions vied for power. After 14 years of civil war, Afghanistan's religious, ethnic, and territorial divisions appeared even more pronounced [Reuters, 5/26/92].

At mid-year the fragile stability was ensured only by the consent of the two main Muslim guerrilla groups: the **Herb-i-Islami,** led by **Gulbuddin Hekmatyar,** which controls areas south of Kabul, together with a coalition led by **Ahmad Shah Masood;** and the forces of **General Abdul Rashid Doestam,** the Uzbek leader of a northern militia that turned against President Najibullah. Not only did tensions persist between the forces led by Masood and the extreme fundamentalist Hekmatyar but there were strains within Masood's own coalition, composed of Iranian and Saudi Arabian-backed factions, northern guerrillas, a group headed by a Sufi religious leader, and an alliance led by **Prof. Sibgatullah Mojadedi.** Mojadedi was proclaimed interim president on April 28 for a period of two months, but he later declared that he intended to remain in office up to two years.

There was speculation among some diplomats that the country could face fragmentation. Masood and his followers are northern Tajiks, while Hekmatyar, a fierce Muslim fundamentalist, is a member of the formerly dominant Pathans, who account for half the country's population. The country is also divided between Sunni Muslims (84 percent) and Shiites (15 percent).

"The militias will be in charge in the north, mujahideen leaders in charge of their respective areas, and there will be a weak government in Kabul pretending to rule," predicted an Asian diplomat [Reuters, 5/26/92]. Further complicating the situation have been attempts by neighboring countries to gain influence by acting through the various factions [*The New York Times*, 5/10/92]. An important element is the **rivalry between Saudi Arabia and Iran,** as well as **Pakistan**'s desire to see Afghanistan as the major transit point for goods moving between the Central Asian republics and the port of Karachi [ibid.]. In April, Boutros-Ghali traveled to neighboring Iran and Pakistan for discussions. "My message was that we must find a quick solution, otherwise what has happened in Yugoslavia may happen tomorrow in Afghanistan," he told reporters on May 18. "Or you may have a kind of situation like in Lebanon, which has lasted 12 or 14 years" [SG/SM/4752].

Despite the May 25 agreement to hold elections, sporadic fighting continued. One source of tension was that Hekmatyar refused to participate in Mojadedi's government, in which Masood was Defense Minister. Among other things, Hekmatyar opposed the interim government's alliance with General Doestam, who had, until recently, supported Najibullah and fought against the now victorious Muslim guerrillas. Doestam also earned Hekmatyar's enmity by opposing the latter's attempts to seize power after Najibullah's fall.

In a further sign of the deep divisions in Afghanistan, on May 29 shrapnel from a rocket hit the plane bringing Mojadedi back from Pakistan. He and 69 others escaped unharmed. Later he accused Communists and fighters loyal to Hekmatyar of the attack [Agence France-Presse 311730]. On June 2 more than 20 people were killed in clashes between Iranian-backed rebels—Hezb-e-Wahadat—and forces loyal to the caretaker government. The rebels, who refused to join the interim ruling coalition, are comprised of eight small guerrilla parties representing Afghanistan's minority Shiite Muslims. They have demanded at least five ministerial posts and three deputy ministries [Associated Press, 6/2/92].

At a time when it appeared the country would continue in the way of Yugoslavia, Mojadedi stepped down peacefully from the office of President on June 28, abandoning his effort to side-step the May 25 agreement [Associated Press, 6/29/92]. The ten-member council that is to guide Afghanistan to national elections handed over power to Burhanuddin Rabbani, leader of Jamiat-i-Islami, one of the strongest guerrilla factions. In his presidential address, Rabbani, an Islamic scholar, stressed the need for unity and consensus. Hekmatyar announced at the same time that his deputy, Ustad Fareed, would become Prime Minister within a week [ibid.].

The transition of power is thought to be the most peaceful in Afghanistan in nearly a century, but religious, political, and ethnic rifts continue to threaten to erupt in violence. While the May 25 agreement between Masood and Hekmatyar outlines tentative plans for elections, it does not address demands of General Doestam for a federal state giving special protection to Uzbeks, Tajiks, and other minorities [Reuters, 5/26/92]. Basic issues, such as whether women have the right to vote, have yet to be decided by the rival groups. And in Kabul there are continued reports of an undercurrent of chaos as looting and sporadic shooting continue. The Muslim guerrillas have been more successful in banning alcohol and forcing women to wear veils.

Following the pullout of Soviet forces in 1989, the United Nations sought to convene an international conference and to implement a peace plan for Afghanistan, but there is much yet to be done. The 14-year conflict created **over 6 million refugees,** who will have to be resettled. The country will also have to be de-mined and its physical and economic infrastructures rebuilt. A report prepared by **Special Rapporteur Felix Ermacora of the Commission on Human Rights** [A/46/606] on November 5, 1991, noted that "the vigilance of the United Nations concerning the situation of human rights in Afghanistan should come to an end only when it is satisfied that free elections leading to the massive return of refugees and to the monitoring of human rights through an independent Afghan legal system have been achieved."

7. Cyprus

Greek and Turkish communities locked in a 28-year stalemate for control over the Mediterranean island of Cyprus had until July 1992 to narrow their differences or face the likely withdrawal by the end of the year of the U.N. peacekeeping force that has separated them since 1964. Now in his last year of office, Secretary-General Javier Pérez de Cuéllar renewed his efforts during May and June to bring Greek and Turkish Cypriot leaders into substantial agreement on all aspects of a settlement; and it was thought at mid-year that the new Secretary-General might recommend convening a high-level meeting of the two sides, with their Greek and Turkish patrons, to conclude an overall framework agreement should talks progress. If this effort fails, however, the refusal of troop-contributing countries to continue to bear the costs of maintaining an unacceptable status quo may force the Secretary-General to recommend the termination of the peacekeeping operation on the divided island. The Security Council might well accept such a proposal, prompted by a growing consensus that the U.N. presence in Cyprus has had the effect of impeding rather than facilitating a resolution to the conflict.

Originally dispatched to prevent a recurrence of the fighting that had erupted between Greek and Turkish Cypriots in the wake of the British decolonization of the island in 1960, the U.N. Peacekeeping Force in Cyprus (UNFICYP) currently patrols a 180-kilometer buffer zone separating the predominantly Greek Republic of Cyprus in the south from the self-proclaimed Turkish Republic of Northern Cyprus. The division of the island dates from 1974, when Turkish forces invaded and occupied the northern 40 percent of the republic in response to a Greek Cypriot coup d'état by militant nationalists who favored Greek annexation of the island. The Turkish zone declared itself an independent sovereign state in 1983, but only Turkey has extended it formal diplomatic recognition. The United Nations continues to seat one Cypriot state, represented by the Greek Cypriot-controlled government in Nicosia, and has negotiated with Turkish Cypriot leaders but not the administration in the north per se.

The Security Council has continuously renewed the mandate of UNFICYP for six-month periods since its inception despite the lack of sustained movement toward a negotiated settlement and the mounting costs of keeping the peace. While most other peacekeeping operations are financed through a combination of assessed and voluntary payments from member states, UNFICYP relies completely on voluntary contributions, which have never been sufficient to meet the one-third of total costs the United Nations has agreed to reimburse to troop-contributing countries. (Sweden withdrew its contingent from the operation in 1987 over this issue.) In requesting another extension of the mandate in May 1991, the Secretary-General underscored the $178.7 million deficit in contributions received to date, which had allowed the United Nations to reimburse troop contributors only through December 1980, and recommended as he had on previous occasions that the Security Council consider financing UNFICYP through assessments [S/22665]. The Council approved the mandate extension on June 14 [S/Res/697 (1991)] and the next day requested that the Secretary-General further study the financing question and report his findings by October [S/Res/698 (1991)].

The Security Council was more assertive in handling the Secretary-General's report on his good offices mission in Cyprus, endorsing on June 28, 1991, his intention to reach final agreement on an outline for an overall settlement at a high-level international meeting of the interested parties [S/22744]. Proposed by **Turkish President Turgut Ozal** in May, the meeting would bring together for the first time the Cypriot communities, Greece, and Turkey to formally approve all eight sections of the U.N.'s long-debated unification plan, provided that all sides were in or close to agreement on all the issues at the outset. To bring negotiations to this point, the Security Council directed the Secretary-General to pursue two further rounds of talks during July and August on the "set of ideas" under consideration since late 1990, aimed at resolving the outstanding questions. It was hoped that the high-level meeting would provide the "impetus" or pressure necessary to establish the "bizonal, bicommunal, and federal" Republic of Cyprus sought by the Security Council since the division of the island.

The visits by U.S. President George Bush to Athens and Ankara in mid-July [*The Christian Science Monitor, 7/24/91*] further catalyzed the peace process and resulted in an August 2 offer to host the proposed U.N. conference in September [*The New York Times, 8/5/91*]. Greece announced the acceptance by all four parties of the American invitation on August 4 [ibid.]. Negotiations reached an impasse on September 11, however, when the Prime Ministers of Greece and Turkey, meeting for the first time, failed to close the gap on several important issues. Speculation in the press centered on the question of territorial adjustments to be made by the Turkish Cypriots, who comprise just 18 percent of the total population but hold 37 percent of the land [ibid., 9/12/91]. The possibility of a September peace conference vanished.

In his October 8 report to the Security Council, the Secretary-General indicated that the talks had broken down over a last-minute demand from the Turkish Cypriot side for guarantees on a "right of secession" from the proposed federation. Arguing that recognizing such a right would be incompatible with his mandate to preserve the "territorial integrity" of Cyprus and would "fundamentally alter" the one state–two communities solution, the Secretary-General nevertheless called the progress achieved on other issues "an important step forward." He recommended that talks resume in November to finalize the set of ideas and expressed confidence that the high-level meeting could be convened before the end of 1991.

By the end of August, U.N. negotiators had worked out a text of ideas so detailed and comprehensive that both Greek and Turkish Cypriot leaders agreed to bypass the outline agreement foreseen by the Security Council and focus on elaborating the overall framework of a final settlement. The two sides were fairly close in four of the eight "headings," or issue areas, contained in the unification plan: overall objectives; guiding principles of federation; powers and functions of the federal government, legislature, and judiciary; and security and guarantee. But they remained apart on displaced persons, the federal executive, territorial adjustments, and transitional arrangements.

The Security Council endorsed the resumption of talks in its **Resolution 716** of October 11 and offered a thinly veiled rebuke to the Turkish side for its attempt to win recognition of a right of secession. According to the resolution, all parties were to refrain from "introducing concepts that are at variance" with the fundamental principles of settlement first delineated by the United Nations in 1975 and accepted by both Cypriot communities in 1977 and 1979. These specifically included the territorial integrity of the Republic of Cyprus and specifically excluded secession. But the Council also addressed itself once again to the longstanding Turkish Cypriot demand for equal standing with the Greek Cypriot Republic by reaffirming that the communities would participate in negotiations on an equal footing and would be politically equal in a reunited Cyprus.

Follow-up talks were postponed due to the fall elections in Turkey; and as the most recent mandate renewal of UNFICYP neared expiration, attention turned once again to financing the operation. In his report on the subject—the third such U.N. study within the year—the Secretary-General proposed a scheme for reducing reimbursements to troop contributors by some 29 percent contingent on the willingness of the Security Council to finance UNFICYP through assessed contributions [S/23144]. Arrearages had grown to $186.1 million, allowing the United Nations to make payments only through June 1981 [S/23263]. Announcing that "necessary agreement" did not currently exist on altering the financial arrangements of UNFICYP [U.N. press release SC/5331, 12/12/91]—perhaps a reference to objections among the permanent membership—the Security

Council renewed the mandate of the operation through June 1992 [S/Res/ 723 (1991)].

Austria and Canada, supplying almost half of the personnel for the 2,100-man peacekeeping operation in Cyprus, immediately announced plans to review their continued participation in the force. They complained that most of the permanent membership—excluding perhaps the United Kingdom, the largest troop contributor to UNFICYP—continued to oppose assessments, despite strong support for them among the majority nonpermanent membership [S/PV. 3022].

The Secretary-General and the four parties in Cyprus were under increasing pressure to conclude an agreement before the threatened withdrawal of UNFICYP removed the major source of stability on the ground. In his good offices report of December 19, 1991, the Secretary-General reiterated that "the framework of a settlement has become clear," and stressed that further work on the issues of territorial adjustments and displaced persons would bring an overall framework agreement—and an international conference—within reach. To prevent future misunderstandings where all sides were already close to agreement, the Secretary-General attempted to clarify two major points. Guarantees of political equality for each community—an issue of extreme importance to the Turkish Cypriots—would not mean "equal numerical participation" in the future federal government, and the security arrangements under discussion would involve the withdrawal of all non-Cypriot forces from the island, a delicate matter for both Greece and Turkey.

The Security Council endorsed these observations on December 23 and stated that "a solution to the Cyprus problem is long overdue" [S/23316]. Pointing out that the "status quo is not an option" and that the maintenance thereof "does not constitute a solution," both the Council and the Secretary-General pressed for concessions from all sides by April. The **United States** likewise underscored the need for compromise and announced its intention to resume diplomatic efforts toward a framework agreement in early January 1992 [U.S. Mission to the U.N. press release 112 (91), 12/24/91]. After separate meetings with Greek and Turkish Cypriot leaders at U.N. Headquarters on January 20–21, Secretary-General Boutros Boutros-Ghali initiated a new round of talks under his sponsorship in early February. President Bush met with **Turkish Prime Minister Suleyman Demirel** on February 11 in Washington, reportedly to elicit a renewed Turkish commitment to an international conference and promises from Ankara for concessions on the territorial and refugee issues [*Cyprus Weekly Diary*, #3/92, 2/11/92].

The February–March talks failed to resolve any of the difficulties noted at the close of negotiations in August 1991 and reported on by the Secretary-General the following October. "Not only had there been no progress," the Secretary-General said in his April 3 report, "but in some areas there had even been regression" [S/23780]. The report did not specify these areas but did say that urgent work was still required on displaced persons and territorial adjustments. The ideas put forward to date contained the "essence of a solution" to the first problem, according to the Secretary-General, but the lack of agreement on a revised boundary between the communities impeded further progress. A reported compromise proposal through which the Turkish Cypriots would surrender some territory but limit the right of return of the 150,000 Greek Cypriots displaced from the north was evidently not accepted. Financial compensation for them and the 60,000 displaced Turkish Cypriots had also been suggested [*The Christian Science Monitor*, 2/3/92].

The United Nations had made considerable progress in settling the Cyprus problem since launching the current effort in March 1990. It had hammered out agreements in principle on previously divisive issues, such as the "three freedoms"—of movement, of settlement, and of property ownership—and made the first mutually acceptable proposals on economic development, including a single membership for Cyprus in the European Community, and a program of action to promote goodwill and closer relations between the communities. But the tendency of all sides to interpret Security Council resolutions according to their individual interests, their unwillingness to abide by long-established principles of settlement, and their desire to introduce conflicting concepts continued to undermine the process [S/23780].

If diplomacy fails to move the parties, perhaps the financial collapse of UNFICYP will do so. In his April 3 report, the Secretary-General notified the Security Council that two of the main troop contributors, later identified as Canada and Denmark [*The New York Times*, 4/12/92], were "unlikely" to be able to continue their participation in the operation for more than another mandate period, due to Council's failure to approve a system of assessed contributions. A third troop contributor was reexamining its role in the force. Noting that other member states could not be expected to offer replacement troops under the current financial arrangements, the Secretary-General warned that UNFICYP would probably not exist, at least at its current strength, beyond 1992. A report on "alternative possibilities" was submitted to the Security Council in May.

The Council underplayed its alarm at this development, neither confirming nor denying the December 1992 deadline set by the Secretary-General but stating only that it would "look forward" to his report [S/Res/750 (1992)]. Unnamed diplomatic sources quoted in the press interpreted this as an effort to jolt Greece and Turkey into making long-needed concessions [*The New York Times*, 4/12/92]. The Security Council was more explicit in its support of the Secretary-General's diplomatic efforts, deciding for the first time to "remain seized of the Cyprus question on an ongoing and direct basis." It also signaled that time might be running out by setting a deadline of its own: The Secretary-General was to pursue "intensive" negotiations during May and June and report on his progress by July "at the latest."

8. Other Colonial and Sovereignty Issues

World War II proved to be the catalyst for a rush to self-rule by colonial peoples, whose aspiration to be rid of the occupying power was fed by the Allies' slogans and stated war aims. A dozen former colonies were admitted to the United Nations between 1955 and 1958, and an additional 17 in 1960. By that year the former colonies were sufficiently numerous to push through the General Assembly a **Declaration on the Granting of Independence to Colonial Countries and Peoples.** In affirming that freedom from colonial domination is a basic right of all peoples, the Declaration put further pressure on the colonial powers to speed up the decolonization process. By the end of the 1960s, U.N. membership had tripled to about 150. Today it stands at 178.

The General Assembly

At its 46th Session, the General Assembly adopted 11 resolutions, 2 "consensuses," and 4 decisions relating to specific decolonization issues, underlining the importance many member states attach to the decolonization issue. At its **43rd Session** in 1988, the General Assembly adopted a resolution by which it declared the period 1990–2000 as the **International Decade for the Eradication of Colonialism.** The 46th General Assembly adopted without a vote a resolution entitled **"International Decade for the Eradication of Colonialism,"** in which it reaffirmed that the peoples of the remaining Non-Self-Governing Territories [NSGTs] have an inalienable right to self-determination and independence in accordance with the U.N. Charter, the Declaration, and other relevant resolutions and decisions [A/Res/46/181]. In adopting the resolution, the Assembly also adopted a plan of action to achieve a world free from colonialism by the beginning of the 21st century [A/46/634/Rev.1]. The plan calls on the **Special Committee on the Situation with Regard to the Implementation of the Declaration on the Granting of Independence to Colonial Countries and Peoples** to prepare periodic analyses of the progress and implementation of the Declaration, to review the impact of the economic and social situation on the constitutional and political advancement of Non-Self-Governing Territories, and organize seminars to review the progress of the plan of action. The resolution also called on the Special Committee to encourage and facilitate the participation of representatives of Non-Self-Governing Territories in regional and international organizations, in specialized agencies of the U.N. system, and in the Special Committee.

The General Assembly reviewed and approved the report of the Special Committee [A/46/23] in a resolution entitled **Implementation of the Declaration on the Granting of Independence to Colonial Countries and Peoples** [A/Res/46/71]. The resolution passed 137–2–22, with the United States and the United Kingdom casting the only two negative votes. The resolution also calls on the Special Committee to continue to seek suitable means for the immediate and full implementation of the Declaration and the International Decade for the Eradication of Colonialism. And it calls on administering powers to terminate military activites in the Territories. In addition, it calls on the Special Committee to formulate specific proposals for the elimination of the "remaining manifestations of colonialism." Those proposals will be discussed at the 47th General Assembly. A similar issue received a General Assembly decision in "Military activities and arrangements by colonial Powers in Territories under their administration which might be impeding the implementation of the Declaration on the Granting of Independence to Colonial Countries and Peoples" [A/Dec/46/419]. On the recommendation of the Assembly's Fourth Committee (Decolonization) and by a vote of 108–34–16, the Assembly adopted this decision, which reiterated "its strong views" that existing bases and installations should be withdrawn. In addition, it requested that "the colonial Territories and areas adjacent thereto should not be used for nuclear testing, dumping of nuclear wastes or deployment of nuclear and other weapons of mass destruction." The issue will be considered again by the 47th General Assembly.

The 47th General Assembly will also be discussing the implementation of a resolution entitled "Information from Non-Self-Governing Territories transmitted under Article 73e of the Charter of the United Nations" [A/Res/46/63], which calls on administering powers to annually transmit information on economic, social, and educational conditions. The United States, the United Kingdom, and France all abstained from that vote (157–0–3). Also on the agenda of the 47th General Assembly is the implementation of a resolution on the **dissemination of information on decolonization** [A/Res/46/72]. The resolution calls on the Secretary-General and all states to continue to collect, prepare, and disseminate publicity about decolonization issues. The resolution passed 143–2–16, with the United States and the United Kingdom voting against it, and other Western countries abstaining. The 47th General Assembly will also be hearing a report of the Secretary-General on the implementation of a resolution on "Offers by Member States of study and training facilities for inhabitants of Non-Self-Governing Territories," which invites all states to provide scholarships for inhabitants of Non-Self-Governing Territories [A/Res/46/66]. The resolution was adopted without a vote.

More controversial, the 46th General Assembly voted to put an issue on its agenda for the 47th General Assembly in a resolution with the near-interminable title "Activities of foreign economic and other interests which are impeding the implementation of the Declaration on the Granting of Independence to Colonial Countries and Peoples in Territories under colonial domination and efforts to eliminate colonialism, apartheid and racial discrimination in southern Africa." Although seemingly general in intent, the resolution is aimed primarily at South Africa and calls on nations to reimpose economic sanctions and an oil embargo on that country. The resolution passed over the objection of the developed countries, making the vote 109-34-16. Another resolution, entitled "Implementation of the Declaration on the Granting of Independence to Colonial Countries and Peoples by the specialized agencies and the international institutions associated with the United Nations," met with a similar fate [A/Res/46/65]. The resolution, which passed by a 115-28-17 vote, calls on the specialized agencies and other organs of the U.N. system to support decolonization. Where the resolution falls foul of the developed countries is in its call for economic sanctions against South Africa. Nevertheless, the item will be on the agenda of the 47th General Assembly. A similar version of the same resolution—minus the South Africa reference—was adopted without a vote as "Cooperation and coordination of specialized agencies and the international institutions associated with the United Nations in their assistance to Non-Self-Governing Territories" [A/Res/46/70].

In addition to the resolutions and decisions, the 46th General Assembly also dealt with eight territory-specific pieces of legislation. On the **"Question of Western Sahara,"** the 46th General Assembly adopted without a vote a resolution that welcomes and congratulates in glowing terms the success of the Secretary-General's brokered cease-fire, the Security Council's peacekeeping mission, and a referendum on the territory's future to take place in 1993 [A/Res/46/67]. The issue will be considered again at the 47th General Assemby. The 46th also passed one consolidated resolution on **American Samoa, Anguilla, Bermuda, British Virgin Islands, Cayman Islands, Guam, Montserrat, Tokelau, Turks and Caicos Islands,** and **U.S. Virgin Islands** [A/Res/46/68]. It also passed decisions on **New Caledonia** [A/Dec/46/69], **East Timor** [A/Dec/46/402], **Falkland Islands (Malvinas)** [A/Dec/46/406], and **St. Helena** [A/Dec/46/422], and consensuses on **Gibraltar** [A/Dec/46/420] and **Pitcairn** [A/Dec/46/421].

The Special Committee on the Situation with Regard to the Implementation of the Declaration on the Granting of Independence to Colonial Countries and Peoples

The Special Committee was established by General Assembly Resolution 1654 (XVI) of November 27, 1961. It was requested to examine and help to implement the Declaration on the Granting of Independence to Colonial Countries and Peoples [A/Res 1810 (XV)]. For over 30 years the Special Committee on decolonization has sought to advance the inalienable rights of all colonial peoples to self-determination and independence, and to promote the full exercise of those rights as set forth in the U.N. Charter and the Declaration on the Granting of Independence to Colonial Countries and Peoples. Since then more than 50 Non-Self-Governing Territories and Trust Territories have exercised their right to self-determination. The large majority have chosen independence, while the others have opted for free association, integration, or other status in conformity with Resolution 1541 (XV).

As originally envisaged, the decolonization committee was to serve as a forum in which representatives of the territories could annually present their views on the degree to which their administering power was fulfilling its obligations. Specific problems would be raised, differences of opinion would be aired, practical solutions would be sought, all with the specific interests of the peoples of the territories in mind. The administering powers agreed to submit to such international scrutiny because they recognized that their long-term interests would be furthered by participation in a constructive, public process designed to promote the discharge of their sacred trust.

For many years the decolonization committee and the administering powers cooperated successfully in achieving the objectives of Chapter XI. Of the more than 70 former Non-Self-Governing Territories that existed prior to 1960, only 18 still remain on the agenda of the decolonization committee. But, in some sense, the decolonization committee has become the victim of its own success. With so few territories remaining under its jurisdiction, the committee began to place its focus elsewhere. According to the U.S. position, instead of dealing with particular problems brought to its attention by representatives of the territories of other interested parties, the committee began to inject extraneous and anachronistic colonial and Communist rhetoric into its debates and resolutions. "The decolonization committee began to assert that the few remaining Non-Self-Governing Territories had failed to achieve a full measure of self-government because of some colonial animus on the part of the administering Powers," argued U.S. Ambassador Shirin Tahir-Kheli in the Fourth Committee [USUN Press Release 48, 10/4/91].

As a result, **all the Western nations have now abandoned the decolonization committee.** Britain withdrew in 1986, observing that while the vast majority of territories it had been responsible for had chosen independence, a small number preferred to remain in close association with the United Kingdom. Although they could modify their choice at any time, it seemed unlikely that any would do so in the near future. In those circumstances, Britain felt that there was no need for the

United Nations to devote its scarce time and resources to the study of these territories' affairs. Britain has ten remaining dependent territories. Norway, the last remaining Western representative, withdrew from the committee on January 1, 1992 [A/AC.109/1096].

As of June 1, 1992, the **Special Committee was composed of 24 members:** Afghanistan, Bulgaria, Chile, China, Congo, Côte d'Ivoire, Cuba, Czechoslovakia, Ethiopia, Fiji, India, Indonesia, Iran, Iraq, Mali, Papua New Guinea, Russian Federation, Sierra Leone, Syria, Trinidad and Tobago, Tunisia, Tanzania, Venezuela, and Yugoslavia [A/AC.109/L.1774]. The **decolonization committee now watches over 18 territories:** Western Sahara, American Samoa, Anguilla, Bermuda, British Virgin Islands, Cayman Islands, Guam, Montserrat, Tokelau, Turks and Caicos Islands, Trust Territory of the Pacific Islands, U.S. Virgin Islands, New Caledonia, Gibraltar, Pitcairn, East Timor, Falkland Islands (Malvinas), and St. Helena. Under Article 73e of the Charter, members of the United Nations that have responsibilities for the administration of territories whose peoples have not attained a full measure of self-government are requested to "transmit regularly to the Secretary-General for information purposes, subject to such limitation as security and constitutional considerations may require, statistical and other information of a technical nature relating to economic, social and educational conditions in the Territories for which they are responsible. . . ."

Bermuda

In November 1991 a Progressive Labor party member of the Bermudian Parliament delivered a motion in the House of Assembly calling for the question of independence to become an issue in the next general election, declaring that "it was a total anachronism we should be seen as a colony." Bermuda's Premier responded that he remained unconvinced that the majority of Bermudians favored independence [A/AC.109/1102].

Noting that no U.N. visiting mission had ever been to Bermuda, the General Assembly called on Britain to facilitate the dispatch of such a mission. The resolution also called on Britain to ensure that the presence of military bases and installations in the territory would not constitute an obstacle to the implementation of the decolonization declaration or hinder the Bermudian population from exercising its right to self-determination and independence. In addition to Britain, the United States and Canada maintain military bases in Bermuda (about a tenth of the total land is currently leased to the United States for military purposes) [A/AC.108/1103].

By its action concerning Bermuda, the General Assembly called on the administering power to ensure the economic and social stability of the territory and to counter problems related to drug trafficking [A/Res/46/

68]. The region has no natural resources "in the conventional sense," and tourism provides 55 percent of its economic activity. Its illegal drug trade has reportedly reached an estimated $70 million a year [A/AC.108/1103].

British Virgin Islands

Named by Christopher Columbus in 1493, the British Virgin Islands are made up of 30 islands and islets, only 16 of which are inhabited. The total population of the islands is about 17,700. In its resolution on the Islands, the General Assembly called on Britain, the administering power, to assist the territory in developing and diversifying the economy. The General Assembly noted with satisfaction the current measures being taken by the territorial government to prevent drug trafficking and money laundering, and urged the United Kingdom to continue its assistance in those endeavors [A/Res/46/68].

With regard to constitutional and political developments, an amendment to the Constitution was proposed last year that would allow legislators to represent the territory in regional affairs. (The Constitution restricts participation in foreign affairs to the governor only.) Regarding the future status of the territory, that question had not been an issue during the campaign for the general election held in 1990. Representatives of the territorial government maintain that the people of the territory wish to preserve the current status, which could only be changed by a constitutional amendment.

The economy of the territory remains dependent on tourism, banking, real estate development, construction, and government services. Agricultural and manufacturing activities play a secondary role. The Islands may graduate to "net contributor status" in the fifth U.N. Development Programme cycle, meaning that the territory may become responsible for paying for its own development projects. During 1991–92 the territorial government planned to invest $59.7 million in its Public Sector Investment Program. One interesting footnote: In May of 1991 the British government decided to abolish the death penalty for murder in its Caribbean dependent territories. Leaders of the territorial government protested the decision and requested that it be reviewed, as the local government had not been consulted [A/AC.109/1100].

Cayman Islands

Administered by Britain, the Cayman Islands is a group of three islands and 25,000 people. Tourism is the main source of revenue for the territory. In 1991 the Governor of the Islands formed a Constitutional Commission to "ascertain and evaluate opinion in the Cayman Islands upon possible paths of constitutional evolution." The members of the

Constitutional Commission released a report last year that states that "residents of the Territory had expressed the sentiment that existing links with the United Kingdom should be maintained and that any constitutional change must not only preserve stability but must also stop appreciably short of full internal self-government, the penultimate stage before independence. There was no wish to alter the present status of the Cayman Islands on which much of the Territory's prosperity may depend" [A/AC.109/1097].

In its resolution on the Cayman Islands, the 46th General Assembly called on Britain to continue the constitutional review process and to promote agricultural development in order to reduce the Islands' dependence on imported food supplies. The resolution also noted with regret that there had not been a U.N. Visiting Mission to the territory in 14 years [A/Res/46/68].

Montserrat

Yet another territory administered by Britain, Montserrat is situated in the Leeward Islands in the eastern Caribbean. The island, which was visited by Columbus in 1493, has a population of 12,000. A new ruling party came to power in late 1991, and though it considers independence inevitable, it has adopted a gradual approach. It has the distinction of having the most advanced constitution of the NSGTs in the Caribbean, but the government and the opposition parties share the view that economic viability should precede political independence. Toward that end, the 46th General Assembly urged Britain to provide the necessary assistance for the training of local personnel and urged the expansion of aid to accelerate the development of the economic and social infrastructure of the territory. Regret was expressed that there had been no U.N. mission to the island in ten years. The resolution also called on Britain to take the necessary steps to help Montserrat gain admission as an associate member of UNESCO.

New Caledonia

New Caledonia is located in the southwest Pacific Ocean between Australia and Fiji and has a population of 164,000. Named after the ancient name of Scotland by Captain James Cook, New Caledonia is a group of islands administered by the French. In December 1986, the General Assembly stated that it considered the islands a Non-Self-Governing Territory. While France disagreed—noting that citizens of New Caledonia were also citizens of France and had the same rights as any other citizen of France—it did agree in the **Matignon Accords** that if the majority of citizens of the islands came out in favor of independence, France would respect that decision.

Toward implementing the referendum envisioned in the Matignon Accords, the parties concerned decided that New Caledonia should vote freely on self-determination in 1998—a vote in which only those who had lived continuously in New Caledonia for ten years or more would be able to participate. Under the terms of the Accords, ratified by 80 percent of the French population in a national referendum in November 1988, the territory should enjoy greater autonomy and be largely administered by its own elected officials. The agreements also made provision for a vigorous policy of economic development and social justice to promote growth and to ensure equal opportunity. In its 46th Session, the General Assembly adopted without a vote a resolution noting the positive work of the French. The 47th General Assembly will also be examining the issue [A/Res/46/69].

Pitcairn

Bigger in legend than in life, the islands that featured in the real mutiny on the HMS *Bounty* have only 59 inhabitants—and most are descendants of castaways from the *Bounty,* who arrived there in 1790. Though only one island is inhabited, the territory actually comprises four islands, situated midway between Australia and South America. Since the independence of Fiji in 1970, overall responsibility for the territory has been vested in the United Kingdom High Commissioner to New Zealand, who is also designated Governor of Pitcairn. Internal affairs of the territory are managed through an Island Council consisting of ten members. At its 46th Session, the General Assembly reaffirmed the inalienable right of the people of Pitcairn to self-determination in conformity with the Declaration on the Granting of Independence to Colonial Countries and Peoples. The Assembly further reaffirmed the responsibility of the administering power to promote the economic and social development of the territory, and urged the administering power to continue to respect the very individual life-style that the people of the territory have chosen [A/Dec/46/421].

The economy of Pitcairn is based on subsistence fishing and gardening and the sale of handicrafts and postage stamps. As the population has been very stable, land use has varied little in recent years. Most imports are for home use. Vessels of one shipping company make approximately four scheduled stops on the island a year. Other cargo vessels make unscheduled calls. Although Britain had examined the possibility of constructing an airstrip to improve communications with the outside world, it decided that the high cost of construction and maintenance made such a project unfeasible. The radio-telephone and telegraph service was in the process of being replaced by a satellite system operated out of New Zealand [A/AC.109/1098].

St. Helena

Situated in the South Atlantic midway between Angola and Brazil, the island of St. Helena has housed several celebrities. It was the home of astronomer Edward Halley and the final residence of the vanquished Napoleon, who was sent there in 1815 and died there six years later. Ecologists love it because of the untouched flora and fauna and abundance of green turtles and sea birds. The main industry is fishing. The sale of postage stamps provides the second largest source of income.

The 46th General Assembly passed a decision on the island by a vote of 120–2–38 calling on Britain to remove its military base from the island of **Ascension,** considered by the United Nations and most member states—but not Britain—as a dependency of St. Helena. Britain had built up the base in the wake of the Falkland Islands dispute. The United States and the United Kingdom cast the only negative votes. The decision also urged Britain to continue to take all necessary steps to ensure speedy implementation of the Declaration on Decolonization. The issue will be debated again during the 47th General Assembly [A/Dec/46/422].

Turks and Caicos Islands

The Turks and Caicos Islands are a group of British-administered islands southeast of the Bahamas and north of the Dominican Republic. Currently, 11,500 people live in the territory, which consists of two groups of islands separated by a deep-water channel. The 1988 Constitution provided for a Governor appointed by the Queen, an Executive Council, and a Legislative Council. The Constitutional Order of 1988 conferred powers of administration on the Governor that were usually those of the elected government. General elections are held every four years.

Acknowledging the relationship between economic viability and the viability of independence, Turks and Caicos Islands have announced their goal to attain economic independence and phase out development aid to the territory by 1996. The Chief Minister of the Islands has called for some $11.5 million per year during the next five years to help achieve that goal. The United Nations Development Programme (UNDP) is currently considering the integration of the requirements for achieving that goal of economic independence into its Third Country Programme for the Turks and Caicos.

The economy of the Islands is based primarily on property development, offshore banking, tourism, the export of fish, and government expenditure. The fishing industry provides all of the territory's exports, while tourism is the major source of revenue. Considerable assistance comes from the United Kingdom, Canada, the European Development Fund, and the Caribbean Development Bank. Several U.N. bodies and specialized agencies provide assistance to the territory, with UNDP as the main source of technical assistance. In order to reduce its economic dependence on external assistance, the government has been expanding the tourist industry and the Islands' role as an international banking center [A/AC.109/1098].

The Trusteeship Council

Palau is the **last remaining U.N. Trust Territory** and the last of the former Trust Territory of the Pacific Islands. By a December 1990 resolution, the Security Council, in light of the entry into force of new status agreements for the Federated States of Micronesia, the Marshall Islands, and the Northern Mariana Islands, determined that the objectives of the Trusteeship Agreement had been fully attained with respect to those three entities of the Trust Territory of the Pacific Islands. Therefore, the Trusteeship Agreement with them was terminated [S/Res/45/683].

Palau is classified as a "strategic area" under Article 83 of the U.N. Charter and is administered under a trusteeship agreement by the United States. In March 1992 a Trusteeship Council Visiting Mission went to Palau to observe current conditions [T/Res/2194 S-XXI]. The mission also discussed the final political status of Palau, which is likely to be decided during the 47th General Assembly. The United States would like to see Palau adopt a Compact of Free Association with the United States, as the Federated States of Micronesia and the Republic of the Marshall Islands have done. So far, however, Palau has failed on seven occasions to ratify a Compact of Free Association.

The impending termination of the trusteeship agreement with Palau would effectively complete the work of the Trusteeship Council. There have been some suggestions that the Trusteeship Council next focus on issues of self-determination. This would avoid the potential problems of amending the U.N. Charter and would allow the Trusteeship Council to deal with the hottest issue of the 1990s: domestic instability as newly liberalized nations undergo a transition toward democracy [David Scheffer, *International Herald Tribune*, 1/31/92]. Others have suggested that the Trusteeship Council take over administration of the environment. Whatever role it will play in the 1990s, the Trusteeship Council has almost completed its 40-year task of overseeing 11 Trust Territories until they can determine their destiny.

II
Arms Control and Disarmament

Nineteen ninety-one began and ended with a world-transforming bang, albeit of different sorts. On January 15, U.S.-led coalition forces along the Saudi border with Kuwait and Iraq were poised to begin the most intense air bombardment of the postwar period, with the aim of reversing the Iraqi invasion of Kuwait and destroying much of Baghdad's offensive military potential. Eleven months later, on Christmas day, Soviet President Mikhail Gorbachev handed over the reins of power, including the nuclear launching codes, to Russia's President Boris Yeltsin and the other 11 presidents of former Soviet republics. In so doing, Gorbachev acknowledged what had become a de facto reality: The Soviet Union had formally ceased to exist as a sovereign entity.

Both these events have had profound implications for arms control and disarmament, and both are also likely to color debate on the issue during the 47th Session of the General Assembly. The war against Iraq raised anew the issue of weapons proliferation as a major concern of the international community. The United Nations Special Commission, which was created by U.N. Security Council Resolution 687 to oversee the disarmament of Iraq's weapons of mass destruction and ballistic missile delivery systems, uncovered a huge and covert Iraqi effort to produce such weapons of mass destruction. At the same time, Baghdad's ability during the 1980s to amass the fourth largest army in the world despite an eight-year war with Iran raised serious questions about the policies of many industrial countries that had been willing to sell military equipment and other dual-use items to sustain Saddam Hussein's bid for regional hegemony.

The collapse of the Soviet Union that followed the failed coup of August 1991 reinforced concerns about the control and disposition of Soviet military forces and, in particular, of its vast arsenal of nuclear weapons. A series of nuclear-reduction initiatives launched by the United States and reciprocated first by President Gorbachev and later by President Yeltsin effectively signaled a reversal in the nuclear arms race. Concomitant with these efforts, the United States offered, and Russia accepted, financial and technical assistance in the safe transportation,

117

secure storage, and sound dismantlement of the former Soviet Union's nuclear inventory, heralding a new era of cooperation between the two former adversaries. The same sense of cooperation was also noticeable throughout the rest of Europe, where efforts to secure ratification of the Treaty on Conventional Forces in Europe (CFE) were accompanied by intense negotiations to achieve agreement on a new set of confidence- and security-building measures, an "Open Skies" Treaty, and a CFE-1A agreement in time for the July 1992 Helsinki Summit of the Conference on Security and Cooperation in Europe.

Many of these events took shape during the 46th Session, and their broader implications were only dimly apparent at the time. This may account for the fact that the latest session was largely devoted to issues raised in earlier years. The one exception concerned the issue of transparency in armament transfers, which had become a major concern in the aftermath of the Gulf War. In the fall of 1991, much of the debate in the First Committee was devoted to setting up a U.N. Register of Conventional Arms to record weapons imports and exports on an annual basis. A resolution to this effect was adopted by the General Assembly in December [A/Res/46/36L].

Although developments in Iraq had raised serious questions about the efficacy of the nuclear nonproliferation regime, there were many encouraging signs of a contrary trend as well. In June 1991, France announced that it would sign the nuclear Non-Proliferation Treaty (NPT), followed in August by China, which signed the treaty in March 1992. With these actions, all recognized nuclear weapons states had joined the NPT regime. There was also positive movement with respect to a number of so-called nuclear threshold states. South Africa signed the NPT in July 1991 and concluded a full-scope safeguards agreement with the International Atomic Energy Agency (IAEA) in September; Brazil and Argentina signed an agreement on the peaceful use of nuclear energy in July and an IAEA inspection agreement in December; and North Korea, which had signed and ratified the NPT in 1985, concluded an agreement with South Korea on denuclearizing the Korean peninsula, signed a full-scope safeguard agreement with the IAEA in January 1992, and ratified the agreement in April. There were also signs that India might be willing to enter into talks with Pakistan, the United States, Russia, and China on the establishment of a Nuclear Weapons-Free Zone in South Asia.

The issue of nuclear testing also received attention during the 46th Session. Although prospects for negotiating a comprehensive test ban treaty remained dim throughout the year, there were a number of positive developments. In October 1991, President Gorbachev announced a one-year testing moratorium, expressing the hope that "in this way a road will be opened up for the earliest and complete cessation of all nuclear testing" [*The New York Times*, 10/6/91]. And in April 1992, France's new Prime Minister, Pierre Bérégovoy, made the surprise announcement that his government would suspend its nuclear testing program in the South Pacific for the remainder of the year [ibid., 4/9/92].

In the Conference on Disarmament (CD), efforts intensified to conclude a chemical weapons convention (CWC) in 1992. Following the U.S. initiative of May 1991—in which President George Bush announced that the United States would destroy its chemical weapons (CW) stock and abandon its right to use chemical weapons, even in retaliation, once the convention had entered into force [ibid., 5/14/91]—negotiations in the Ad Hoc Committee on Chemical Weapons of the CD sought to overcome remaining differences over challenge inspections, cost, and other issues. These proceeded apace, and by mid-1992 there was a high probability that the CD would report to the General Assembly that a draft convention had been successfully negotiated.

In the area of biological weapons (BW), the Third Review Conference of the Parties to the Convention on the Prohibition of the Development, Production and Stockpiling of Bacteriological (Biological) and Toxin Weapons and on Their Destruction—informally known as the Biological Weapons Convention—convened in September 1991. It made significant progress in a number of areas, including agreement on additional confidence-building measures and verification and inspection measures.

The profound implications for arms control of the disintegration of the Soviet Union are likely to be more apparent in the 47th Session than in the 46th. Member states may be expected to explore ways of capitalizing on the recent changes, encouraging further progress in nuclear, chemical and biological weapons, and conventional arms control and disarmament negotiations. While progress to date will probably be welcomed, many nations are also likely to insist that the major powers take additional measures in the nuclear field, particularly in the area of testing. At the same time, the major powers will likely insist on devising more stringent measures to halt and reverse the proliferation of weapons of mass destruction—an issue already raised during the meeting of the heads of state and government of the U.N. Security Council on January 31, 1992 [ibid., 2/1/92].

1. Nuclear Arms Control and Disarmament

By the time of the 46th Session of the General Assembly, the U.S.-Soviet nuclear arms control agenda had been unalterably transformed—a fact that was to some extent recognized in the General Assembly's resolution on "Bilateral Nuclear-Arms Negotiations" [A/Res/46/36J]. During the **Mos-**

cow Summit in late July 1991, Presidents Bush and Gorbachev had finally signed the **Treaty on the Reduction and Limitation of Strategic Offensive Arms** (better known as **START**), which had been under negotiation for over nine years. Under the treaty, whose details had been known for some time [A Global Agenda: Issues Before the 46th General Assembly of the United Nations, pp. 78–79], both sides agreed for the first time actually to reduce their strategic offensive forces by 30–35 percent.

The importance of START, and even prospects for its ratification, were thrown in doubt by the Moscow coup of August 1991. The success of the coup would have raised serious questions in the U.S. Senate about the advisability of ratifying the agreement. Its failure, on the other hand, called into question the nature of the U.S. treaty partner, since the collapse of the coup was soon followed by the disintegration of the Soviet Union itself. Soviet nuclear forces and facilities affected by the treaty were deployed on the territory of what were now four independent states: Belarus, Kazakhstan, Russia, and Ukraine. Although all four pledged to uphold the Soviet Union's international obligations, including ratification of START [The New York Times, 12/23/91], who would actually sign and ratify this bilateral treaty remained uncertain. A compromise worked out by the four states, under which Russia would become the U.S. treaty partner and the other three states would sign a legally binding agreement with Moscow to guarantee their adherence to the treaty to the extent it affected forces and facilities on their territory, collapsed in March 1992 when Ukraine insisted that it wanted to be a full and equal treaty partner [Arms Control Today 22, no. 2 (3/92), p. 21; The Washington Times, 4/12/92].

In April 1992 the Bush administration for the first time intervened actively in the negotiations among the four states to resolve the issue of who would sign and ratify the START Treaty. In meetings with officials of each of the four states, it suggested that a new protocol be signed by the four states and the United States that would identify the four states as the U.S. treaty partner and commit the three non-Russian states both to join the NPT as non-nuclear weapon states and to remove all nuclear weapons from their soil by the end of the seven-year START implementation period [The Washington Post, 4/29/92].

A protocol to this effect was signed by the four former Soviet republics and the United States in Lisbon on May 23, 1992. Under the protocol, all four states are named as the treaty partner of the United States. In addition, Belarus, Kazakhstan, and Ukraine have committed to destroying by no later than 1999 all systems covered by the treaty that are deployed on their soil. Finally, the three new states also pledged to join the NPT "in the shortest time possible" [The New York Times, 5/24/92]. The signing of the protocol paves the way for START ratification later in the year—an event that is sure to elicit praise and support during the 47th Session of the U.N. General Assembly.

While the modalities of securing START's entry into force have occupied lawyers on all sides of the issue, nuclear arms control as such was being propelled into different and far more radical directions. Fueled by concern about the control over and disposition of the vast Soviet nuclear arsenal—which consisted of some 27,000 weapons spread over much of the territory of the USSR—the Bush administration launched a major initiative on September 27, 1991, to eliminate many of the least controllable of these forces: tactical nuclear weapons deployed on land and at sea [ibid., 9/28/91]. One week later, President Gorbachev responded positively, reciprocating the unilateral steps announced by President Bush and suggesting matching initiatives in other areas [ibid., 10/6/91].

The **Bush-Gorbachev proposals on nuclear weapons** included the following elements: the elimination of all ground-based tactical nuclear weapons; the removal of all nuclear weapons (including nuclear sea-launched cruise missiles [SLCMs]) from surface ships and attack submarines, destroying many and consolidating the remainder; the standing down from alert of all strategic bombers and those intercontinental ballistic missiles (ICBMs) scheduled for elimination under START; and the cancellation of major strategic modernization programs, including mobile missiles and short-range attack missiles. Bush further proposed a negotiated ban on multi-warhead or MIRVed land-based missiles. Gorbachev also proposed the elimination of all naval nuclear weapons on a reciprocal basis; the removal of tactical nuclear bombs and missiles from air force units; a negotiated 50 percent cut in post-START strategic force levels; and a reciprocal ban on the production of fissile material. Both sides also agreed to enter discussions on the possible deployment of strategic defenses to defend against limited ballistic missile attacks.

With the final collapse of the Soviet Union in December and the establishment of the Commonwealth of Independent States—a loose confederation of 11 of the 12 former Soviet republics—the United States moved to supplement its earlier initiative on tactical nuclear forces with a new proposal to cut strategic forces. On January 28, 1992, President Bush announced that the United States would halt almost all remaining strategic modernization programs. He also said that as part of a negotiated ban on all land-based MIRVed missiles, the United States would unilaterally reduce its strategic forces to about 4,700 weapons by eliminating the MX missile, removing two of three warheads from Minuteman missiles, reducing warheads on U.S. submarine-launched ballistic missiles (SLBMs) by one-third, and converting a "substantial portion" of strategic bombers to conventional use. At the same time, President Bush continued to insist on the need to increase spending for the **Strategic Defense Initiative (SDI)** in order to deploy a defense system capable of defending the United States against limited missile attack [*The New York Times*, 1/29/92].

In speeches over Moscow television and in the U.N. Security Council in the days immediately following, President Yeltsin welcomed the new U.S. initiative while committing Russia to all the unilateral steps announced by Gorbachev the previous October [ibid., 1/30/92, 2/1/92]. And he added some significant initiatives of his own, including a proposal to end almost all strategic modernization programs; a proposal to reduce strategic offensive arms to 2,000–2,500 on each side; a suggestion to create an international agency to ensure the reduction of nuclear weapons, gradually placing under its control the entire nuclear fuel cycle of all countries; and a proposal to create a global defense system for the world community based on a reorientation of the SDI program and Russian defense technology.

Within just four months of negotiations a new arms-reduction agreement was reached during the **Bush-Yeltsin Summit** in Washington on June 17, 1992. Under the agreement, U.S. and Russian nuclear forces will be cut to 3,000–3,500 weapons on each side within a decade. This represents an unprecedented cut of 70 percent from current levels. To reach this historic agreement, both sides compromised on their initial positions. The United States agreed to a lower overall force level than it had proposed earlier, and also accepted a limit of 1,750 warheads on SLBMs—half the number it had planned under START. Russia, for its part, agreed to eliminate all MIRVed land-based missiles, including the SS-18—long the backbone of its strategic force [*The New York Times*, 6/18/92].

Together, these U.S. and Russian initiatives represented a dramatic reversal of the nuclear arms race. The new climate of relations between the erstwhile adversaries was further underscored by an intensive cooperative effort to ensure the safety, security, and environmentally sound destruction of nuclear weapons. High-level discussions on **safety, security, and dismantlement (the SSD talks)** were initiated in November 1991 and propelled forward by a congressional decision to allocate $400 million of U.S. Defense Department funds to assist in these efforts [*The Washington Post*, 11/28/91]. Further expert-level discussions resulted in agreement to expend U.S. funds for the construction of storage containers for fissile materials and warhead components, the redesign of special rail cars for secure transportation, the provision of kevlar or bullet-proof blankets to cover warheads and components during transit, assistance in nuclear accident planning and warhead-accounting methods, and the establishment of scientific clearing houses designed to match weapon scientists with proposals for non-military research [ibid., 4/27/92].

The 47th General Assembly is likely to acknowledge the fundamental transformation of the bilateral nuclear arms control agenda. In the past year the United States and Russia have clearly demonstrated an awareness that radical reductions in nuclear armaments are both possible and necessary. At the same time, the 47th Session is likely to encourage the two countries, as well as the other nuclear powers, to negotiate further reductions in their respective nuclear forces, cease nuclear testing in all environments, and halt the production of fissile materials for nuclear weapons and nuclear explosive devices—steps that were urged during the 46th Session as well [A/Res/46/29; A/Res/46/36D; A/Res/46/36J].

2. European Security

By something of a tradition, the 46th Session paid little attention to European security questions. It welcomed progress on arms control and disarmament issues and encouraged states party to the Conventional Forces in Europe (CFE) Treaty to hasten its entry into force [A/Res/46/36G]. Although most of 1991 was devoted to consolidating the arms control gains of previous years, the months leading up to the **July 1992 Helsinki Summit of the Conference on Security and Cooperation in Europe (CSCE)** saw significant progress in a number of areas, including negotiations on CFE, Open Skies, and additional confidence- and security-building measures (CSBMs).

Having resolved differences over treaty interpretation in June 1991, the 22 **CFE Treaty** signatories moved in the summer to secure its ratification. By December, most had done so, but, as in the case of START, entry into force was thrown into doubt by the disintegration of the Soviet Union. In January 1992, all former Soviet republics with territory in the area of application committed themselves to signing and ratifying the treaty [*Arms Control Today* 22, no. 1(1-2/92), p.44]. Doing so, however, depended on agreement among these states on how to divide force entitlements that belonged to the Soviet Union under the treaty. Although negotiations were protracted, the new states concerned reached agreement on this issue in mid-May [*The New York Times*, 5/16/92]. Agreement opened the way for an extraordinary conference of all CFE parties, convened in Oslo in early June, which in turn agreed to amend the CFE Treaty to reflect the fact that one of its parties—the Soviet Union—had dissolved into separate states. The treaty's entry into force was expected to coincide with the CSCE Summit in Helsinki, July 9–11, 1992.

The run-up to the CSCE Summit also saw final agreement on an Open Skies Treaty and a new CSBM accord, known as the Vienna Document 1992. The **Open Skies Treaty** had been under negotiation since 1989, when President Bush first proposed it. It was signed in March 1992 by 25 states, including all CFE signatories, Russia, Ukraine, Belarus, and Georgia, and will be open to signature by all other CSCE participating states [ibid., 3/21/92]. Under the treaty, parties will have the right, within certain preset quotas, to overfly the territory of other states periodically, with no exemptions for sensitive sites. The inspected party can decide whose aircraft will be used, but the inspecting party can decide what equipment is to be employed, including optical and video cameras, infrared line scanners, and synthetic aperature radars. The data collected will be available to all signatories in raw form, thus providing far more information than would a single flight by a single country [*Defense News*, 4/6/92, p.36].

The **Vienna Document 1992** builds on earlier CSBM agreements concluded in Stockholm in 1986 and in Vienna in 1990. The Document, which was signed by all CSCE participating states in March 1992, adds a number of significant provisions to these earlier agreements. One has to do with the exchange of technical information and the demonstration of major new weapon systems deployed in the area of application; another prohibits exercises involving more than 40,000 troops and 900 battle tanks more than once every two years; a third lowers the ceilings on the level of military activities requiring notification; and still another requires prior notification of the movement of forces out of garrison.

In the months leading up to the July summit in Helsinki, the CSCE participating states sought to build on the achievement of prior years by negotiating a mandate for a **CSCE Forum for Security Cooperation** in which new arms control negotiations will take place, additional conflict prevention measures will be devised, and an ongoing dialogue on security building will be established [*BASIC Reports*, no. 21, 4/20/92]. The issues to be addressed will likely include additional CSBMs, subregional force reductions, defense conversion, the role of the military in democratic societies, cooperative force planning and defense budgeting, weapons proliferation and export controls, mediation and arbitration services, peacekeeping, and defensive restructuring.

Although European security has nearly vanished as a topic of discussion within the General Assembly, the entry into force of the CFE Treaty, the successful conclusion of the Open Skies and Vienna CSBM negotiations, and the establishment of the CSCE Forum for Security Cooperation at the Helsinki Summit are likely to be welcomed as further evidence of the renewed sense of cooperation in Europe. The 47th Session may also point to the European experience as evidence that confrontation can be replaced by cooperation through the concerted effort of all states within a region to build confidence and security, lower military spending and force levels, and engage in an ongoing dialogue on defense and security issues.

3. The U.N. Special Commission

On April 3, 1991, the U.N. **Security Council** passed **Resolution 687** declaring a cease-fire in the Gulf War. Section C of the resolution dealt with Iraq's obligations in the area of weapons of mass destruction and ballistic missiles. Specifically, it decided that Iraq must confirm unconditionally its obligations under the 1925 **Geneva Protocol for the Prohibition of the Use in War of Asphyxiating, Poisonous or Other Gases, and of Bacteriological Methods of Warfare** and the 1968 **nuclear Non-Proliferation Treaty** and go on to ratify the 1972 **Biological Weapons Convention (BWC)**. It further decided that Iraq must accept unconditionally the "destruction, removal, or rendering harmless, under international supervision" of all chemical and biological weapon (CBW) stocks and agents and related facilities and all ballistic missiles with ranges greater than 150 kilometers and related facilities. With respect to nuclear capabilities, the resolution decided that Iraq "unconditionally agree not to acquire or develop nuclear-weapons-usable material" or any subsystems or components or related facilities, and must place all its "nuclear-weapons-usable materials under the exclusive control, for custody and removal, of the IAEA." The Security Council also called on the U.N. Secretary-General to develop a plan for the ongoing monitoring and verification of Iraq's compliance with these measures. Implementation of these measures was to be undertaken by a newly created U.N. Special Commission (UNSCOM).

The activities of UNSCOM and the International Atomic Energy Agency (IAEA) in the year after the adoption of Resolution 687 revealed that Iraq had embarked on an extensive program to acquire and deploy weapons of mass destruction and ballistic missiles. Despite Baghdad's obstruction and repeated failure to comply with U.N. Security Council resolutions, a series of intrusive and short-notice on-site inspections uncovered large stockpiles of undeclared capabilities and an intricate network of research, development, and production facilities in each weapons area. Much of this capacity has since been destroyed, although significant uncertainties remain in all four areas of weapons development.

In the ballistic missile area, UNSCOM has supervised the destruction of 62 ballistic missiles, 18 fixed-missile launch-pads, 10 mobile launchers, 11 decoy missiles, 32 warheads, 127 missile-storage support vehicles, a substantial amount of rocket fuel, an assembled 350-mm supergun, components for 350-mm and 1,000-mm superguns, and a ton of supergun propellants. Inspectors have also confirmed the destruction of missile-repair and production facilities by coalition bombing [S/23165, 10/25/91, p.5]. Following a demarche by the Security Council in March 1992, in part because of Iraq's refusal to destroy remaining ballistic missile production and facilities, Iraq declared that an additional 89 ballistic missiles had been destroyed previously. This new information was subsequently verified by UNSCOM inspectors [*The Washington Post*, 3/21/92, 3/24/92].

In the chemical weapons area, Iraqi declarations and subsequent inspections revealed that Iraq possessed some 46,000 filled CW munitions, including 10,780 122-mm rocket warheads; 1,776 aerial bombs; 12,634 155-mm artillery shells; 30 ballistic missile warheads; and 20,000 120-mm mortar shells. The latter were filled with the tear gas CS, the others with a variety of nerve agents and mustard gas. Iraq also had 280 tons of mustard agent and 75 tons of nerve agent stored in bulk form and nearly 80,000 unfilled munitions that could be used to deliver chemical agents [S/23472,1/24/92, pp.22–23]. Finally, in March 1992, Iraq declared that it had on hand another 45 missile warheads that it claimed to have destroyed earlier [*Chemical and Engineering News*, 4/20/92, p. 16]. Many of the unfilled munitions have been destroyed already, but the actual incineration of mustard and tear gases and the neutralization of nerve gases—to commence in the summer of 1992, in facilities built by Iraq under U.N. supervision—is expected to last 12 to 18 months [ibid.].

In the biological weapons area, Iraq initially denied that it had a BW capability or program, but upon further inspection it admitted to a military research program that could have been used for both defensive and offensive purposes. The micro-organisms involved in this program included anthrax, botulin toxin, and gas gangere. Although UNSCOM inspections have not found any biological weapons or facilities for filling weapons, UNSCOM has concluded that the research effort under way "logically would have included a plan for a [BW] development and production component" [S/23165, 10/25/91, p. 29].

The most surprising and disturbing findings were in the nuclear weapons area. Following initial denials by Baghdad that it was pursuing a nuclear weapons program, Iraq declared on July 7, 1991, that it had pursued three undeclared uranium-enrichment programs—electronic magnetic isotope separation, centrifuge-based technology, and chemical separation—and, on July 18, the **IAEA Board of Governors** declared that Iraq had violated the safeguard agreements it had signed with the IAEA. The U.N. Security Council followed up on August 15 with a resolution affirming that Iraq's failure to subject its uranium-enrichment program to IAEA safeguards "constitutes a breach of its international obligations" [S/Res/707(1991)]. Subsequently, the IAEA discovered another series of operations that violated Iraq's obligations under the NPT, including the irradiation of undeclared fuel elements, the separation of small quantities of plutonium, the procurement of components sufficient for thousands of centrifuges, and covert research on weaponization [S/23514, 1/25/92, pp. 17–20]. In the past year the IAEA has removed or destroyed most of these materials and facilities and has also forced Iraq to destroy the nuclear complex at al-Athir, where much of the research and development work relating to Iraq's nuclear weapons research had taken place [S/23295, 12/17/91; *The Washington Post*, 4/8/92].

The experience in Iraq has been a sobering one for the international community. It has demonstrated the inadequacy of the existing IAEA inspection practices and highlighted the dangers of exporting dual-use items to a country bent on acquiring weapons of mass destruction. Remarkably, the General Assembly paid little attention to these developments at its 46th Session. This could change in the 47th Session, when members may cite the Iraq experience as reason to move more expeditiously toward the establishment in the Middle East of a zone free of all weapons of mass destruction, as both the General Assembly [A/Res/46/30] and the Security Council [S/Res/687(1991)] have urged.

4. Nuclear Proliferation and Nuclear Weapons-Free Zones

The experience with Iraq has had a salutary effect on the nuclear non-proliferation regime. Not only is it enhancing efforts to strengthen the inspection and safeguards regimes of the IAEA, but it began a trend to "deproliferation" in quite a few regions. In South America, southern Africa, and the Korean peninsula, so-called nuclear-threshold states are taking steps to assure their neighbors that they will not seek to develop the bomb. The possibilities for progress in South Asia also improved as India moved slowly from outright rejection of the idea of a nuclear weapons-free zone (NWFZ) in the region to an indication of interest in attending talks on the subject with Pakistan, China, Russia, and the United States. The General Assembly addressed many of these issues at the 46th Session, and the 47th Session is likely to reiterate its support for nuclear weapons-free zones in various regions.

Iraq's clear violation of its obligations under the nuclear Non-Proliferation Treaty (NPT) has led the IAEA to consider ways of strengthening its inspection and safeguards regime. Meeting in late February 1992, the Agency's Board of Governors reaffirmed the IAEA's right to conduct **"special inspections"** of suspect sites and facilities to determine whether undeclared fissile materials might be present. Although this right has been enshrined in all IAEA safeguard agreements signed with member countries, the IAEA has never conducted such an inspection without the invitation of a host country. The board also decided to change regulations governing the provision of information on new nuclear facilities. It now requires member states to provide the IAEA with design information on new installations as soon as a construction decision is made. Previously, it required this information only 180 days prior to the introduction of nuclear materials. Finally, the board deferred until June 1992 a decision on whether to expand a registry for data on the transfer of nuclear and nuclear-related commodities. Under this provision, suppliers and recipients would be required to notify the IAEA when nuclear materials, sensitive equipment (such as for enrichment and reprocessing technologies), and even some non-nuclear materials are transferred [*Arms Control Today* 22, no. 3 (4/92), p. 27].

In addition to strengthening the IAEA inspection regime, the Gulf War has also resulted in renewed efforts to control the export of technologies that may be used to produce nuclear weapons. On April 3, 1992, the 27-nation **Nuclear Suppliers Group (NSG),** which includes most of the world's nuclear technology exporters, issued new guidelines to limit the export of so-called "dual-use" technologies that have both civilian and military applications. Items to be controlled were listed in an annex containing some 67 categories, including equipment for uranium isotope separation, heavy water production plants, implosion system development, explosives, and nuclear testing. Under the new guidelines the NSG members agreed not to transfer items on the list unless the item was to be employed in safeguarded facilities. Any equipment exported must also be subject to "end-user" assurances, and the supplier must be granted a veto over any possible retransfer [ibid., p. 19].

Although these measures to enhance the **IAEA safeguards regime** and strengthen export controls were stimulated primarily by a fear of growing nuclear proliferation, 1991 was also the year in which a new trend—nuclear deproliferation—became evident. The two remaining declared nuclear powers—China and France—signed the NPT, while Russia, as the Soviet successor state, reaffirmed its obligations as a nuclear weapons state under the treaty. Five southern African countries also acceded to the NPT: Mozambique, Tanzania, Zambia, Zimbabwe, and, most significant, South Africa. A number of the former Soviet republics, including the three Baltic states—Estonia, Latvia, and Lithuania—have also joined the NPT, while Belarus, Kazakhstan, and Ukraine have pledged to do so shortly. Between the beginning of 1991 and mid-1992, therefore, the number of state parties to the NPT had risen to 151 from 141.

The deproliferation trend was also demonstrated in many of the regions in which proposals for the establishment of NWFZs have long been supported by the General Assembly. Most noteworthy was the progress in northeast Asia, where, on December 31, 1991, North and South Korea signed a **Joint Declaration for a Non-Nuclear Korean Peninsula** [*The New York Times*, 1/1/92]—this within two weeks of agreement on a nonaggression pact [ibid., 12/13/91]. Under the nuclear declaration, the two countries agreed neither to "test, produce, receive, possess, store or deploy nuclear weapons" nor to "possess facilities for nuclear reprocessing and uranium enrichment." These commitments would be verified through on-site inspections of facilities. The declaration paved the way for Pyongyang (which had acceded to the NPT in 1985) to sign the IAEA safeguards agreement as required. It did this on January 30, 1992, and formally ratified the agreement on April 9. In May, Pyongyang presented the IAEA with a 100-page description of its nuclear program, revealing among other things that it had a "radiochemical" laboratory designed for research on separating plutonium from spent fuel. A subsequent visit to this and other sites by the IAEA Director General, Hans Blix, further revealed that North Korea had produced a small amount of plutonium and that, when fully operational, the "radiochemical" laboratory was really a reprocessing facility [ibid., 5/7/92]. However, the openness displayed by North Korea in this instance, and its willingness to sign and fulfill other commitments, suggests the increasing likelihood that the Korean peninsula will become free of nuclear weapons by the end of the year.

Similarly promising have been recent developments in Latin America, where on July 18, 1991, Argentina and Brazil signed an **Agreement for the Exclusively Peaceful Use of Nuclear Energy** [CD/1117, 1/22/92]. Under this and previous agreements, the two countries agreed to forgo the military use of nuclear energy (except for the propulsion of nuclear submarines), to submit their facilities to joint inspections by one another and the IAEA, and to take steps to ensure that the 1967 **Treaty for the Prohibition of Nuclear Weapons in Latin America** (also known as the **Treaty of Tlatelolco**) enters into full force. A safeguards agreement between the two countries and the IAEA was signed on December 13, 1991 [CD/1118, 1/22/92]. In February 1992, Argentina and Brazil further announced that they would submit some amendments to the text of the Treaty of Tlatelolco that were largely technical in nature [A/47/92, 2/19/92]. Once submitted and accepted by the other parties to the treaty, Brazil and Argentina will become party to the Treaty of Tlatelolco, leaving Cuba as the lone nonparty in the region. The establishment of a nuclear weapons-free zone in Latin America was further enhanced by the decision of France to ratify **Additional Protocol I** of the treaty, under which it finally agreed neither to emplace nuclear weapons in nor to transfer them through the treaty area. For the 46th General Assembly, the French decision meant that—for the first time in years—the First Committee did not act on a draft resolution calling on France to ratify the protocol [A/46/664, 1/21/91]. The 47th Session is likely to welcome these developments while calling on Cuba to sign and ratify the treaty.

The 46th Session of the General Assembly did address the issue of a **Nuclear Weapons-Free Zone in South Asia**, again reaffirming its endorsement in principle of the concept [A/Res/46/31]. What was noteworthy this time, however, was the fact that the Soviet Union voted in favor of the resolution, rather than, as in previous years, abstaining. This decision followed Moscow's endorsement of a proposal by Nawaz Sharif, Prime Minister of Pakistan, for talks among India, Pakistan, China, the Soviet Union, and the United States on the establishment of a South Asian NWFZ [CD/1091, 7/24/91]. The Pakistani proposal, which was endorsed by China, Russia, and the United States (but not India), has since become the main vehicle for dealing with the nuclear question on the Indian subcontinent. Both Moscow's decision to endorse the five-power talks and the General Assembly resolution have further isolated India on this issue. Although New Delhi still formally opposes such talks, it has eased its opposition somewhat, holding out the prospect of some kind of discussion on the issue in the course of the year [*The New York Times*, 3/11/92]. This apparent willingness to change policy followed the successful implementation of the agreement between India and Pakistan to exchange data on the location of their respective nuclear installations as part of their 1988 agreement not to attack each other's facilities [*The Washington Post*, 1/2/92].

The decision by **South Africa** to accede to the NPT and submit its facilities to IAEA safeguards changed somewhat the tone of debate on this issue at the 46th Session. Rather than condemning South Africa, the General Assembly passed a resolution on the "Nuclear Capability of South Africa" that called upon South Africa to comply with the safeguards agreement by, among other things, disclosing its nuclear facilities and materials in conformity with its obligation under NPT; and it requested the IAEA to ensure early implementation of the safeguards agreement it signed with South Africa in September [A/Res/46/34A]. The 46th Session also reiterated past Assemblies' calls for implementation of the **Declaration on the Denuclearization of Africa,** which was adopted by the heads of state and government of the Organization of African Unity (OAU) in July 1964 [A/Res/46/34B]. The 47th Session will receive and most likely discuss a report by the group of experts set up jointly by the OAU and the United Nations on the implementation of the OAU declaration.

Reviewing the issues of a **nuclear weapons-free zone in the Middle East** at its 46th Session, the General Assembly again urged all states in the region to consider taking practical and urgent steps for implementing a NWFZ in the Middle East; called upon all states that had not yet done so to place all their nuclear facilities under IAEA safeguards; urged states in the region to adhere to the NPT; invited them to forswear the development, production, testing, or acquisition of nuclear weapons and to forbid the stationing of nuclear weapons on their territory; requested the Secretary-General to conduct further consultations with states in the region and other concerned states; and decided to take up the matter once more at the 47th Session [A/Res/46/30]. In another resolution, the 46th Session further reiterated its "grave concern" about Israeli nuclear armaments and its military cooperation with South Africa and decided to include an item on "Israeli nuclear armament" on the agenda of the 47th Session [A/Res/46/39].

5. Nuclear Testing

The 46th Session returned to the issue of nuclear testing in two resolutions. One called upon all parties to the **Treaty Banning Nuclear**

Weapon Tests in the Atmosphere, in Outer Space, and Under Water to participate in the Amendment Conference for the achievement of a **Comprehensive Test Ban Treaty** (CTBT) and urged all states, especially nuclear weapons states that had not yet done so, to adhere to the treaty [A/Res/46/28]. The other resolution reaffirmed the General Assembly's conviction that a treaty to achieve the prohibition of all nuclear-test explosions by all states in all environments for all time is a matter of priority. To this end, it urged the **Conference on Disarmament** to intensify its work on the issue, particularly as concerns the structure and scope of verification and compliance, and also urged the nuclear weapons states to agree to appropriate verifiable and militarily significant interim measures, with a view to concluding a CTBT [A/Res/46/28].

The 47th Session, which is to discuss both issues, is likely to pay particular attention to the question of nuclear testing in light of the Russian and French decisions to suspend all tests until the end of the year. While the Soviet Union and, now, Russia have continued to support the negotiation of a CTBT, the French decision to suspend its testing program in the Pacific was surprising—all the more so because France has not signed the **Limited Test Ban Treaty** (LTBT) and has consistently voted against General Assembly resolutions calling for a CTBT. The change in French attitude may have contributed to a renewed debate in the United States on the issue. In May it was reported that the Bush administration was considering various testing restraint options, ranging from a 50 percent reduction in annual tests (from six to three) to a virtual halt in testing by 1995 [*The Washington Post*, 5/24/92]. Depending on the outcome of these deliberations as well as of discussions on this issue between Presidents Bush and Yeltsin during the Washington Summit in June 1992, the General Assembly is likely to endorse a measured approach to the complete cessation, through interim steps, of nuclear testing in all environments.

6. Chemical and Biological Weapons

Prospects for completing negotiations on a **chemical weapons convention (CWC)** within the Conference on Disarmament's (CD) **Ad Hoc Committee on Chemical Weapons** appear to have brightened following U.S. President George Bush's announcement of May 12, 1991, that the nation would forswear the use of chemical weapons for any reason and destroy its entire CW stockpile once a convention had entered into force [*The New York Times*, 5/14/91]. As part of his announcement the President urged that negotiations on a CWC be completed within 12 months—a timetable that was endorsed by the 46th General Assembly [A/Res/46/35C].

It soon became clear, however, that a number of important issues had to be resolved before negotiations could be completed. Prime among these were challenge inspections of undeclared sites. In July 1991 the United States, joined by Australia, Japan, and the United Kingdom, introduced a new working paper in the Ad Hoc Committee that stepped back from the long-standing U.S. position in favor of "anytime-any-where" challenge inspections [CD/CW/WP.352, 7/15/91]. Under the new proposal, up to a week could elapse between the notification of an inspection and the time it actually began; monitoring of the site's exit points could not begin until three days after notification; and the inspected country could choose one of four access options, only one of which provides direct access on the ground within the suspected site.

The new proposal got a mixed reception, with many members of the so-called Western group criticizing the United States for stepping back from a more intrusive inspection regime. After months of discussion, significant modifications were proposed in a new overall draft treaty text submitted by Australia. Under the Australian text, no more than five days could elapse between notification and the inspection itself; exit monitoring would begin no later than 48 hours after notification; and, rather than choosing from a list of "access options," the inspected country must allow inspectors direct access to the suspected site (although the extent of access thereafter remains subject to negotiation between the host country and the inspectors) [*Arms Control Today* 22, no. 3 (4/92), p. 20].

The Australian draft treaty text also proposed compromise language on a number of other controversial issues, including verification of the civilian chemical weapons industry, composition of the Executive Council that will oversee the convention's implementation, and cost-sharing arrangements. In late June 1992 the Chairman of the Ad Hoc Committee circulated a final draft text to the CD members in the belief that a final text would be initialed in August. It can therefore be expected that the CD will report to the 47th General Assembly that the convention is ready for signature. The Assembly can similarly be expected to endorse the draft convention overwhelmingly.

The 46th Session welcomed the results of the **Third Review Conference of the Parties of the Convention on the Prohibition of the Development, Production and Stockpiling of Bacteriological (Biological) and Toxin Weapons and on Their Destruction,** which took place in September 1991 [A/Res/46/35A]. The states parties to the BWC agreed in the Final Declaration of the Third Review Conference to expand existing confidence-building measures regarding the declaration of past activities in offensive and/or defensive biological research development programs and of facilities engaged in vaccine production. The Final Declaration also announced agreement on establishing an ad hoc group of governmental experts to identify and examine potential verification measures from a scientific and technical standpoint on the basis of a number of criteria agreed upon by the Conference [BWC/Conf.III/23/II, 9/27/91]. The 47th Session is likely to address this issue by noting the progress made by the ad hoc verification group, while urging states that have not yet done so to submit data on their past and present BW research activities as part of the confidence-building measures agreed to in the Final Declaration.

7. Arms Transfers and Transparency

Among the most important issues addressed by the 46th Session, and one that is likely to receive much renewed attention during the 47th, was the issue of transparency in arms transfers. Discussions on this issue resulted in the establishment of a **U.N. conventional arms registry** to record information supplied by member states on their arms imports and exports in the preceding year. Moreover, throughout the year the five permanent members of the Security Council (the Perm Five)—China, France, Great Britain, the Soviet Union (later Russia), and the United States—met a number of times to develop guidelines for arms transfers to the Middle East. Both these developments reflected concern with the arms trade and its potential for aggravating regional tensions and conflicts.

In his Middle East Arms Control Initiative announced in May 1991, President Bush proposed that the Perm Five meet to devise guidelines for restraints on destabilizing transfers of conventional weapons, weapons of mass destruction, and associated technologies [*White House Fact Sheet on Middle East Arms Control Initiative*, 5/29/91]. An initial meeting in Paris, July 8–9, 1991, resulted in agreement among the five that they would "observe rules of restraint" in transferring weapons to the Middle East and that they intended to establish guidelines to this effect at their next meeting [*Arms Control Today* 21, no. 7 (9/91), p. 27].

The second Perm Five meeting, held in London in October, led to the adoption of a number of general guidelines for arms transfers to the region, including a pledge to avoid transfers that would increase tensions or contribute to instability, introduce destabilizing capabilities, or be incompatible with strengthening legitimate security and defense needs. In addition, the five agreed to "make arrangements to exchange information [on arms sales] for the purpose of meaningful consultation," although they failed to agree on whether the exchange should be made prior to or after the transfers had been made [ibid., no. 9 (11/91), pp. 15, 22]. A third Perm Five meeting in Washington in May 1992 similarly failed to reach agreement on when notification should be given. Again China was alone among the Perm Five in insisting that information be exchanged only after transfers are made [*The Washington Post*, 5/30/92].

The deliberations of the First Committee at the 46th Session proved more successful. The idea of an arms sale registry, which the **League of Nations** acted on and administered from 1925 to 1938, was strongly endorsed by the U.N. Secretary-General in his report to the 46th General Assembly on increasing the transparency of arms transfers [A/46/301, annex]. Debate in the First Committee on a draft resolution introduced by the 12 European Community countries and Japan [A/C.1/49/L.18] highlighted a major difference between the North and the South, with the former concentrating on arms transfers and the latter insisting that data submitted to the registry include information on weapons holdings, stockpiles, and production [*Arms Control Today* 21, no. 9 (11/91), p. 22]. In the end, a compromise was reached whereby the information to be recorded in the registry would "include data on international arms transfers as well as information provided by Member States on military holdings, procurement through national production and relevant policies" [A/C.1/46/L.18/Rev.1, reprinted in A/46/673, 11/29/91, p. 24].

The 46th Session adopted a resolution on "Transparency in Armaments" that established a **Registry of Conventional Arms** for the purposes outlined above (only Cuba and Iraq abstained; China was absent) [A/Res/46/36L]. The Annex to the resolution specifies that data be included on transfers of the following armaments: battle tanks, armored combat vehicles, large-caliber artillery systems, combat aircraft, attack helicopters, warships, and missiles or missile systems. The resolution calls upon members to provide data on the preceding year's arms transfers and invites them to include information on their military holdings and procurement. It further calls on the Secretary-General to prepare "a report on the modalities for the early expansion of the scope of the Registry by the addition of further categories of equipment and inclusion of data on military holdings and procurement through national production." This report will be discussed at the 47th Session and, depending on its conclusions, may result in the expansion of the Registry to include data not only on arms transfers but also on national holdings and annual weapons production. If only for this reason, transparency in armaments is likely to be a lively topic of debate during the 47th Session.

III
Economics and Development

1. Overview: A Time of Change, Turbulence, Conflict, Worry, Risk—and Promise—in International Economic Relations

The end of the bipolar cold war era occurred at summer's end 1991 with breathtaking swiftness and drama, as a chastened Soviet **President Mikhail Gorbachev dissolved the Communist party of the Soviet Union.** Yet, despite the heady preparatory years of détente and liberal reform, the first culmination of which came in 1989 atop a "liberated" Berlin Wall, some leading Western governments, especially that of the United States, appeared genuinely unready for a new world in which economic matters would gain precedence over military and security concerns. And so it happened that the early months of the long-sought and long-awaited post-cold war era came to be characterized less by its intrinsic promise of economic cooperation and prosperity than by conflict, worry, and a heightened sense of economic risk.

Change seemed not only everywhere apparent but in many instances simply amazing—not only in its pace but in its direction and magnitude. Leading the way was the Soviet Union—and subsequently Russia. Liberal economic reform was the order of the day, as both the last Soviet President, Mikhail Gorbachev, and the first Russian President, **Boris Yeltsin,** rejected Marxist-Leninist attitudes toward private property and foreign investment and declared their country open to foreign business. However, the economic revolution was not limited to the former Soviet Union, or even Eastern Europe. **India** made a dramatic departure from its long-standing hostility toward economic liberalism. Astonishingly, the Indian government allowed Coca-Cola and, later, the IBM Corporation, to return as investors. In **Sweden,** the left-of-center Social Democrats were replaced by a center-right coalition led by Prime Minister Carl Bildt, who immediately set about dismantling both the welfare state and the barriers to international trade and investment, and moreover set the country firmly on a fast track toward membership in the European Community (discussed below). Sweden was, to varying degrees, joined

135

in its interest in affiliating with the EC by other members of the **European Free Trade Area (EFTA),** all of whom ultimately reached agreement with the EC on creation of a special economic relationship and the creation of a 19-nation free trade zone known as the **European Economic Area (EEA).** China, finally abandoning its post-Tiananmen Square defensiveness, returned—perhaps predictably—to the fold of economic liberalization [*Financial Times*, 2/21/92; *The New York Times*, 2/24/92; *The Wall Street Journal*, 3/2/92].

There were more surprises, however. In **South Africa,** African National Congress (ANC) President **Nelson Mandela** announced that, once in power, the ANC would honor South Africa's external debts and would, in addition, welcome and protect foreign investment [*Financial Times*, 2/8/92, 2/9/92]. **The United Nations Conference on Trade and Development (UNCTAD),** in a major break with its past, accepted, adopted, and began promoting free trade principles, and undertook to find ways to reduce the costs associated with trading with developing countries [ibid., 2/27/92]. **Ethiopia's** new non-Communist rulers also pledged allegiance to liberal trade ideals [ibid., 1/25/92, 1/26/92]. And even **North Korea's** isolated Stalinist regime opened the door to foreign investment [*The Wall Street Journal*, 5/12/92, A1].

Change was not limited to the developing and formerly socialist countries. Interesting developments occurred in the industrialized countries as well. **The United States,** for example, after hesitating, lowered its barriers to **trade with the former Soviet republics.** Western attitudes toward **foreign aid** or economic development assistance also began to change, though not always in the same way. In the United States, for example, a general reorientation toward domestic concerns—entirely legitimate, at least in moderation—was accompanied by a new hostility toward foreign aid [*The Boston Globe*, 11/17/92]. Sweden's new government displayed no distaste for foreign aid but increased the number and types of conditions recipient countries were required to satisfy [*Financial Times*, 1/10/92]. In **Great Britain,** on the other hand, the spring 1992 election campaign, which ultimately returned **Prime Minister John Major** to office, revealed strong public support in that country for more foreign assistance [ibid., 3/18/92].

Turbulence accompanied many of the changes of 1991–92. Ethnic violence erupted in many places in Central and Eastern Europe and among the members of the new Commonwealth of Independent States, as discussed elsewhere in this volume. Radical programs designed to bring about an immediate shift from socialist to capitalist economic organization produced dislocation in many instances, and anger and consternation in others. Even the "stable" West was not immune. In the United States, **President George Bush** faced a discontented electorate, weary of recession and no longer persuaded by warnings of imminent foreign dangers. At one point, American **anti-Japanese sentiment** seemed to spin out of control; and in April and May 1992 the city of Los Angeles (where, as discussed below, a few months earlier anti-Japanese sentiment had prompted the cancellation of a major contract for subway cars awarded to a Japanese firm) experienced the country's most destructive race riot since the 1960s, sparked by African-American anger at the U.S. system of justice and, to some degree, politics. In **France,** the electorate rattled **President François Mitterrand,** prompting him to change prime ministers [*The Wall Street Journal,* 4/3/92]. In Britain, it seemed until election day that Prime Minister Major would be defeated. In **Japan,** scandal and financial market instability (the latter not entirely unrelated to the former) threatened to destabilize both the ruling Liberal Democratic Party (LDP) and the much-vaunted Japanese economy. Separately, **anti-American sentiment** exploded from various parts of Japanese government and society. In **Italy,** forming a government proved nearly impossible; while in **Canada Prime Minister Brian Mulroney**'s popularity ratings seemed to be sinking to the single-digit level. And, finally, in **Germany,** discontented voters and workers shook **Chancellor Helmut Kohl**'s government to its foundations, prompting several high-level resignations, including that of longtime **Foreign Minister Hans-Dietrich Genscher** [*Financial Times,* 4/28/92].

Given the above, it was perhaps inevitable that **conflict,** including confrontation and stalemate, would come to characterize the period. The United States—now the sole military superpower, but in economic terms much closer in size and power to the European Community and Japan— was at the center of many of the conflicts. Whether that was due mainly to its undeniably great size and power and expansive interests or to the suddenly distinct instead of blurred ideological differences with other major actors is not clear. Also not clear is whether in most of these conflicts the United States was "wrong." In a number of them, however, the United States did appear either to stand outside an apparent consensus among its peers or to contradict recognized norms or standards of behavior—situations that tend to generate tensions in political relationships.

The lengthy list of conflicts begins with tussling among the members of the **Group of Seven** economic summit countries: the United States, Germany, Japan, the United Kingdom, France, Canada, and Italy. Disagreements focused on two areas of concern: (1) how to assist the former Communist and later simply the former Soviet republics, most of which by late 1991 were members of the Commonwealth of Independent States, led by Russia; and (2) how to manage inflation-unemployment tradeoffs in the world economy. Both are discussed in greater detail below. Perhaps the most central conflict, if not necessarily the most spectacular, involved principally the United States and the **European**

Community and the issue of agricultural subsidies, the reform of which constitutes the centerpiece of the deadlocked Uruguay Round of multilateral trade negotiations. The United States also openly engaged its other two major trading partners in trade disputes. With **Japan** there was a very public head-of-government-level spat over the importation of U.S.-made autos and auto parts into Japan [*The New York Times*, 1/10/92]. There were also government-level disputes over trade in semiconductors (a seemingly never-ending story) [*Financial Times*, 3/10/92] and the North American content of Honda autos manufactured in Canada under the U.S.-Canada Free Trade Agreement [ibid., 3/4/92]. In addition, lower-level disputes erupted over the aforementioned purchase of subway cars manufactured by a Japanese firm, Sumitomo, by the Los Angeles Metropolitan Transit Agency [*The Wall Street Journal*, 4/22/92], and over possible Japanese (nongovernmental) part-ownership of an American baseball team, the Seattle Mariners.

With **Canada,** its neighbor and largest economic partner, the United States found itself embroiled in confrontations over the aforementioned Honda autos [ibid., 3/6/92], softwood lumber exports to the United States [*The New York Times*, 3/7/92], and trade in beer [*Financial Times*, 12/30/91; *The New York Times*, 4/26/92]. The United States also fought with China over its handling of patents and copyrights [*The Wall Street Journal*, 11/27/91], with the EC over oilseed subsidies [*Financial Times*, 5/1/92], and with France over a civil air agreement [ibid., 5/6/92]. It also took on India, despite India's conversion to economic liberalism [*The Wall Street Journal*, 2/27/92], and Thailand [*Financial Times*, 12/3/91, 2/28/92] and Taiwan [*The Wall Street Journal*, 5/1/92] over various trade and trade-related issues.

Elsewhere, the **European Community and Japan** skirmished briefly over the rate at which Japanese cars might be imported into Europe [*Financial Times*, 4/25/92, 4/26/92], and the EC warned Japan about resorting to bilateralism to preserve Japan's position in the U.S. market [ibid., 3/11/92]. Finally, there were not entirely unexpected elements of **North-South conflict,** related in some degree to the anticipated June 1992 **Earth Summit** (U.N. Conference on Environment and Development [UNCED]) at which the developed countries were expected to ask the developing countries to develop "sustainably," and the developing countries were in turn expected to ask for financial support or compensation for doing so [*Financial Times*, 4/30/92].

Worry and a sense of risk formed an ominous backdrop to the frenzy of activity, much of it troubling, at center-stage. While there was much over which to worry, **the global economy** and its principal component parts tended to dominate. That was because the leading economies, the world's engines of growth, all seemed to be "out of tune and sputtering," as *The New York Times* put it [4/26/92]. It was one thing for the United States, the United Kingdom, and Canada to be in recession simultaneously [see *A Global Agenda: Issues/46*] and quite another for the United States, the United Kingdom, Canada, Germany, and Japan to experience simultaneous slowdowns. To some, Japan's situation seemed especially threatening, especially considering Germany's tight monetary policies. Therefore, speculation about a possible global recession increased [Leonard Silk, *The New York Times*, 4/3/92]. Other worries focused on the world trading system, deadlocked at the Uruguay Round of the General Agreement on Tariffs and Trade (GATT) and rapidly subdividing, or so it seemed, into possibly protectionist if not belligerent regional blocs. Similarly, there was a persistent fear that the United States in particular would, especially in the face of record-high Japanese trade surpluses, abandon multilateral free trade and pursue bilateral or "minilateral" managed trade [*Financial Times*, 1/17/92; *The New York Times*, 3/13/92], under which quantitative allocations would be made and markets divided. In short, the world seemed to some to be perched between some kind of "new world disorder" and a relatively orderly world economic system in which international markets would not operate relatively freely but come instead under the sway of governments.

Perhaps the greatest irony was that this turmoil occurred at a seemingly unparalleled moment of promise for global prosperity and peace. With the demise of Soviet communism and the rapid spread of liberal economic (and political) ideology virtually throughout the world, with only a few conspicuous exceptions, the stage seemed to be set for the creation of a truly integrated world economy. It appeared that most countries would be democratic and, therefore, oriented toward individual rights—both economic and political—and toward peace. Although some saw emerging trade blocs as a step backward (for example, Columbia University and GATT economist Jagdish Bhagwati), others (for example, MIT economist Rudiger Dornbusch) saw them as an important stepping-stone toward a liberal, integrated global community. Those who took a positive view could not but be encouraged by the creation of the **European Economic Area (EEA)**, a combination of the EC and European Free Trade Area (EFTA), and by the prospect of eventual Polish, Czechoslovakian, and Hungarian membership in an enlarged European Community incorporating EFTA states as well.

While some worried that the **Uruguay Round** agenda was too full, others calculated the potential benefits of a successful conclusion. One estimate came in at $195 billion the first full year [*Financial Times*, 4/21/92]. Others calculated the value of a **North American Free Trade Agreement** at $24 billion annually in the early years [ibid., 2/28/92]. Other hopeful signs were reported, among them apparent U.S. voter support for North American free trade [*The Wall Street Journal*, 4/21/92] and opposition to protectionism. A new pragmatism was detected at the **International Monetary Fund (IMF)**, and the president of the **World Bank** declared himself committed to delivering aid to the poor [ibid., 4/28/92]. The World Bank also promised to watch the arms budget of aid recipients [*The New York Times*, 5/11/92], and a move was afoot in the European Community to relax rules requiring aid recipients to buy EC goods [*Financial Times*, 2/21/92]. The United States moved to restore economic ties with Vietnam [*The Wall Street Journal*, 4/30/92]; international business executives expressed support for UNCED [*The New York Times*, 5/8/92]; and a Gallup poll taken in advance of the Earth Summit found most respondents willing to forgo some economic benefits in order to preserve the environment [*The Wall Street Journal*, 5/6/92].

2. The World Economy: Retrospect and Prospect

By registering the first negative annual change in world real gross domestic product since the end of World War II, −0.3 percent [IMF, *World Economic Outlook*, hereafter *WEO*, 5/92], 1991 decisively marked **the termination of an almost decade-long period of sustained economic growth,** at least among the developed countries. That period had begun after the previous recession, a painful but inflation-crushing one during 1981–82. As mentioned in *Issues/46*, by the late 1980s Germany, Japan, Canada, and the United States had once again consciously adopted anti-inflationary policies. Those policies were not prompted by oil market and related money supply developments, as they had been in 1974–75 and 1980–81 (indeed, oil prices had surprisingly collapsed in the mid-1980s and had recovered to only moderate levels by 1989–90), but instead by expansionary fiscal policies adopted in each of the principal economies for different reasons. These governments saw the fruits of their efforts mainly in the U.S., Canadian, and British recessions of mid-1990, which some policy-makers, especially in the United States, Canada, and the United Kingdom, hoped and expected would end about one year later, with inflationary tendencies having been suppressed.

By the spring of 1991, however, it became clear that neither the German nor the Japanese monetary authorities were willing to accommodate the expansionary wishes of U.S., Canadian, and British policy-makers. Left to their own devices, each of the latter acted according to its own situation. The United States, lacking flexibility in fiscal policy because of burgeoning fiscal deficits, began to relax monetary policy; it did so aggressively in the fourth quarter of 1991 and first quarter of 1992, though seemingly with little effect on credit markets, and the recession persisted. Canada opted to maintain a strict anti-inflationary, pro-Canadian dollar stance of tight monetary and fiscal policy. As a result, especially given sluggish U.S. demand for Canadian exports, Canadian unemployment remained high. The United Kingdom adopted a similar package of policies, aimed at protecting sterling's position in the European Monetary System bands while dampening inflation. British unemployment, therefore, also continued to rise following a "pronounced labor market shakeout" that began at the end of 1990 [OECD, *Economic Outlook*, hereafter *Economic Outlook*, 12/91].

The contractionary tendencies generated by a sudden and unexpected drop in demand for credit in the United States, and the relatively restrictive Canadian and British policies, were compounded by the German and Japanese anti-inflationary macroeconomic strategies. Germany, of course, found it necessary to grapple with the inflationary ramifications of rebuilding eastern Germany virtually from the ground up, a task expected to cost some 1 trillion marks by the year 2000. For the most part, tight German monetary policy has been the principal anti-inflationary instrument. However, higher direct and indirect taxes have also been introduced to help finance the reconstruction of the former East Germany [ibid.]. The taxes have in turn led to demands for large wage increases by powerful German private and public sector trade unions. In Japan, demand for both domestic and foreign goods and services slowed significantly as monetary policy was tightened from about 1990 onward to counter inflationary pressures. (It should be borne in mind, however, that Japan's threshold of inflation tolerance is, at about 2 to 2.5 percent, much lower than that of the United States. That is one reason why U.S. policy-makers maintain that Japan has, and perhaps Germany has also, much more freedom to adopt expansionary policies than the United States, where inflation doesn't really matter for many until it reaches the 5–6 percent level.)

Table III–1
World Output, 1989–93

	1989	1990	1991	1992*	1993*
Output (percentage of annual change)					
World	3.3	2.2	−0.3	1.4	3.6
Advanced industrial countries	3.3	2.6	0.8	1.8	3.3
United States	2.5	1.0	−0.7	1.6	3.5
Germany	3.8	4.5	3.2	2.0	3.0
Japan	4.7	5.6	4.5	2.2	3.9
Developing countries	3.2	1.0	3.3	6.7	5.4
Africa	3.5	2.1	1.4	2.7	3.0
Asia	5.4	5.5	5.8	5.5	3.7
Middle East	4.6	0.7	0.4	15.0	7.3
Latin America	1.4	−0.9	2.8	4.7	2.2
Eastern Europe	−0.7	−7.9	−16.6	−1.0	3.9
Former USSR	3.0	−1.9	−17.0	−17.0	n/a

Source: IMF, *World Economic Outook*, 5/92, Table A1.
*Estimate.

World output in 1991 was also reduced by economic restructuring in **Eastern Europe**—Poland, Czechoslovakia, Hungary—and economic "de-structuring" in the Soviet Union, which by year's end had ceased to exist and was replaced by the Commonwealth of Independent States (CIS), sans the Baltic republics and Georgia. According to the *World Economic Outlook,* output in both Eastern Europe and the Soviet Union/ CIS fell about 17 percent in 1991.

Finally, the **developing countries** as a group were unable to contribute substantially (1.4 percent) to global economic growth in 1991. A clear exception to that general observation was to be found in the performance of the **Asian developing countries,** which recorded an impressive growth rate of 5.8 percent [*WEO, 5/92*]. Thus, 1991 became a "trough" year in the global business cycle.

With a disappointing year behind them, the world's principal economic analysts and policy-makers turned their attention to recovery and the slope of the path toward the next "peak." The key question was, naturally, the speed of the early phase of the recovery. The relative optimism revealed by the *World Economic Outlook* and some other prognosticators in late 1991 had been dampened noticeably by spring 1992. Why? According to the May 1992 *World Economic Outlook,* the principal negative influences were **worsening consumer confidence** in most industrial countries; **increased taxation and high interest rates** in Germany, which have resulted in high interest rates elsewhere in Europe; and **reduced spending on business investment in Japan** [4/23/92]. There was a good deal of public speculation, especially among U.S. policy-makers, about the possibility of a truly global recession. By April, however, that prospect was being downplayed by the IMF's Managing Director, Michel Camdessus [*The New York Times, 4/20/92*], and some other analysts [*The Wall Street Journal, 4/17/92*].

As for the world economy's **1993** prospects, there is broad agreement among analysts that it will be **a year of relatively strong recovery.** According to the IMF and OECD, the major economies will again become synchronized in 1993 and will grow at about the same annual rate, ranging from about 3.0 percent to 3.5 percent, with Japan performing somewhat better than average and Germany and the European Community as a whole faring somewhat worse [*WEO, 5/92; Economic Outlook,* 12/91].

Worth noting is that conditions in neither oil nor non-energy commodity markets are seen as negatively affecting global growth prospects. However, depressed non-energy commodity prices (coffee, for example, recently dipped to a 17-year low [*The New York Times, 4/17/92*]) are hurting developing countries' prospects even though they help suppress inflation in the developed world. The price of oil, which when high can wreak havoc on both developed and non-oil-producing developing countries, has been fluctuating between about $17 and $21 per barrel, a price range neither too high for developed country consumers nor too low for producers—although it is generally thought to be too low for environmentalists. The **Organization of Petroleum Exporting Countries (OPEC)** has essentially accepted—and indeed with **Saudi Arabia**'s leadership it has created—the prevailing price level. Some of the organization's members are dissatisfied with their production quota, however, including **Kuwait,** which with the Gulf War behind it is seeking an increase in its production quota [ibid., 4/20/92]. **Iraq,** of course, has been unable to sell openly much of its oil; yet its return to production and export almost certainly will not be deferred indefinitely. Thus, for the time being at least, the underlying pressure on oil prices is downward not upward. There were some problems in foreign exchange markets, however. On the one hand, the European Monetary System has been declared by some observers to be on the verge of breakdown [*The Economist,* 5/2/92]. The British, for example, have wrestled with the possibility of a devaluation. On the other hand, the historically low exchange value of the Japanese yen seems to have become problematic in connection with Japan's worldwide trade deficit. The exchange rate may be one reason why the Japanese do not import as much as many economists and others think they should. Japan's under-importation, if it exists, limits the economic growth-through-trade opportunities of all of its trading partners. Additional problems influencing Japan's growth and, therefore, its production, consumption, and imports may be seen in problems currently affecting the Japanese stock market and, through it, Japanese banks and other multinational enterprises.

The Group of Seven

Since the mid-1970s, management of the world economy has been the province of seven states—the United States, Germany, Japan, the United Kingdom, France, Canada, and Italy—the so-called **Group of Seven** economic summit countries, **also known as the G7.** With the demise of the Soviet Union and the end of the cold war, there was speculation and even apprehension in some quarters that the Group of Seven, which had in any event always discussed and cooperated on political as well as economic issues, would claim or exert a right to manage international political and military—in addition to economic—relations (see, for example, James Morgan, "Rip van Winkle's New World Order," *Financial Times,* April 25–26, 1992, in which the author claims that "the fall of the Soviet Bloc has left the IMF and G7 to rule the world and create a new imperial age"). Recent experience suggests that both the speculation and the fear were unfounded. On the one hand, the G7 lacks the institutional capacity to manage political relations in all or even most parts of the world. On the other hand, the G7 has displayed, both in recent times and in more distant ones, a good deal of disunity, which tends to render virtually impossible the kind of rapid decision-making and action that quickly changing situations demand.

As discussed both in *Issues/46* and below, disagreement among the G7 in 1991–92 was especially evident with respect to **macroeconomic policy**. There were and continue to be major differences in the area of **trade relations**, however, specifically regarding European Community agricultural subsidies, and **foreign aid policy**, particularly regarding the former Soviet Union. These were downplayed at the mid-July 1991 economic summit in London, however, and the conference was rather subdued compared to some earlier gatherings. Some observers attributed the low-key nature of the meeting to a shared recognition that approaching elections in several member countries limited their ability to make major changes. Nevertheless, the summit ultimately generated a great deal of interest and debate by inviting **Soviet President Mikhail Gorbachev** to present a proposal for Western assistance. This prospect provoked heated debate among G7 members, some of whom wanted to be very forthcoming and others of whom wanted to wait and see. Gorbachev was warmly welcomed in any case, made his presentation, and received a good deal of attention from his listeners and the media but little concrete support. The G7 agreed to "associate" Soviet membership in the IMF but little more. (The Soviets, for their part, promptly ignored the "associate" qualification and applied for full membership [*The Economist*, 8/3/91].) Debate over the issue of what to do about the Soviet Union intensified in September and October, following the abortive mid-August coup against Gorbachev and the dissolution of the Soviet Communist party. At the annual meetings of the IMF and World Bank in Bangkok, Thailand, the G7 were reported as being "bitterly divided" over how to handle the Soviet economic crisis [*Financial Times*, 10/15/91].

In January 1992 the United States succeeded in persuading Japan to commit, at least in principle, to spur economic growth by reducing taxes, increasing government spending, or lowering interest rates. The United States then sought the support of other G7 members, especially Germany, which was pursuing a very restrictive monetary policy [ibid., 1/9/92]. According to various reports, Germany acknowledged that there was in fact a growth problem, but was reluctant nevertheless to adopt a pro-growth policy. Germany's stance effectively eliminated the ability of other European states, especially France, to pursue an expansionary policy. However, in a surprise turn of events, G7 finance ministers, meeting in Garden City, New York, in late January 1992, agreed in principle to concentrate more on growth. It was, as one account stated, "a significant improvement on recent efforts at economic policy coordination" [ibid., 1/27/92]. Shortly afterward, however, Germany's ability to follow through was significantly reduced by two factors: first, a renewed commitment by the Bundesbank to fight what from a German perspective is a skyrocketing inflation rate, reaching 4.61 percent in April 1992 [*Financial Times*, 5/26/92], and which was not only becoming a threat to the envisioned single European currency but was also damaging Germany's reputation abroad; and, second, the settlement of a vigorously fought wage dispute, whereby at mid-1992 some union wages had been settled in excess of the 5 percent limit seen by the Bundesbank as necessary to maintain control over inflationary pressures.

Japan seemed to be having the opposite experience: A flurry of economic statistics showed the Japanese economy headed toward recession [*The Economist*, 2/29/92; *The New York Times*, 3/9/92]. Some expected a major shift away from Japan's policy of hedging its commitment to growth, but no such shift occurred. And at a late April meeting of G7 finance ministers held in conjunction with the spring meetings of the IMF and World Bank, Japan—not Germany, for once—came under intense pressure from other G7 members to adopt more expansionary policies [*The Wall Street Journal*, 4/27/92; *Financial Times*, 4/28/92]. As the July 1992 G7 Summit in Munich, Germany, approached, the United States pronounced itself satisfied with both Japanese and German macroeconomic policies [*The New York Times*, 6/30/92], and planned to focus instead on trade issues [*The Wall Street Journal*, 7/3/92]. The Europeans preferred to emphasize aid to Russia, especially considering that Russian President Yeltsin was expected to come to Munich. All G7 members appeared to benefit from a long-awaited settlement between Russia and the IMF just two days before the meetings began [*The New York Times*, 7/6/92].

United States

As anticipated in *Issues/46*, the performance of the U.S. economy was the focus of global concern in 1991 and 1992. There was a good deal of hope, perhaps more than expectation, that a U.S. recovery beginning in the second half of 1991 would lead the world into recovery. In fact, however, U.S. economic performance was disappointing. Growth in 1991, projected by the IMF in October 1990 to reach 1.7 percent, came in at −0.7 percent. Growth in 1992, projected in October 1991 to climb to 3.0 percent, is now projected to reach 1.6 percent. In other words, the beginning of genuine recovery from the U.S. recession that began in mid-1990 has been pushed back by about one year—to mid-1992. What happened? According to the OECD [*Economic Outlook*, 12/91], a nascent recovery that began in April 1991, led by consumers and homebuilders, stalled in August and September in the midst of credit supply problems in the banking industry. The **Federal Reserve** reacted by lowering the Federal Funds rate several times and later reducing the discount rate—perhaps the most symbolic indicator of the Fed's wishes—to lows of 3.5 percent, rates not seen since the early 1960s [*The New York Times*, 12/21/91]. President Bush, about to launch his campaign for reelection, came under harsh criticism and intense pressure regarding his management of the economy. He responded by proposing mildly stimulative measures in his late-January 1992 State of the Union message to Congress. Bush argued for moderation because, notwithstanding high and rising unemployment statistics (7.1 percent in December 1991 [*The New York Times*, 1/11/92] en route to 7.3 percent in March [ibid., 4/4/92]), there were signs that a genuine, sustained recovery was almost under way. And, indeed, there was some confirmation of this as early as February. Positive indicators continued to be reported throughout the spring months, boosting not only growth prospects for the economy but President Bush's reelection prospects as well. Still, a number of analysts contended that the recovery would be too anemic to provide much comfort to unemployed Americans, unemployed persons abroad, or even President Bush and his campaign team [ibid., 5/11/92]. The latter view was essentially confirmed in early July 1992, when the U.S. unemployment rate leaped to 7.8 percent. Although the Federal Reserve responded by lowering the discount rate to 3 percent—its lowest rate since 1963—a "triple dip" recession had suddenly become a genuine possibility. Prospects for 1993 were significantly brighter, however. The IMF projected U.S. growth in 1993 at a respectable 3.5 percent, attributing its optimism to low and falling inflation, which allows for lower interest rates; the absence of commodity market disturbances; the end of the pessimism and lack of confidence associated with the Gulf War; reductions in consumer and business debt; and the improving performance of developing countries [WEO, 5/92].

Germany

The record of strong—and, more recently, unexpectedly strong—(West) German economic growth compiled during the past several years began to weaken at mid-year 1991 as the German government began raising taxes to help finance the reconstruction of eastern Germany, and the Bundesbank continued to pursue a very restrictive monetary policy to try to contain reconstruction-related inflation. That weakness lowered Germany's rate of growth from 4.5 percent in 1990 to about 3.2 percent in 1991 [WEO, 10/91, 5/92; *Economic Outlook*, 12/91]. The slower-growth phenomenon continued into 1992, leading to forecasts of only 2.0 percent growth for that year [WEO, 5/92]. More positively, real growth should rise to about 3.0 percent in 1992 as German inflation falls and demand for German exports increases in line with the anticipated global recovery [ibid.].

The German economic situation has become complex and difficult for virtually all involved. Several major forces are colliding with one another, the principal ones being the unification process, which, as mentioned above, is a historic but very expensive political achievement, and the wishes of German workers either to maintain or to achieve a high standard of living. Financing the integration of the Eastern economy and people into the West therefore poses a dilemma for the government of Chancellor Kohl. On the one hand, it would be politically popular, at least in the short run, to avoid raising taxes. However, a massive increase in public spending unaccompanied by a tax increase would invite inflation, something the German people generally, and the fiercely independent Bundesbank particularly, abhor. Therefore, taxes were eventually raised. That helped reduce inflationary pressures, but also provoked demands for inflationary wage increases.

The government could have, of course, resisted the wage demands by refusing to grant them, at least to public sector employees, but doing so would have provoked—and in April–May 1992 did provoke—widespread strikes, which could potentially reduce overall economic growth and hurt Germany's image as a stable place to do business. The government can also try to attract foreign investment to help finance projects in eastern Germany, and it is doing so. The country's privatization agency, the **Treuhandanstalt,** has reportedly sold half of the companies assigned to it. However, it may find it increasingly difficult to sell the others [*Economic Outlook,* 12/91]. Yet another complication is the disparity between western Germany, where wages are high and unemployment low, and eastern Germany, where unemployment remains very high. This situation has both social and political ramifications that are troubling for Germans in general and Chancellor Kohl in particular.

Japan

Japan has recorded impressively high rates of growth (ranging from 4.3 to 6.2 percent) in every year since 1984 but one (1986). In early 1991 the rapid rate of expansion began to slow in response to measures taken by the Bank of Japan, begun in August 1990, to restrain the strong growth of domestic demand, preempt inflationary pressures arising from tightening labor markets, and resist the tendency toward higher land prices [*Economic Outlook,* 12/90, 12/91]. In July 1991, once the Bank of Japan confirmed that its restrictive policies had brought about the desired changes, i.e., receding inflation and decelerating output, the Bank relaxed its policies. However, the credit markets did not respond as expected because of special circumstances in the banking sector, with the result that monetary and credit conditions remained relatively restrictive [ibid., 12/91]. As a consequence, the business investment climate deteriorated, with negative implications for some sectors of the economy. For this and other reasons, the rate of growth of Japan's gross national product declined from 5.4

percent in 1990 to 4.5 percent in 1991 [WEO, 5/92]. The decline might have been even larger, if not for a sharp improvement in the current account balance as merchandise imports fell and exports rose. Monetary policy continued in a relatively relaxed stance in late 1991 and into 1992, permitting Japan to join the United States in a pro-growth commitment. However, the country's monetary aggregates stubbornly continued to refuse to respond, and the rate of growth of Japan's money supply fell, by some measures to record lows [*The Economist*, 2/29/92], making the Bank of Japan the target of renewed international criticism, especially in light of the country's surging trade and current account surpluses. The Bank of Japan finally responded in April 1992 by lowering the discount rate.

Separately, the government of Japan was at pains to explain to its economic partners that plummeting real estate and stock prices would not undermine the Japanese financial system, something that might quickly destabilize international financial markets. The Japanese economy was expected to expand by only 2.2 percent in 1992. However, a firm recovery was forecast for 1993, when growth is expected to reach 3.9 percent [WEO, 5/92].

Other G7 Economies

In response to restrictive policies introduced in 1988, the rate of growth of the **United Kingdom**'s economy declined for three consecutive years, falling from 4.3 percent in 1988 to −2.2 percent in 1991 [WEO, 5/91, 5/92]. The decline turned out to be "Britain's longest since World War II" [*The Wall Street Journal*, 2/21/92]. British macroeconomic policy is guided by the goals of keeping the pound sterling within its European Monetary System banks and by attaining sustained low inflation [*Economic Outlook*, 12/91]. The first objective requires keeping British interest rates in close proximity to high German interest rates, which tends to dampen economic activity in the United Kingdom.

France's situation, though perhaps not ideal from the French perspective, is nevertheless quite respectable, even if the economy's growth rate was only 1.4 percent in 1991 and is projected to be only 2.1 percent for 1992. According to the OECD, "France's overall macroeconomic performance relative to its European partners has been good and is likely to remain so." Inflation is low, the public deficit and level of indebtedness are also relatively low, and the current account deficit is modest and expected to be reduced [ibid.].

Canada entered a period of economic recession in mid-1990. The recession was brought about by a firm anti-inflationary monetary policy directed by the Bank of Canada. That policy was to have been supported by fiscal policy as well, but for reasons to some degree beyond control of the government, much less support has been provided than was expected. This has left monetary policy to bear most of the policy burden. Though not as deep as the 1981–82 recession, the current recession has been more pronounced and geographically concentrated, i.e., in the province of Ontario [ibid.]. In addition, the course of the Canadian economy appears to have paralleled that of the United States by starting into recovery in mid-1991 only to appear to stall in the second half of the year. The Canadian economy grew by about 0.5 percent in 1990 and then contracted by −1.1 percent in 1991. It is projected to expand by a respectable, though moderate by historical standards, 3.1 percent in 1992 and 4.1 percent in 1993 as the U.S. recovery proceeds and somewhat easier monetary policy allows the housing sector to come back. Canadians will continue to face a number of constraints, however, as macroeconomic policy remains cautious with a view toward creating wage, price, and fiscal conditions conducive to long-term productivity and competitiveness.

Italy faced its third consecutive year of slowing economic activity in 1991. As in the United Kingdom, interest rates have been kept high to keep the lira's exchange rate within the Exchange Rate Mechanism (ERM) limits of the European Monetary System [ibid.]. Italy is also hobbled by a fiscal deficit that is too large and that siphons off investment capital. In addition, non-bank capital began flowing out of Italy in mid-1991. The Italian economy is expected to grow by about 2.0 percent in 1992 and 2.5 percent in 1993, well below its potential, according to the OECD [ibid.].

Newly Industrializing and Other Developing Economies

According to the World Bank's annual report, *Global Economic Prospects and the Developing Countries*, the aggregate gross domestic product of the developing countries grew by 1.9 percent in 1991, the same as in 1990. Worse, per capita incomes declined for the second consecutive year, the first time that has happened since 1965. The Bank attributed this situation to four factors: first, wars disrupted economic activity in many developing areas; second, economic dislocation accompanied the fundamental political and economic changes in Eastern Europe and the former Soviet Union; third, as reported above, growth slowed in the major industrial countries; and fourth, several major developing countries, including Brazil and Zaire, made poor progress on economic reforms.

More happily, the **East Asian** developing economies grew rapidly, averaging almost 7.0 percent in 1990–91. **Thailand** recorded an impressive 8.2 percent rate of expansion, and **China**'s growth rate reached 7.0 percent in 1991. The four Asian "tigers"—**Hong Kong, Singapore, South Korea,** and **Taiwan**—grew by 6.2 percent in 1991 and are forecast to grow at about the same rate in 1992 [WEO, 10/91]. **Latin America** also did well in 1991, registering a regional growth rate of 2.6 percent, the same as in the previous year. Elsewhere, growth increased marginally in **sub-Saharan Africa** in 1991, to 2.3 percent, but is expected to increase more in 1992, to 3.4 percent, not far below the projected developing country average of 3.9 percent. **South Asian** developing countries are expected to experience a decline in growth in 1992 (2.8 percent) from 1991 (3.6 percent) before rebounding to a strong 5.0 percent in 1993. The **Middle East and North Africa**, negatively affected by the 1991 Gulf conflict, recorded negative growth of −1.9 percent in 1991 but should bounce back to 4.9 percent in 1992.

The World Bank study is generally optimistic about the prospects of developing countries during the decade of the 1990s. Its optimism is based on the expectation of improved developing country access to developed country markets as a result of the Uruguay Round negotiations and/or the various free trade arrangements being negotiated (discussed below), the likelihood of higher rates of growth in the industrial countries than has occurred the last few years, and improved policies in the developing countries. One of the countries that best represents the new situation and strategies of developing countries is **Mexico**. In just a few years Mexico has radically changed its policies toward trade and investment and toward the domestic economy. All have been liberalized. Moreover, Mexico is on the verge of completing negotiations for a historic **North American Free Trade Agreement** with the United States and Canada. Mexico's economic performance and its prospects have improved dramatically because of initiatives taken at home and abroad. According to the World Bank, economic prospects for developing countries depend mainly on their domestic economic policies, although their prospects are certainly affected by the outlook for the world economy and developments in world trading and financial systems.

Eastern Europe and the Commonwealth of Independent States

The IMF, in its *World Economic Outlook* of October 1991, surveyed economic conditions and prospects in **Eastern Europe and the (former) Soviet Union**. The situation it describes is, overall, a dismal one, although islands of promise can be found. To begin, production dropped so sharply in Eastern Europe and the former Soviet Union in the first half of 1991 that output projections had to be revised downward considerably. The rate of production is estimated to have declined between 14 percent [note by the Secretary-General, E/1992/IMF/1] and 17 percent [WEO, 5/92]. In any case, this steep decline followed sizable declines the previous year. A number of special factors have contributed to the situation. First, stabilization and reform programs are in effect in such countries as **Bulgaria**,

Czechoslovakia, Hungary, Poland, and **Romania.** These programs usually entail the closure of economically nonviable firms and, thus, the termination of their production. Second, in most countries there is a climate of general uncertainty, declining real wages, and tight macroeconomic policy. Third, social and political upheavals have disrupted supply links. Finally, intraregional trade between former members of the Council for Mutual Economic Assistance (CMEA or COMECON) has been disrupted [*WEO*, 10/91]. The latter development has been extremely costly to the region, because at least 20 percent of trade—volume and value— was lost as imports into the former Soviet Union declined by about 40 percent [GATT per *Financial Times*, 3/18/92; World Bank: *Global Economic Prospects*].

Among the non-former Soviet East and Central European states, **Poland** had by late spring 1992 become perhaps the most controversial aid applicant. Poland was able to secure IMF approval of its budget proposal and economic plan and was scheduled to receive $2.5 billion in IMF support. However, the Polish Sejm, or parliament, which since October 1991 has had representatives of some 24 political parties, essentially reneged on the country's pledge to the IMF by voting a major increase in public spending that would send the deficit soaring above the IMF's limit. As of mid-May 1992 the fate of the $2.5 billion loan, as well as the rescheduling of some $11.5 billion, was in doubt. Moreover, Poland's President, **Lech Walesa,** had lost patience with the Sejm and proposed a major expansion of presidential powers to deal with the political crisis over economic reform [*The Times* (London), 5/8/92; *The Economist*, 5/9/92].

Analysts predict that in 1992 the **former Soviet Union,** now the **Commonwealth of Independent States (CIS)** plus the **Baltic republics** and **Georgia,** will suffer another major decrease in output, on the order of 12 to 17 percent. **Russia** has initiated radical pro-market reforms. On January 1, 1992, the government lifted price controls on a number of goods, provoking an outcry among the populace [*Financial Times*, 1/2/92, 1/3/92, 1/18/92]. The government made some concessions, which in turn slowed the reform somewhat and drew warnings from the G7. Despite significant pressure from the Russian parliament, the government essentially stayed the course into the spring months. The Russian government vigorously welcomed direct foreign investment while seeking and receiving emergency food and other assistance from the West. It and the other governments of the Commonwealth of Independent States also entered into negotiations with the IMF with a view toward membership. By late April agreement had been reached, making the members of the CIS eligible for crucial IMF and World Bank support. Along with price reform, the Russian government assigned priority to stabilization and convertibility of its currency, the ruble. To this end the IMF, the G7, and Russia designed a $24 billion fund to help generate and maintain confidence in the ruble's exchange value. Interestingly, the ruble's exchange rate had already begun to stabilize, and indeed to appreciate, even before the agreement was announced [*The New York Times*, 2/25/92], as a consequence of the reformist policies being pursued. The IMF noted with regret in its May 1992 *World Economic Outlook* that, in contrast to Russia, the other members of the CIS (except Ukraine) have not yet initiated reform programs and, therefore, have yet to begin the inevitable transition to a market economy. The Fund urged them to initiate bold and comprehensive reform as soon as possible [*Financial Times*, 4/23/92].

3. External Debt: Problem for Some, Crisis for Others

The World Bank, in *World Debt Tables, 1991–92*, observed that important differences had emerged across groups of indebted developing countries. Three types of debtor countries were identifiable: middle-income, lower-middle-income, and lower-income. The recent experience of each differed significantly, according to the Bank.

Middle-income countries with access to debt-reduction provisions of the Brady Plan (see *Issues/46*) had been able to reduce their eligible commercial bank debt by about 25 percent. The confidence of investors—especially domestic ones—had improved, and access to international capital markets had been regained. Included in this group were Costa Rica, Mexico, the Philippines, Uruguay, and Venezuela, with Nigeria as a potential member in the near future.

Lower-middle-income countries had enjoyed some flexibility on the part of the Paris Club representatives of official creditors. This flexibility appeared to have been prompted by the Group of Seven, which had taken an interest in the special situation of such lower-middle-income countries as Poland and Egypt (the former important as a Central European symbol of change from socialism to capitalism, the latter an important Middle Eastern supporter of the Gulf War against Iraq in late 1990 and early 1991). Both these countries were treated to exceptional debt relief of up to 50 percent in present value terms. The Group of Seven claimed to be interested in the welfare of other countries with similar debt and economic circumstances, but the importance of the political criterion in the first two cases may have contributed to a lack of clarity about the Group's actual intentions.

The experience of **lower-income countries** was not fundamentally different with respect to official interest in their difficulties. However, their economic situation is fundamentally different, especially from that of the middle-income countries today. According to the World Bank, official support for adjustment programs for low-income countries has been progressively strengthened in recent years. New concessional

Table III-2
Selected External Debt Indicators

	1981	1985	1990	1991*
Total external debt, all developing countries (US$ billions)	751	1,046	1,355	1,351

Country	Debt Outstanding 1990, US$ billions	Debt Service 1990, US$ billions	Debt/GNP 1990 (%)
Argentina	61.1	5.1	61.7
Brazil	116.2	7.4	22.8
Mexico	96.8	12.1	42.1
Poland	49.4	1.0	82.4
Nigeria	36.1	3.0	117.9
Venezuela	33.3	4.3	71.0

Share of 1990 total debt by region (%)

Latin America and the Caribbean	33.7
East Asia and the Pacific	18.3
Europe and the Mediterranean	14.4
Sub-Saharan Africa	13.6
Middle East and North Africa	11.0
South Asia	9.0

Source: World Bank, *World Debt Tables, 1991–92*, Tables 1.1, 1.3, 1.5.
*Estimate.

money has been provided, as has debt relief through cancellation of official debt and through rescheduling under the so-called Toronto terms, adopted by the Paris Club in 1988. The impact of Toronto-terms reschedulings was modest, however, and in September 1990 then-British Chancellor of the Exchequer John Major proposed the so-called Trinidad terms. Under this provision, a once-and-for-all reduction in the debt stock would be effected, with the amount determined on a case-by-case basis. The expected benchmark would be about two-thirds reduction in bilateral official debt, most of it concessional in any case. Continuing on a case-by-case basis using the Trinidad terms seems desirable for many countries. For certain others, however, even the Trinidad terms are insufficient. As the World Bank observed, the issue has arisen as to whether some countries, such as Mozambique, Somalia, and Sudan, all in Africa, can service existing debt burdens on a sustainable basis. Their cases clearly call for extraordinary measures.

The **U.N. Secretary-General**, in "External Debt Crisis and Development: A Report on the Recent Evolution of the International Debt Strategy" [A/46/415, 9/18/91], presented a less charitable view of the efforts of the developed countries to address developing countries' persisting debt troubles. The report denied that lending increased substantially, and claimed that the observed increase in total indebtedness, taken by the

World Bank as a positive sign, was in fact a negative one. There had been no improvement in the debt indicators of developing countries, the report claimed, though that may have been due principally to global macroeconomic factors. The report also conceded that various groupings of developing countries had had different experiences.

The Secretary-General's report focused on debt owed to official bilateral creditors, not to commercial lenders, because, the report said, debt owed to official creditors constitutes a major share of the total debt of least-developed and other low-income countries. The report expresses great dissatisfaction not only with the Toronto terms but also with the Trinidad terms praised by the World Bank. These initiatives and others, the report maintains, "fall short of meeting overall international cash flow and investment needs for adequate growth of indebted countries." After examining debt owed to commercial banks and debt owed to multilateral institutions, the report offered several conclusions: first, that some progress has been registered but that success has been limited; second, that despite signs that lending may resume (not necessarily to governments initially) it would be premature to assert that the end of the crisis is near; third, that, overall, prospects for augmented private capital inflows in the near future are limited; fourth, that private foreign direct investment (FDI) can meet only a portion of the needs for development finance; and, fifth, that increased international cooperation is called for either to augment the flow of international capital to heavily developing countries or to help reduce their financial needs.

4. Economic Development: Issues and Initiatives

In this period of fundamental political change and worldwide economic reorientation, developed countries and multilateral agencies are reviewing, reassessing, and revising their development assistance objectives, policies, and programs. There is, of course, widespread concern that without the Communist threat as a rationale, assistance to developing countries will decline. However, according to the OECD's Development Assistance Committee (DAC), that did not occur, at least during 1990. On the contrary, there was **an increase in overall official development assistance** (ODA) flows [OECD, DAC, *Development Co-operation*, 1991]. The increase was attributable, the DAC said, to increases in ODA by the United States (which replaced Japan as the largest donor), Japan, France, Austria, Norway, Switzerland, Germany, and Belgium. The DAC's new Chairman, **Alexander R. Love,** remained cautious, however, and reminded the development community that its financial support would be especially important as many developing countries grappled with economic reform and political evolution. The Chairman noted that, despite the increase in total aid, the average ODA-to-GNP ratio remained essentially unchanged at 0.35 percent, well below the U.N.'s ODA target of 0.7 percent. Consistent with the general trend toward market-based economies in developing and transitioning countries, the development community has focused more on **participatory development and the private sector**, which has resulted in, among other things, strong development community interest in the **microenterprise** concept. Also, consistent with heightened concern about the global environment, as well as poverty, the development community has once again begun to focus on **slowing population growth.**

Eastern Europe and the Commonwealth of Independent States

In regional terms, Eastern and Central Europe have jumped to the head of the development assistance queue. This is in large part because of the revolutionary nature of those countries' shift from socialism to capitalism. While interest has run high since 1989 in helping non-former-Soviet states such as Poland, Czechoslovakia, and Hungary (as well as East Germany, for which the former West German government has taken

Table III-3
Selected Overseas Development Assistance Indicators

Sources of Overseas Development Assistance, 1990

Country	US$ Amount (billions)	Percent of GNP
United States	11.4	0.21
Japan	9.1	0.31
France	6.6	0.55
Germany	6.3	0.42
Italy	3.4	0.32
United Kingdom	2.6	0.27
Netherlands	2.6	0.94
Canada	2.5	0.44
Sweden	2.0	0.90
Norway	1.2	1.17
Denmark	1.2	0.93

Geographical Distribution of Overseas Development Assistance, 1989–90, percentage of total

	Sub-Saharan Africa	South Asia	Other Asia	Middle East	Latin America & Caribbean
Bilateral	34.3	11.8	21.2	18.4	14.5
Multilateral	6.7	5.5	26.6	52.5	8.7
Total	34.4	14.4	19.5	18.7	13.0

Source: OECD, Development Assistance Committee (DAC), *Development Cooperation, 1991*, Tables 1 and 9.

responsibility), there was persistent disagreement and ambivalence in the West concerning whether and how to assist the "new" Soviet Union that had evolved under President Mikhail Gorbachev. That changed, first, when the Soviet Communist party was disbanded in August–September 1991 and, finally, when Russia and the Commonwealth of Independent States officially succeeded the Soviet Union in late December 1991. At that time the focus of the Western debate shifted from whether the former Soviet Union might once again threaten the West to whether Russia was genuinely and irrevocably committed to economic reform. In October 1991 the G7, after squabbling over how to proceed, approved a modest debt-relief package for the then-Soviet Union.

By early 1992, enthusiasm for helping Russia had increased significantly, even in the United States, where in late January 1992 President Bush hosted an **international conference on aid to Russia and other members of the CIS.** Thereafter, there was clear if not necessarily steady movement toward membership in the IMF and World Bank for Russia and Ukraine. U.S. support for Russia in particular was spurred in March by a memorandum, bitingly critical of President Bush, written and publicized by former President **Richard M. Nixon** [*The New York Times*, 3/10/92]. In April, Russia and Ukraine were approved for full membership in the world's two central international financial institutions. The IMF estimated that Russia would require $44 billion in 1992 to stabilize the ruble and the economy. While most members of the G7 promptly pledged contributions, **Japan** did not, complaining that the process had been unsatisfactory from Japan's point of view because of outstanding Japanese claims against the former Soviet Union and its successor [ibid., 4/19/92]. However, in May, Japan, while continuing to withhold financial support from Russia, agreed to provide loans and equity investment to Eastern and Central European countries [ibid., 5/16/92].

The Least Developed

According to **K. K. S. Dadzie, Secretary-General of UNCTAD,** the U.N. agency that has responsibility within the U.N. system for reviewing and appraising the U.N.'s Programme of Action for the (57) Least Developed Countries (whose populations total at least 500 million), it may appear that the Least Developed Countries are sliding into a pattern of decline and stagnation [UNCTAD, *The Least Developed Countries, 1991 Report*]. However, he maintains, a steady improvement in living standards has been attained by 11 of those countries (with populations totaling 58 million), and an additional six countries (with populations totaling 124 million) have realized modest gains in per capita gross domestic product. Moreover, said Dadzie, this occurred during a period of singular turmoil in the international economy. Therefore, there are grounds for hope, provided the correct lessons are drawn from the experience of various Least Developed Countries. Among those lessons are (1) that these countries should implement national policies and measures conducive to long-term and sustainable development, the promotion of individual initiative, and the participation of all their people in the development process, and (2) that specific international support measures, including ODA, debt relief, and external trade, can play a significant role.

Development and Environment

The **U.N. Conference on Environment and Development (UNCED)** was held in Rio de Janeiro in June 1992. There, as expected, the leaders of virtually all nations, both developed and developing, addressed the question of how to promote development without reducing the economic and other opportunities of current—and especially of future—generations. The political dynamic underlying UNCED was far more complex than in some other North-South negotiations. In this instance, North-North and South-South were often as important as North-South relations. At the preparatory meetings, for example, the United States tended to adopt positions that were less forthcoming than those of most of the other developed nations [*The New York Times*, 2/18/92]. And, on the other side, Malaysia tended to adopt positions more radical than those of most developing countries [*Financial Times*, 4/30/92]. Well before the conference began, consensus had already been reached that the alleged dichotomy between development and environment was false [see, for example, World Bank: *World Development Report, 1992*]. As the World Bank put it, environment and development are complementary: Without adequate environmental protection, development will be undermined; without development, environmental protection will fail [ibid.]. And as the **Rio Declaration on Environment and Development** stated, ". . . eradicating poverty is an indispensable requirement for sustainable development" [*The New York Times*, 4/5/92].

At issue, then, were on the one hand goals and timetables—especially for developed countries—and on the other hand financial and technology transfers to the developing countries. Agreement on both was reached before the conference, with goals and timetables made voluntary at the insistence of the United States. Financial and technology transfers—above and beyond normal development assistance—were agreed to, at least in principle, by the developed world. It was estimated that overseas development assistance would have to increase by $75 billion annually to a total of $125 billion to meet the developing countries' environmental protection costs [ibid., 4/5/92]. However, it was widely understood that in the current unfavorable economic environment actual annual increases would be on the order of $5–$10 billion [ibid., 3/2/92]. Separately, the World

Bank, U.N. Development Programme (UNDP), and U.N. Environmental Programme (UNEP) established a $1.5 billion **Global Environmental Facility (GEF),** the expansion of which to about $5 billion was supported by UNCED Secretary-General Maurice Strong [ibid.] and a number of countries, although the United States apparently was not one of them [ibid., 5/21/92].

5. Trade and the Trading System

International Trade 1991

The rate of growth of **world export volume,** which had been expected to remain unchanged in 1991 from the 1990 level of 5.0 percent, fell instead to either 3.0 percent [GATT, as reported by *The Wall Street Journal* and *Financial Times*, 3/18/92] or 3.3 percent [*WEO*, 5/92], but in either case its lowest level since the post-recession year 1983, and the third consecutive drop. The decline was attributed principally to recessions in North America and much of Europe, although the possibility that protectionist measures contributed substantially to the situation could not be ruled out and, therefore, lent credence to arguments supporting successful completion of the Uruguay Round negotiations, discussed below. The news was not all bad, however. Trade growth continued to outpace general output, which was negative (−0.3 percent) during the same period. Trade in services performed better than merchandise trade. And the six leading **Asian developing country exporters** (Hong Kong, Malaysia, Singapore, South Korea, Taiwan, and Thailand) turned out to be "the most dynamic element" in world trade in 1991. The value of their exports rose between 10 and 20 percent, and that of their imports between 8 and 30 percent. Overall, the value of world merchandise exports rose only 1.5 percent to $3,530 billion, compared to a 13.5 percent increase in 1990. **The United States,** its merchandise exports again surging, **replaced Germany as the world's leading exporter.** The two have alternated in first place since 1986. Japan, France, and Britain completed the top five in 1991. World export growth in 1992 is expected to be either 4.0 percent [GATT, per *Financial Times*, 3/18/92] or 5.0 percent [*WEO*, 5/92], neither especially high nor especially low compared to recent experience, but in any case substantially higher than projected overall output (1.4 percent). Trade, in short, contributes substantially to global economic growth already and could contribute even more if the comprehensive multilateral trade negotiations under way since 1986 were to succeed.

Table III-4

Merchandise Exports, 1991 Value; Share of World Total and Exports Per Capita

Country	Value ($ billions)	Share (percent)	Exports per capita ($)
TOTAL	3,524	100.0%	N/A
United States	422	12.0	1,693
Germany	403	11.0	5,195
Japan	307	9.0	2,551
France	213	6.0	3,865
Britain	185	5.0	3,232
Italy	N/A	N/A	2,962
Holland	134	3.8	8,896
Canada	127	3.6	4,864
Belgium/Luxembourg	119	3.4	11,448
Hong Kong*	99	2.8	16,749
Former Soviet Union	N/A	N/A	270
Taiwan	N/A	N/A	3,735
China	72	2.0	563
South Korea	72	2.0	1,683
Switzerland	62	1.8	9,381

Source: GATT, United Nations, *Nikkei Weekly, The Economist,* 4/18/92.
*Includes re-exports.

The International Trading System

The Uruguay Round

Despite firm commitments by the Group of Seven and other members of the OECD to complete the Uruguay Round of multilateral trade negotiations—launched in 1986, scheduled to terminate in December 1990, and extended until December 1991—and despite concessions on agricultural subsidies made by U.S. President George Bush in a meeting in The Hague in November 1991 [Reuters, 11/11/91], **no agreement was reached** before the new deadline. Nevertheless, the negotiations continued well into 1992, though with no end in sight despite occasional glimpses of the proverbial light at the end of the tunnel. The principal sticking point remained **European agricultural subsidies,** although there were other points of contention as well. As the end-of-December 1991 deadline approached with the talks deadlocked, GATT's Director-General, **Arthur Dunkel**—who in early December had announced that he would not seek reelection to his post after 1992—offered a comprehensive draft agreement for consideration by the parties. The United States reluctantly accepted it as a basis for further negotiation [*Financial Times,* 12/23/91], but the Europeans rejected the agricultural subsidies provisions [ibid., 12/24/91]. In January the two principal antagonists continued to exchange accusations, and in the process the focus of the dispute grew to include bilateralism (with its potential for managed trade) and later regionalism in U.S. trade policy and the U.S. position on intellectual property rights and trade in services [ibid., 1/22/92]. The saga continued into February, when U.S. Vice President **Dan Quayle,** on a European tour, allegedly linked continued U.S. participation in NATO to European compromise on agricultural policy [ibid., 2/19/92], a linkage that the United States promptly denied. In late March, German **Chancellor Kohl** discussed the situation with President Bush in Washington but the deadlock persisted, as it did when European Community President **Jacques Delors** also visited the U.S. President. U.S. officials blamed intra-EC politics for the deadlock, while EC officials suggested that Bush's ability to make concessions might be restricted until the November 1992 presidential election, in which he is seeking a second term. Despite U.S. hopes, no breakthrough was expected at the July 1992 Summit in Munich [*The New York Times,* 7/5/92].

After the Uruguay Round

Speculation has already turned to the next round of talks, on the by now heroic assumption that the current round will conclude successfully. Several proposals for topics to be considered at the next round have been put forward. One, by U.S. Senator Max Baucus, is for a so-called **"Green Round"** that would focus on the relationship between trade and the environment [*Greenwire,* 10/31/91], also discussed below. A second suggestion is that the next round should consider **competition policy.** This recommendation followed an announcement by the U.S. Justice Department of a policy change to allow greater enforcement of U.S. antitrust laws against foreign companies and cartels that try to limit U.S. exports on the world market. Some Japanese industries were alarmed because of a suspicion that they would be the principal targets of the new policy, despite U.S. denials that such was the likelihood [*The New York Times,* 4/4/92]. The European Community also expressed serious concern about the apparent quantum expansion of U.S. extraterritorial activity, and proposed negotiations to address the question [*Financial Times,* 2/3/92]. A third proposal is for a round to consider rationalizing **taxes on corporations** internationally [*The Economist,* 1/18/92]. A fourth proposal is for a round to focus on **the international arms trade** [*The Wall Street Journal,* 3/16/92].

Regional Blocs

The proliferation of regional economic arrangements since the mid-1980s has been a source of alarm or of angst for some analysts of international economic relations and for others a source of pleasure and pride. The **United States** has entered into free trade agreements with **Israel** and **Canada,** and is negotiating a **North American Free Trade Agreement**

(NAFTA) with **Canada and Mexico.** President Bush has also proposed a hemisphere-wide free trade area under his **Enterprise for the Americas Initiative** (EAI). It was reported in May 1992 that the United States and **Chile** were preparing to negotiate a free trade agreement under the auspices of the EAI [*Financial Times*, 5/2/92, 5/3/92]. It was also reported that the NAFTA negotiations had accelerated such that a complete agreement was now likely by summer 1992, possibly as early as June. Congressional approval in calendar year 1992 was said to remain unlikely, though not impossible [*The New York Times*, 5/8/92].

At the same time, the **European Community** has proceeded with plans to create a single market by the end of 1992. In this regard the mid-December 1991 EC summit meeting at **Maastricht,** Netherlands, is generally viewed as an important milestone. There the leaders of the Twelve agreed, among other things, to the goal of **a common currency,** the ecu, by the year 2000 and to the creation of a **European central bank.** They also agreed to cooperate much more closely on political matters. The **United Kingdom** sought and obtained the right to opt out of aspects of Economic and Monetary Union, and rejected EC-established guidelines for social policy, even though all the others accepted them. The United Kingdom may be taking comfort in the fact that since Maastricht there have been frequent reports that one Community member or another, or its electorate, is having second thoughts about Economic and Monetary Union [*The New York Times*, 4/19/92]. This was confirmed in early June 1992, when Danish voters refused to ratify the Maastricht agreement [*Financial Times*, 6/3/92]. Separately, the EC entered into an agreement with three former East-bloc countries—**Poland, Czechoslovakia, and Hungary**—regarding economic relations [*Financial Times*, 2/27/92], and also reached agreement with former **European Free Trade Area** (EFTA) members to create a European free trade zone known as the **European Economic Area** (EEA) [ibid., 5/2–3/92]. The EFTA countries are expected to become full members of the EC if they wish to do so. Poland, Czechoslovakia, and Hungary may one day follow. German Chancellor Kohl has argued, however, that the former Soviet republics should not be offered or granted full membership [ibid., 4/4–5/92].

Regional economic cooperation in **East Asia,** the subject of a great deal of speculation since the U.S. initiatives with Canada and Mexico, has also taken root. Two organizations are vying for leadership in this regard, although it appears that they may be moving toward a formal, instead of the current informal, merger. The first is the **Asia-Pacific Economic Co-operation** forum (APEC). Organized in 1989 on the initiative of Australia, it is the larger and more broadly based of the two, though it is also technically the newest. APEC has 15 members: the six members of the Association of Southeast Asian Nations (ASEAN), i.e., Indonesia, Thailand, the Philippines, Malaysia, Singapore, and Brunei, plus Japan, South Korea, Australia, New Zealand, the United States, Canada, China, Taiwan, and Hong Kong. The other association is ASEAN itself, which has existed as a forum for southeast Asian political consultation for many years. ASEAN is now exploring the possibility of expanded economic cooperation among its members. However, there seems to be substantial support outside ASEAN for making APEC, to which ASEAN members belong in any case, the principal regional economic organization. The United States, incidentally, has offered strong political support to both, but seems to see APEC as the more useful economic association.

Trade and the Developing Countries

A New Liberalism Among Developing Countries

It is no small irony that liberal international trade has "caught on" among developing countries just when the liberal world trading system faces the greatest challenges to its viability since World War II. While trade liberalization negotiations among the giants of international commerce— the United States, European Community, Japan, and Canada—remain deadlocked and teetering on the edge of failure, many developing countries are surprising the developed world (and perhaps themselves) by adopting liberal trade and other economic policies, sometimes in cooperation with other developing countries and sometimes even unilaterally. As UNCTAD Secretary-General Dadzie observed, just when the "developed market-economy countries have forfeited their position in the vanguard of trade liberalization, some developing countries and economies in transition (such as Chile, Mexico, and Poland) have assumed the pioneering role, with many others following their example. Recent years have seen a widespread movement among developing countries toward trade liberalization, both unilaterally and within trading groups" [UNCTAD, *Trade and Development Report, 1991*]. GATT confirmed this observation by reporting that 51 of the 63 countries that have announced trade liberalization measures since 1986 are either developing or transition economies [GATT, per *Financial Times*, 3/18/92]. UNCTAD is very much concerned about the **eroding commitment to trade liberalization in the developed world,** something that has taken several forms. One, discussed below, is regional preferential trading arrangements or blocs, which have largely excluded developing countries. A second is "the panoply of non-tariff barriers that faces a large proportion of the exports from developing to developed countries" [*Trade and Development Report, 1991*]. A third, related to the first and second, is the reduced commitment of developed countries to a properly functioning multilateral system. A fourth is stubbornly low non-fuel commodity prices; and a fifth is the apparent trend toward the use of trade policy measures for environmental purposes without giving consideration to the special conditions and developmental requirements of developing countries [UNCTAD VIII Conference Report, "A New Partnership for Development: The Cartagena Commitment," 2/92].

Some of UNCTAD's concern was directed not to developed but to developing countries. The UNCTAD VIII Conference Report, cited above, acknowledges and validates the "growing recognition of the importance of the market and the private sector for the efficient functioning of economies at all stages of development." Also important, notes the report, are personal freedom, personal security, participation of the population in economic and political processes, and good management in both the public and private sectors. UNCTAD also declares that economic cooperation among developing countries (ECDC) is more important now than ever. The organization proclaims itself ready and willing, as an institution, to adapt urgently to the new global political and economic environment.

Regionalism and the Developing Countries

Contemporary UNCTAD reports contain frequent references to the rapid rate at which regional trading blocs in Western Europe, North America, and East Asia—blocs that tend to exclude or disable developing countries—are either forming or consolidating. The General Assembly also took notice and adopted, on recommendation of the Second Committee, a resolution [A/Res/46/145, 3/2/92] calling for special attention to activities promoting regional economic integration among the developing countries and requesting that the regional commissions and UNCTAD help identify, prepare, and implement specific projects to facilitate such integration.

Trade and Environment

Some 20 years after GATT established a **working group on the relationship between trade and environmental issues,** that group held its first meeting. Dormant for so long, the trade/environment nexus leaped to the top of the international agenda in 1991 when a GATT panel considered and ruled on a dispute between the United States and Mexico. The U.S. government had in 1990 been forced by a U.S. judge, who cited the U.S. Marine Mammal Protection Act (MMPA), as amended, to enforce an import ban on tuna harvested in a way that entailed the deaths of too many dolphins. In August 1991 the GATT panel ruled that the U.S. ban was inconsistent with the GATT charter. Together, the ban and the panel's ruling sparked a heated international debate about GATT's role with respect to environmental protection and sustainable growth and development. GATT responded by reviving its working group on environment [*Financial Times*, 10/9/91]. The GATT secretariat later issued a detailed report, concluding that GATT rules do not prevent governments from adopting policies to safeguard their own domestic environment or block regional or global policies, although "trade measures are seldom likely to be the best way to secure environmental objectives and, indeed could be counterproductive." It also warns sternly against the use of unilateral trade measures to offset the competitive effects of different environmental standards, and maintains that there is serious risk of environmental issues and concerns being exploited by trade protectionist interests [GATT, "Trade and Environment," 2/92]. **Environmentalists,** especially in the United States, rejected the secretariat's recommendations. The **U.S. Congress** also rejected GATT's conclusions and left the offending law in place. The U.S. tuna ban remained in force while bilateral and "minilateral" arrangements were worked out between the United States and tuna-exporting countries willing to modify their practices [*Financial Times*, 3/19/92; *The New York Times*, 5/12/92].

6. Transnational Corporations and the Global Economy

Growing Importance of Foreign Direct Investment

As the **U.N. Centre on Transnational Corporations (UNCTC)** pointed out in its 1991 Annual Report, "fundamental changes in the world economy—including the spread of policies to give a greater role to the private sector and the market, the globalization of industries, heightened technological competition, and economic regionalization—are placing transnational corporations (TNCs) at the vortex of international economic relations." Poorer countries in particular, the report declared, are turning insistently to richer ones for foreign direct investment (FDI). Unfortunately for the developing countries, **most foreign direct investment** (i.e., four-fifths of stocks and annual flows) **involves three industrialized actors**—the United States, the European Community, and Japan, or "the Triad."

The UNCTC, in an important and revealing publication, *World Investment Report, 1991: The Triad in Foreign Direct Investment*, (1) describes global trends in foreign direct investment, (2) examines how the relative importance of individual Triad members changed during the 1980s, (3) looks at the interrelationships of FDI with trade, technology, and finance, (4) raises the issue of governance, and (5) analyzes the implications for developing countries, with special attention to the LDCs. According to the study, the global stock of FDI reached about $1.5 trillion in 1989 and the annual flow amounted to $196 billion. **FDI**

nearly tripled between 1984 and 1987, the Centre found, and then increased by another 20 percent in both 1988 and 1989. The number of outward investors increased, with Japan at the forefront. Investments abroad by Japanese transnational corporations increased at an annual rate of 62 percent from 1985 to 1989, according to the Centre. Other new outward investors included Singapore, Hong Kong, and Taiwan. The share of developed countries in worldwide inflows reached 81 percent during 1985–89, while the developing countries' share fell from 25 percent to 19 percent during the same period, despite an overall rise in the size of the flow. Elsewhere it was noted that in 1991 the heavy outflow of FDI from Japan dropped dramatically [*The New York Times*, 4/25/92] and Japanese firms even became takeover targets of investors from Europe, the United States, and other countries [*The Economist*, 3/22/92]. According to the UNCTC's report, a transformation also occurred in the sectoral composition of both the flows and stocks of FDI. Previously concentrated in raw materials, other primary products, and resource-based manufacturing, FDI now centers on services, including financial services, transportation and tourism, and technology-intensive manufacturing.

In both the *World Investment Report* and a separate publication, "Government Policies and Foreign Direct Investment" [UNCTC Current Studies, Series A, No. 17], the Centre investigates international as well as national policies and policy changes affecting FDI. While such international policy changes (such as efforts currently under way in the Uruguay Round of

Table III-5
Intra-Triad Foreign Direct Investment, 1988–89, and Selected Investment Indicators

Item	Stock 1988 (*$billions*)	Annual Flow Growth Rate Average 1985–89
Japanese investment in the US	$ 53.4	102.2%
US investment in Japan	17.9	36.1
US investment in the EC	131.1	24.3
EC investment in the US	193.9	84.5
Japanese investment in the EC	12.5	46.0
EC investment in Japan	1.7	46.0
Worldwide stock of foreign direct investment, 1989		US$ 1,500 billion
Foreign direct investment outflows, total 1989		US$ 196 billion
Average annual rate of growth of worldwide investment outflows, 1983–89		29%
Developed countries' share of worldwide investment outflows, 1985–89		81%
Developing countries' share of worldwide investment, average 1985–89		19%

Source: UNCTC, *World Investment Report, 1991.*

multilateral trade negotiations to liberalize FDI in services and to limit Trade-Related Investment Measures [TRIMs]) are interesting, the national policy changes are, in many cases, breathtaking. For example, as the Centre notes, by the end of 1990 virtually all countries of **Central and Eastern Europe** had passed new legislation encouraging FDI, especially in formerly government-owned enterprises that were being privatized. The **former Soviet Union** turned previous practice on its head by permitting 100 percent foreign ownership of enterprises. And the Soviet Union's successor, **Russia,** went even further by opening its oil industry to foreign investors. **India, Mexico, South Korea, and China** all declared FDI welcome, as did **Albania, Mongolia, and North Korea,** among many others. Noting that new policies are not enough to guarantee a substantial inflow of FDI, the Centre considered policy implications for improving investment flows to developing countries. The Centre identified in this regard a need for coordinated public policies by host countries, home countries, and international institutions. The Least Developed Countries, which typically receive extremely low volumes of FDI, require even more extensive measures, including active promotion of investment opportunities and the development of infrastructure, human resources, and entrepreneurship.

Transnational Banks and Banking

The spectacular failure of the **Bank of Credit and Commerce International (BCCI)** in 1991—adversely affecting over a million customers in more than 400 branches in 73 countries—accentuated two realities, according to the UNCTC. First, the financial sector is by far the most internationalized of all economic sectors. Second, it is the sector in which the absence of a framework of international governance is most keenly felt [UNCTC: "Annual Activities of UNCTC for 1991"]. The Centre believed that the collapse of BCCI raised a number of fundamental questions relating to transnational enterprise, including how to deal with the failure of a transnational corporation and how to protect the innocent parties affected by the failure. To address these and other important related questions, the Centre organized a meeting of a **group of experts** in London in late November 1991. The experts' 24-page report, which was sent to 60 central banks for their consideration, is **highly critical of the country-by-country approach adopted by a number of major countries,** including the United States, in addressing the problem. The swift seizure and shutdown of BCCI, the report said, undermined some Third World countries, including Nigeria, Jamaica, Bangladesh, and Zambia, and increased the risk that depositors would suffer large losses. The report recommends a more coordinated international settlement process in comparable future situations [*The New York Times*, 2/5/92].

Regional Economic Integration, Transnational Corporations, and Developing Countries in the 1990s

The UNCTC, mindful along with other U.N. bodies of the rapidly advancing trend toward regional economic integration and the central roles of multinational enterprises and FDI in the evolving international economic structure, conducted a study of integration programs in Europe, North America, and a number of developing country regions. The study, published as "Regional Integration and Transnational Corporations in the 1990s: Europe 1992, North America, and Developing Countries" [UNCTC Current Studies, Series A, No. 15], focuses on the impact of regional economic integration on the behavior of transnational corporations and the implications for FDI flows into and among the developing countries. Of particular interest are the study's conclusions regarding the implications of the Europe 1992 program and the U.S.-Canada Free Trade Agreement for FDI in the developing countries. According to the study, the principal FDI implications of EC 1992 are trade-related and challenging. As is generally believed with respect to all of the European Community's trading partners, the plan for a single market will have both negative and positive trade effects, with the net effect dependent on actual EC policies. Export-oriented FDI in developing countries could weaken, the report maintains, if the EC implements policies are designed to promote European sourcing. On the other hand, FDI flows into developing countries could rise sharply if the new single market is kept open to imports of components and final goods from non-EC countries. The U.S.-Canada Free Trade Agreement, which entered into force in January 1989, is expected to have the greatest impact on FDI in developing countries in the automobile sector, according to the study. Because of higher effective North American-content requirements than under the existing U.S.-Canada Automotive Agreement, or Auto Pact, the agreement is biased toward new investment in the United States and Canada, especially the latter. However, major auto manufacturers based in the United States exceed the content requirements by a wide margin and could increase their sourcing from developing countries without violating the agreement. Unfortunately, the study does not incorporate the implications of replacing the U.S.-Canada bilateral agreement with a three-way North American Free Trade Agreement (NAFTA) now being negotiated among the United States, Canada, and Mexico, a developing country.

Transnational Corporations and Sustainable Development

Among the many important activities of the UNCTC during 1991 was a contribution to the preparations for the United Nations Conference on

Environment and Development (UNCED), which took the form of a report, "Transnational Corporations and Sustainable Development: Recommendations of the Executive Director" [E/C.10/1992/2]. The report began by noting that certain specific roles and responsibilities of transnational corporations ensue from their unique management aspects, corporate networks, technological resources, and international consequences of their decision-making. It is clear, therefore, the report suggested, that transnational corporations can make a substantial contribution to sustainable development. However, the report continued, it was also clear that that potential was far from being realized. And in response to Economic and Social Council (ECOSOC) Resolution 1991/55 of July 26, 1991, UNCTC undertook to prepare recommendations concerning the cooperation of transnational corporations for the protection and enhancement of the environment in all countries. Before formulating or passing on recommendations for action, the Centre compiled, in consultation with progressive elements of the international business community, a list of environmental objectives for international companies. Those objectives include:

- clear corporate environmental management policies;
- risk and hazard minimization;
- environmentally sounder consumption patterns;
- full-cost environmental accounting; and
- environmental conventions, standards, and guidelines.

Among the many possible activities transnational corporations might engage in to achieve those objectives are:

- overseeing the integration of environmental criteria into the firm's complete range of products, processes, and services;
- giving preference to corporate investment in funds and investments that are compatible with sustainable growth;
- sponsoring training programs for host country managers and employees on environmental protection, resource management, and sustainable development;
- promoting product durability and longevity through company-wide quality control programs; and
- redefining assets and liability boundaries in order to include public goods, such as air and water quality and biodiversity, in a manner consistent with sustainable development.

U.N. Restructuring and the Work Program of the Centre on Transnational Corporations

One of the first actions taken by the new Secretary-General of the United Nations, **Boutros Boutros-Ghali,** upon succeeding Javier Pérez de Cuéllar in January 1992 was to approve a **sweeping reorganization, or restructuring, of the U.N. Secretariat,** the essence of which Pérez de Cuéllar had recommended. Fourteen senior posts were abolished and top-level administrators reshuffled. Twelve offices and departments were slated for dissolution, among them the **U.N. Centre on Transnational Corporations.** Although the reform plan was not new and was supported by a consensus among members on the need to streamline and update the Secretariat's operations and prepare it for assuming greater responsibilities, there was nevertheless a great deal of shock and, in some cases, disappointment bordering on despair. Delegates from the Third World and environmentalists were especially distressed. According to one report, they "detected a clear trend towards enhancing the world body's role in peacekeeping operations and preventive diplomacy with a proportionate lessening of emphasis on economic and social development" [Inter Press News Service, 2/7/92].

Much regret, if not outrage, followed the decision to cease the operations of the UNCTC as an autonomous unit. According to reports, the Centre's operations would be incorporated into a new economic development department, along with the also-abolished Department of Technical Cooperation for Development, Department of International Economic and Social Affairs, Office of the Director-General for Development and International Economic Cooperation, and the Center for Science and Technology. (The new department was to be headed by **Under-Secretary-General Ji Chaozhu** of China.) Martin Khor, a spokesman for the Penang-based Third World Network (TWN), asserted that under the United Nations' restructuring program the departments best suited for tackling the growing development and environment problems had been either eliminated or reduced in size. He singled out, it was reported, the diminishing powers of the U.N. Centre on Transnational Corporations, "bearing in mind that transnational corporations (TNCs) are the biggest players in much of the global problems relating to the environment" [Inter Press News Service, 3/12/92].

According to the Secretary-General's office, the functions and duties of the abolished departments and offices were to continue in the new organizational framework. The annual report of the Centre [E/C.10/1992/9] showed it to have been actively involved in such endeavors as assisting and conducting joint studies with UNCTAD, the World Bank, the OECD, UNCED, UNIDO, the ILO, the IMF, and GATT, among other multilateral agencies. The Centre has produced numerous important publications, including but not limited to those mentioned above. It has also convened ad hoc groups of experts on various topics and supported efforts to formulate a code of conduct for transnational corporations; international standards of accounting and reporting; and international, regional, and bilateral agreements relating to transnational corporations.

In support of developing countries' interests, the Centre has also investigated ways of minimizing the negative effects of transnational corporations and enhancing their contribution to development; explored measures to strengthen the negotiating capacity of governments in their relations with transnational corporations; conducted economic and legal analyses of host country policies; helped, through EMPRETEC, to promote small and medium-sized enterprises in developing countries; and analyzed the political, social, environmental, and cultural impact of transnational corporations on host developing countries. Finally, the Centre considered the transnational banking industry, as mentioned above; studied the role and impact of transnational service corporations on host developing countries; and, importantly, provided technical cooperation to strengthen the capabilities of host developing countries in dealing with transnational corporations. This has been important not only throughout the developing but also in the newly emerging market economies of Central and Eastern Europe and the Commonwealth of Independent States [ibid.].

IV
Global Resource Management

1. Environment and Sustainable Development

When the 44th General Assembly decided to convene a **United Nations Conference on Environment and Development (UNCED)**—to be held in Rio de Janeiro, Brazil, June 3–14, 1992—it set in motion a negotiating process of enormous scope and complexity. In March 1990 governments, regional organizations, U.N. agencies, and a plethora of nongovernmental organizations began in earnest to prepare for a conference that would attempt to address virtually every environmental and developmental issue, from ozone depletion to poverty.

UNCED marks the 20th anniversary of the 1972 U.N. Conference on the Human Environment, which was held in Stockholm and which gave birth to the **U.N. Environment Programme (UNEP)**. Since that conference, both developed and developing countries have come to see that prospects for sustained economic growth are threatened by the failure of traditional development strategies to take the environment into account. "The [conference] will focus on the changes that we must make to ensure global environmental and economic security," said **UNCED Secretary-General Maurice Strong**. "The stakes are high—nothing less than the survival of life on earth" [*Development Forum* 19, no. 2, 3–4, 1991].

The mandate of the conference is to devise strategies for halting environmental degradation and promoting sustainable development worldwide [A/Res/44/228]—a tall order for some 178 countries whose economic and environmental priorities are far from uniform. The agreements to be signed or adopted in Rio are expected to include a declaration containing the basic principles of conduct to ensure a sustainable future; Agenda 21, a far-reaching action plan for promoting sustainable development up to and beyond the year 2000; a nonbinding statement on forest principles; and conventions on climate change and biodiversity.

A **Preparatory Committee** comprised of delegations from U.N. member states and the heads of the specialized agencies was established by the 44th General Assembly to negotiate the draft agreements to be adopted in Rio. Owing partly to the size of the negotiating body and to the scope of its mandate, two of the four negotiating sessions, or PrepComs, saw little in the way of negotiation. In attempting to address every issue on the agenda at **PrepCom I** (held in Nairobi, August 6–30, 1990), no one issue could be addressed in any depth. Notwithstanding the shortage of time, most delegations lacked the background information necessary for substantive debate. By the end of the session the committee had requested more than 70 background reports from the Conference Secretary-General on environmental issues and related economic issues to be submitted to the second and third PrepComs in Geneva, March 18–April 15 and August 30–September 4, 1991.

PrepCom II followed the pattern of PrepCom I, with many of the decisions taking the form of requests for more information from the UNCED Secretary-General. Much of the committee's work during the month-long session was devoted to reviewing the reports of the secretariat and to defining the issues to be addressed in Agenda 21 [For details of PrepCom II deliberations, see *A Global Agenda: Issues Before the 46th General Assembly of the United Nations*, pp. 151–52]. Frustrated by the lack of progress, a U.S. official commented that "large assembly settings, the use of translators, and time constraints make it difficult to take concrete steps forward" [Interview with *Issues/47*].

Logistical problems were only part of the story. When negotiations finally commenced at the **third PrepCom,** North-South tensions proved to be a formidable obstacle to progress. At issue was the lack of balance being accorded to environmental and developmental issues in UNCED deliberations. "The narrow environmental agenda stressed by some industrialized countries takes a rather myopic view of the whole problem," a representative from Pakistan told the 46th General Assembly after PrepCom III concluded. "Environment has to be studied in the larger context of the economic and development crisis facing developing countries" [U.N. press release GA/EF/2530, 11/19/91].

Just how obstructive an issue the environment-development balance had become was evident in negotiations on a consolidated draft of principles, compiled by the conference secretariat. Even the title of the document was the source of long and heated debate. Developing countries argued that the name "Earth Charter" neglected the developmental component of the conference, and insisted that it be renamed the **Rio Declaration on Environment and Development.** Negotiations on the actual text of the document had barely begun before the Group of 77 developing countries (G-77) attempted to shift debate to a draft of their own, arguing that the consolidated draft did not address many of their concerns. Because of a procedural dispute over which of the drafts was to be considered first, negotiation of the Rio Declaration was postponed until the **final PrepCom** in New York (March 2–April 3, 1992), where it was decided that the G-77 draft would be used as the starting point for negotiations.

The political struggle between North and South over the contents of the declaration continued into the final hours of PrepCom IV. Whereas most of the industrialized countries hoped to see a short statement of lofty principles, developing countries insisted on a pragmatic, detailed declaration that would, among other things, insulate their weak economies from the economic costs of environmental management.

Many of the principles contained in the G-77 draft—in whole or in part—faced strong opposition from industrialized countries, who argued that the document was overly negative in tone and unbalanced in its treatment of environmental and developmental issues. Specifically, they objected to text that placed the blame for environmental problems with the North; called on industrialized countries to reduce and eliminate unsustainable production and consumption patterns; and called for differentiated environmental standards along economic lines.

By the end of March a consensus was reached on only two principles—one concerning public participation in the promotion of sustainable development, and the other concerning the role of women in particular [*Earth Summit News*, Vol. 1, No. 22, 3/30/92]. In a last-ditch effort to produce a compromise document, **Committee Chairman Tommy Koh of Singapore** formed a small negotiating group consisting of 16 regional or bloc representatives, and won their consent to remove from the draft every bracket (the indicators of a lack of consensus) before session's end.

The final draft adopted by the PrepCom marked a victory for the developing countries, since it incorporated most of the G-77 proposals in some shape or form. In particular, the document affirms the right to development (a principle long opposed by the United States in U.N. forums), and recognizes that the North and South are not equally responsible for the world's environmental problems and, thus, do not share equally the burden of addressing them. A highly contentious principle calling on states to "reduce and eliminate unsustainable patterns of production and consumption and promote appropriate demographic policies" escaped deletion, although the United States remains opposed to it [A/CONF.151/PC/WG.III/L.33/Rev.1, 4/2/92; U.N. press release ENV/DEV/108, 4/4/92]. The developing countries, for their part, agreed to remove their proposed text on environmental damage caused by weapons of mass destruction (strongly opposed by the United States, the United Kingdom, and others) and text that blamed the North for environmental degradation [A/CONF.151/PC/WG.III/L.20/Rev.1].

The draft declaration incorporates a number of principles which, though nonbinding, provide standards for national behavior. Among these is the **"precautionary principle,"** which would deny nations the opportunity to use scientific uncertainty as justification for continued practices considered harmful to the environment. (Such a justification was recently used by the United States to block agreement on international targets for the reduction of carbon dioxide emissions—a main cause of global warming—during negotiations on the climate convention that is to be signed in Rio.) The draft calls on states to cooperate "in an expeditious and more determined manner" to develop international law regarding liability and compensation for transboundary damage to the environment [L.33/Rev.1]. Among the national actions to be taken, the declaration calls on states to undertake environmental impact statements and to promote the use of economic instruments to combat environmental degradation, taking into account the **"polluter pays" principle.**

Agenda 21

"Unwieldy" has been the term most frequently used by nongovernmental observers and delegates alike to describe negotiations on the action plan, Agenda 21. During PrepCom IV alone, 24 million pages of documentation had been circulated [*Earth Summit Bulletin* 1, no. 26, 4/4/92]. (Considering that it took eight years to negotiate a package of agreements for just one of the issues covered in Agenda 21—oceans—before the 1982 Law of the Sea treaty could be opened for signature, the progress made by the UNCED Preparatory Committee is in some ways remarkable.) The non-legally binding document is intended to provide the basic framework for integrating environment and development into decision-making at local, national, and international levels.

The draft approved by PrepCom IV is a mammoth 800-page document, containing 40 chapters that cover 112 topics. Chapters are divided into four sections: Social and Economic Dimensions of Promoting Sustainable Development; Conservation and Management of Resources for Development; Strengthening the Role of Major Groups; and Means of Implementation.

The progress made in negotiating the action plan has varied from issue to issue, but the pattern of both developing and developed countries has been to block proposals that are perceived as threatening to their national interests. Some sections have been criticized by nongovernmental observers as being little more than a rehashing of already existing programs, declarations, and legal instruments, while others—such as those dealing with institutions and nongovernmental participation—have been widely viewed as innovative.

Contentious North-South debate on consumption patterns, deforestation, technology transfer, and financial resources did not abate at the final PrepCom, and these sections remain heavily, if not almost entirely, bracketed. By late May, delegates had yet to decide whether the Rio conference should adopt Agenda 21 chapter-by-chapter or as a package.

Toxic Chemicals; Hazardous, Solid, and Radioactive Wastes

As the primary receptacles for the North's toxic wastes, developing countries have been pushing for inclusion in Agenda 21 the endorsement of a complete ban on the transboundary movement of hazardous wastes. In January 1991 every African state except South Africa signed the **Bamako Convention,** which bans trade in all hazardous wastes. Movement for such a ban in South and Central America gained momentum in March 1992, when a memo from a World Bank chief economist was leaked to the press, intimating that the Bank might want to consider encouraging waste transfers to the South, where long-term environmental and health considerations are given less of a priority [*The Christian Science Monitor*, 3/10/92]. Many of these nations have already enacted laws banning or severely restricting waste imports—the bulk of which come from the United States—but such laws have proved difficult to enforce.

Proposals for an international agreement on toxic waste trafficking were blocked by the United States. The final text adopted by PrepCom IV takes note of the fact that no such agreement exists, and proposes activities to improve the detection and prevention of illegal traffic in toxic chemicals [A/CONF.151/PC/WG.II/L.30; U.N. press release, ENV/DEV/103, 4/2/92]. Calling the text "unbalanced, vague, and lacking a committed approach," a representative of Malaysia told the committee that "it was a matter of regret" that the text did not commit nations to negotiating an international agreement [ibid.].

Even more contentious an issue was the management of radioactive wastes. At PrepCom III the United States bracketed all proposals on the subject, arguing that UNCED was an inappropriate forum for discussing the issue [*The InterDependent* 18, no. 1, 1–2/92]. Despite warnings from the United States and Japan about a lack of consensus, the text adopted at PrepCom IV sets out a range of activities that governments should take to ensure "the safe and environmentally sound management of radioactive wastes" [A/CONF.151/PC/WG.II/L.27 and Corr.1]. The United States won removal of a section dealing with military waste, and bracketed text that discourages the storage or disposal of radioactive wastes near the marine environment.

Negotiations on environmentally sound management of solid wastes were comparatively uncontroversial. Developing countries opposed setting international targets and timetables, arguing that many nations lacked the economic and technical capacity to meet such targets. In a compromise, footnotes were added to the final text, which tie the incorporation of targets to the outcome of negotiations on technology and financial assistance to aid developing countries in meeting UNCED agreements. The text calls on industrialized and developing countries to put in place a national recycling program by the year 2000 and 2010, respectively. By the year 1995 and the year 2005, industrialized and developing countries respectively should ensure that at least 50 percent of all sewage, waste water, and solid wastes are disposed of in conformity with national and international guidelines, with the aim of meeting these guidelines for all such wastes by the year 2025. The text also calls on countries to reduce the production of agrochemical wastes by the year 2000 [A/CONF.151/PC/WG.II/L.26 and Corr.1].

Desertification, Agriculture, and Rural Development

Desertification currently affects about a sixth of the world's population and a quarter of the planet's total land area. The most severely affected region is Africa, where overpopulation, overgrazing, and the farming of marginal land are turning ever-wider rangeland to desert. The **"Common African Position"** on UNCED that was adopted at the Second African Ministerial Conference on Environment and Development (held in Côte d'Ivoire, November 11–14, 1991) called on the Preparatory Committee to incorporate into Agenda 21 an agreement to pursue an **International Convention on Halting Desertification in Africa** [A/Conf.151/PC/WG.I/L.39/ Rev. 1].

Less than a week before PrepCom IV was to convene, the Global Coalition for Africa, in collaboration with the U.N. Department of Economic and Social Development, brought together ministers and high-level officials from African and northern donor nations for an exchange of views on the African Common Position [U.N. press release ENV/DEV/104, 4/2/ 92]. The two-day ministerial meeting, held in New York on March 29–30, 1992, did much to strengthen the African position in PrepCom negotiations, where support was won from every industrialized country except the United States for a convention on desertification. The text on desertification that was adopted by PrepCom IV closely mirrors the African Group's proposals in the attention paid to the relationship between poverty and land degradation, and to the need for developing local, national, and regional monitoring and assessment capabilities. Emphasizing the importance of local participation, the text calls on governments to support community-based people's organizations, and to adopt national policies that would promote a decentralized approach to land-resource management.

According to an expert group convened by the World Bank, the U.N. Development Program (UNDP), and the Food and Agriculture Organization (FAO), developing countries will need to produce 3 percent more food every year just to keep up with expanded population and demand [U.N. note to correspondents, Note No. 4988, 3/31/92]. A central objective of the Agenda 21 chapter on "sustainable agriculture and rural development" is to achieve food security for present and future generations while at the same time preventing further land degradation. A critical factor in land degradation is land tenure. Commonly, in many developing countries the most fertile land is owned by large landholders whose crops are grown for export, forcing the rural poor to overwork marginal land in order to eke out a living. A politically sensitive issue, land tenure was treated with vague rhetoric in Agenda 21. Governments are encouraged to implement policies to influence land tenure and property rights "in a positive way" [A/Conf.151/PC/WG.I/L.42 and Corr.1]. Text calling on governments to harmonize agricultural trade policies remained in brackets. Other program areas address pesticide use, rural energy development, and genetic resource conservation.

Forests

Negotiations on a nonbinding set of forest principles have been mired in North-South disputes. The heavily bracketed document adopted by PrepCom IV raised doubts that an agreement would be adopted in Rio.

The industrialized countries, led by the United States, hold the view that the document should affirm the shared stake of nations in forest management, and should include internationally accepted guidelines. Developing countries have sought to immunize themselves from international commitments, proposing text that guarantees their "sovereign and inalienable right to use, manage, and develop their forests in accordance with their development needs," and bracketing text referring to future negotiations on a forest convention [A/CONF.1511/PC/WG.I/L.46]. Another point of contention was the G-77's proposal that the document recognize the North's overconsumption of forests. "Who was better placed to address the issue," asked Shri Kamal Nath, Minister for Environment and Forests of India, "a Third World villager who cuts firewood to cook a meagre meal, or an affluent citizen whose lifestyle is unsustainable?" [U.N. press release ENV/DEV/101, 4/1/92]. Nearly a third of the principles in the draft document, proposed by developing countries and bracketed by the developed, deal with the traditionally contentious North-South issues: debt, trade, and aid.

Freshwater Resources

From eastern Africa to the western United States, freshwater shortages are cropping up in regions across the globe as ever-increasing demand pushes sources to the limit. In 1990 the World Bank predicted that at current rates of consumption, water demands in Israel, Jordan, and the West Bank would exceed all renewable supplies within six years [*State of the World, 1990*, p. 48].

"There is now no longer an unlimited supply of freshwater, and international competition for it is growing," Mostafa Tolba, Executive

Director of UNEP, told some 500 experts attending an **International Conference on Water and the Environment,** sponsored by the World Meteorological Organization (WMO) [U.N. Non-Governmental Liaison Service, *E&D File 1992,* no. 21, 2/92]. The conference, held on January 26–31, 1992, in Dublin, lent much needed expertise to diplomats negotiating Agenda 21.

At the request of the UNCED committee, participants addressed a wide array of subjects in the conference report, including integrated water resource development and management, water resources assessment, and water supply for urban and rural development. The text adopted by PrepCom IV lays out action programs for these areas, and sets a number of timetables and targets, ranging from the year 2000 to 2005, for establishing national assessment and management programs [A/CONF/151.PC/WG.II/L.17/Rev.1; U.N. press release ENV/DEV/101, 4/1/92]. All targets were bracketed, pending the outcome of negotiations on financial and technological assistance for developing countries.

Oceans, Seas, and Coastal Areas

This chapter was the subject of lengthy and often difficult negotiations, in part because of the breadth and complexity of the subject. Program areas—many of which have their basis in the 1982 Law of the Sea Treaty—include integrated management and sustainable development of coastal areas (a subject of great concern, since 60 percent of the world's population is expected to live in coastal areas by the year 2000); marine environmental protection; living marine resources; critical uncertainties (which deal mainly with the potential effects of climate change); strengthening international institutions; and sustainable development of islands. (See also "Law of the Sea" section for more on these issues.)

Left unresolved by PrepCom IV was the issue of managing straddling and highly migratory species on the high seas. Canada, which hopes to curb fishing by the European Community next to its **Exclusive Economic Zone (EEZ)** in the North Atlantic, has been pushing for greater management control over these species in high seas adjacent to its and other nations' EEZs. The bracketed text calls for cooperative measures between states whose nationals fish for such stocks and the coastal states in whose EEZs such stocks occur.

In a landmark resolution of the 46th General Assembly, governments agreed to a global moratorium on all large-scale high seas **driftnet fishing** by December 31, 1992, with a 50 percent reduction to be achieved by January 1 [A/Res/46/215]. PrepCom IV, however, was unable to reach agreement on text calling for international cooperation in the development of agreed criteria for the use of selective fishing gear and practices to minimize waste of catch in targeted and nontargeted species.

Atmosphere

As the primary root of smog, acid rain, and (predicted) global warming, energy production and consumption have been a central focus of atmosphere negotiations. They have also been among the most contentious. Developing countries sought to emphasize the special obligations of industrialized countries to establish energy policies restricting consumption of fossil fuels, since the North consumes the lion's share of the world's supply. Although the United States blocked any overt distinction between North and South in the text, the *intent* of the text clearly reflects such a distinction: The aim is to halt unsustainable patterns of production and consumption patterns and to assist developing countries in their transition to environmentally sound energy systems.

The United States and the Arab oil-producing nations successfully blocked agreement on even the most innocuous of proposals designed to **reduce fossil fuel use.** Remaining in brackets was text calling for the study and development of economic instruments to improve energy efficiency; formulation of objectives or policies relating to energy production and consumption; promotion of the use of economic instruments; and strengthening of energy standards [A/CONF.151/PC/WG.I/L.47]. A proposal to create a new U.N. agency to promote energy conservation was abandoned in favor of less specific text stating that a global-level institutional response will be required, and that there is presently "no U.N. agency responsible for the whole range of energy issues within the United Nations."

Agreement was reached on a number of activities designed to combat the adverse environmental effects of the transport and industrial sectors. The United States withdrew earlier objections to the promotion of economic mechanisms to discourage large fuel-consuming and polluting vehicles. Governments are to encourage industry to develop more energy-efficient products and processes and to "develop, improve, and apply environmental impact assessments" [ibid.].

In early February 1992 scientists detected alarming concentrations of **ozone-depleting chlorofluorocarbons (CFCs) and halons over the North Pole,** sending shock waves through Europe and North America. These substances are believed to have already produced an "ozone hole" over Antarctica, permitting dangerous levels of ultraviolet radiation to penetrate the earth's atmosphere. Similar damage to the ozone layer over the North Pole would mean that more radiation would penetrate over the United States, Canada, and the European nations. These and other nations agreed in 1990 to phase out CFC production by the year 2000 when they signed on to amendments to the **1987 Montreal Protocol on Substances that Deplete the Ozone Layer.** The new evidence prompted Germany, Denmark, and the Netherlands to move up the deadline to 1994, the European Community to 1995, and the United States to 1996.

Agenda 21 calls on nations to ratify the Montreal Protocol and its 1990 amendments, and urges replacement of all ozone-depleting products with substitutes that are neither ozone-depleting nor greenhouse gases. The substitutes currently being employed also deplete the ozone, but at a slower rate than do CFCs. The United States bracketed text on environmentally sound substitutes.

"Cross-Sectoral" Issues

A number of Agenda 21 chapters deal with "cross-sectoral" issues—issues that cut across a number of environment and development concerns. Among these are the protection and promotion of human health, rural and urban human settlement development, education, poverty, consumption and production patterns, and international economic issues.

International Economy. The economies of much of the developing world depend upon the export of their natural resources, and adverse price trends—not to mention the Third World's heavy debt burdens and slow rates of economic growth—do not allow these countries to make long-term investments aimed at protecting the environment. One of the most important sections of Agenda 21, **"International policies to accelerate sustainable development in developing countries, and related domestic policies,"** was also one of the most hackneyed. Most of the language can be found in the 1990 U.N. Declaration on International Economic Cooperation and a plethora of U.N. resolutions on trade, debt, and other development concerns.

Among the shorter chapters, it calls for market-oriented macroeconomic reforms in developing countries, but offers no new initiatives in the areas of trade and debt relief. Governments are asked to encourage international and regional economic institutions to elaborate studies on the relationship between trade and the environment; to ensure that environmental standards do not constitute unjustifiable discrimination in trade; and to develop and clarify the relationship between multilateral environmental measures and the provisions of the General Agreement on Tariffs and Trade (GATT). Members of the European Community bracketed text affirming the need to remove existing trade distortions in agriculture—a key issue for developing countries as well as for the United States. The United States, following its standard operating procedure for negotiations on development assistance, bracketed text calling on the North to meet targets for overseas development assistance.

Poverty, Consumption, and Population. Alleviating poverty, halting unsustainable consumption patterns, and controlling population growth are the stuff of sustainable development. No environmental problem will be adequately addressed without progress on these three fronts.

This much could be agreed upon by delegates negotiating sections on **"Combating poverty, changing consumption patterns, and demographic dynamics and sustainability."** When it came to making international commitments in these areas, negotiations bore little fruit. Much of the text on consumption is bracketed because the U.S. administration strongly opposes any language that would infer the need for change in the lifestyle of its citizens. Governments are urged to develop a policy framework to promote sustainable consumption and production patterns that would include environmentally sound pricing and measures to increase energy and resource efficiency and minimize wastes [A/CONF.151/ PC/L.68]. Policies and action programs on population are urged only "where appropriate," owing to continued southern resistance to international commitments in this area. The section on poverty urges governments to focus on "the empowerment of local and community groups" in carrying out poverty-eradication programs.

Institutional Mechanisms. If Agenda 21 is to be more than a political statement, institutional arrangements must be created to coordinate and monitor its implementation. In Rio, governments were asked to choose between two options for a follow-up mechanism to UNCED: A high-level **sustainable development commission** that would report directly to the General Assembly on substantive issues, and through the Economic and Social Council (ECOSOC) on matters related to coodination; or a **revitalized ECOSOC** [CPR.3/Rev.3]. Both structures provide for direct input from nongovernmental organizations and citizens groups, and the business, scientific, and academic communities. It will be left to the **47th General Assembly** to decide on the modalities of operation, regardless of which option is chosen.

The chapter affirms that strong and effective leadership on the part of the U.N. Secretary-General is crucial, since he/she would be the focal point of follow-up efforts within the U.N. system. The Administrative Committee on Coordination (ACC), which is headed by the Secretary-General, will be given the task of monitoring, coordinating, and supervising efforts within the U.N. system. The PrepCom has left it to the Secretary-General to recommend the creation of a high-level advisory board of eminent persons. The proposed advisory board, whose members would be appointed by the Secretary-General and would act in their personal capacities, would lend their expertise on environment and development to the Secretary-General and to intergovernmental bodies within the U.N. system. The chapter also calls for strengthening and enhancing the role of UNEP and UNDP.

Nongovernmental Organizations (NGOs). The UNCED process is without precedent in the level of nongovernmental involvement at local, national, regional, and international levels. Even before NGOs were given formal entree into the process, they established an International Facilitating Committee (IFC), based in Geneva, to assist organizations and networks in defining their roles vis-à-vis UNCED; to serve as an information clearinghouse; to provide a forum for dialogue among the independent sectors; to promote fair and effective participation in UNCED on behalf of the independent sectors; and to assist the Brazilian NGO forum in promoting and facilitating a parallel "people's conference" in Brazil.

In the United States, 200 private citizens and NGO representatives met in the nation's capital on October 21–22, 1990, to establish the **U.S. Citizens' Network on UNCED,** a body serving many of the same functions on the national level as the IFC serves on the global level. The many U.S. constituencies involved in the process have been convening public hearings and conferences across the nation, generating policy proposals for the U.S. government, and working to garner the attention of the media on UNCED negotiations.

All "relevant" NGOs received a formal invitation from the 45th General Assembly to make written submissions to the conference secretariat and to address PrepCom sessions, upon the approval of the PrepCom Chairman. These guidelines were extended to the conference itself by the 46th General Assembly. While most delegations recognized the value of the NGO community as a source of expertise and an agent for modifying public behavior and consumption patterns, some developing country delegations sought to restrict NGO participation because, said one observer, they "did not want their own nongovernmental organizations interfering in the deliberations" [interview with *Issues/47*]. By PrepCom IV, 1,838 nongovernmental representatives had been accredited to participate in the process.

To the dismay of many, however, only government delegates were permitted in closed sessions and in many of the informal sessions, where some of the most important negotiations took place. Nonetheless, NGOs had ready access to delegates in the lounges and corridors, and many groups held briefings with the official delegations of their home countries. A strong supporter of NGO access to both plenary and informal sessions, the U.S. government included 24 NGO observers (rotating on a weekly basis) in its own delegation to PrepCom IV.

The UNCED process, and the agreements reached in Rio, may help shape a more participatory United Nations of the future. As was mentioned, the independent sector will play a direct role in any new institutional mechanism assigned to follow-up UNCED. The chapter on "major groups" that was adopted by PrepCom IV elaborates national and international strategies for strengthening the role of nine sectors in facilitating the objectives of Agenda 21. The nine include women, youth, indigenous people, NGOs, farmers, local authorities, trade unions, business and industry, and the science and technology community. According to the draft text, all intergovernmental organizations and national governments are to promote and allow NGOs and their networks to contribute to the review and evaluation of Agenda 21 implementation programs, and are to provide access for NGOs to accurate and timely data concerning these programs [A/Conf.151/PC/L.72].

Governments are called on to implement strategies for eliminating obstacles to women's full participation in sustainable development by the year 2000. By 1993 governments are to have established procedures for allowing consultation and possible participation of youth in decision-making processes related to the environment at local, national, and regional levels. A number of actions are called for to empower indigenous people, including the adoption or strengthening of "appropriate policies and/or legal instruments" aimed at protecting indigenous intellectual and cultural property and the right to preserve customary and administrative systems and practices—a proposal bracketed by France.

Financial Resource and Technology Transfers. Financial resource and technology transfers from North to South—unquestionably the most divisive issues in the UNCED debate—may ultimately determine the conference's success or failure, since developing countries have made it clear that without external assistance they will not be able to integrate environmental protection into their development policies in any effective way. Developing countries have footnoted a number of Agenda 21 activities with a qualifier stating that their participation is dependent upon the outcome of negotiations on these two issues.

In the days before the final PrepCom, Secretary-General Strong announced that developing countries would need $125 billion a year in aid to pay for the new environmental programs, $70 billion more than all the financial assistance they now receive [*The New York Times*, 3/2/92]. Acknowledging that raising such a sum is unrealistic, he stated that an initial commitment of $5 to $10 billion a year should be the aim. Each chapter of Agenda 21 contains the Secretary-General's estimated partial price tag, which would together total $125 billion over a number of years. All such estimates are in brackets.

At PrepCom IV, financial negotiations ended in deadlock, raising doubts that an agreement can be reached in Rio. The G-77 held firm in its call for "new and additional funds" to cover the "incremental costs" of Agenda 21 agreements "with no reallocation of existing multilateral or bilateral financial flows" [A/CONF.151/PC/L.41/Rev.1]. Most industrialized countries acknowledge in principle that new and additional aid flows will be necessary, but reject the demand that there be no reallocation of existing overseas development assistance.

Industrialized countries have also rejected southern demands for the creation of a special fund to which contributions would be mandatory. The proposed fund would give all parties an equal voice regarding project selection and the administration of funds. The preferred funding mechanism of the industrialized countries is the **Global Environment Facility (GEF)**—a three-year pilot project launched in 1990 by the World Bank, UNEP, and the U.N. Development Programme to fund developing-country projects in four areas: climate, biodiversity, ozone depletion, and water pollution. The Third World finds the GEF lacking in transparency, accountability, and southern participation in decision-making; and it points out that despite the facility's three organization sponsors, the actual manager is the World Bank, whose governing structure is dominated by the major powers.

The final session of the **Intergovernmental Negotiating Committee (INC) on climate change,** held in New York from April 30 to May 8, breathed new life into the negotiations on financial mechanisms. The INC, responsible for negotiating a framework convention on climate for the Rio conference, is distinct from the PrepCom, but both have been mired in disputes over financing. In the final hours of climate negotiations, the G-77 agreed that the GEF should be "the international entity entrusted" with assisting the developing countries in meeting their obligations to the climate agreement [A/C.237/L.14/Add.6]. The draft convention calls for the GEF to be restructured so as to ensure balanced representation and transparency in its governance. While this agreement pertains only to the climate convention, it may signal a change in the South's position in support of a new funding mechanism for Agenda 21.

In a meeting held in Washington, D.C., on April 29–30, developed and developing countries reached agreement on a plan to restructure the GEF. The participation of developing countries in decision-making was to be enhanced through the creation of a Participants' Assembly that would take decisions on the basis of consensus. In the event that a consensus could not be reached, "a voting system would be used that guarantees an equitable representation of southern interests while giving due weight to the funding efforts of donor countries" [GEF press release, 5/1/92]. The scope of projects considered eligible for GEF funding was broadened considerably to include "programs and projects that are country driven and consistent with national priorities designed to support sustainable development."

The sticking point in PrepCom negotiations on technology concerns the conditions under which developing countries are to obtain it. The South has remained steadfast in the demand for the transfer of environmentally sound technology on a "preferential and non-commercial basis," while the United States and other developed countries have empha-sized the primary role of the private sector in developing and transferring these technologies.

At issue is the question of intellectual property rights. The United States and others argue that governments have a limited ability to promote technology transfer since many of these technologies are proprietary or the property of those who develop it. Another key issue in the technol-ogy debate is financing. Developed countries bracketed text calling for the provision of financial resources to assist developing countries in acquiring environmentally sound technologies [A/Conf.151/PC/L.69].

Framework Convention on Climate

The need to address global warming took on a sense of urgency with the release of three authoritative reports by the **International Panel on Climate Change (IPCC)** in the spring of 1990. The IPCC was established by UNEP and the World Meteorological Organization in 1988 to coor-dinate and unify the world's scientific and policy-making communities to address climate change. The panel concluded that a warming of the global climate by 2° to 5°C could be expected over the next century if no action was taken to curb greenhouse gas emissions (primarily carbon dioxide, but also methane, CFCs, and nitrous oxides, among others). By 1992 all the world's major Global Circulation Models had predicted a warming that is 10 to 100 times faster than ecosystems have ever faced before [*International Environmental Issues*, Greenpeace International, 2–3/92]. Sea level rise, storm surges and coastal flooding, drought and desertification, and severe ecological disruption are among the predicted impacts of global warming for different parts of the world.

At the **Second World Climate Conference,** held in Geneva from October 29 to November 7, 1990, 135 nations agreed that nothing short of a global convention would suffice to reverse predicted warming trends. Every industrialized nation except the United States had already pledged to cut back carbon emissions by the time formal negotiations had begun in February 1991. The framework convention on climate change, one of two legally binding agreements to be signed in Rio, was widely predicted to be the centerpiece of the conference. To the disappointment of developing and developed nations alike, the draft framework convention that emerged from the sixth and final negotiating session was devoid of targets and timetables to combat global warming. "Nothing in this convention requires action," lamented a representative from the Natural Resources Defense Council. "It's a political statement."

From the outset of negotiations, the U.S. government refused to join the European Community, Canada, Australia, New Zealand, and Japan in agreeing to stabilize carbon emissions at 1990 levels by the year 2000.

Brushing aside the predictions of most scientists, the Bush administration has argued that the scientific evidence of a warming trend is not sufficient to warrant actions that would have an adverse effect on the U.S. economy. (The administration has stated at the same time that the nation is likely to reach the proposed targets, but nevertheless remains opposed to including them in a convention.) The United States found a sympathetic ear among oil-producing southern nations, who feared that commitments to stabilize emissions would reduce demand for oil from the North.

"They're protecting their turf," said a delegate from Samoa. "They have economic interests at stake" [U.N. press conference]. Samoa is among the 36 islands and nations with low-lying coastal areas that comprise the **Alliance of Small Island States (AOSIS)**—a transregional group that has been lobbying vigorously for a strong convention, and one in which the industrialized countries commit themselves to stabilize emissions by the year 2000. As a result of sea level rise, cyclones, coral bleaching, and coastal flooding, "several dozen cultures are at risk, possibly within one or two generations," warned a delegate from Jamaica.

Despite heavy pressure from its northern allies, AOSIS, and other nations, the U.S. position ultimately prevailed. Using its leverage as the world's largest emitter of greenhouse gases, the United States reportedly threatened not to sign the agreement if it included targets and timetables for emissions reductions. Since the nation's factories, cars, and electric utilities account for 20 percent of the world's man-made carbon emissions, most nations wanted the United States to be a party to any treaty they sign.

The compromise draft calls on developed country parties to "adopt national policies and take corresponding measures on the mitigation of climate change," and recognizes the importance of "returning individually or jointly to their 1990 levels" of carbon emissions and other greenhouse gases. The text gives national governments discretion in the adoption of such policies, as a consequence of the "differences in these Parties' starting points and approaches, economic structures and resource bases, [and] the need to maintain strong and sustainable growth . . ." [Future A/AC.237/L.14/Add.6]. Like the draft Agenda 21, the convention states that the participation of developing countries "will depend on the effective implementation by developed country Parties of their commitments under the Convention related to financial resources and transfer of technology." These commitments include the provision of new and additional resources through a restructured GEF to meet "the agreed full costs incurred by developing country Parties in complying" with the agreement.

The convention does not indicate any steps that nations are to take after the year 2000, but it sets up a reporting and review process to assess the adequacy of the convention. The first review conference will convene within six months of its entry into force, at which time the convention may be amended.

At the conclusion of negotiations, both developed and developing countries expressed disappointment over the lack of specific commitments by industrialized countries to stabilize emissions. "The convention was to have been the centerpiece of the Rio summit, but it has not been negotiated in a spirit of true partnership," INC representative Renji Sathia of Malaysia told the committee at the session's conclusion. Referring to the U.S. role in negotiations, he added that "key parts [of the draft] had been virtually dictated on a take-it-or-leave-it basis—another manifestation of the so-called new international order" [U.N. press release, ENV/DEV/118, 5/9/92]. The Malaysian delegate said that his government will not sign the treaty because of its inadequacies in dealing with climate change. It is unclear whether other developing nations will join Malaysia in refusing to sign.

Biodiversity

"It is clear that biodiversity—the ecosystems, species, and genes that together make life on earth both pleasant and possible—is collapsing at nothing less than mind-boggling rates," reports the Worldwatch Institute, based in Washington, D.C. [*State of the World 1992*, p. 9]. Pollution, overharvesting, the inappropriate introduction of species into an ecosystem, and the pressures of population growth are the root causes of biological impoverishment. Deforestation alone condemns to extinction at least one species of bird, mammal, or plant daily [ibid.].

Mounting global concern over such loss prompted UNEP in 1988 to initiate deliberations aimed at achieving an international legal instrument on biological diversity. Based on the work of **UNEP's Ad Hoc Working Group of Legal and Technical Experts on Biological Diversity**, the UNCED PrepCom decided that such a legal instrument should be negotiated in time for signature in Rio.

At the closing of its sixth and penultimate session, held February 6–15 in Nairobi, the INC on biodiversity had reached agreement or near agreement on 29 of the 43 articles to be contained in the convention [U.N. press release, ENV/DEV/89, 3/2/92]. "Although I feel cautiously optimistic, I think a major breakthrough has been achieved at this session," commented INC Chairman Vincente Sanchez. "We accomplished a lot more than we thought we would at the beginning of the session" [UNEP news release 1992/8, 2/17/92]. The final negotiating session took place in Nairobi on May 11–19.

Many of the major themes in negotiations on climate and on Agenda 21 are shared by those on biodiversity. Financing and technology transfer (biotechnology, in the context of biodiversity negotiations) are the main points of contention; national actions, rather than international actions, are the preference of most governments for preserving biological diversity. The draft convention emphasizes the sovereign right of countries to exploit their biological resources pursuant to their own environmental policies, but recognizes that the conservation of biodiversity is the common concern of all humankind and requires international cooperation. The convention calls on contracting parties, according to their particular capabilities, to develop national strategies to regulate or manage biological resources, whether or not they are within protected areas; establish a system of protected areas; rehabilitate and restore degraded ecosystems; prevent the introduction of, and control or eradicate, alien species that threaten ecosystems; support the participation of local populations in implementing remedial measures; and encourage cooperation with the private sector [UNEP/Bio.Div/N7-INC.5/2].

Remaining wholly or partially in brackets are several far-reaching measures for minimizing the adverse effects of projects or policies on biodiversity. Parties are to require environmental impact assessments for proposed projects that are likely to affect biodiversity, *"whether within or beyond the limits of national jurisdiction"*; and they are to be responsible for the cost of avoiding or minimizing damage inflicted by activities within their jurisdiction on the biodiversity of areas outside their jurisdiction. Bracketed text calls on the conference of parties to adopt protocols setting rules of procedure related to liability and compensation.

Developing countries have been pushing for a link between biodiversity and biotechnology in treaty negotiations, hoping to get access to biotechnology as a quid pro quo for increased efforts to conserve biological resources within their borders. The technology and expertise necessary to economically profit from biodiversity is found in developed countries, whereas most of the world's biodiversity is found in developing countries. Developing countries want some form of compensation for the biodiversity preserved by them and used by pharmaceutical companies in the North at great profit. A recent agreement between the pharmaceutical company Merck, Sharpe, and Dohme and the government of Costa Rica may have set a precedent for cooperation in this area. In return for the nonexclusive rights to search for compounds that may have medicinal value, Costa Rica will receive part of the royalties derived from any products developed that use these compounds [*Network '92*, no. 9, 8/91].

The draft convention, which contains alternative bracketed proposals, calls on the parties "to [ensure priority access] [promote and advance fair and equitable access], especially to developing countries, to the results and benefits arising from biotechnologies based upon genetic resources [originate in/and or] provided by contracting parties." The heavily bracketed article on financial mechanisms, based on a G-77 proposal, calls for the establishment of a **Biological Diversity Fund** for the achievement of convention objectives by developing countries.

The Rio Conference: A Brief Overview

In June 1992 world attention focused on Rio de Janeiro, where 118 heads of state backed by thousands of negotiators gathered to conclude the agreements painstakingly negotiated over the previous two years. Reflecting the environment's newfound prominence on the international agenda, over 150 nations signed conventions on climate change and biological diversity—a milestone considering that only 14 nations signed the Vienna convention to protect the ozone layer when it was first presented in 1985. Consensus was reached on three additional nonbinding agreements intended to meld the world's environmental and economic priorities.

UNCED marked the isolation of the world's sole remaining super-power as much as it did a renewed commitment by other nations to tackle the world's environmental problems. Citing concerns about intellectual property rights, the United States refused to sign the biodiversity treaty. Other industrialized countries, too, had reservations, but considered them to be outweighed by the benefits of the treaty. European governments set themselves further apart from the United States when they signed a statement in Rio pledging to stabilize carbon emissions at 1990 levels by the year 2000.

The conference, which was attended by 8,000 journalists and more than 15,000 representatives of NGOs and grass-roots citizens' groups, served to elevate the concept of sustainable development. "Much more than 12 days ago, the world today is aware that the questions of environment and development cannot be treated separately," President Fernando Collor de Mello of Brazil told delegates at the closing of the conference [*The New York Times*, 5/15/92].

At the same time, however, UNCED offered a glimpse at the difficult challenges that lay ahead as nations attempt to build a more sustainable international society. The fragility of the new consensus reached in Rio was underscored by the decision of governments not to reopen debate on the Rio Declaration on Environment and Development, a set of 27 principles intended to guide nations in the pursuit of sustainable development. The product of protracted and at times torturous debate, the Declaration represented a very delicate compromise between the developed North and the developing South. Upon its adoption, UNCED Secretary-General Maurice Strong and U.N. Secretary-General Boutros Boutros-Ghali each praised the document as an important achievement, but called on states to negotiate a more inspirational and legally progressive "Earth Charter" for adoption on the 50th Anniversary of the United Nations in 1995 [*The InterDependent* 18, no. 3, Summer 1992].

Governments had less success in charting an inspired global course for preserving the world's forests. In negotiations on the "non-legally binding authoritative statement of principles for a global consensus on the management, conservation, and sustainable development of all types of forests," the United States and other industrialized nations failed to win a commitment from developing countries to eventually turn these principles into a binding treaty. Led by Malaysia, whose economy depends heavily on its timber industry, developing countries insisted on watering down any principle that could be interpreted as weakening their sovereign right to exploit their resources. The agreement reached recognizes the value of the forest "to the environment as a whole," and calls on nations to manage their forests "on the basis of environmentally sound guidelines" as well as "national development policies and priorities" [The Earth Summit Bulletin, 5/17/92].

Eleventh-hour compromises made by both developed and developing countries enabled governments to adopt Agenda 21, a comprehensive action plan to promote sustainable development on local, national, and global levels. After initially blocking the proposal, the United States moved to accept Agenda 21 text that calls for the establishment of an Intergovernmental Negotiating Committee, under the auspices of the General Assembly, to elaborate a convention on desertification. In another compromise, the United States withdrew objections to a chapter dealing with one of the most fundamental tenets of sustainable development: the need to change unsustainable patterns of production and consumption that lead to environmental degradation.

One of the most important achievements was an agreement to create a U.N. Commission on Sustainable Development at the 47th Session of the General Assembly. The new Commission, which will report to ECOSOC, is intended to provide a regular forum to review the progress of nations and international organizations toward the goals agreed to at the conference, as well as to maintain global attention on sustainable development issues not adequately addressed at UNCED. Praising the agreement, NGO observers noted that the new Commission will help to hold governments accountable to the commitments made in Rio. Agenda 21 also reaffirms and expands the roles of UNEP as the primary environmental catalyst within the U.N. system, and calls for broader participation of major groups in decision-making, from the grass-roots level to the new Commission on Sustainable Development.

Less fruitful were negotiations on financial resources. The G-77 hoped to win a commitment by donor nations to meet the long-established target of 0.07 percent of their Gross National Product to development assistance by the year 2000, as well as a "substantial initial commitment" at UNCED to assist developing countries in meeting the financial costs of implementing Agenda 21 [Earth Summit Update, no. 10, 5/92]. In the end the Group accepted a compromise that fell far short of these goals. The agreement calls only on those nations already committed to achieving the 0.07 percent target to do so "as soon as possible," thus excluding the

United States; and the new pledges made by donor nations in Rio fall far short of what many observers believe is needed. Of the $6–$7 billion in commitments, observers estimate that only $2 million represents new aid [*The New York Times*, 5/15/92]. Thus far, only $55–$75 million has been earmarked for Agenda 21 agreements.

"Expectations of UNCED may not have been fully met, but there is a renewed sense of urgency and purpose and a determination to work for a more equitable and environmentally sound world order," Muhammad Nawaz Sharif, Prime Minister of Pakistan, stated at the closing of the conference [U.N. press release ENV/DEV/151, 5/15/92]. The UNCED products, though less far-reaching than many had hoped, nevertheless represent an important starting point in a process of reconciling the world's diverging economic and ecological priorities.

2. Food and Agriculture

Every year the world produces enough cereal grain or grain equivalent, the basic food staple, to provide an adequate diet for everyone on the planet. But every year about half a billion people, mainly women and children—twice the U.S. population—face starvation. Although the 1991–92 cereal crops will still be sufficient to feed everybody, production is expected to fall by about 4 percent, largely because of declines in North America and Eastern Europe.

Of the nearly 2 billion tons of cereal crops produced annually, the industrialized world is responsible for more than two-fifths; almost half of the rest is rice, which is consumed mainly by people in the developing world. Just over 9 percent of the total—mostly in the form of wheat, maize, and other feed grains—is traded internationally, and 0.5 percent is donated overseas. The rest is consumed by people or animals in the region or country in which it is grown.

The food and agriculture picture for the past year has held little encouragement for the majority of the world's people, who are the poor and the hungry. Consumption of cereal grains exceeded production for the third consecutive year [FAO, *Food Outlook*, no. 3, 1992] and wheat prices rose sharply. About 40 percent of total cereal consumption (mainly maize) and most of the soybean consumption (the major nongrain crop) were used to feed animals whose products (meat, milk, and eggs) rarely reached the tables of the poor.

Although early forecasts for 1992–93 suggest a modest (2.5–3 percent) increase in cereal production, most of this increase is expected in the industrialized countries, and most of the growth in cereal trade will probably reflect larger imports by China and the states of the former Soviet Union. The worst drought of this century is projected for southern and eastern Africa [ibid.], where production has been lagging behind consumption for more than a decade now. UNICEF estimates that a quarter of a million children die each year from malnutrition and the diseases to which this condition renders them vulnerable. Some 17 million refugees from war, famine, and other disasters are constantly at risk of malnutrition [U.S. Committee for Refugees, *World Refugee Survey 1992*, p. 33 (Table 1)].

The **World Food Council (WFC)**, the United Nations' highest policy body in the food and agriculture area, convened its 17th session in Helsingør, Denmark, June 5–8, 1991. The documents prepared for this meeting framed a policy discussion about food security that went considerably beyond the food and agriculture sector—the original mandate of the Council. These documents dealt with such matters as the economic integration of Western Europe, political changes in Eastern Europe, the GATT negotiations, the Gulf War, the decline in official development assistance, and the global economic environment, and considered their implications for action on world hunger.

When the Council's report on the 17th session was submitted to the General Assembly [A/46/19], its language was sadly familiar:

> We are deeply concerned about the deteriorating situation of hunger and malnutrition in the world. Some 45 million people—30 million of them in Africa—are threatened by famine, many of them refugees displaced by war and civil strife. . . . Less visible, but no less tragic, is the continuing crisis of chronic hunger and malnutrition affecting a growing number of men, women and children around the world. In developing countries, one out of three children under the age of five is malnourished. Malnutrition and common, preventable diseases kill 40,000 of them each day. . . .

It had become clear in previous sessions of the Council that while consensus could be achieved on the general goals—combating famine, chronic hunger, malnutrition, and nutritional diseases [A/44/10, Part I]—implementing them was more difficult by far, mainly for lack of political will. In its report on the 17th session, the Council therefore stated that "We must now focus our energies on mobilizing the political determination—as well as the financial and, particularly, human resources—to translate consensus into effective policies and programmes" [A/46/19].

The Council appears to be well aware of its own limitations and those of the U.N. system. It points out the necessity of increasing external assistance and of using it more effectively. It acknowledges the significance of the outcome of the Uruguay Round of the GATT negotiations and recognizes that the development policies of multilateral aid donors and the commercial policies of industries, banks, and trading corporations will have more impact on food security than will any program directly focused on the food and agriculture sector. And yet, while conceding that "economic growth" is essential to the effort to reduce hunger and poverty, the Council nevertheless underscores its conviction that "hungry people in the affected countries and elsewhere cannot wait for an upturn in the global economic fortunes."

A dozen years ago—somewhat late in its history but ahead of most of the rest of the world—the Council noted its deep concern "about the increasing deterioration of our natural resource base, which is jeopardizing the food security of future generations." "The deterioration of the environment," it continued, "is linked to unsustainable development patterns in many countries, particularly in the developed ones." To a considerable extent this finding is reflected in the outcome of the April 1991 Conference on Agriculture and the Environment, jointly sponsored by the Food and Agriculture Organization of the United Nations (FAO) and the government of the Netherlands, which discussed strategies and goals for sustainable agriculture and rural development. Although the World Food Council itself has not specifically endorsed the concept of **sustainable agriculture,** it does stress the importance of preserving the resource base "through the adoption of efficient management, good agricultural practices and use of non-toxic inputs." The World Bank too is speaking about the importance of careful management of agricultural resources both to feed increasing populations and to reduce environmental damage [World Bank, *World Development Report 1992*, p. 134 passim].

The world food problem has not been viewed as a major General Assembly agenda item for several years, although it is dealt with directly by several U.N. agencies—FAO, the International Fund for Agricultural Development (IFAD), the World Food Programme (WFP), and the World Food Council—and indirectly by the World Health Organization, the U.N. Environment Programme (UNEP), the U.N. Development Programme (UNDP), UNICEF, the U.N. High Commissioner for Refugees, and the World Bank Group, the regional banks, and the International Monetary Fund (IMF). In 1991, however, the **General Assembly** took action, revising the general regulations of the World Food Programme and increasing the size of the WFP's Committee on Food Aid Policies and Programmes from 30 to 42 members [A/Res/46/22], but its impact remains uncertain. The 46th Assembly also accepted the Second Committee's report on Desertification and Drought and ordered that it be transmitted to the Preparatory Committee for the U.N. Conference on Environment and Development (UNCED) for its fourth session [A/Res/46/161]. This report had grown out of a report by the Secretary-General on the situation of countries stricken by desertification and drought in Africa [A/46/268].

None of this, however, is likely to have much effect on the actual distribution of food. According to FAO, the cereal import needs of the developing countries (excluding Eastern Europe) are expected to increase by 7 million tons, but the **level of food aid** from all sources in 1991–92 (including the United States, which supplies four-fifths of all world food aid) is expected to fall about 300,000 tons, declining to 10.4 million tons. FAO points out that this is "well below the levels provided to these countries during previous years [and] . . . will cover only 15 percent of their total cereal imports" [*Food Outlook*, no. 3, 1992]. In view of this disparity, the General Assembly adopted its largest voluntary contribution target to date for WFP's 1993–94 period—$1.5 billion—"of which not less than one third should be in cash and/or services" [A/Res/46/200]. Five months later, a joint study by the World Bank and the Russian Federation concluded that the states of the former Soviet Union alone will need $6 billion in food aid for the remainder of 1992 [*World Bank News*, 4/9/92].

Agriculture is one of the more contentious sectors of the economy, as the stalemate on the Uruguay Round of GATT negotiations has shown. Although **trade in food products,** which makes up 75 percent of agricultural trade, has declined steadily since World War II, the agriculture sector continues to be vital for many countries, accounting for 15 percent of GDP in developing countries as a group and for more than a third of GDP in sub-Saharan Africa [*UNCTAD Trade and Development Report*, Part III, Chapter II, passim]. Developing countries must also rely on agriculture for 50 to 100 percent of export earnings. At the same time, these countries' share of the market in agricultural exports has consistently declined over the past two decades, and the developing world has little weight in the GATT negotiations on agriculture, which reflect mainly competition between the United States and the European Community for dominance in this trade sector. It remains to be seen whether the elimination of the industrialized countries' **export subsidies,** which have largely frozen the developing countries out of their "natural" markets in the industrialized world, will reduce the penetration of the First World's highly capitalized agriculture into the Third World's home markets.

There is also concern that the **integration of Eastern Europe and the states of the former Soviet Union into the international market economy,** which has been slower than many had hoped, will shrink the funds available to the developing countries from commercial and official sources. The developing countries are already transferring financial resources to the rest of the world—$39 billion in 1990, according to the *U.N. World Economic Survey, 1991* [Table IV.1]—much of which is financed by new borrowing. The prospect of lower availability of such funds will force those countries into an even heavier emphasis on exports and will reduce food production for domestic needs.

Although there is serious hunger and malnutrition in Iraq and Afghanistan as a result of war and its aftermath, and in Haiti because of what are called "unsettled conditions," a poor harvest, and depletion of stocks, the most serious regional shortages are in Africa. Never the primary focus of world attention, **Africa** faces an increasingly uncertain future unless external aid increases and unless there is genuine progress toward democracy in South Africa. Lack of financial resources, military and civil conflict, government inexperience and corruption, inefficient state enterprises, erratic weather and climate, a fragile agricultural industry, rapid population growth, and decreasing political and strategic importance as the cold war fades into history—all inhibit development and perpetuate hunger on the African continent. Even countries that are usually exporters of cereal grains, such as South Africa and Zimbabwe, will have to import feed grains in particular; and the total import requirement for the subregion may triple, to more than 6 million tons [*Food Outlook*, no. 3, 1992]. FAO points out that the condition of ports and railroads places its own limitations on food distribution, and that because of the poor harvest, the food aid programs that depend in part on supplies from within the subregion will be hard put to sustain themselves.

In the policy area, however, there seems to be a convergence of several development trends, which may lead to implementation of the rather idealistic yet unanimous **Universal Declaration on the Eradication of Hunger and Malnutrition** adopted at the 1974 U.N. World Food Conference in Rome and accepted by the General Assembly. This declaration proclaims that "Every man, woman, and child has the inalienable right to be free from hunger and malnutrition in order to develop fully and maintain their [sic] physical and mental faculties."

At the 1991 **World Food Day** ceremony—held every October 16 to renew the World Food Conference's pledge—the Secretary-General spoke of the occasion's broader context: "World Food Day reminds us," he said, "that without food for all, the call for economic and social development will have a hollow ring. And, without significant progress in alleviating hunger and poverty, there can be no real peace for millions of our fellow human beings" [SG/SM/4640, 10/18/91].

In January 1992 the new Secretary-General, Boutros Boutros-Ghali, applied this principle to the effort to empower rural women. The Secretary-General pointed out that "rural women were responsible for more than half of all food production in the developing world . . . and that no development strategy could be considered truly participatory unless rural women's economic roles and requirements become an integral part of its design" [IFAD/450]. The statement was made in the context of the Secretary-General's endorsement of an International Fund for Agricultural Development conference on this subject, held in Geneva in February 1992. IFAD's analysis of the problem in 114 nations shows that the number of poor rural women has increased by 50 percent in the past 20 years, that 16 million landless women care for 80 million family members, that women make the key decisions on nutrition, education, and consumption, that the economic contribution of women is consistently underestimated, and that women suffer many forms of discrimination. IFAD also reported that "since rural residents make up the vast majority of most developing nations, their lack of purchasing power poses a serious hindrance to the growth of manufacturing and service industries, slowing down overall output, growth and capital accumulation" [IFAD press release, 2/6/92]. In short, without the empowerment of women, especially rural women, development in the poorer countries is unlikely.

IFAD has been particularly active in the area of environmentally sustainable agriculture. In April 1992 its Governing Council received a report on the implementation of "a framework of operations entailing the application of environmental principles and criteria [and addressing] the environmental aspects of rural poverty alleviation" [IFAD, GC 14/L.9/Rev.1]. Sustainable resource management is the key criterion for these projects, and IFAD recognizes that it has a large educational task with respect to both donors and beneficiaries, as well as a "dearth of information for sound project design." Nevertheless, projects have been approved and are under way in 14 countries.

Agriculture had a prominent place on the agenda of the U.N. Conference on Environment and Development (UNCED) in Rio de Janeiro, June 3–14, 1992. In the least-developed countries, agriculture is equivalent to development itself; and in all countries (whether the land is worked by agribusinesses or by poor peasants) farming is a major contributor to environmental damage, which inevitably affects development.

Scheduled for the days after UNCED were two other major meetings with a bearing on the world food situation. The first of these—the 18th session of the World Food Council, June 23–26, to be led by a new president, the Agriculture Minister of Iran—would be paying particular attention to migration and food security, to the state of the GATT negotiations, to hunger-alleviation targets in domestic programs, and to the impact of the East European situation on food security in developing countries. Continuing a discussion on the need for a "new Green Revolution" begun two years before, the government ministers at this Nairobi meeting were also expected to have a "frank and open discussion" on how to "move from commitment to action to eradicate hunger" [WFC/1992/1].

In November comes the second of these post-UNCED meetings—a joint FAO-WHO International Conference on Nutrition in Rome, for which governments have been preparing "country papers" on the nutritional situation within their borders. Whether there is to be a major conference in 1994 to mark the 20th anniversary of the World Food Conference has yet to be determined. That conference had proclaimed the end of world hunger in ten years—a far more elusive goal than it appeared at the time, involving as it does not only supply-side inputs, such as land, water, energy, and technology, but environmental and social considerations as well. The widely heralded Green Revolution that increased yields and produced abundant harvests has not brought food security. It is UNCED, however, that might well be this decade's key event in advancing the cause of food security, since it will be educating the world about the nature of development and focusing public attention on the "limits of growth" for the first time since the Club of Rome published its report of that title two decades ago.

3. Population

World population will increase during the 1990s at a record rate of nearly 100 million people per year, causing the current population of 5.48 billion to almost double by the middle of the next century according to the U.N. Population Fund (UNFPA) in its 1992 *State of World Population* report released in April.

The "medium," or most likely, **projection of population growth** puts total world population at 8.5 billion people by 2025, at 10 billion by 2050, and on a plateau of just over 11.6 billion by 2150. It assumes that the average number of children born in developing countries will decline gradually and stabilize at replacement level over the next 35 to 55 years. The figure for stable population under the medium projection is 1.4 billion higher than under the 1980 projection, which showed population stabilizing at 10.2 billion [UNFPA, *State of World Population*, 1992, p. 2].

The number of people added to the world population will average 97 million a year for the next decade (the highest in history and the population equivalent of another United States every two-and-a-half years) and 90 million a year through 2025. Ninety-seven percent of this population growth will occur in Africa, Asia, and Latin America.

The Population Division of the U.N. Department of Economic and Social Development recently published a series of long-range projections that examines possible population scenarios up to the year 2150 [United Nations, *Long-range World Population Projections—Two Centuries of Population Growth, 1950–2150*, 1992]. The range of the new projections is daunting, but actions taken during this decade can have a restraining effect on ultimate population size.

One of the most striking points to be drawn from these projections is the large variation in population size resulting from relatively small changes in the total fertility rate (the average number of children per woman). For example, if fertility does not stabilize at replacement level but stays just 5 percent higher (2.17 children per woman instead of 2.1), the difference would be more than 9 billion people added to the earth's population (20.8 billion versus 11.5 billion in the year 2150). And if fertility remained constant at today's rate of 3.4, world population would reach the absurd level of 694 billion by 2150 ["New UN Projections Show Uncertainty of Future World," *Population Today*, 2/92].

Developing countries have improved living conditions for an increasing proportion of their populations, but the absolute number of poor, illiterate, and malnourished people has continued to climb [*State of World Population*, pp. 3–5]. According to a World Bank estimate, the *percentage* of people living in poverty in developing countries fell from 52 percent in 1970 to 44 percent in 1985; yet, as a result of population growth, the *number* of people living in poverty increased to 1.156 billion, up 212 million since 1970. And although the proportion of people who are malnourished dropped, there were 50 million more chronically hungry people in the mid-1980s than there were at the end of the 1960s. At the recent International Conference on Water and the Environment in Dublin, experts noted that over a billion people did not have access to safe water and sanitation in 1990 despite programs that provided about 1.5 billion people with water and 750 million more with sanitation in the 1980s [*Population*, 2/92]. Similar trends are seen in school enrollments, literacy, housing, and health care.

Not all development trends are negative, and some improvements in the quality of life around the world are worth noting. A World Health Organization (WHO) report prepared for the 45th World Health Assembly in Geneva noted significant gains in life expectancy and declines in infant mortality and childhood diseases. Average life expectancy worldwide is 65 years, up one-and-a-half years since 1985. Infant mortality fell from 76 deaths per 1,000 live births in 1985 to 68 deaths per 1,000 in 1990. Deaths from childhood diseases are down sharply, thanks in large part to a major immunization campaign by international agencies. Most impressive is the drop in measles deaths from 2 million to 800,000 between 1985 and 1990 [*The Washington Post*, 5/9/92].

Countries that succeeded in slowing population growth saw the benefits in the 1980s. Between 1965 and 1980 rapid population growth appeared to pose no problem for economic growth, but in 41 developing countries with slower population growth in the 1980s (2.4 percent per year), incomes grew 1.23 percent annually, while in the 41 countries with faster population growth (3 percent per year), incomes fell by 1.25 percent annually [*State of World Population*, p. 7]. UNFPA research also shows, however, that countries with slower population growth in the 1965–80 period saw incomes grow 1.8 percent a year faster in the 1980s than did the countries with faster population growth in 1965–80. The size of a country's foreign debt in 1980, the most obvious alternative explanation, was found to have no correlation with income growth in the 1980s. Another study found that countries with slower population growth tended to have higher savings and investment ratios [ibid.].

Family planning programs are also beneficial to the health of women and children. An estimated 500,000 women die each year—one every minute—from pregnancy and childbirth-related causes. Family planning could prevent a quarter to a third of these deaths. Such programs could also save the lives of several million children annually by helping women to avoid high-risk and often unwanted births, especially when those births are spaced less than two years apart or when the woman is too young or too old, or has had three or more children [UNICEF, *State of the World's Children*, 1992, p. 59].

As the positive impact of lower population growth rates on human welfare and economic development becomes clearer, countries are devoting more attention and resources to family planning. The results of an international survey of 88 countries undertaken by the Population Council, with support from UNFPA, show a dramatic increase in and better implementation of family planning program efforts between 1982 and 1989 ["Family Planning Programs: Efforts and Results, 1982–1989," *Studies in Family Planning*, 11–12/91]. Between 1975 and 1990, 19 out of 88 countries experienced 30 to 50 percent declines in family size and an additional 26 countries had declines of 15 to 29 percent. The results show unequivocally that family planning program efforts are strongly related to declines in fertility, independent of social and economic factors. Total fertility rates declined on average by about 6 percent in countries with weak or nonexistent programs, by 24 percent in countries with moderate programs, and by 33 percent in countries with strong programs.

The analysis reaffirms earlier findings that both organized family planning efforts and the socioeconomic setting play major roles in fertility decline and that the socioeconomic setting can itself be a factor in a country's ability to launch a successful program. Fertility decline was sharpest in countries that ranked high on both social setting and program effort. Only a few countries in the study with low levels of development had a strong or moderate program effort (Bangladesh, Nepal, India, and Vietnam). The authors conclude that the formidable task of significantly increasing the overall number of contraceptive users can probably be achieved if developing countries continue to strengthen their family planning activities, including those of the private sector, as they did during the period 1982–89.

The challenge facing family planning programs over the next decade is immense. During the decade of the 1990s the number of couples of childbearing age will increase by about 18 million per year—a record. At the same time, a growing proportion of women say they want to stop or postpone childbearing (the proportion now approaches three-quarters in many countries). These facts, taken together, fuel the extraordinary growth in unmet demand for family planning. Of approximately 300 million couples who do not yet have access to safe and effective modern contraception, at least 125 million want help in planning smaller families, and field studies indicate more would use such services if they were available [Population Crisis Committee, *Report on Progress Toward World Population Stabilization*, 1990].

Studies show that for **world population to stabilize** at less than double its current level, the number of contraceptive users will have to increase by the end of this decade, from 360 million to 880 million couples. Spending on family planning in developing countries will also have to rise, from $4.6 billion to about $10.5 billion in constant dollars, with about half to be raised from donor countries [ibid.; estimate of current expenditures from all sources based on UNFPA's draft *Global Population Assistance Report 1990*].

The scientific community is now convinced that human populations are already beginning to threaten the planet's ability to support life under current technology use and patterns of consumption. In an unusual joint statement, the prestigious National Academy of Sciences and the Royal Society of London recently declared: "If current predictions of population growth prove accurate and patterns of human activity on the planet remain unchanged, science and technology may not be able to prevent either irreversible degradation of the environment or continued poverty for much of the world" ["Population Growth, Resource Consumption, and a Sustainable World," 2/26/92].

The **U.N. Conference on Environment and Development** (UNCED) in June 1992 was intended to change a number of old patterns by establishing principles (an Earth Charter) and action plans (Agenda 21) that begin with a recognition of the interrelationship of widespread poverty and environmental degradation. Although the 44th General Assembly's resolution establishing the conference did not include any reference to population matters, the next Assembly emphasized the importance of "addressing the relationship between demographic pressures and unsustainable consumption patterns and environmental degradation during the preparatory process of the United Nations Conference on Environment and Development . . ." [A/Res/45/216].

Nonetheless, governments continued to disagree on the importance of the population issue at UNCED. Many of the developing nations believed, for example, that the Preparatory Committee was giving too little weight to the development side of the UNCED agenda and that the effect of focusing attention on population problems would be to shift the blame for environmental degradation unfairly, away from the First World's industries and consumption patterns and over to the Third World. The latter also saw such a shift as adding to their difficulty in making a case for debt-relief, technology transfer, and increased aid flows from the industrialized nations to help underwrite the cost of sustainable development. A number of developing countries maintained that the international population conference, scheduled for 1994, was a more appropriate forum for discussing population issues in any case [*E Magazine*, 5–6/92].

By the final UNCED Preparatory Committee meeting in New York in March 1992, population had received attention throughout Agenda 21, which now included a separate chapter on "Demographic Dynamics and Sustainability." However, when the U.S. delegation moved to delete references to overconsumption by the developed countries, the Group of 77, representing the political interests of the developing world, deleted most references to population as an important factor in environmental degradation [*The Washington Post*, 4/12/92]. The draft Agenda 21 presented to the delegates at UNCED in June also made no specific mention of "family planning" or "contraception"—this as a result of vigorous lobbying by the Vatican, with the support of Argentina, the Philippines, and a few other governments [ibid., 4/30/92], and of the fact that the New York preparatory meeting operated by consensus, allowing the Holy See to hold out for acceptable wording. Nor does the document offer any concrete recommendations for programs to deal with global population problems or for the funds to address them.

The way in which population and environment have been addressed at UNCED could influence deliberations at the **U.N. International Conference on Population and Development** in 1994. The Economic and Social Council adopted a resolution calling for this third decennial population conference [E/1991/93]. Previous population conferences have been held in Bucharest in 1974 and Mexico City in 1984. The site for the conference has yet to be determined. Official offers to host the conference have been received from Tunisia, Egypt, and Turkey. Tunisia, initially thought to be the front-runner, has withdrawn its invitation. Dr. Nafis Sadik, Executive Director of UNFPA, will serve as the conference secretary-general.

The main tasks of the population conference will be to revise the **World Population Plan of Action,** which outlines the international community's response to the global population problem, taking into account changing demographic and political trends since 1984, and to identify future courses of action and priorities. During 1992 and 1993 a number of preparatory meetings will be held at the regional level and among intergovernmental and nongovernmental organizations. In addition, a series of six expert group meetings will be held around the world on the following subjects: population, environment, and development; population policies and programs; population and women; family planning, health, and family well-being; population growth and demographic structure; and population distribution and migration ["Report of the Ad Hoc Task Force on the International Conference on Population and Development," 1/92].

Despite the mounting evidence that world population will probably double and could triple without a large infusion of resources, political controversies in one major donor country, the **United States,** threaten to undermine the global consensus on the need to expand family planning and population programs. Ignoring calls for better international cooperation, the United States continues to deny funds to UNFPA, an institution it was instrumental in establishing over 20 years ago, because of UNFPA's program in **China.** In 1985 the U.S. Agency for International Development (AID) withheld $10 million of a $46 million contribution earmarked for UNFPA, claiming that the organization was comanaging China's population program and that the Chinese program relied on coercive abortion and involuntary sterilization to implement its "one child per couple" policy. In the seven years since, AID has withheld the entire $25–$30 million budgeted annually for UNFPA. The decision for 1992 is forthcoming.

As the basis for its decisions to withhold funds, AID has cited an amendment—part of a supplemental foreign aid appropriations bill in 1985—prohibiting U.S. funding of any organization that "supports or participates in the management of a program of coercive abortion or involuntary sterilization." AID has continued to maintain that the activities neither of the Chinese government nor of UNFPA have changed sufficiently to warrant renewed U.S. support. UNFPA has repeatedly pointed out that it does not support abortion in China or anywhere else in the world, since it does not consider abortion a method of family planning, and it denies the charge that it "manages" China's program.

The size of UNFPA's contribution relative to the Chinese government's expenditures ($10 million versus $1 billion annually, or 1 percent of the total) and the number of UNFPA staff in Beijing relative to the size of the State Family Planning Commission (4 versus 160,000 family planning workers, plus numerous volunteers scattered throughout the countryside) suggest that allegations about UNFPA helping to "manage" the Chinese program are not credible. Of the funds that have been allocated by UNFPA for projects under the five-year program that began in 1990, only 1 percent has gone directly to the government of China, with the remainder channeled through "executing" agencies, such as the World Health Organization (WHO), UNICEF, Food and Agriculture Organization, and nongovernmental organizations [UNFPA, "Facts About UNFPA and China," 10/90].

Critics of Washington's policy have long maintained that U.S. birth control opponents have never been able to produce evidence of UNFPA complicity. Prior to 1989 the United States had never formally expressed concern about the China program in the U.N. Development Programme/ UNFPA Governing Council, the appropriate institutional forum. The Governing Council approved five-year programs for China in 1980 and 1984, and subsequent annual meetings were notable for the absence of any expressions of concern about the China program. Many critics of

U.S. policy marshal these facts to support their contention that the withdrawal of U.S. funding from UNFPA remains primarily a concession to a vocal domestic political constituency rather than an expression of concern about alleged human rights violations in China.

Defenders of UNFPA believe that the Fund plays a positive role by strengthening voluntarism in the Chinese population program. Since 1980, UNFPA has supported modern contraceptive production to improve the typically low quality of contraceptives manufactured in China. The wide availability of higher quality contraceptives promotes voluntary participation in the population program by reducing the incidence of unplanned pregnancies resulting from contraceptive failures and discontinuation of use. For example, one study of the impact of Chinese women replacing primitive steel rings with modern copper-bearing IUDs, manufactured by two factories built with UNFPA support, estimates that 324,000 unplanned pregnancies, many of which would be aborted, are prevented each year [personal communication, 11/89].

UNFPA is currently in the third year of a $57 million assistance program in China for the period 1990–94, approved by the 48-member Governing Council in June 1989. The program concentrates on three areas: contraceptive production and research, maternal and child health programs, and the training of demographers. Assisting in the implementation of major components of the new program will be UNICEF and WHO [DP/FPA/CP/48].

The composition of the new program eliminated some of the UNFPA-funded activities in China that the U.S. government found most objectionable in the past, such as technical assistance in census-taking and other demographic data collection and analysis. Despite these UNFPA and Chinese efforts at accommodation, the U.S. delegate at the Governing Council expressed strong opposition to the new cycle of assistance to China.

In response to the Bush administration's refusal to restore U.S. support to UNFPA, family planning supporters in the U.S. Congress have been attempting to pass legislation to force AID to fund UNFPA. An amendment to the Fiscal Year 1990 foreign aid appropriations bill, sponsored by Senator Barbara Mikulski (D–Md.), earmarked $15 million for UNFPA and stipulated that UNFPA was to maintain the U.S. funds in a segregated account, none of which could be used in China. The Mikulski amendment was adopted by both houses of Congress as a reasonable compromise to break the impasse over UNFPA funding. It was sent to President Bush as part of a $14 billion foreign aid appropriations bill. Rather than sign the bill with the Mikulski amendment, President Bush vetoed the entire legislative package.

Since the Tiananmen Square massacre of pro-democracy demonstrators in 1989, supporters of UNFPA have sought to disassociate the issue from China and focus on the other 140 countries to which UNFPA is attempting to provide family planning services even in the absence of U.S. funds. In 1991, language drafted by Representative Bill Green (R–N.Y.) built on the Mikulski approach and further required that U.S. funds be used only for the purchase of contraceptives and that UNFPA allow no increase in its approved budget of $57 million for work in China during 1990–94. The provision also stipulated that if UNFPA increased its funding to China above the $57 million level, the entire contribution would be returned to the U.S. Treasury.

Green's provision, contained in the House appropriations bill, was matched by language in the House-Senate agreement on the foreign aid authorization bill. In an additional compromise, worked out by Senator Alan Simpson (R–Wyo.), all disbursements of U.S. funds by UNFPA were to be subject to the approval of the U.S. ambassador to the United Nations. Some international observers viewed this surrender of control to a single donor government a breach of the principles of multilateralism, but Simpson, a member of the Senate's Republican leadership, believed that he had negotiated an agreement acceptable to President Bush. In the end, the White House threatened to renew its veto of UNFPA funding, and neither the authorization nor the appropriations bill reached the President's desk.

The United States remains the only major industrial country that does not contribute to UNFPA—this despite a recent poll commissioned by the Population Crisis Committee showing that over 90 percent of Americans think that poverty and other social problems will worsen if rapid population growth continues unchecked, and that close to three-fifths (58 percent) of Americans believe that the U.S. government should resume funding of UNFPA. A surprisingly large proportion of voters (43 percent) stated that they would be less likely to vote for a candidate opposed to U.S. foreign aid for family planning [Gordon S. Black Corp., *U.S. Attitudes on Population*, 3/92].

Despite the absence of U.S. participation, **contributions from other donors** continue to increase. UNFPA expects to receive an estimated $230 million in 1992, up from $221 million in 1991 [UNFPA press release, 2/92], due to an increase in support by several countries—most notably the United Kingdom, which raised its contribution by 50 percent in 1990. The Netherlands and Norway made supplementary grants to their 1991 contributions. But adjusted for inflation, contributions have failed to keep pace with inflation. UNFPA's program allocations in 1992 will fall far short of the more than $550 million in requests for assistance it has received from developing nations [*Population*, 12/91].

At the **International Forum on Population in the 21st Century**, held in Amsterdam in November 1989, 79 governments—both donors and developing countries—agreed to double the amount of funds available for population programs. The hope was to reach $9 billion by the end of the century, with the aim of stabilizing world population at an early date. Approximately $1 billion of this money would be channeled through UNFPA. The target was endorsed by the UNFPA Governing Council and the Development Assistance Committee of the Organization for Economic Cooperation and Development in 1990. UNFPA is still well short of that goal.

The winners of the **U.N. Population Award** for 1992 are J.R.D. Tata, a leading Indian industrialist who pioneered family planning services for his employees; and the Population Council, a major social science and biomedical research and training institution, which has helped to develop such new contraceptive methods as copper T-380A intrauterine device and the new implant Norplant [ibid., 2/92].

4. Law of the Sea

As the tenth anniversary of the 1982 **Law of the Sea (LOS) Convention** approached, there were indications that the treaty might enter into force within the year or not much after. Six nations ratified the treaty in 1991, raising the number of ratifications to 51 (a total of 159 countries had taken the preliminary step of signing the document). The LOS Convention enters into force one year after the 60th country submits its articles of ratification.

When the Convention does enter into force, its institutions will come to life as well: the **International Seabed Authority (ISA)**—the body charged with regulating deep-seabed mining—to be based in Kingston, Jamaica; and the 21-member **International Tribunal on the Law of the Sea (ITLOS)**, in Hamburg, Germany. With the single exception of Iceland, however, the only countries to have ratified the Convention thus far are developing countries that account as a group for less than 5 percent of U.N. assessed contributions. Noted one observer, the LOS Convention could well enter into force "for a group of almost exclusively Third World states, which would encounter insurmountable difficulties" as they tried to invigorate these institutions [*A Global Agenda: Issues Before the 46th General Assembly of the United Nations*, p. 158].

The ninth session of the **Preparatory Committee (PrepCom)** for the ISA and ITLOS made some progress in defining the modalities of operation of the LOS institutions, but the developed and the developing countries remain at odds over the extent of these bodies' authority to regulate and intervene where deep-seabed mining is concerned, as well as over particular LOS provisions affecting mining. The developed countries, which advocate a scaled-back institutional structure and a market-oriented approach, prefer not to give the Authority strong regulatory powers.

The PrepCom approved the applications of China and a group of Eastern European countries for registration as **Pioneer Investors** in deep-seabed mining. Registered Pioneer Investors receive exclusive rights to explore the mineral potential of specified seabed areas, assuming certain obligations in exchange. After considerable debate, China was granted a status similar to India's and will provide free training to some personnel of the future Enterprise (the ISA's own, intergovernmental mining company) but will not be required to take on some other First World-investor obligations [LOS/PCN/117]. The PrepCom's various committees also considered draft environmental provisions for seabed mining, joint-venture options for the Enterprise, rules for a finance committee to assist the ISA, and estimates of ISA's operational costs [LOS/PCN/92].

The failure of PrepComs to resolve the more divisive issues related to **deep-seabed mining** gave rise to the series of informal consultations initiated by U.N. Secretary-General Javier Pérez de Cuéllar in mid-1990. Four such consultative sessions were held in 1991 and were attended by some 30 delegations—including the United States, which is not a treaty signatory. At the third of these sessions, in March 1991, delegates agreed to reconsider a variety of issues in light of such developments as the disintegration of the Soviet Union, the collapse of communism, and the current market prices for the minerals to be extracted. Among those issues were the costs of the Convention to state parties, the Enterprise, the review conference, technology transfers, limits on production, a compensation fund, financial terms of contracts, and environmental impacts.

There was general agreement that costs to state parties should be minimized and that the institutions' modalities of operation should evolve over time. A prime candidate for this evolutionary approach is the Enterprise, since it is not expected to carry out actual mining activities for some years. The governmental representatives at the March consultative session also agreed that the drafting of detailed production controls could be postponed as well, until such time as there is a real possibility of seabed production. The fall in demand for some of the principal seabed metals, and particularly the drop in the price of copper (which is expected to account for a third of deep-seabed mining revenues), has made large-scale deep-seabed mining unlikely until well into the next century.

Less progress was made on the thorny issue of decision-making. The United Nations' new Secretary-General, Boutros Boutros-Ghali, agreed to pick up where his predecessor left off, scheduling his first informal session on the LOS convention for June 1992.

Delegates to the 46th Session of the General Assembly carefully—and successfully—revised the wording of the **annual resolution on LOS** to avoid a negative vote from the United States [A/Res/46/78]. Washington traditionally opposes Assembly pronouncements on the Convention because they call for ratification without modification. Now, explaining why the United States joined Ecuador, Germany, Israel, Peru, the United Kingdom, and Venezuela in merely abstaining from the voting, U.S. Permanent Representative to the U.N. Thomas Pickering said: "This resolution departs from earlier resolutions [in] its acknowledgment for the first time that political and economic changes, particularly growing reliance on market principles, underscore the need to reevaluate matters in the seabed mining regime in light of the issues of concern to some states [A/46/PV.70, 12/30/91]. The resolution passed by a vote of 140–1 (Turkey).

In a historic move, the 46th Session also passed a resolution—this by consensus—calling for a 50 percent reduction of driftnet fishing by June 30, 1992, and a total moratorium on this practice by the end of the year [A/Res/46/215]. The Secretary-General was asked to report to the 47th Session on the implementation of this self-enforcing resolution. A 1989 resolution had called for a temporary suspension of driftnet fishing in the South Pacific and a review of the use of driftnets on the high seas. The U.N. Office of Ocean Affairs had prepared for the 45th Assembly an extensive report on the environmental dangers of driftnet fishing [A/45/663], with a follow-up report for the 46th [A/46/645/Add.6], and these documents gave momentum to the call for a moratorium.

The restructuring of the U.N. Secretariat by the new Secretary-General early in 1992 abolished the position of Under-Secretary-General for Ocean Affairs, held by Satya Nandan. Under-Secretary-General for Legal Affairs Carl-August Fleischhauer was given oversight responsibility for the **Office of Ocean Affairs** and Jean-Pierre Lévy was named Director of the Office. Mr. Fleischhauer informed the tenth session of the PrepCom that the restructuring did not imply any change in U.N. policy on maritime affairs and would not affect the informal meetings of the Secretary-General. The Office of Ocean Affairs continues to service the PrepCom, monitor trends in the implementation of the LOS Convention, and provide assistance to developing countries in preparing ocean policies and legislation.

Serving as an important forum for deliberations on LOS issues were the negotiations leading up to the **U.N. Conference on Environment and Development (UNCED)** in Rio de Janeiro, June 3–14. The most divisive issue in UNCED negotiations on oceans was how to protect fish stocks that straddle two different jurisdictions: an Exclusive Economic Zone, with one set of provisions; and the high seas, with another. Whereas some coastal states want to extend their jurisdiction, the better to manage depleting stocks, some nations with high-seas fishing fleets have opposed this idea on the grounds that high-seas resources are held in common. The U.S. proposed that these "**straddling stocks**" be dealt with on a unified regional basis, but the proposal was seen by some states as limiting the jurisdiction of coastal states. Since no agreement was reached at the final negotiating session before the Rio meeting, UNCED was scheduled to consider convening a future U.N. conference to deal with the issue.

Under the LOS Convention, states have the obligation to protect and preserve the marine environment as well as the duty to manage and conserve living marine resources. Agenda 21, the UNCED action plan for promoting sustainable development, recognizes the importance of the Convention, stating that it "provides the international basis upon which to pursue the protection and sustainable development of the marine and coastal environment and its resources" [A/Conf.151/PC/WG.II/L.25/Rev.1]. To deal with **land-based non-point source pollution,** such as agricultural run-off, Agenda 21 calls on UNEP to convene, at the earliest practicable date, an intergovernmental meeting on protecting the marine environment from land-based activities. (See Environment section for further discussion of marine issues on the UNCED agenda.)

5. Antarctica

The ninth year of General Assembly debate on the question of Antarctica once again ended in deadlock over the traditional two-part resolution: While a majority of the Assembly approved the resolution, only one party to the **Antarctic Treaty** (Guatemala) actually participated in the vote on part one [A/Res/46/41A], and only seven in the vote on part two, which simply calls for the exclusion of the "*apartheid* regime" of South Africa from **Antarctic Treaty Consultative Party Meetings (ATCMs)** [A/Res/46/41B]. Germany, speaking on behalf of the parties to the treaty, urged that consideration of the question of Antarctica proceed on the basis of consensus. For years the General Assembly has put its Antarctic resolution to a formal vote rather than seek a compromise resolution to which the treaty parties could agree. Consequently, many parties have refrained from participating in the vote.

A number of developing countries that are not parties to the treaty maintain that the United Nations, and not a gathering of a few dozen signatories, is the most appropriate body for conducting and supervising scientific research in Antarctica, "which must be preserved as the common heritage of all mankind" [statement by Dr. John William Ashe, representative of Antigua and Barbuda to the U.N., 11/26/91]. These countries focused debate on the significance of Antarctica as "mankind's last terrestrial frontier," arguing that the time is ripe for action through the United Nations to promote the natural use and development of marine living resources and to combat

the threats posed by climate change, ozone depletion, and marine pollu-
tion [statement by Kushairi Redzuan, Deputy Permanent Representative of Malaysia to the U.N., 11/
26/91]. Most of the nonsignatories welcomed the new Protocol on Environ-
mental Protection that was signed by Antarctic Treaty parties in Madrid,
calling it a "positive step," but noted that such areas as enforcement,
liability, tourism, and conservation of marine living resources are not
adequately dealt with in the protocol.

Part one of the 46th Session's Antarctic resolution once again
expresses regret that the **Antarctic Treaty Consultative Parties (ATCPs)**
have not invited the Secretary-General or his representative to their
meetings, and requests that the ATCPs deposit information with the
United Nations on "all aspects of Antarctica." Reflecting the views of
the nonsignatories, the resolution acknowledges with appreciation the
signing of the Madrid environmental protocol, but expresses disappointment over the fact that the protocol was not negotiated with the full
participation of the international community and, moreover, lacks monitoring and implementation mechanisms to ensure compliance. The resolution underscores the need for universal participation in negotiating a
convention to establish Antarctica as a nature reserve, or world park, and
advocates reducing the number of scientific stations on the continent
[A/Res/46/41A].

In response to requests by the 45th Session, the Secretary-General
submitted three reports to the 46th. A brief report concerning apartheid
contains Germany's response on behalf of the treaty parties, which
reiterates their call on the General Assembly to seek compromise and
consensus when dealing with the question of Antarctica [A/46/512]. A
second report assesses the feasibility of establishing **a U.N.-sponsored
research station in Antarctica.** The report concludes that, given the
already existing level of international cooperation in Antarctica scientific
research, establishment of such a station "presents a formidable endeavor" and "a complicated exercise" [A/46/583]. The third report concerns
the state of the Antarctic environment and its impact on the global
system. It concludes that increased scientific activities, evidence of an
ozone hole over Antarctica, and speculation about mineral exploitation
have led to increased public concern about "the dangers which human
activities may pose to the Antarctic environment and to the global
system" [A/46/590].

The Secretary-General was asked by the 46th Session of the General
Assembly to prepare three reports for the 47th: an annual report on the
state of the environment in Antarctica; a report evaluating information
and documents deposited with the United Nations by the ATCPs; and a
report on actions taken to exclude the South African regime from
ATCMs. The Secretary-General was also asked to explore the feasibility

of providing Antarctic-related materials through the U.N. Department of Public Information.

Antarctic Treaty membership grew by only one in 1991 with Guatemala's accession to the treaty on July 31 as a Non-Consultative Party (NCP). NCPs are contracting parties that have not sought to qualify themselves as Consultative Parties by "conducting substantial research activity [in Antarctica], such as the establishment of a scientific station or the dispatch of a scientific expedition" [Antarctic Treaty, Article IX, para. 2]. Of the 40 parties to the treaty, 14 are NCPs, which have observer status in ATCMs and cannot vote.

The **XI special ATCM** convened in Madrid from April 22 to 30 and from June 10 to 22, 1991, to hammer out final details of a comprehensive environmental protection agreement for Antarctica. Returning to Madrid on October 4, the ATCPs adopted the **Protocol on Environmental Protection to the Antarctic Treaty** and opened it for signature [Ant. Doc. XI ATSM/2]. Negotiated over three years, this protocol and its annexes constitute the most comprehensive multilateral instrument on the protection of the environment to date. It must await the ratification of all ATCPs before entering into force.

The prospects for adoption had been temporarily dimmed by the United States during the June meeting in Madrid. Washington alone refused to endorse the draft protocol, arguing that in requiring a consensus of the parties to lift the 50-year moratorium on mining, the protocol amounted to a de facto permanent ban on mining [*The New York Times*, 5/23/91]. A new formula requiring only a three-quarters majority proved acceptable to the United States, and on July 3 the Bush administration announced its intention to sign [White House press release, 4/3/91].

The protocol represents a significant shift by the ATCPs away from support for the possible exploitation of minerals in the region and toward support for the preservation of Antarctica as an international conservation zone. Two years after the adoption of the **Convention on the Regulation of Antarctic Mineral Resource Activities (CRAMRA)**, Antarctica has been designated a "natural reserve, devoted to peace and science."

The Madrid protocol establishes fundamental environmental principles for planning and conduct of all activities (except fishing), and establishes a **Committee on Environmental Protection.** This committee is responsible for advising ATCMs and formulating recommendations with regard to the protocol's implementation but has no decision-making authority. All activities are to be subject to environmental-impact assessment procedures.

Article VII of the protocol prohibits all **commercial mining** activities, but subsequent amendment and modification procedures imply that the ban may not be unconditional. The protocol may be modified at any time, provided all ATCPs agree; and after 50 years an amendment proposed at a Review Conference requires the agreement of only three-quarters of the original ATCPs for adoption and three-quarters of all ATCPs for ratification. However, the prohibition on mining cannot be lifted until a legally binding regime has been established to regulate mineral resources.

No mineral deposits of commercial interest have yet been discovered in Antarctica, although there is circumstantial evidence of offshore oil. Even if major discoveries were made, the exorbitant costs of extraction in and transport from this remote, forbidding region means that it could take decades for any venture to become economically feasible.

The protocol includes four annexes that reinforce and more precisely define measures previously adopted by the ATCPs as Antarctic Treaty "recommendations," including those pertaining to conservation of Antarctic flora and fauna, assessments of the environmental impacts of proposed activities, marine pollution control, and waste management and disposal. The obligations contained in the annexes concerning environmental-impact assessments, emergency-response measures, and prohibition of mineral activities are subject to compulsory dispute-settlement procedures, as are the obligations set forth in the protocol itself. Draft annexes relating to **tourism** and to designated protected areas were considered at the XVI regular ATCM in Bonn, October 7–18, 1991.

The protocol stresses Antarctica's **intrinsic wilderness value** and its role in the conduct of **global scientific research.** Its provisions reassert the Antarctic Treaty's call for cooperative activities in scientific research, the sharing of facilities, preparation of environmental-impact assessments, pollution prevention, and environmental protection.

ATCPs made significant progress toward early ratification of the protocol when they gathered in Bonn for the XVI regular ATCM. Negotiations were completed on a new annex regarding a Protected Area System, and it was agreed that, in the future, Consultative Meetings would be held annually. However, no formal arrangements were negotiated for carrying out joint inspections of research stations in Antarctica, nor was serious consideration given to the possible establishment of the Committee on Environmental Protection prior to the ratification of the protocol. Negotiations also failed to establish a secretariat for the Treaty system and liability rules under the protocol.

The XVI ATCM reached agreement on 13 recommendations, ten of which relate to implementing the new annex. The Protected Areas System is divided into two categories: **Antarctic Specially Protected Areas (ASPAs),** which will remain free from human interference; and **Antarctic Specially Managed Areas (ASMAs),** which will provide for multiple-use coordination of activities. Other recommendations deal with exchange of information, accessibility of geophysical data, and the convening of an informal meeting to discuss regulating tourism.

At the tenth annual meeting of the 21-member Commission of the **Convention for Conservation of Antarctic Marine Living Resources (CCAMLR)**, held at its headquarters in Hobart, Tasmania, Australia, from October 21 to November 1, 1991, 15 new conservation measures were adopted, most of which concerned prohibitions on fishing of designated species around **South Georgia Island**. Most significant was the consensus agreement on a management policy for the **krill fishery**. The policy applies the precautionary principle in stating that, in the absence of essential data, very conservative catch limits are warranted. Conservation Measure 32/X places a catch limit of 1.5 million tons of krill around South Georgia in any fishing season. Also noteworthy was the prohibition of **driftnet fishing** within the Convention Area to minimize the incidental mortality of seabirds and other vulnerable species.

6. International Space Year

On December 8, 1989, the General Assembly endorsed the initiative of the international scientific community to designate **1992** as **International Space Year (ISY)**. The year was proposed in 1985 by the U.S. Congress to commemorate the 500th anniversary of Columbus's voyage to the New World and the 35th anniversary of the launching of the first space satellite.

Since the United Nations is only one of many organizations sponsoring ISY activities, the General Assembly outlined two distinctive goals for its own participation: First, ISY should promote international cooperation in space technology, "taking into particular account the needs of developing countries"; second, the **U.N. Programme on Space Applications** should be used as the vehicle for promoting such international cooperation during ISY. The Space Applications program has its own small budget, but there is no money in the regular U.N. budget for ISY, whose activities must be financed by voluntary contributions [A/Res/44/46].

To meet these goals the Department of Political and Security Council Affairs' Outer Space Affairs Division (OSAD—redesignated the Office of Outer Space Affairs in the Secretariat reorganization of 1992) said that the U.N. will focus on three areas: resource management, long-term education, and public education [*The Participation of The United Nations System in International Space Year*, 5/91]. OSAD expressed the hope that these activities would encourage the international community, especially developing countries, "not only to participate in the applications of space technology but also to undertake programmes that could contribute to the understanding, management, and the safeguarding of the global environment, to the solution of local and transnational environmental problems, and to the development of the technology to meet local needs."

In its 1991 report, the General Assembly's **Committee on the Peaceful Uses of Outer Space (COPUOS)** stated that "United Nations ISY activities were being planned to be complementary to the activities of international organizations" and called attention to "the primary focus of ISY activities on the use of space technology for studying and monitoring the global environment" [A/46/20], as recommended by the 45th General Assembly and reiterated by the 46th. The latter also recommended that COPUOS, as well as its Scientific and Technical Subcommittee, dedicate at least one meeting of their annual sessions to ISY [A/Res/46/45].

Following the General Assembly's lead, the Scientific and Technical Subcommittee opened its 29th session with a day-long meeting on February 24, 1992, to commemorate ISY. The special meeting was organized by the Committee on Space Research (COSPAR) of the International Council of Scientific Unions (ICSU) and the International Astronautical Federation (IAF). Among its major speakers was Hubert Curien, Chairman of the **Space Agency Forum for International Space Year (SAFISY)**—the team of 28 space agencies and 8 affiliated organizations that is promoting the unrestricted flow of data amassed via remote sensing and the use of this data for the sustainable development of Earth's resources. The commemorative events included a speech on Space Flight and Global Unification, a panel discussion on Space and the Global Change Program, and a symposium on Space Technology and the Earth's Environment, which touched on such topics as global warming, natural disasters, and the use of satellites in monitoring climate and rain forests [A/AC.105/513].

In its most recent reports on U.N. participation in ISY, COPUOS lists 23 projects, conferences, and exhibitions between September 1991 and the summer of 1993 that the United Nations is cosponsoring with a host of member states, international agencies, and nongovernmental organizations [A/AC.105/445/Adds. 6 and 7].

Activities in the first ISY priority area, **resource management,** kicked off in September 1991, when the United States hosted a month-long training course in South Dakota that focused on the use of space science in gathering and analyzing environmental data. From September 23 to 27, 1991, the Chinese government, the U.N.'s Economic and Social Commission for Asia and the Pacific (ESCAP), the U.N. Disaster Relief Organization (UNDRO), and the U.N. Educational, Scientific and Cultural Organization (UNESCO) held a conference in Beijing on using satellite technology to forecast and control the effects of natural disasters. From October 3 to 5, the government of Canada and the International

Astronautic Federation held a workshop on identifying space technologies that can be utilized by developing countries.

At a March 1992 workshop in Ecuador, cohosted with Japan, Latin American government administrators received instruction on the use of space technology for resource development and environmental management. The German space agency (DARA), the Commission of the European Communities (CEC), and the European Space Agency (ESA) held a similar conference later in the spring [A/AC.105/445/Add.7]. Also on the ISY calendar was a U.S.-hosted 1992 summer conference in Boulder, Colorado, to assess the needs of developing countries in the use of remote sensing technology [A/AC.105/445/Add.6]. The International Society for Photogammetry and Remote Sensing (ISPRS) held a workshop on data analysis in August in Washington, D.C., followed several weeks later by an IAF/COSPAR-sponsored meeting of the World Space Congress.

Among several long-term resource-management projects is one jointly sponsored by France, the U.N. Development Programme (UNDP), and the Indian Ocean Marine Affairs Co-operation Council, which will use space-acquired data to study and protect marine resources in the Indian Ocean region. (Designs were completed in 1991.) At the same time the ESA was assessing project proposals to use its data for development programs in Africa; and the United Nations was awaiting the essays of several authors for a booklet summarizing the world body's various space-related development programs.

ISY activities will continue beyond 1992. Scheduled for 1993 are the Indonesian government's conference on space technology, the ESA's Africa Space Conference, and Greece's international seminar on space communications.

In the second priority area, **long-term education,** the United Nations has cosponsored a series of workshops, conferences, and instructional aids for educators in developing countries. The most ambitious project in this area is the effort by the World Meteorological Organization (WMO), the Food and Agriculture Organization (FAO), and UNESCO to establish **Centres for Space Science and Technology Education.** These centers, which are still in the planning stage, will be organized in existing educational institutions in four regions: Africa, Asia and the Pacific, Latin America and the Caribbean, and Western Asia. In the spring of 1992 educators from developing countries journeyed to Sweden for a month-long training course on incorporating developments in remote sensing technology in their curricula. The United Nations and the International Centre for Theoretical Physics (ICTP) have tentatively arranged a conference on "Bridging the Information Gap in Space Science and Technology", to explore ways of collecting and distributing current literature on space technology in developing countries. (The ICTP recycles some 50,000 science and math books each year, which are donated to educational institutions in 90 countries.)

The ongoing **U.N. Programme on Space Applications** has fulfilled its role as the primary vehicle for long-term education—and more, since its goals are similar to those of the ISY. The Space Applications program, mandated on December 10, 1982, provides a variety of fellowships, workshops, technical advice and training, and space-related information to member states and regional institutions; and seeks to promote greater cooperation among developed and developing countries [A/AC.105/497].

Indeed, many of this program's seminars, workshops, and conferences appear on the ISY calendar of events, while others, seemingly equally pertinent to the theme of ISY, do not. "There is some overlap," said Ralph Chipman, Chief of the Committee Services and Research section of Outer Space Affairs, who noted that the criterion for defining an activity of the Programme on Space Applications as part of the ISY effort was its relation to the ISY themes of remote sensing technology and environmental monitoring. The classification, he admitted, is "somewhat arbitrary." Certainly the effect is to make it difficult to assess the program's actual role in ISY. Chipman points out that with a two-year budget of only $345,900 [A/AC.105/497], the program's activities, whether classified as ISY-related or not, are heavily dependent on voluntary contributions [interview with *A Global Agenda: Issues Before the 47th Session of the General Assembly*].

In an effort to meet the third objective of ISY, **public education,** the United Nations launched a series of seminars, lectures, and publications designed to stimulate interest in outer space among children and the general public. A number of scheduled events have been postponed or canceled for **lack of funds.** Production of seven videos about space technology has been held up, as has a special satellite telecast originally scheduled for June 1992. And an exhibition scheduled to be mounted at U.N. Headquarters was still facing a $1.5 million shortfall just weeks before its scheduled opening in summer 1992.

Finally, despite ISY's emphasis on the environment, it became increasingly clear as the U.N. Conference on Environment and Development approached (June 3–14, 1992) that outer space issues would be slighted on the Conference agenda. "There's very little connection right now," said Chipman a month before UNCED was to open in Rio. "The agenda has been narrowed . . . and questions of technology for monitoring the environment have been virtually ignored" [ibid.].

V

Human Rights and Social Issues

1. Human Rights

In 1993 the United Nations will convene a World Conference on Human Rights, the first such gathering since 1968, when the nations of the world met in Teheran and adopted decisions that shaped the human rights program of the United Nations as they moved from the promotional stage (adoption of standards) to a protectionist stage (implementation of standards). The mandate of the Conference, its scope, and its agenda can be as critical—if not more so—to the shape of the U.N.'s human rights program in the future.

The end of East-West confrontation at the United Nations has not ended the controversy over the activities of the human rights program. On the contrary, the countries most likely to commit human rights violations have continued their efforts to keep the programs small, ineffective, and abstract. And many states continue to oppose the approach of the Western group, which wants to see the implementation mechanisms strengthened. These issues are expected to surface and be sorted out at—or before—the World Conference.

Because the 47th Session of the General Assembly is that body's last opportunity to set the direction of the World Conference, its deliberations on some of the broad issues likely to stir controversy at the Conference will be particularly important. Among these are the role of the thematic rapporteurs and working groups of the Commission on Human Rights, the relationship of human rights and development, and future directions of the human rights program.

The 45th General Assembly authorized the World Conference [A/Res/45/155], which was the idea of former Under-Secretary-General Jan Martenson, who headed the U.N.'s human rights programs until February 1992, when the new Secretary-General appointed Antoine Blanca, the U.N.'s former Director General for International Economic Cooperation, to the post. The Assembly set forth six objectives of the World Conference, which have defined its scope ever since:

1. To review and assess progress in the field of human rights since

the adoption of the Universal Declaration of Human rights, identifying obstacles to progress and the ways in which they can be overcome;

2. To examine the relation between development and the enjoyment by all of economic, social, and cultural rights as well as of civil and political rights, recognizing the importance of creating the conditions that will allow peoples everywhere to enjoy these rights, as set out in the international covenants on human rights;

3. To examine ways and means to improve the implementation of existing human rights standards and instruments;

4. To evaluate the effectiveness of the methods and mechanisms used by the United Nations in the field of human rights;

5. To formulate concrete recommendations for improving the effectiveness of U.N. activities and mechanisms in the field of human rights through programs aimed at promoting, encouraging, and monitoring respect for human rights and fundamental freedoms; and

6. To make recommendations for ensuring the necessary financial and other resources for the U.N. activities that are designed to promote and protect human rights and fundamental freedoms.

The General Assembly's Unique Role

The General Assembly's role in human rights has, by and large, been neglected by scholars and nongovernmental activists, who have tended to concentrate the Commission on Human Rights and its expert Subcommission on Prevention of Discrimination and Protection of Minorities. But as a universal membership body located at the center of the U.N.'s operations, the General Assembly remains in many ways the key to the expansion and success of the U.N.'s activities on behalf of human rights. The General Assembly supervises the human rights programs and is the final arbiter of the standards adopted, issues addressed, and the proportion and kind of administrative and budgetary resources that will be devoted to the U.N. human rights machinery. This is nowhere more visible than in the six objectives set forth for the World Conference.

The General Assembly often approves decisions made by subsidiary human rights bodies, but it also often instructs those bodies on how to address new problems or resolves highly controversial issues—structural, political, and substantive. Meeting just six weeks before the Commission on Human Rights holds its session, the General Assembly is often the place for political negotiations on the controversial elements of country resolutions that the Commission later adopts.

The General Assembly's unique capacity to explore linkages between human rights and other major issues, such as development or women's rights, gives it a unique coordinating role in New York, at the center of U.N. activities. Divergent views about the shape of the 1993 World

Conference on Human Rights, the monitoring of free elections, the priority attached to violations-focused mechanisms, the activity of non-governmental organizations in the U.N.'s human rights work, and the "right to development" are but a few of the topics that have been sorted out in the General Assembly in recent years.

The U.N. Human Rights Machinery

The 53-member Commission on Human Rights, composed of government representatives, has established a variety of implementational mechanisms. "Working Groups" that engage in drafting standards are currently preparing draft declarations on disappearances, on the rights of members of minority groups, and on human rights defenders. One Working Group (discussed later) examines situations of gross violations processed through the so-called "1503" confidential procedure.

But the most innovative creations of the Commission are the "special procedures"—the thematic and country mechanisms called, variously, "working groups" and "special rapporteurs"—set up for one, two, or three years, to investigate and take effective action both on human rights problems worldwide and on situations in particular countries. As of mid-1992, five such special mechanisms examined and often took emergency action on individual cases falling into their mandated "thematic issue"—the working groups on (a) enforced or involuntary disappearances and (b) arbitrary detention; and the special rapporteurs on (c) summary or arbitrary executions, (d) torture, and (e) religious intolerance. Two other "thematic rapporteurs" address the problems of mercenaries and the sale of children but do not intercede in individual cases as the other five do. Meanwhile special rapporteurs (or "representatives" or "experts") have been appointed to report to the Commission on human rights situations—and violations—in Afghanistan, Cuba, El Salvador, Iran, Iraq, Myanmar (Burma), Haiti, and Equatorial Guinea. Of these, several will present interim reports to the Assembly in 1992. Afghanistan, El Salvador, and Iran (absent in 1991), and Iraq are returnees; all the others (save Equatorial Guinea, which reports only to the Commission) will come before the Assembly for the first time. Additionally, a Working Group established in 1967 continues to study and report on South Africa. One of the important distinctions made by the Commission is that those who serve on these "special procedures" are appointed in their individual capacity as experts, not as government representatives.

Other working groups and rapporteurs add to the U.N.'s human rights work, but they are the creations of the **Subcommission on Prevention of Discrimination and Protection of Minorities ("the Subcommission")**. At the end of its 1991 session the Subcommission had working groups on complaints concerning consistent patterns of gross violations of human rights (where the screening of the "1503" confidential communications on human rights violations begin), on contemporary forms of slavery, on indigenous populations, on detention, and on the methods of work of the Subcommission. It also had 19 special studies or reports in progress, conducted by its members or former members, who are often called "special rapporteurs," although their role is rather different from that of their namesakes at the Commission. Five of these reports address discrimination of minorities; two of the studies and a drafting initiative are focused on indigenous peoples, another study focuses on peaceful solutions of minority problems, and yet another on discrimination against persons infected with the HIV virus. The other topics reveal the breadth of subjects covered at the Subcommission: annual reports on (a) banks doing business with South Africa, and (b) countries that have proclaimed states of emergency; studies on the impunity of perpetrators of violations of human rights and on a victim's right to restitution; examinations of freedom of expression, the right to a fair trial, the independence of the judiciary, and the detention of U.N. staff members, as well as of such subjects as human rights and youth, detained juveniles, traditional health practices harmful to women, the realization of economic and social rights, the right to adequate housing, and human rights and the environment.

In addition to the political bodies cited above, each of the U.N.'s six principal human rights treaties now establishes an independent supervisory committee composed of expert members who monitor compliance. (There is no supervisory mechanism for the **Genocide Convention,** and the **Convention on Migrant Workers** has yet to come into force.) The treaty bodies include:

- International Covenant on Civil and Political Rights: Human Rights Committee (18 members).
- International Covenant on Economic, Social and Cultural Rights: Committee on Economic, Social and Cultural Rights (18 members).
- International Convention on the Elimination of All Forms of Racial Discrimination: Committee on the Elimination of All Forms of Racial Discrimination ("CERD"—18 members).
- Convention against Torture and Other Cruel, Inhuman or Degrading Treatment or Punishment: Committee against Torture ("CAT"—10 members).
- Convention on the Rights of the Child: Committee on the Rights of the Child ("CRC"—10 members).
- Convention on the Elimination of All Forms of Discrimination against Women: Committee on the Elimination of All Forms of Discrimination against Women ("CEDAW"—23 members).

These committees examine reports officially submitted by the countries that are party to the treaties, and may make general comments or recommendations about the treaty. They report annually to the General Assembly, although all but the Economic and Social Rights Committee are technically independent bodies set up by the treaties and thus independent of the U.N. Charter. But because the treaties are dependent on the U.N. for logistical support and personnel, they are generally regarded as bodies functioning within the general framework of the U.N. system. The Economic and Social Rights Committee is a subsidiary body of ECOSOC.

The controversy over the World Conference, which had already held two preparatory meetings by the time ECOSOC met in July 1992, focused largely on the agenda and priorities attached to the different subjects. The Western group, now joined by the Eastern group countries, has emphasized the need to focus precisely on the strengthening of the rapporteurs, special mechanisms, and treaty committees, and to assure their proper financing. But a groundswell of concern from the Group of 77 (G-77) developing countries focuses on the issue of development—and on the right to development. At the core of all this is whether the programs will indeed be strengthened or emasculated.

Disappearances

The 47th General Assembly will again address the phenomenon of "disappearances" when it considers whether to approve the **draft Declaration on Enforced or Involuntary Disappearances** that has now been completed and endorsed by the Commission on Human Rights [E/CN.4/ 1992/19/Rev.1]. At the same time, it will consider the Report of the Commission's **Working Group on Disappearances** [E/CN.4/1992/18 and Corr.1 and Add.1].

The Working Group was the first of the U.N. specialized "theme mechanisms" set up by the Commission on Human Rights in 1980, and the first to begin to intervene with governments for information on behalf of individual victims and their families.

Disappearances occur when individuals are seized, often by persons in plainclothes and either in government service or protected by government agencies, and never seen or heard from again. The government denies any knowledge of the individuals or any responsibility for their whereabouts. The practice eliminates victims, terrorizes and causes anguish among family and friends, renders the government unaccountable, and flouts all international guarantees of personal liberty and due process.

In 1991 the General Assembly again expressed its concern about the practice of forced or involuntary disappearances [A/Res/46/125]. It welcomed completion of the draft declaration and encouraged the Commission on Human Rights to transmit it promptly, as was done. As before, the

General Assembly expressed anguish at the suffering of the families of the disappeared. The Working Group has been particularly concerned about reports of intimidation of relatives of the disappeared who contact the Working Group, and in 1990 it instituted a new **"prompt intervention"** procedure to help defend them. In its current report, however, the Working Group expresses concern that this procedure is not being utilized effectively and encourages greater attentiveness to it.

Pursuing a strictly "non-accusatory approach," focused on finding out what happened to the victim rather than placing blame on governments or specific officials, the Working Group has examined disappearances throughout the world. In its 12 years it has asked some 45 governments to explain more than 25,000 cases of disappearances. In 1991 the Group reported taking action on 4,800 out of a total of 17,000 case submissions it received (almost as many as it had addressed in its entire history—and certainly up from 1990, when it had taken action on 987 of 3,864 cases received). Of the 1991 cases, 3,841 are attributable to Sri Lanka, which now holds the dubious distinction of being the state with the largest number of disappearances considered by the Working Group.

In 1991, three members of the Group traveled to Sri Lanka to undertake consultations and investigations regarding disappearances. In their report [E/CN.4/1992/18/Add.1] they provide details on the conflicts in the country that have led to the deterioration in human rights and the increase in disappearances, on the legal and judicial systems (including problems with habeas corpus), and on the meetings they had with government officials as well as with representatives of nongovernmental organizations and with relatives of victims. They noted that government policy not to ask questions or prosecute armed forces fighting the insurgency has encouraged a climate of impunity. The Group's conclusions and recommendations to the government seem almost benign in comparison to the enormity of the disappearance horrors facing the country. The Commission debate on this topic, like the debates the Working Group has criticized in past years, all but ignored the report. If Sweden called for a follow-up visit to Sri Lanka, Britain, expressing concern over the "appalling" violations, nonetheless spoke of the "commendable efforts" of the government "to rectify abuses of the past." Other countries to which the Group has been invited include El Salvador and Ecuador.

The Group has previously explained that while only 7–8 percent of all disappearance cases it has adopted have been formally clarified, the rate rises to 25 percent when it comes to cases submitted promptly and taken up within three months of the actual "disappearance." Yet it reports that, like its new "prompt intervention" procedure, its regular **"urgent action"** procedure is not being used enough at present.

Of the 1991 caseload, the countries with the largest number of new reported disappearances after Sri Lanka were:

Iraq (370 cases, of which 142 occurred in 1991).
Peru (154 new cases, of which 117 occurred in 1991).
Morocco (115 new cases, of which 101 occurred in 1991).
Indonesia (111 new cases, of which 27 occurred in 1991).

It is interesting to note the sharp decline in reported cases of disappearances in several other countries that previously had widespread disappearances, including two (Colombia and Philippines) visited by the group:

Iran (40 new cases, of which 2 occurred in 1991, compared to 58/7 in 1990).
Guatemala (33 new cases, of which 30 occurred in 1991, compared to 86/74 in 1990).
El Salvador (46 new cases, of which 30 occurred in 1991, compared to 24/7 in 1990).
Colombia (25 new cases, of which 20 occurred in 1991, compared to 108/82 in 1990).
The Philippines (9 new cases, of which 5 occurred in 1991, compared to 54/43 in 1990).

Despite these statistics, the Group has made vigorous efforts to draw attention to the shortage of resources devoted to its work and the work of the entire "special procedures" section, which coordinates activities for all of the thematic and country-specific rapporteurs and working groups. It has highlighted the thousands of cases it would not act upon because of staff resource limitations to date.

The Group, which previously stated that it plans to pursue the results of its visits more effectively, reported that a number of its specific recommendations following missions to the countries recently have been put into effect, citing among those doing so the Philippines, Peru, and Colombia.

The Working Group had endorsed the draft declaration on disappearances, which defines and would specifically outlaw the practice. In the past the Group has been the U.N. agency most openly critical of government efforts to grant impunity to perpetrators of disappearances. Now it reports that it has begun an effort to solicit ideas and recommendations on this subject from nongovernmental organizations with which it works.

Religious Intolerance

The General Assembly will again consider measures to end religious intolerance, a matter examined by another "thematic" rapporteur, Angelo Vidal d'Almeida Ribeiro of Portugal. The **Special Rapporteur on Religious Intolerance** was established in 1985 by the Commission on Human Rights, and his mandate has been extended since then by consensus. The Rapporteur's reports address individual country situations and contain excerpts from his correspondence with them and their replies, if any.

In his latest report [E/CN.4/1992/52] Ribeiro provides information on his correspondence with 25 governments in 1991 regarding allegations of religious discrimination or intolerance "inconsistent with the provisions of the Declaration" that have reached him. A total of 13 governments replied—10 for 1991 inquiries and 3 for earlier ones, making his response rate higher than that of other "thematic rapporteurs." Wherever relevant, the Rapporteur presents the government's reply verbatim and without comment.

Among the countries (and religious minorities) cited in the Rapporteur's 1992 report are:

- China, for persecuting Tibetan monks and nuns as well as arrests of Catholic clergy.
- Cuba, for denying prisoners religious literature.
- Egypt, for actions against Coptic Christians, including imprisonment and torture of persons involved in conversions from Islam to Christianity, and measures against their churches and associations.
- Iran, for discrimination against Baha'is as well as against Zoroastrians and Assyrians.
- Iraq, in the longest country-specific section in this (or any other) Rapporteur's report, for actions against the Shi'a religious community, including persecution and killing of religious leaders and scholars, systematic destruction of religious educational institutions, destruction or damage to numerous holy shrines and mosques, etc. (Allegations of more than 20,000 killings are noted. Pages of names are followed by an Iraqi reply, which is followed by additional pages of names of alleged victims of incidents.)
- Pakistan, for persecution of Ahmadis, including killings, destruction of villages, closing of newspapers, etc.
- Saudi Arabia, for discrimination against non-Islamic persons and measures against Shi'a Muslims.
- Sudan, for reports that apostasy from Islam is punishable by death sentence.
- Syria, for discrimination against its Jewish communities, whose

members are forbidden to travel, emigrate, and vote, and who suffer other restrictions.
- United States, for an Oregon case in which two drug rehabilitation counselors, members of the Native American Church, were dismissed and denied unemployment compensation because they had taken peyote, a hallucinogenic substance, in a religious ceremony.

In the past, the Rapporteur has noted that infringement of religious freedoms usually results in infringements of other human rights, including extrajudicial killings in clashes with other religious groups or even with government security forces, and infringement of the rights to physical integrity and freedom of movement and expression.

This year Mr. Ribeiro continues his report and analysis of another 25 replies to a questionnaire he has circulated to governments. His total respondents to date number 60. He inquired systematically about distinctions in national legislation concerning religious groups, treatment of believers and nonbelievers, and measures that might protect religious minorities; about reciprocity for foreigners, conscientious objection, clashes between religious groups; and about action against expressions of "extremist or fanatical" opinions related to religious groups, as well as remedies and conciliation mechanisms.

The Rapporteur's 15-page analysis of the replies (about which the Irish delegation at the Commission on Human Rights—long the leading sponsor of the United Nations' religious resolutions—offered the gentle criticism that a more systematic analysis is still needed) noted that many countries' replies were so brief as to prevent a "conclusive insight" into the government's position on a given topic. Most countries failed to distinguish specific distinctions between religions, religious sects, and religious associations. The Rapporteur noted that only Western countries referred to the "negative freedom" of holding no religious belief, and he expressed his opinion that the rights of nonbelievers should be guaranteed. He discussed the problems of discrimination against minorities *within* a religion, and of minority religious groups in a country with a majority or state religion.

Like the other theme rapporteurs, Mr. Ribeiro does not comment on the replies, nor offer country-specific recommendations for alleviating infringements of religious freedoms. Still, he has previously characterized his inquiries as situations "which seemed to involve a departure from the provisions of the Declaration," and has found that such government actions "have persistently occurred in most regions of the world." Where positive results have been seen, as in East and Central Europe and the former republics of the USSR, he welcomes and praises the progress. But the Rapporteur addresses some of the most sensitive issues for many societies—discrimination against religious groups and, often, against minorities—and trains the spotlight of international scrutiny on them.

By consensus, the 46th General Assembly largely reiterated its concerns on religious intolerance of the past several years [A/Res/46/136]. It supported efforts to continue a wide array of promotional measures to implement the Declaration on the Elimination of All Forms of Intolerance based on Religion or Belief, the principal instrument in this area.

In his report, the Rapporteur again endorses the idea of moving toward a binding instrument on religious tolerance. Both the General Assembly and the Commission, however, have continued to reply with caution to proposals about drafting a new binding instrument on religion, although a number on nongovernmental organizations remain enthusiastic in support of the idea. The main point of governmental reluctance continues to be the worry that any new convention will further erode the standards stated in the Declaration on Religious Intolerance and other instruments.

Working Group on Arbitrary Detention

A new, regionally balanced **"Working Group"** of five experts was established in 1991 by the Commission on Human Rights to study and take action in instances of **arbitrary detention** [Res. 1991/42]. This new mechanism, which held two meetings in 1991, can be said to complete the U.N. Commission's coverage of major human rights violations now addressed by "thematic mechanisms."

Observers have looked to the new Working Group to take action on the cases of political prisoners (or "prisoners of conscience") worldwide, and to intervene on behalf of the United Nations to assure that these prisoners' detention and trial is based on international standards of due process and humane treatment or that they are released. The fact that this mechanism will be worldwide in its coverage adds an important dimension to the work of the United Nations in actually trying to put an end to egregious rights abuses.

The new Working Group got off to a speedy start, adopting its methods of work, principles applicable to its examination of alleged arbitrary detentions, and a questionnaire for complainants to submit. Its first report [E/CN.4/1992/20] lists some 235 cases in 22 countries on which it transmitted information to governments between its initial meetings in October and December 1991.

The Working Group's initial report on its activities is not very transparent as to the cases adopted. It describes its actions chronologically and presents only the names of persons whose cases were reported back *by governments* with the indication that the individual had been released or the case otherwise decided. The countries approached were

Bhutan (6 cases), China (20), Cuba (64), Egypt (1), Iran (9), Israel (2), Republic of Korea (1), Laos (2), Libya (9), Malawi (3), Morocco (24), Myanmar (3), Peru (1), Saudi Arabia (1), Sudan (18), Syria (60), Tanzania (2), Tunisia (2), Turkey (2), Uganda (1), Chile (3), and Mexico (1). According to the report, eight countries have already sent replies to the Working Group—a remarkably high response rate in a mere three months of operation. The Group was told that a number of the persons cited had been amnestied or otherwise released. Once a person is released, for whatever reason, the Group drops the case—and presumably drops its interest in whether or not the detention was "arbitrary."

However, the legal principles set forth by the group as the criteria by which it judges its work are well thought out and fairly rigorous. In presenting them, and a questionnaire for complaints, the Group's report is considerably more transparent and precise than was the report of the Disappearances Working Group in its early years, or are the reports of other thematic mechanisms even today.

At the Commission on Human Rights, the Chairman/Rapporteur of the Working Group, Louis Joinet of France, drew attention to the Group's major difference from similar mechanisms: For the others, the violations addressed are prohibited in all circumstances. This is not the case for detentions per se, and therefore the Group's challenge is not in verifying the detention itself but in determining *whether or not it is legal*. Second, the Group has been tasked to *investigate* cases, whereas other mechanisms are only to study various questions. Third, the Group is called upon to examine whether national legislation is compatible with international instruments in this area.

Most governments spoke positively of the Group at the Commission on Human Rights, although it remains to be seen how this new thematic mechanism will be received at the next General Assembly session by those to whom it sends large numbers of allegations.

Summary and Arbitrary Executions

In 1992, S. Amos Wako of Kenya, the U.N. **Special Rapporteur on Summary or Arbitrary Executions** for ten years, announced his resignation from that key post, since he was now Attorney General of his own country. As the second major "thematic mechanism" established by the U.N. Commission on Human Rights in 1982, the Special Rapporteur's annual reports has addressed ways to combat summary and arbitrary executions but has also detailed numerous cases he raised with governments.

These submissions of Mr. Wako's have shown special concern about massive killings—both those conducted by governments and those by death squads operating outside the law. Governmental use of the death penalty against political opponents was reported in thousands of cases, ignoring national laws that grant the accused due process rights to a lawyer or to an appeal.

Since 1982, the Commission, the General Assembly, and Mr. Wako have expanded the scope of the Rapporteur's concern. His mandate has grown from a scholarly focus on *actual* deaths to an activist effort to do something about *imminent* deaths. He inquires about death penalty cases without legal safeguards, and about suspicious deaths at the hands of governments or their agents.

In his latest report [E/CN.4/1992/30 and Add. 1] Mr. Wako reviews the first decade of the Rapporteur's activities. He discusses his mandate and its growth, citing his own techniques and the responses of governments, and notes that, during ten years in office, he had addressed letters or appeals to over 100 states. He recalls that he had identified the following practices as falling within his mandate: death threats, deaths in custody, executions following inadequate trial or judicial procedures, and extralegal executions in situations of armed conflict. A key area of his concern continues to be deaths as a result of torture; abuse of force by police, military, or other government institutions; and assault by individuals or paramilitary groups acting with official collusion or connivance as well as by bodies that oppose the government or are outside its control.

In earlier reports Mr. Wako stated that summary and arbitrary executions have occurred in all world regions. What they had in common, he told the Commission on Human Rights in his last appearance, was the "opposition, or perceived opposition, of the victims to those who wielded political or economic power." He also mentioned the increased occurrence of summary and arbitrary executions in internal conflicts, and he noted that the violation of human rights was often a warning signal that summary or arbitrary executions could occur if the problems were not remedied [E/CN.4/1992/SR. 33].

Most of Mr. Wako's 1992 report consists of specific documentation, including names and dates, about cases he has raised with governments and the replies, if any. Over the years, and particularly in the last two years, Mr. Wako saw the number of cases reported to him grow dramatically, because, he speculates, his mandate was better known worldwide. In fact, only a fraction of these incoming cases ended in cables or letters from the Rapporteur, but that fraction had increased in recent years. In his report he notes that "most of the allegations concerning summary or arbitrary executions and death threats . . . are presented by nongovernmental organizations" but that "some governments" have presented allegations of executions, attributing these to opposing forces [para. 622].

In 1991, Mr. Wako contacted a total of 65 governments—about 174 communications, both "urgent" and regular. This was up from the 49 contacted in 1990, and up even more dramatically from the 9 contacted in 1982. During the last year of his mandate, Mr. Wako reports that the number of urgent appeals alone nearly doubled, reaching 125 in 1991. These were addressed to 44 countries (compared to 9 countries in 1982) and concerned 345 identified cases [E/CN.4/1992/30, para. 616]. Later, he says that in 1991 he sent still other requests to 49 governments, for information about 4,200 specific cases of death threats [para. 624].

As in the past, the Rapporteur draws attention to governments that "systematically fail to reply" to his communications, listing Chad, Haiti, Libya, Pakistan (since 1989), Somalia, South Africa, Thailand, Uganda, and Zaire [para. 636]. And, as in the past, if many of the governments contacted by the Rapporteur are often mentioned in U.N. human rights bodies, some are rarely discussed in such forums. Among the situations cited in the 1992 report were:

- **Algeria,** concerning death sentences for economic crimes.
- **Argentina,** concerning death threats.
- **Brazil,** concerning death threats.
- **China,** concerning imminent executions.
- **Colombia,** concerning killings of political, union, peasant, and indigenous leaders, among others, some carried out by paramilitary groups.
- **Cuba,** concerning deaths in custody or at the hands of police officers.
- **Guatemala,** concerning executions of members of trade unions, political opposition groups, and organizations representing indigenous peoples, as well as of human rights activists, peasants, students, academics, and street children.
- **India,** concerning 401 cases of alleged executions by armed forces in Jammu and Kashmir, Punjab, and Uttar Pradesh.
- **Iraq,** concerning killings of Kurds and Shiites.
- **Paraguay,** concerning death threats in connection with judicial inquiries into previous violations of human rights.
- **Peru,** concerning death threats, summary executions, and human rights abuses and the impunity of the perpetrators of these acts.
- **Sudan,** concerning summary trials and legal proceedings as well as killings of civilians in connection with the internal conflict.
- **Soviet Union,** concerning killings in Lithuania and in Tbilisi, Georgia.
- **Yugoslavia,** concerning clashes with demonstrators in Belgrade and killings of civilians in civil war.

Governments responses vary from silence to denial of the event itself (or denial that the execution in question was summary or arbitrary) to counter-accusations against the victims. There are also promises to investigate and punish those responsible or to supply information on investigations in progress. (Mr. Wako drew attention to the U.N.'s need to "increase both the material and human resources" of the Centre for Human Rights in Geneva.) Alike with other thematic mechanisms, little or no information is presented in the reports on follow-up measures once a government has replied. The Rapporteur does not evaluate or comment upon the government responses.

As before, the Rapporteur stresses the importance of missions, or **on-site visits,** calling these "the most effective method available to the Special Rapporteur for evaluating the veracity of allegations received" and for understanding the context as well. He has made visits to Suriname (1984, 1986, and 1989), Uganda (1986), Colombia (1989), and Zaire (1991). He reports having received recent invitations from Peru and Sri Lanka, and thanks all these countries.

In 1992, Mr. Wako released a report on his May 1991 **mission to Zaire,** which dwarfs in size and sophistication all previous mission reports by the Rapporteur and his colleagues. Amounting to 101 pages, it presents a legal justification of the Rapporteur's mandate in Zaire; a historical overview of the country's situation, details of events on the campus of the University of Lubumbashi in connection with the "so-called massacre," and an analysis of these details and of inquiries into the case; and it goes on to offer specific conclusions and recommendations. Wako concludes that he has "strong reason to believe that the Government of Zaire ordered or authorized the operation of two attack groups on the University of Lubumbashi" on May 11–12, 1990, and that "the disposition reached in the judgement" of the Supreme Court of Zaire did not fully discharge the obligation of the government under international human rights standards.

When the 45th General Assembly discussed the report of Mr. Wako back in 1990, it adopted a resolution that "strongly condemns" the practice of summary and arbitrary executions, "appeals urgently" for effective action to combat them, and asks the Rapporteur to respond effectively to information presented to him [A/Res/45/162]. Despite the importance of the subject matter and the strong language used, the 46th General Assembly did not discuss the report directly, having decided that it would consider the topic only in even years.

As before, the debate at the 48th Commission on Human Rights in 1992 touched only cursorily on the Rapporteur's work. Because it falls under the extensive "gross violations" item along with the reports of country rapporteurs and numerous emergent crises, there is little sustained attention to the Rapporteur's findings or recommendations. Over the years, the Commission has offered little or no guidance in its debate or its resolutions on the questions the Rapporteur has posed about the scope of his work. Among the reasons for this is the lack of time devoted to discussion of the Rapporteur's report and mandate. The 48th Commission on Human Rights' Resolution 72 extended the mandate of the Special Rapporteur by three years, called for the appointment of "an individual of recognized international standing" to succeed Mr. Wako, and requested the Special Rapporteur to pay "special attention to executions of children" in the next report.

To improve the effectiveness of the Rapporteur's work, some nongovernmental organizations have drawn attention to the need for country-specific recommendations and follow-up. More sustained interaction with the governments in question, and regular and more routine follow-up, could help. To date, governments have done nothing to support the Rapporteur's request for support in establishing some form of sanction against governments that fail repeatedly to respond to his requests. Commission and General Assembly encouragement of "cooperation" by governments has only a limited impact.

Torture

The U.N.'s efforts to prevent human rights violations have focused heavily on eradicating torture. Another thematic mechanism of the Commission on Human Rights is the **Special Rapporteur on Torture**, who examines the phenomenon of torture, takes action on emergency reports of torture cases worldwide, and examines the current situation and prevention of torture in other countries, visiting some upon their request.

As part of the rationalized plan for the agenda of the Third Committee of the 47th General Assembly, reports will be received from the **Committee against Torture (CAT)**, a treaty body that monitors compliance with the **Convention against Torture**, and the Assembly will also review the status of the low-key **Voluntary Fund for Victims of Torture**. However, as in the past, the 46th General Assembly did not consider the highly regarded work of the **Special Rapporteur on Torture** in its resolutions, in contrast to its past endorsement of other major "thematic mechanisms" and core issues addressed at the Commission. This may prove to be a dangerous omission, if storm signals that arose in the Commission on Human Rights in February 1991 continue to grow. Concern about torture has long been at the center of international efforts, including those of the General Assembly, to protect human rights. Fatigue at so many resolutions coming before the General Assembly is at best an unsatisfactory reason for giving the Commission on Human Rights exclusive jurisdiction over the subject. (The 46th General Assembly did adopt a pro forma resolution urging governments to contribute to the Voluntary Fund [A/46/110].)

The Special Rapporteur on Torture, Professor Peter Kooijmans of the Netherlands, intervenes in an attempt to stop instances of torture and asks governments to clarify other detailed allegations concerning torture; since 1984 he has recommended an array of international and national measures that would diminish the practice of torture. The Special Rapporteur noted that he continued to receive "an alarming number" of allegations of cases of torture worldwide during 1991. His annual report to the Commission on Human Rights [E/CN.4/1992/17] amounted to 107 pages, mostly detailing specific case allegations and his correspondence with governments about them, plus his follow-up measures on past visits to countries, conclusions, and recommendations. A 21-page supplement [E/CN.4/1992/17] discusses his November 1991 trip to Indonesia and East Timor (see below).

The Rapporteur's 1991 report describes his 64 urgent communications in 1991 on 287 individual cases to 31 countries, among them China, Cuba, Egypt, Greece, Kenya, the Philippines, Sudan, Tunisia, Turkey, the Soviet Union (regarding Azerbaijani treatment of Armenian detainees], and Zaire. Of the full group, 16 countries—about half—replied. According to the Under-Secretary for Human Rights, Jan Martenson, replies were received concerning 30 percent of the cases that actually occurred in 1991.

The Rapporteur's 1991 report also describes a total of 65 countries, up from 52 in 1990 and 48 in 1989, with whom the Rapporteur conducted correspondence about individual cases and situations involving torture, details of which are noted in the text. A country will be listed whether it received one allegation (as in the case of India and Togo) or 97 (El Salvador); whether a single paragraph is devoted to it (United Kingdom and Malaysia) or 12 pages (as occurred this year for Turkey, which received 14 urgent appeals along with other letters from Professor Kooijmans). Professor Kooijmans reveals that 39 of the countries with which he conducted "correspondence" had replied in some form by publication date, which continues an upward trend in replies. But responses are sometimes vacuous, simply asserting that the allegations are baseless or "sheer nonsense." Sometimes the replies are unintentionally revealing, as in the 1990 Saudi Arabian response to the Rapporteur's charges that a number of persons had their hands and arms amputated as a punishment. The Saudi government stated that no sentence had ever been issued to amputate an arm: "only the hand is amputated if the accusation is proved and following a confession. . . ." Or in 1991, when Israel explained that the charges that a prisoner had been "beaten with clubs all over his body" were disproven by medical doctors, who found only two bruises; and that those who inflicted them were being sought but could not be identified "owing to the number of policemen who were involved in different stages of this case."

Few governments provide details of any investigations that occur, and few undertake independent inquiries. In the past, the Rapporteur has suggested that details be provided in replies. This year he again encourages countries to invite him to examine the charges in person, and he notes that no country has yet taken up his suggestion.

Professor Kooijmans notes the lack of follow-up correspondence to his earlier on-site recommendations to the governments of Peru and Honduras, but he welcomed information from Turkey and the Philippines, which he visited in 1990, and from Guatemala after the report was completed. The Rapporteur reiterates that the primary purpose of his visits are consultative and preventative—not accusatory or investigative. He welcomed an invitation from Djibouti.

At the conclusion of his report, the Rapporteur reminds the Commission on Human Rights that torture is "the most intimate of human rights violations," normally taking place in isolation and with the torturer deliberately anonymous, as the victim is often hooded or blindfolded. He stresses the important role of the judicial branch of government as "the last bastion for the protection of the citizen's basic rights" in upholding the prohibition against torture. Regretting judicial lack of awareness of the role it can play, he emphasizes the importance of judicial control and supervision of detainees, and the key role of immediate access to legal counsel. Stressing preventive measures, as he has in the past, he draws special attention to the on-site investigative visits to detention facilities by the independent experts of the **European Committee for the Prevention of Torture**. He reminds governments that "they cannot leave the fight against torture to the treaty-based bodies" and must continuously "hold accountable" governments that permit torture to occur. He even includes the uncharacteristically undiplomatic suggestion (in a U.N. document) that third parties can exert "diplomatic pressure," among other means.

At the 1991 Commission on Human Rights a revised version of the 1980 Costa Rican proposal for an optional protocol to the Torture Convention [E/CN.4/1991/66] to permit periodic "preventive" visits to detention centers was tabled and discussed by a number of governments. Although it became a separate agenda item in 1992, the Commission nonetheless stressed the "importance of instituting" such a system of visits in its resolution on the Torture Rapporteur's report [1992/32]. In addition, in Commission resolution 1992/43, it decided to establish a two-week intersessional Working Group to develop an optional protocol based on the Costa Rican draft, and to consider the experiences of similar systems by other international or regional bodies. If the General Assembly chooses to adopt a resolution on the Torture Convention in 1992 that addresses anything other than its financial structure, it would be important to add support for the effort to establish the system of visits through the optional protocol.

Among the Rapporteur's other recommendations on ending torture "stressed" in the Commission's 1992 resolution are the need for the judiciary to "play an active role" in guaranteeing rights to detainees, the need to provide detainees with "prompt" access to a lawyer and to ensure the right to initiate proceedings on the lawfulness of his detention, as well as the need for measures to outlaw incommunicado detention; to conduct interrogations only at official interrogation centers (where names of interrogators are recorded and blindfolding and hooding are forbidden); to establish national ombudsman-type authorities or human rights commissions with investigative or prosecutory powers to examine complaints of torture independently; to take "strict measures" against medical professionals who collaborate in torture; and, whenever complaints of torture are found to be justified, to see to it that "the perpetrators should be severely punished, especially the official in charge of the place of detention where the torture" took place.

As before, the Commission emphasizes the importance of training programs for law enforcement personnel and the need to utilize U.N. advisory services programs to educate and improve behavior by police and law enforcement and other officials.

East Timor. Professor Kooijmans sums up his findings on his two-week visit to East Timor and Indonesia by stating that he "cannot avoid the conclusion that torture occurs in Indonesia" [E/CN,4/1992/17, Add.1, para. 73]. Nonetheless, he also states that "Basic human rights, including the right to physical and mental integrity, are guaranteed by the Indonesian State philosophy and legislation. Whether these basic rights are actually respected however, seems questionable, in particular in those areas where there is civil unrest" [ibid., para.78]. As he has done during other visits, Professor Kooijmans presents a list of recommendations to the government: calling for accession to international human rights treaties; urging efforts to bring about greater awareness in the judiciary of their role in enforcing protections of human rights of citizens; suggesting that the independent Attorney General's office and the judiciary supervise the legality of arrests and the regularity of criminal investigating procedures; calling for the repeal of the Anti-Subversion Law, which lacks clarity and is duplicative of other legal provisions; urging establishment of a national commission on human rights and an authority with independent investigative powers to which human rights victims can file complaints and of a system for preventive visits to detention centers and punishment of officials found guilty of committing or condoning torture; and giving jurisdiction over offenses committed by military officials to the civilian courts. Commenting on this report to the Commission, the Indonesian government's representative suggested that Kooijmans was unfamiliar with existing complaint mechanisms in Indonesia, noted that Indonesia was cooperating with the **Secretary-General's Personal Envoy**, Amos Wako, himself the Special Rapporteur on Summary and Arbitrary Executions, sent to study the November 1991 incident, and expressed his government's view that it was unacceptable that the Rapporteur's report was commented upon on Dutch radio *before* it had even been made available in Geneva [E/CN.4/1992/SR.25]. He criticized the Rapporteur for discussing freedom of expression and other human rights topics in Indonesia in his report, as these were, he charged, outside the Rapporteur's mandate.

The Special Rapporteur was actually in East Timor on November 12 when security troops opened fire on a crowd marching to a cemetery where one of the victims of a prior incident was buried, killing anywhere from the official 19 to unofficial estimates of 50–60 persons and wounding many others. The Rapporteur, who was not an eyewitness to the Dili incident, expressed his "astonishment and disappointment" that the Timorese authorities did not promptly inform him of the incident. Once he learned of it, he appealed for all those detained to be treated humanely, and asked Indonesian authorities to permit international observers to participate in the investigation of the incident. This was opposed on the grounds it constituted "interference in the internal affairs" of Indonesia. As he was about to leave East Timor as scheduled on November 13, 1991, he was refused permission to visit the hospital where the wounded were being treated, on the grounds that it would be misinterpreted as U.N. "endorsement of anti-government" forces and could lead to more rioting.

The Dili massacre—and the fact that the incident took place while the U.N. Rapporteur was present—seemed to crystallize international criticism of the human rights situation in East Timor for the first time. Portugal and a number of its former dependencies began commenting on the situation at the 46th General Assembly. Even though the Subcommission has asked the 1991 Commission to examine gross violations on the island occupied by Indonesian forces since 1975, it had taken no action. But now, in 1992, the situation was different. Not only had the Dili massacre occurred, but Portugal was in the rare position of holding the presidency of the European Community as well as membership on the Commission on Human Rights. As a result, a strong draft resolution was tabled by the Community and a weaker "consensus" Chairman's statement, which followed most of its major points, was agreed to and read out to the Commission.

The statement expresses "serious concern" over the human rights situation in East Timor and "strongly deplores" the Dili incident. It welcomes Indonesia's setting up of a commission of inquiry to look into the deaths and to clarify the fate of those unaccounted for. It expresses encouragement over the Indonesian government's "disciplinary measures and military court proceedings" to bring to trial and punish those responsible. It calls for humane treatment of all those detained in connection with the incident and the release "without delay" of those not involved in violence. In a surprising political statement, the Chairman's text encourages the Secretary-General to continue to use his "good offices" for achieving "a just, comprehensive, and internationally acceptable settlement of the question of East Timor." Urging the government of Indonesia to improve human rights in East Timor, it "commends" Professor Kooijman's report and urges the Indonesian government "to implement its recommendations" and "looks forward to a report thereon"—from whom it does not say, although it later calls on the Secretary-General to keep the Commission informed in 1993.

It is unlikely that the 47th General Assembly will do more than hear comments on the situation in East Timor, but the attention to human rights in a new situation—in one of Asia's largest and most powerful countries—is a significant accomplishment in which the Torture Rapporteur's role has been and no doubt will continue to be significant.

Attacks on the Thematic Mechanisms

One of the greatest achievements of the United Nations in establishing machinery to protect human rights has been the appointment of the thematic working groups and special rapporteurs. As noted above with regard to the 1993 World Conference on Human Rights, one of the important aims of the pro-human rights bloc at the United Nations has been to find ways to strengthen this machinery. Many (but not all) of these mechanisms were established by consensus, and it has become the rule that they are extended by consensus. Slowly, it has become possible to extend each mandate from one year to two—as part of the regular budgetary cycle—and an agreement was reached at the 1990 ECOSOC session that once the Human Rights Commission was expanded to 53 members, the thematic mechanisms would be extended for three-year periods. This is part of an effort to enable them to function more independently, to assure financial and permanent (full-time) staff support, and to develop their activities.

This agreement was challenged this year in February 1992, when the Philippines—a country mentioned in the reports of all the thematic mechanisms and visited in 1990 by two of them (Torture, Disappearances)—began an assault at the Commission. It began modestly enough: When the Special Rapporteur on Religion was under discussion, the Philippines' representative proposed that the mechanism's activities be taken over by the Subcommission or the "Centre for Human Rights" itself, since the original intention was for special rapporteurs to be "temporary" mechanisms. No one else commented or supported this view and nothing happened. Less than a week later the Commission was in the process of adopting a resolution on its newest thematic mechanism, the Working Group on Arbitrary Detention, and the Philippines was one of the sponsors of the resolution, which was adopted without a vote. The renewal of the group's three-year mandate (1991–94) was not at issue. But less than an hour later, at the same meeting, the resolution on the Torture Rapporteur came up for a vote. The Philippines' delegate dredged up the old East German (and Soviet) argument that the rapporteurial mechanism was duplicative of the treaty body, the Committee against Torture, and that it should be renewed for only one year so it could "wind up [its] affairs." After all, he opined, the Rapporteur himself said his recommendations repeated those in prior reports, and "that meant there was not much more he could do other than to continue receiving and monitoring alleged cases of torture and communicating with the governments concerned" [E/CN.4/1992/SR.47, para. 67]. A groundswell of support emerged promptly from Indonesia, Iran, India, and Nigeria. Cuba went further: The Commission should "review the mandates of the special rapporteurs [all of them] on an annual basis." Syria said the resolution should not refer to a single region's [Europe's] experience fighting torture. China agreed, noting afterwards that it also agreed with the Philippines that the Torture Rapporteur's mandate should be renewed "by one year only, to enable him to complete his work" [ibid., para. 76]. After a lunch break Pakistan continued to support the critical position, but others spoke up: Belgium, France, the United Kingdom, Australia, Portugal, Canada, all from the Western Group, as well as a number of Latin American representatives of democracies that had overcome years of problems with regimes run by torturers—including Chile, Argentina, Uruguay, Brazil, Mexico, Venezuela, and even Peru—with some helpful support from Japan, the Russian Federation, and Senegal. Japan's Deputy U.N. Ambassador Sezaki summed up most eloquently: "Of all the means at the disposal of the Commission, the Special Rapporteur approach was one of the most effective, and his [Kooijman's] report showed that he could display creativity and imagination in his recommendations without going to extremes. Two Special Rapporteurs had already had their mandates extended for three years, and [there was] no reason why an exception should be made in the case of . . . torture. If resources were inadequate, it would be preferable to reduce the mandate of the Special Rapporteur on mercenaries. . . . [There was] no reason why" the mandate should not be renewed for "three, six or even nine years" [SR.48, para. 8]. Numerous speakers pointed out that the mechanisms were not duplicative, but complementary, that the Convention was applicable only to those 60 or more states that had adhered to it (perhaps a third of all countries), that torture was a particularly heinous crime that must be combatted, that ECOSOC had reached an agreement that should not be overturned lightly, and that budgetary constraints and timing would otherwise severely hamper the Rapporteur's efforts to combat torture. In retreat, the Philippines' representative said he had never meant to "in any way imply" his country regarded torture as of minor importance, but had simply wished to reduce duplication. And after Mexico clearly detailed why and how there was no duplication, China noted that a consensus was now emerging, and stated it was only trying to make it unnecessary for governments to reply to multiple requests from differing bodies, experts, etc. The mandate was extended for three years—by consensus.

This was not the last of this topic. Although the Philippines was silent later that day when the mandate of the Working Group on Disappearances was extended by consensus for three years, it sent another shot across the rapporteurs' bow a week later when the mandate of the Special Rapporteur on Summary and Arbitrary Executions came up. Proposing only a one-year extension, the Philippines suggested that the new Crime Commission could handle the subject of summary and arbitrary executions just fine, that the Special Rapporteur "only" undertakes monitoring and contacts with governments, and that his recommendations need no follow up. No one else spoke or commented, and the original resolution was adopted by consensus.

These attacks appear to reflect a strong view, particularly in the Asian group, that the special rapporteurs are not welcome instrumentalities of the Commission. In contrast, the fact that both regionally balanced thematic working groups were renewed without comment or opposition suggests greater support for such (more expensive) procedures, which operate on a more consensual basis. There may be another aspect to this: The Philippines had responded to the Torture Rapporteur's recommendations this year, and the measures adopted—including repeal of the nettlesome Presidential Decree 1850, new measures regarding the release from custody aimed at minimizing disappearances, and a list of 42 members of the military convicted of serious human rights violations—were cited in his report. But he said nothing publicly about them, nor did he speak favorably of them in the report or in his oral remarks. Whether the Philippines' actions were motivated more by substance than by diplomatic pique is hard to know. However, it seems clear that resistance to the rapporteurs will rise again—in the General Assembly as it prepares for the World Conference or at the Conference itself.

Convention against Torture

A binding 1984 treaty, the Convention against Torture formally criminalizes torture. This treaty is monitored by the Committee against

Torture (CAT), which meets twice annually. Its next report will be reviewed by the 47th General Assembly and will in the future be considered only in even years. It was not the subject of a resolution at the 46th General Assembly.

The Convention against Torture had 64 states parties at the end of 1991, an increase from 55 the previous year. Another 15 had signed but had not formally ratified. Reports on compliance with the Convention are reviewed by the Committee in public session. CAT, the Convention's only implementational mechanism, is similar to the mechanisms under other U.N. human rights treaties, although many observers believe it may develop stricter enforcement procedures than those of other treaty supervisory bodies because it contains strong optional procedures.

At the meeting of states parties to the Convention in November 1991 in Geneva, elections to the Committee produced no Asian member. In the past, an expert from the Philippines had served. After he chose not to run, China put forward its own candidate. Sometime back, when CAT reviewed China's first report, it had seriously criticized the practices of the People's Republic and asked China to submit an additional report with more detailed information (as had been the case with some other states parties, including Egypt, Cameroon, and Chile). Since that time China has attacked CAT publicly in various human rights bodies. Now, when CAT held elections, China's representative—though the sole candidate from Asia—received too few votes to qualify. Some activist nongovernmental organizations had, in fact, urged the states parties to vote for others as a form of protest. This marks the first time that China has not been elected to a seat it sought on a U.N. human rights body.

The 47th General Assembly will consider steps to assure full funding of the Committee. In 1991 the Assembly took a major step toward obtaining full financing of CAT and the CERD from the regular U.N. budget [A/Res/46/111], inviting the meetings of state parties to the two treaties to consider amendments that would allow for full funding. The state parties to the Racial Convention, meeting in January 1992, approved such action. The Convention against Torture has the more onerous requirement that states parties must themselves pay for *all* expenses of the Committee, including its meetings, documents, and staff. The resultant uncertainty of cash flow, the poor experiences of other treaty bodies with a pay-as-you-go provision, and curtailment of CAT meeting time during its first year have focused attention on this problem. With support for reform expressed by the 46th General Assembly, and with the United States having ratified the Convention (though still awaiting the passage of implementing legislation before becoming a party), it appears probable that the 47th General Assembly will continue to move ahead on the financial side of this issue.

The Relationship of Human Rights and Development

Ironically, as the East-West conflict over human rights has waned, tensions between North and South have become more pronounced in U.N. human rights bodies. These conflicts will be addressed again at the 47th General Assembly, particulary in Third Committee deliberations about the 1993 World Conference on Human Rights, and the annual debate on the right to development, but they will no doubt also surface again in Second Committee debates on UNDP's *Human Development Report* (see below).

While affirmation of the importance of democracy, free elections, and respect for human rights has since 1989 acquired a prominence it never previously enjoyed, differences have resurfaced, with developing countries stressing the need to concentrate attention on economic and social rights and, in particular, on the right to development. **China** has led the way on behalf of the developing countries, pressing successfully for the General Assembly to include the relationship between development and human rights as one of the priority topics at the 1993 World Conference on Human Rights.

Since the United Nations's earliest years, members of the world body have argued about which rights are preeminent: civil and political rights (e.g., the right to be free from torture and arbitrary arrest, to choose a religion, to exercise freedom of expression and association) or economic and social rights (e.g., the right to food, education, and medical care). The Universal Declaration on Human Rights, adopted in 1948, had proclaimed both kinds of rights, but treaties following the Declaration separated the two.

When the Soviet Union and its allies argued vehemently that economic and social rights have priority over the other rights, it was widely understood that this was a means of whitewashing the fact that they simply had no intention of implementing civil and political rights guarantees. (Their simultaneous invocation of "non-interference in internal affairs" and "sovereignty" as barriers to the development of effective U.N. human rights monitoring only served to confirm this view. China and Cuba's repetition of these formulas does the same today.) Yet, even before the cold war ended, the Soviet Union had abandoned its argument of preeminence in favor of the formula that both sets of rights are interrelated, interdependent, and, in some formulations, indivisible. Western countries, often reluctantly (and revealing differences among them), acknowledged the need to devote attention to economic and social rights questions, but routinely stressed that development must be based on full respect for civil and political rights.

While Third World nations also accepted language affirming indivisibility, with few exceptions they stressed the preeminence of economic and social rights issues in the development process. While seeking to direct the policies and actions of the North in ways that would be favorable to economic development goals, the South also wanted no "interference" or constraints on its own actions at home. Predictably, this led to a standoff that has continued to the present. First raised in 1972, the "right to development" was by 1986 an entrenched agenda item at the United Nations, with its own Working Group and a separate instrument: The **Declaration on the Right to Development,** adopted by the General Assembly, establishes the right to development as an "inalienable" right of every person and all peoples, and simultaneously encompasses economic, social, cultural, *and* civil and political rights. The Declaration sets forth various general obligations for states in giving effect to the right, emphasizing the need to ensure equality of opportunity and citing popular participation as a key entitlement.

The concept has been controversial, in no small measure because of its use as a diversionary tactic. Vociferous Eastern group support for this approach in its early years only reinforced the view that this was designed to diminish any U.N. achievements in the human rights sphere. Opponents of the concept charge it with being "intellectually amorphous" and an excuse for blaming the "failure of Third World development on exploitation rather than on root causes, such as the lack of individual freedom or political accountability." Inability to measure when the right to development is "realized" only compounds this [M. Abram, *Harvard Human Rights Journal*, 1991, pp. 76–77ff.]. Proponents of the right to development, however, see this open-endedness as a strength of the Declaration, reflecting the different views of its drafters and the complexity of the subject matter addressed, which allows the concept to be interpreted flexibly [P. Alston, *Melbourne University Law Review*, 12/91, pp. 220–21]. They note the difficulty in measuring all human rights, and suggest the Declaration's provisions can be measured best by disaggregating it into its component parts: the specific rights of the two covenants.

In this debate, the **U.S. government** has been the most outspoken: It does not recognize a "right" to development, insisting that human rights may only limit state action, not provide international entitlements. (Since 1981 the United States has also opposed the concept of economic and social rights, arguing that they too are simply social goals, however worthy.)

Presentations at the 1992 session of the Commission on Human Rights in Geneva, revealed the range and variety of views on this subject and their lack of depth. For example, in a period piece speech, China's representative at the Commission declared that the right to development is primarily a collective right to be realized only when countries are freed from the exploitation of racism, colonialism, and foreign aggression. Unless development comes first, he argued, human rights are but an "empty aspiration" [E/CN.4/1992/SR.13]. Unlike other speakers, including several from the Third World, he offered no specific proposals as to how to measure, monitor, or implement the right to development. Pakistan's representative, virtually alone in using Marxist terminology at the Commission, declared that the right to development is the foundation on which the "superstructure" of all human rights could be based [ibid.]. In contrast, Colombia, Senegal, Madagascar, and some other speakers at the Commission proposed specific mechanisms, focused on a need for greater expert analysis of new development challenges, called for greater cooperation among the U.N. agencies and bodies concerned with development and with human rights, and called for serious reporting on issues and concrete recommendations.

Where some, such as Kenya (under fire by traditional aid donors for its severe human rights abuses) railed against "conditioning" of aid on human rights practices, other countries took a more nuanced approach. Many Western states spoke of the importance of popular participation in the development process, mentioning that this required not just "consultation" but free elections and democratic decision-making. Yet Madagascar, which called for "absolute priority" on development issues at the 1993 World Conference, asked for greater recognition (read: financial assistance) to those Third World states that had moved to bring genuine democracy to their countries in recent years. The representative warned that popular disappointment that democracy had not alleviated poverty might bring a reaction against democracy itself, and that more development aid was now urgent. Mexico reminded the donor states that only development would bring real stability to the South.

Where France called for concentration on the relationship of development and human rights practices at the national level (finding international efforts to prescribe development or human rights formulas insufficiently sensitive to the views of the people themselves), others, notably Nigeria, continued to argue that the appropriate focus is not on national violations of human rights but, rather, on the hostility of the international environment to national development, including the protection of human rights.

After assuring the Third World that it would continue to be attentive to its legitimate aspirations, the Russian Federation suggested that the very concept of the right to development needs further development. The Commission, Russia argued, should focus on legal and standard-setting questions, leaving "purely economic issues" to other "appropriate" U.N. bodies. Others, notably Australia, have taken a different position— arguing that the isolation of human rights matters in bodies separated from real development policies is an artificial distinction wrought by the cold war, and that the time is at hand to explore the linkages seriously and in a nonconfrontational setting. Speaking before the Commission on

Human Rights, Australia's representative proposed that the Commission organize expert seminars that explore the linkage of development with, for example, the rights to literacy, free expression, and popular participation in decision-making. Noting that the International Labour Organisation and UNICEF already had incorporated human rights concerns into their technical cooperation programs, he proposed that other U.N. development agencies be encouraged to do the same [E/CN.4/1992/SR.15]. For all the controversy sparked by UNDP's *Human Development Report* and its Human Freedom Index (see below), he welcomed it as an attempt to break down the artificial separation of these subjects. Because this will be the last General Assembly session before the 1993 World Conference, the 47th General Assembly's consideration of *implementation* of the Declaration on the Right to Development may become more focused than past exhortations on the subject.

In 1990 a "Global Consultation" on the Right to Development recommended establishment of a high-level independent expert panel to report annually on the progress in implementing the Declaration. That Consultation also called for the development of criteria by which to assess progress in establishing the right to development, for measures to promote wider knowledge about the right, and for ongoing studies of activities incompatible with the right. Yet some sympathetic critics have questioned whether the United Nations should really add one more oversight body to the seven existing treaty bodies, which are themselves insufficiently funded and staffed and which already need consolidation to minimize duplication. One specialist has proposed that the Commission on Human Rights provide its members with regular surveys of current trends in development thinking and practices pursued by international development agencies. Clearly, what has been missing from the U.N. debates on development and human rights has been input from genuine experts, including input from other development bodies.

UNDP's *Human Development Report* and Human Freedom Index

Although it has been and will no doubt continue to be discussed in the Second—not the Third—Committee of the General Assembly, UNDP's *Human Development Report* will provide the setting for some of the most ferocious debates on the relationship of human rights and development, and on whether it is acceptable for any U.N. agency—including development ones—to rank and measure the human rights performances of states.

The 1991 *Human Development Report* included a **Human Freedom Index,** which ranked countries by name. Though it acknowledged that the measurement of human freedom was not well-developed or easily quantified into usable multivariate indices, the Report nonetheless based itself *totally* upon a commercially published, 1986 study by a British author, which was not only selective in its coverage of rights but which made a number of dubious quantitative assumptions (e.g., that being subjected to indefinite detention without charge is equivalent to being subjected to torture but three times worse than having to read censored news media). But it was the listing of countries—in rank order—in a publication of the U.N.'s primary development agency that provoked the greatest protest from developing countries. At first, at UNDP's June 1991 Governing Council session, they called upon UNDP's Administrator, William Draper III, to abandon the Report. Later, in a compromise, the Governing Council adopted a resolution asking him to undertake regional consultations to bring the concerns and priorities of the developing countries into consideration as the next report was drafted [Res. 91/6]. Later, some would assert that they had been promised the Index would not be repeated [DP/1992/13, para. 28(g)].

At the 46th General Assembly developing country concerns were reiterated in the debate, and then again—following UNDP consultations among human rights experts on November 19–20, which revealed that UNDP still planned to include human rights matters in its 1992 report— in a resolution introduced by Malaysia on December 2, at the very end of the Second Committee's deliberations [A/C.2/46/SR.53]. The draft resolution called on UNDP to drop the Human Freedom Index—in essence, identifying human rights rankings as unacceptable. Eventually this was revised to a moderate resolution, which cited divergent views about the Human Freedom Index but noted Mr. Draper's "intention" to report on the outcome of the regional consultations so that the Governing Council could make decisions—prior to the publication of the 1992 Report—that took into account these views and those expressed at the Governing Council session in February 1992 [A/Res/46/218].

During the Second Committee debate a number of Asian countries, particularly Laos, Vietnam, Indonesia, and China, vociferously denounced the Human Freedom Index, using such words as "unacceptable," "inaccurate," "inappropriate," and "insensitive." Typically, **China** went the farthest, stating that the Report had "referred to issues that were beyond the mandate of UNDP and had no direct bearing on development." Further, in objecting to the Human Freedom Index specifically, China stated that "any attempt to quantify human rights was unscientific and inconsistent with the spirit of the Charter and the relevant provisions of international human rights instruments" [A/C.2/1991/SR.35].

At the **Special UNDP Governing Council Session** in February 1992 the subject was addressed further. UNDP noted that some developing countries had expressed major concern about the use that some donors might make of the indices in the report, particularly the Human Freedom

Index, "for purposes of aid conditionality" [DP/1992/13]. Indeed, this theme was reiterated in a massive rejection of the report and the Index expressed by the Pakistani ambassador on behalf of the **Group of 77.** Other arguments were that there is no universally agreed definition of freedom, that those used in the 1991 Report were Western interpretations, that there had been no consultation, and that UNDP had no mandate to address such issues; and that the Centre for Human Rights and the Commission were more appropriate forums for these matters. The Chinese representative—stating that he had agreed to the consensus resolution in the General Assembly only as a great concession—declared that his country would never accept inclusion of these issues in UNDP's work. The European Community and the United States spoke up on behalf of the Report, and in particular the concept that human rights concerns must be part of the development debate. Like UNDP's administrator, they argued that although precise measurement may not yet have been achieved, the efforts to develop an index on human freedom would help inform policy debates. After they adjourned to form a closed working group, the issue was thrashed about and a compromise was sought. Here, however, although they were quiet in the public debate, there was strong Latin opposition to the Index. The European Community refused to abandon its support for including human rights factors in the development debate, and the Governing Council deferred further consideration of the matter until its June 1992 session.

In the meantime, UNDP issued its third *Human Development Report* in April. There, it abandoned the Human Freedom Index—technically meeting the concerns of the developing countries—but it offered instead a new **Political Freedom Index (PFI).** After a very carefully balanced discussion of the arguments made by "many people" about economic and social rights as opposed to civil and political rights, the Report argued that the two had to be measured separately. It had attempted to measure economic and social rights in its **Human Development Index (HDI),** but separated political freedom because political freedom, which can fluctuate radically, operates on a different timescale than is the case with "economic and social achievements," which tend to be stable over time. Further, the Report argues that the HDI depends partly on a country's economic opportunities, whereas the PFI does not. "Countries do not have to censor the press or torture prisoners just because they are poor. But a poor country that made substantial progress in freedom could not hope to see this reflected in a dramatic improvement in its ranking in a *combined* index like the HDI" [*Human Development Report 1992*, p. 29, italics added].

In dramatic contrast to its 1991 study, the 1992 Report seems to bend over backwards to address the limitations of its data base in constructing the Political Freedom Index, the indicators it uses, the problems inherent in data sources themselves, and how the UNDP team quantified and weighted the information. In the process it inadvertently raises questions about the reliability of information collected—even by the U.N. Centre for Human Rights and the Commission on Human Rights. In a clear bow to Third World sensitivities, and reminding the reader of long-standing excuses proffered by human rights violators the world over, the Report asserts that negative information about rights violations must be balanced against "positive achievements" of a country and examined in a "dynamic, historical and cultural context" [ibid., p. 30]. Much more work, it argues, is needed to "ensure more comprehensive, objective and up-to-date sources of information." Moreover, the Report carefully sets out areas needing further research, and expresses the hope that, over time, it will become more universally accepted and able to be linked with the HDI and other indices.

The Report's timidity is further illustrated by the fact that, unlike 1991, there is no listing of countries. After all the methodological caveats, the PFI is presented in aggregate terms, showing how countries at various levels of human development, income, political freedom, and industrialization rank in their treatment of the five issue clusters examined by the Index: personal security, rule of law, freedom of expression, political participation, and equality of opportunity. What are the Report's conclusions from all of this?

- that of the 104 countries studied, equal parts have high, medium, and low levels of freedom, but that more countries "will be moving to higher scores";
- that political freedom and human development "seem to move in tandem";
- that the level of per capita income and the extent of democratic freedoms seem to be correlated; but that as income levels fall, freedom does not decline, so "even poor countries can enjoy a high level of freedom"; and
- that the world has made great progress in advancing political participation, free elections, and equality of opportunity, but that the human rights abuses most frequently cited are in the nature of torture and other violations of physical integrity.

The debate will no doubt continue to rage over whether, as U.S. Ambassador Kenneth Blackwell has stated, these matters are best dealt with in the Second Committee of the General Assembly and in discussions of UNDP or at the Commission on Human Rights. In contrast, developing countries have argued that the proper forum for such discussions is the (less influential) Commission on Human Rights, and that UNDP has no mandate to take on these issues. The 1992 Commission on Human Rights, in its Third World-sponsored resolution on the right to development [Res. 1992/3] (adopted 43-1 with 3 abstentions, the United States opposing), recognized the Commission "as an appropriate forum to discuss questions of development and its relation to the rights of the individual." This language carefully identifies the Commission as "an" appropriate forum, not the *only* one, and further recognizes the idea that human rights questions do indeed have a role in development, specifically citing the rights of the *individual*.

No doubt this is only part of a long process of bringing the human rights dimension into U.N. development debates.

Country Situations

Many governments and nongovernmental organizations feared that the expansion of the Commission on Human Rights from 43 to 53 members in 1992, with all of the new members from the developing world, would mark the end of country resolutions (some called it the "end of human rights history" at the United Nations) and that only the thematic mechanisms would survive. Ironically, the country resolutions continued (and were even marked by several additions and the strengthening of some mandates), while a new attack was launched against the thematic mechanisms.

Of the 22 countries cited (17 publicly and 5 privately) at the 48th Commission on Human Rights in 1992, only **East Timor/Indonesia** and **Sri Lanka** were new this year, and both of these were addressed in consensus "chairman's statements," rather than generating resolutions or rapporteurs. Several mechanisms are new: Special Rapporteurs for Burma, Equatorial Guinea, and Haiti in public; and an "independent expert" for Sudan under the **1503 procedure** (the equivalent of a special rapporteur, but the report and findings remain "confidential"; examination of the situations in Somalia, Chad, Bahrain, and Zaire continue under this heading). Furthermore, two other contentious public country investigations were upheld (Cuba and Iran).

Human rights advocates are quick to note that only three of the countries cited were first-timers, and that many "gross violators" escaped international scrutiny this year, among them **Syria**, which was dropped from consideration under the 1503 procedure; and **Kuwait**, whose Special Repporteur was discontinued because his mandate had applied only to the period of Iraqi occupation. The human rights advocates also point out that when criticism of the situation in **China/Tibet** was brought to a vote, it went down in defeat.

Iraq

The Human Rights Commission and the General Assembly, ending years of silence about Iraq's human rights record, now condemn the government's atrocities. Yet the number of member states that abstained from the Iraq vote in the Commission has grown since 1991 (the 1992 vote was 35–1–16), perhaps indicating increasing Third World discomfort with the treatment of Iraq at the United Nations. Indeed, Iraq itself was elected to the Commission during the 1992 enlargement.

The Commission's **Special Rapporteur,** Max van der Stoel of the Netherlands, prepared a chilling report [E/CN.4/1992/31], and the sheer scope and viciousness of the abuses he cites cannot fail to shock even the most hardened observer. The Rapporteur presents evidence that **summary executions** and the **arbitrary detention** of political and religious opponents of the regime continue "on a mass scale," often women and children. He also presents evidence that **torture** is used widely to extract confessions, from children as well as from adults. He had received the names of over 17,000 disappeared persons, and the **Kurds** put the total of Kurdish disappeared alone at 180,000 or so. "While that figure might seem wildly exaggerated," van der Stoel reported to the Commission, "it was becoming less and less unrealistic" [E/CN.4/1992/SR.35].

The Rapporteur himself described as "particularly shocking" the evidence that "thousands of **Kurdish and Assyrian villages had been destroyed**" and, prior to the Gulf conflict, subjected to **chemical attacks.** He also cites persecution of **Turkomans,** and of **Shiites** and particularly their clergy—whose numbers, he reports, were reduced from 8,000–9,000 to 800 in the 20 years that preceded the 1991 uprisings. Those who remain are believed either under arrest or among the "disappeared."

The Special Rapporteur concluded that, except for members of the ruling Baath party and the security forces, "all sections of the Iraqi population had been subjected to severe repressive measures." And van der Stoel stated, with unusual candor in a U.N. human rights report, that "the fundamental problem" is the subordination of the entire state structure to one aim: ensuring the unrestricted rule of the Baath party and its leader, Saddam Hussein. The Rapporteur noted the caution with which he had assembled and weighed the evidence presented to him, and expressed fear for the government opponents in the country's southern marshes, where the Iraqi army was still concentrated.

Following his many conclusions and his recommendations to the government, the Special Rapporteur proposed a new action by the Commission: the dispatch of a **team of human rights monitors** to Iraq. Iraqi citizens are in daily danger, he explained, and mere condemnation by the United Nations is not enough. The Commission failed to endorse the Rapporteur's suggestion, merely requesting that Mr. van der Stoel "develop" his proposal "for an exceptional response" "in consultation" with the Secretary-General, and report on it to the 47th General Assembly [Res. 1992/71].

In spring 1992 the Belgian delegation circulated the van der Stoel report to the members of the Security Council, the body apt to be most directly involved in any plan to send a human rights monitoring mission in Iraq. And, in fact, human rights verification is part of the U.N. monitoring of peace settlements in El Salvador and Cambodia in particular. So far, however, there appears little interest in the proposal in the Iraq case.

Cuba

For the first time ever, the 47th General Assembly will be presented with an official report on human rights conditions in Cuba, prepared by a newly appointed **Special Rapporteur on Cuba.** This Rapporteur's existence and his reports to both the General Assembly and the Human Rights Commission are a result of persistent U.S. efforts to bring Cuba under U.N. scrutiny. The campaign, begun in the mid-1980s, became the top (some have said the only) priority for Washington in U.N. human rights bodies.

In 1988, as the U.S. quest for a Commission resolution critical of Cuba's human rights record seemed near success, Cuba invited the United Nations to send a regionally balanced group to the island, offering its full cooperation with the team. The Commission accepted the invitation and avoided criticizing Cuba in a resolution that year. After the six-member group issued its 400-page report, the Commission adopted a bland resolution asking the U.N. Secretary-General to maintain "direct contacts" with Cuba. The U.S. quest continued [see *A Global Agenda: Issues Before the 46th General Assembly of the United Nations*], and by 1991 the United States had put its full diplomatic machinery behind the prospect of a resolution on Cuba. A "Special Representative" of the Secretary-General was now given the job of maintaining "direct contacts" not only with the government of Cuba but also—a U.N. first—with the "citizens" of the country. Cuba denounced the resolution and stated that it would not cooperate.

The Secretary-General appointed Rafael Rivas Posada of Colombia, who submitted a report to the 1992 Commission. He reveals that Cuba refused to reply to his letters and diplomatic contacts and that, as a result, he "had to limit his activities to receiving information supplied by the citizens of Cuba." He notes that Cuba's noncooperation meant that he could not check the veracity of the complaints presented to him. Here, as elsewhere, Mr. Rivas Posada seems about to concede the field to Cuba. He states that only in the absence of an "official version of events" do the complaints "merit the attention of the international community," and he goes on to note that the government of Cuba is "duly fulfilling its obligations" to reply to communications sent by the Commission on Human Rights under *other* thematic procedures. On another occasion, he acknowledges that allegations of acts against dissidents have increased "alarmingly," but sees this as a limited problem. He concludes that, "although it is not possible to speak of a general, massive, and indiscriminate pattern of official violation of citizens' rights, there are nonetheless sufficient grounds for signalling the absence of guarantees" of such rights [E/CN.4/1992/27, para. 28]. And he appears to suggest that there are mitigating circumstances—prominently, current economic conditions—for human rights violations in Cuba. He ends his remarks by calling "the economic and political context . . . the subject of passionate debate and . . . almost unique in the extent to which it renders immensely difficult any attempt at an objective and impartial appraisal that goes beyond the continuing controversy reflected daily in the media" [para. 32].

Despite these limp conclusions, the documentation of abuses, which comprised 23 of the report's 35 pages, was enough to boost the U.S. case against Cuba. This documentation drew attention to the postvisit harassment and imprisonment of persons who gave testimony to the 1988 U.N. team. The Special Representative had printed the allegations, with names and other details, concerning killings, torture (commonly beatings by prison guards), and other abuses of the prison population, as well as allegations of restrictions on the right to leave, arbitrary arrest and detention, job dismissals, and restrictions on free expression and association, particularly in the case of human rights defense or advocacy groups.

The text of the 1992 Cuba resolution was the strongest yet, and the vote the most decisive: 23–8–21 [Res. 1992/61]. The post of Special Representative of the Secretary-General has been upgraded to that of Special Rapporteur of the Commission on Human Rights itself.

Iran

The **Special Representative on Iran,** Reynaldo Galindo Pohl of El Salvador, made his third visit to Iran at the end of 1991—but only after the European Community, the sponsors of past Iran resolutions, threatened to raise the Iranian question at the 46th General Assembly if the government continued to refuse him access. After the visit he declared that "no appreciable progress" had been made in the human rights situation in that country.

In a lengthy section of the new report [E/CN.4/1992/34], the Representative details case allegations made to him. He then reports on his visit to Iran, with an equally detailed account of each meeting. The most vivid and important of these recount his visits to the notorious Evin and Gorhardasht prisons. Galindo Pohl notes that he presented lists of prisoners with whom he wished to meet but was given long explanations about why it was not possible to see many of them—the nub of which was that they were still "under investigation." When he noted that the International Committee of the Red Cross (ICRC) would have access to all prisoners at any time, he was told bluntly that the ICRC had nothing to do with him.

The Special Representative details the allegations of **summary trials and maltreatment** provided by prisoners he was able to interview. And minutes after being told categorically that there were no political prisoners in Gorhardasht, he found and interviewed several.

Galindo Pohl raised numerous concerns with Iranian officials. Prominent among these was the **lack of guarantees of due process of law,** discriminatory treatment of groups of citizens because of their religious beliefs (notably Baha'is), lack of independent associations, and the absence of a climate of legal security and guarantees of freedom of expression—all of which he and the Commission later identified as the "main weaknesses" of the human rights situation in Iran. He also noted that application of the death penalty, rather than diminishing, had increased.

The Special Representative was told by Iran that the country had been praised by international agencies for its efforts to fight drug traffickers, and that it was they, not political opponents, who were being sentenced to death. He was reminded, in essence, that economic and social rights take priority over the civil and political rights that are the Representative's concern. And he was warned that if he commented on new allegations of human rights violations, or so much as drew conclusions or recommended continuance of his mandate, he would be violating the terms of the mandate and the political compromise that had been struck at the 1991 Commission on Human Rights.

Representative Galindo Pohl pointed out that his mandate came from the Commission resolution, not behind-the-scenes deals of which he knew nothing; that his job was to examine human rights conditions; that the issues with which he was concerned were those he had been examining for several years; and that he would draw his own expert conclusions. Further, evaluating the progress made on each of his prior recommendations—as he was mandated to do—and concluding that there had been "no appreciable progress" in the human rights situation in Iran, he recommended extension of the mandate. Along the way he noted where promises and assurances had been made but not fulfilled.

At issue in the 1992 Commission on Human Rights was the 1991 recommendation to call a halt to the rapporteurship for Iran if "progress" continued. In the end, a strong resolution was adopted by a decisive vote (22–12–15). It renewed the Representative's mandate for another year and reinstated an interim report to the General Assembly.

Myanmar (Burma)

Buoyed by **Aung San Suu Kyi**'s receipt of the 1991 Nobel Peace Prize, the 46th General Assembly adopted its first resolution publicly criticizing Burma's "grave human rights situation" and calling for "early improvement" [A/Res/46/132]. In the quest for its adoption by *consensus*, however, the text was watered down to such an extent that it expressed no criticism of the Myanmar military government, nor was there now even the expression of concern about "continued deprivation of liberty of a number of democratically elected political leaders." Although eight European countries announced they would withdraw their co-sponsorship of the text, activists anticipated—correctly, as it turned out—that the General Assembly's action would set the stage for public consideration of the Burma question in the Commission on Human Rights. Until this time it had been addressed in the confidential "1503" procedure.

And indeed the 1992 Commission decided, not by vote but by rare consensus, that it would appoint a **Special Rapporteur** "to establish direct contacts with the Government and the people of Myanmar, including political leaders deprived of their liberty, their families and lawyers" with a view to examining the human rights situation and "any progress . . . towards the transfer of power to a civilian government and the drafting of a new constitution . . . and the restoration of human rights" [Res. 1992/58]. The Commission resolution—for which regional powers, such as India, were enlisted as co-sponsors—is specific about human rights conditions in Myanmar, mentioning the Nobel Laureate who was under house arrest (and, at that time, still deprived of family visits), the **lack of progress in honoring the 1990 general election results,** the **detention of many political leaders,** the "oppressive measures directed, in particular, at minority groups," and the 80,000 **Myanmar Muslim refugees** who had left for Bangladesh. It calls on the government to "lift the restraining orders" on political leaders, to release those who are detained, to provide fair trial and other due process guarantees, to allow the ICRC access to prisons, to reopen the universities, and to "accelerate the process of transition to democracy."

After the Commission, Burmese leaders took several steps that allow some hope for an improved situation. Among these steps were the release of some political prisoners and the granting of permission to the family of Aung San Suu Kyi to pay her a visit. The General Assembly's Third Committee will be considering the interim report of the Special Rapporteur on Burma at the 47th Session.

Other Countries

The 46th General Assembly's resolutions on **Afghanistan** and **El Salvador** were relatively straightforward, although it was widely understood that the political peace processes in both countries, and particularly the Salvadoran peace treaty, take precedence over any Commission human rights action. The Commission, as a result of Latin-bloc negotiating solidarity, downgraded the El Salvador Special Representative to the level of Expert.

The 1992 Commission ended **Romania's** Special Rapporteur, although the government must report to the Commission in 1993. The Rapporteur's study had been quite detailed and troubling, but the European sponsors of the Commission resolution wanted to recognize the progress made in the country. Another Commission resolution addressed once more the human rights situation in **Albania,** calling attention to the need for free elections and respect for the rights of minorities. A new resolution at the Commission addressed harassment of the **Roma (gypsies)** in Eastern Europe. Germany had put forward an amendment (defeated overwhelmingly) that would have denied various rights and protections to those in another country temporarily.

The Commission ended its consideration of **Equatorial Guinea** and **Haiti** under the "advisory services" category (where states are placed allegedly at their own request) and will be considering them under the "gross violations" item, giving each a Special Rapporteur. Equatorial Guinea has come under "advisory services" for over a decade, with no impact on the human rights situation in the country. The only African country outside of South Africa to be considered under the "gross violations" item, its Rapporteur will be reporting to the 1993 Commission. Haiti's Special Rapporteur will present an interim report to the 47th General Assembly.

In the case of **Guatemala,** the Commission decided to continue the services of an Expert under advisory services and expressed "profound concern" over human rights violations "despite the efforts of the government."

Emergency Procedure

The slowness of U.N. action in a number of fast-breaking situations led to Austria's 1992 proposal for a mechanism that will allow the Commission to respond to human rights emergencies and to recommend investigation and action. Ironically, the response to the proposal on emergencies was to resume consideration a year later [Res. 1992/55].

According to the proposal, in an emergency situation the Chairman of the Commission could ask members of the Commission to approve the dispatch of a regionally balanced group of five persons to investigate the reported violation(s). Upon receiving the group's report, the Commission would decide whether to undertake a follow-up. The controversy surrounding the proposal has to do with the question of whether, if the emergency arises between Commission sessions, this mechanism could be activated by the Bureau (the officers) of the Commission.

Although the decision to defer discussion until the 1993 Commission disappointed many human rights activists, they noted the fact that the proposal itself had not been watered down and that it had enlisted 44 cosponsors. Many suggest that the matter will be finally resolved at the World Conference.

The World Conference

Because political pressure is brought to bear on the country rapporteur mechanisms every year, and because of continuing criticism that selective use is made of these mechanisms, the opinion has been growing that thematic mechanisms—each of which takes a global view of the problem—might be more effective and acceptable. Advocates of the thematic approach have noted that these innovative mechanisms endorsed by consensus at the Commission on Human Rights have dramatically expanded U.N. human rights fact-finding, reporting, and implementation of standards. In carrying out their mandates, the theme rapporteurs and working groups have, by and large, expanded what the United Nations can do in the human rights area.

The special thematic mechanisms are important because they intervene on a timely and urgent basis in individual cases all over the world, often when there is still some time to prevent violations. In addition, the thematic special rapporteurs (but not the Disappearances Working Group or, so far, the Arbitrary Detentions Group) make essential information public, including the names of individual victims. The Disappearance Group makes its information—other than names—public; the Detentions Group has revealed some names once persons are released. The theme mechanisms are comprised of experts who serve in their own capacity, and not as government delegates; they utilize information from all relevant sources, including nongovernmental organizations; and they have continually and constructively expanded their mandates and scope of concern, often making recommendations that stretch the bounds of current thinking and practice.

The rapporteurs and working groups, however, are the first to point out that their ability to halt torture, executions, or disappearances has been quite limited so far. With the exception of the Disappearances Group, the mechanisms have not engaged in systematic case follow-up; and the sanctions available to them remain nothing more than the publicity and exposure of their reports.

Nonetheless, few would deny the substantial contribution made by the thematic rapporteurs' information and fact-finding activities. The international community receives a detailed annual account on each of the phenomena under scrutiny. One of the drawbacks here is that the international community does not receive much information about subsequent actions by governments or about what each rapporteur thinks can be done about unresolved cases.

At the same time, the thematic mechanisms have painfully limited resources at their disposal. The staff for each thematic rapporteur consists only of a single full-time professional and a half-time assistant—clearly inadequate in the face of growing caseloads and the need for more effective follow-up. Both the retiring Special Rapporteur on Summary and Arbitrary Executions and one member of the Disappearances Working Group have appealed to the World Conference's Preparatory Committee for increased financial and human resources for the thematic mechanisms. The resource constraints also limit the rapporteurs to a single on-site investigation annually.

The U.N. financial watchdogs have been unwilling to provide additional financial support. Ensuring more substantial resources for the theme mechanisms is another of the key problems to be ironed out in advance of the 1993 World Conference on Human Rights.

Standard-Setting

Two important new standards have been sent to the 47th General Assembly for its consideration and adoption.

Declaration on the Rights of Minorities

The product of 14 years of drafting, the declaration was pushed through at the initiative of East European countries, Ukraine, and the Russian Federation. It is the first universal instrument of its kind. Previous instruments have focused not on minority protections but on the equality of treatment of all citizens. The declaration, which was described by the Russian delegation as "a minimum," calls on states to "protect the existence and . . . identity of minorities," and gives *persons* belonging to minorities the explicit "right to participate effectively in decisions on the national and . . . regional level" that concern them.

Declaration on Disappearances

This declaration worked its way through the U.N. process rather quickly as a result of the outrage expressed by nongovernmental organizations and Latin American groups of families of the disappeared at various amnesty laws and at the impunity of perpetrators of disappearances. The declaration is the first instrument to define a "disappearance" as a human rights violation and aims at assuring legal safeguards against disappearances in domestic law. Article 14 establishes a duty to prosecute perpetrators of disappearances criminally, and Article 17 establishes that disappearances are "a continuing offence as long as the perpetrators continue to conceal the fate and the whereabouts of persons who have disappeared and these facts remain unclarified."

2. Refugees

The rise of virulent strains of nationalism and the rash of tribal and other ethnic struggles worldwide have caused renewed suffering for millions, swelling the numbers of refugees dramatically. At the same time, some refugees began their trip home as the end of the superpower conflict opened the way for the displaced and dispossessed people of South Africa, Angola, Mozambique, and Cambodia to begin regaining their past lives.

There remain some 17 million refugees in various parts of the world, almost half of whom have little hope of returning home, according to the **U.N. High Commissioner for Refugees (UNHCR), Sodako Ogata.** "Altogether we have about 20 refugee situations with prospects for repatriation," said Mrs. Ogata, adding that the outlook remains bleak for some 8 million refugees elsewhere, at least in the near-term [Reuters, Tokyo, 4/2/92]. In 1991 Western Europe was confronted with a flood of refugees seeking political asylum—570,000 compared to an annual average of 30,000 in the late 1970s and 40,000 in the 1980s. The influx has spurred a backlash against refugees in many countries, and the current recession has only exacerbated the tension. According to Ogata, resettlement of refugees is becoming more difficult to achieve because increasing numbers are viewed as economic migrants.

The **former Yugoslavia** is the scene of great tragedy for refugees and displaced people. The United Nations reported that more than 500,000 people were displaced—two-thirds of them women and children—during the winter of 1991 [S/23280, 12/11/91]. During the spring 1992 fighting in **Bosnia and Herzegovina** at least 520,000 more people were displaced, some 320,000 of whom have taken refuge in neighboring republics. Today's inter-ethnic warfare seems even less likely to respect the rights of civilians than were yesterday's wars among nations.

Voicing his frustration with the Yugoslav conflict, U.N. Secretary-General Boutros Boutros-Ghali stated in a report that "the international community's efforts to bring succor to these suffering people are greatly obstructed by the warring parties, whose demographic objectives they may frustrate" [ibid.]. At one stage a UNHCR convoy had to negotiate its way through 90 roadblocks between Zagreb and Sarajevo, "many of them manned by undisciplined and drunken soldiers of undetermined political affiliation and not responsible to any identifiable central authority," the report went on. "Relief supplies are stolen, vehicles hijacked, and international aid workers threatened and abused."

In 1991 and the first half of 1992, the office of the UNHCR was stretched to its limit as it dealt with the emergency exodus of 1.5 million **Iraqis and Kurds,** forcing a doubling of its budget at a time when compassion for refugees was cooling among Western nations. Ogata has tried to broaden and deepen the work of UNHCR beyond its original mandate of providing protection for refugees by helping with voluntary resettlement and trying to prevent crisis situations from producing new floods of refugees.

At the 42nd session of the UNHCR Executive Committee (EX-COM), Ogata drew attention to the poor conditions in which the majority of the world's refugees are forced to live, and declared that the right to return to one's homeland merited as much recognition as the right to seek asylum abroad. She reaffirmed her determination to pursue voluntary repatriation as the preferred solution to refugee problems.

The issue of voluntary repatriation, however, is a thorny one for the UNHCR. Even though the right of people to leave their country and return is a basic tenet, it does not always work out that way in practice. It can be difficult to ascertain the degree of voluntariness for all refugees in any given situation. Moreover, there are times when conditions in the country of origin are such that safety is not absolute and guarantees are not effectively extended [EXCOM, Subcommittee of the Whole on International Protection, 4/1/92].

The UNHCR says it is developing a set of universal guidelines on voluntary repatriation for the international community. These guidelines are aimed at gaining international consensus on basic principles on the roles and responsibilities for those involved in repatriation. Aided by these guidelines, the UNHCR intends to address the danger faced by refugees repatriated to mined areas, the difficulty of apportioning scarce land among repatriates, and problems of access or return to previously occupied land.

In a variety of news interviews over the past year, Ogata has pointed out that she has broken all records of previous High Commissioners in the hectic pace she has set. In her first year in office she visited 27 countries and made a largely favorable impression as she set about rebuilding the organization after years of neglect and mismanagement. But however much Ogata has championed the cause of refugees, she has not managed to push the refugee issue to the top of the new global agenda. (It still does not garner the kind of attention that environment and disarmament receive, for example.)

UNHCR continues to face the problem of attempting to **separate economic migrants from political refugees.** The Commission considers a refugee to be someone forced to flee to save life and liberty, not someone seeking economic possibilities in a new land. Ogata was therefore highly critical of the U.S. government for its handling of the Haitian refugee situation after the democratically elected government of Jean-Bertrand Aristide was overthrown in a bloody coup. On February 3, 1992, Ogata publicly condemned the United States for resuming the forced repatriation of Haitian refugees.

In Hong Kong the UNHCR participated in the repatriation of so-called "double-backers," that is, refugees who voluntarily returned (with UNHCR assistance) only to flee again. The problem of economic migrants being forcibly returned to their homelands is a difficult one for the UNHCR, if only because decisions on who is to return are generally made in a hurried and arbitrary manner. Although European countries are suffering from "refugee fatigue," very few asylum-seekers are returned from these countries once they have entered. Many are left in limbo for years while immigration authorities use "the difficulties and indignities of the application process as a deterrent" [*Financial Times*, 3/2/92].

In all, some 660,000 people applied for asylum in the group of 16 industrialized nations in 1991—a 22 percent increase from the previous year. Coping with this influx has been very expensive for the industrialized countries, which, in 1991, spent $7–$8 billion to deal with Third World and East European asylum-seekers, according to the Intergovernmental Interior Ministries Secretariat, an international government-backed immigration office in Geneva. This approximates a seventh of annual development aid channeled from the industrialized West to the world's poorest nations, which in 1990 totaled $54 billion. The amount spent on asylum was some 50 percent higher than in the previous year, underlining the growing bureaucratic costs of caring for the refugees of war-torn countries.

Europe continues to be the destination for most asylum-seekers from the rapidly disintegrating former Yugoslavia, and for many from Africa and Asia as well. The 13 European countries in the Geneva secretariat received 543,600 asylum applications last year, a rise of 27 percent from 1990's total of 426,100. Germany alone accounts for about 40 percent of all asylum requests. The 1991 cost to Germany of handling these refugees was at least $4 billion, according to Bonn's Interior Ministry.

Barbara Harrell Bond, Director of Oxford University's Refugee Studies Programme, blames the UNHCR, as well as nongovernmental organizations, for the high costs of handling refugees. Harrell Bond argues that current policies tend to perpetuate problems by imposing a dependency culture on refugees, forcing them to live in camps and to rely on distributions of emergency aid, instead of encouraging them to use their skills to become self-supporting and make a contribution to the host economy in the process [ibid.].

Among the success stories cited by Harrell Bond is Cyprus, where the government met the housing needs of the refugees and placed emphasis on labor-intensive policies, thus using the situation as "a catalyst for the reconstruction of its economy." In Nepal, Tibetan refugees were encouraged to use their carpet-making skills for which they were paid a wage, rather than relying on food aid. Within 30 years this policy had "created employment for thousands of others, [and today] carpet-making is the largest manufacturing industry in Nepal, with foreign currency earnings of $50 million annually" [ibid.].

Harrell Bond contrasts these cases with the "normal" approach in which host governments set up special offices to handle refugees: "The maintenance of these offices depends on the continued existence of visible concentrations of people who attract funds earmarked for refugees. The result has been a perpetuation of a population labelled refugees, left living in limbo, sometimes behind barbed wire, and dependent for their survival on relief." Such bureaucratic interests were demonstrated on the day the Afghanistan peace accord was signed: "Several hundred Pakistani government employees petitioned their parliament demanding to know what would happen to their employment if the refugees went home" [ibid.]. Harrell Bond claims that in the future, governments should adopt a "development," rather than a "relief" approach, with the implication that the refugees should be settled on a semipermament basis even though their most basic wish is to go home.

For the moment, UNHCR is doing everything it can to protect refugees on all continents. In **Africa**, increasing internal conflict and instability have spawned great population movements. There were major influxes into Malawi from Mozambique; into Côte d'Ivoire, Guinea, and Sierra Leone from Liberia; and into Kenya from countries in the Horn of Africa. The impact of such movements on host nations in Africa has been particularly severe, since many are themselves impoverished and cannot bear the burden of refugees. For the Horn of Africa, a region traditionally plagued by crises, this has been especially true. The UNHCR assisted some 50,000 Ethiopians—mostly soldiers—who arrived in the Kassala area at the end of May 1991. Another 130,000 Sudanese refugees living in Ethiopian camps fled to southeastern Sudan. Meanwhile, a horrific war being waged in Somalia between sub-clans sent some 600,000 refugees into eastern Ethiopia. The UNHCR spent a total of $225.9 million on assistance in Africa in 1991.

In southwest Asia and the Middle East, UNHCR activities were dominated by the impact of the Gulf War. Some two million Iraqis were uprooted as a result of the war and subsequent civil unrest. "This constitutes one of the most tragic refugee situations in recent history,"

Ogata stated in her 1990–91 report to the General Assembly [A/AC.96/774, parts V & VI]. Some 1.3 million displaced people took refuge inside Iran, and an additional 430,000 had to be accommodated in makeshift tents along the Turkish-Iraqi border because of Istanbul's refusal to allow Iraqi Kurds to enter its territory. After a massive international relief effort, backed up by the military protection of the allied forces, many Kurds returned to Iraq. Some 7,000 decided to remain in Turkey, and 220,000 are still in Iran. An estimated 550,000 of the Kurds who returned are still displaced within their own country because of the Iraqi army's blockade of much of Kurdistan and the economic embargo on the region.

In another troubled region of the Arab world, the failure of the United Nations to organize a referendum on the future of Western Sahara has left many Saharans impatiently waiting to return home.

The victory of the Afghan guerrillas in the latter part of May 1992 paved the way for the rapid return of refugees from Pakistan and Iran, and the UNHCR has plans to spend more than $14 million in assistance. The U.N.'s humanitarian role in Afghanistan came under a cloud with the publication of a leaked draft auditor's report, which suggested that millions of dollars in aid had gone astray and were still unaccounted for because of poor accounting procedures in earlier years [The Independent, 11/19/91]. The eight-page summary dealt with the **U.N. Humanitarian and Economic Assistance Programmes in Afghanistan**, known as Operation Salaam. A later report—which the United Nations refused to make public—apparently exonerated all U.N. officials in the episode. The allegations in the initial report, which included suggestions of black market activities by U.N. staff and of contracts given without seeking competitive bids, left a sour taste in the mouths of many prominent aid donors.

In Asia, refugee policy comes under the **Comprehensive Plan of Action**, which covers the return of boat people from Indochina who have been determined migrants rather than true refugees. Most of the 9,300 Vietnamese asylum-seekers arriving in Southeast Asia in the first half of 1991 (a 33 percent drop from the previous year) landed in Hong Kong, which in mid-1992 sought to resume the forced return of most of the 54,000 boat people in local camps [The New York Times, 5/13/92]. In Cambodia, efforts began in 1992 to repatriate some of the 320,000 Cambodians from Thailand. Satellite images were taken by the French firm, Spot Images, to produce land-use maps indicating where the refugees might be resettled, and efforts were made to ensure that the refugees were given the chance to choose their final destination.

The crackdown by the military authorities in Myanmar (formerly Burma) led some 200,000 Muslim refugees to flee from that country into neighboring Bangladesh. Myanmar, a predominantly Buddhist country of 40 million, has been a pariah of the international community since

September 1990, when the military refused to hand over power to the democratically elected government.

Central America saw the repatriation of some 35,464 refugees to Nicaragua, along with 18,883 members of the contra resistance. Seven countries participated in a regional plan to benefit the populations uprooted by years of civil war here and elsewhere in Central America.

U.S. treatment of Haiti's boat people came under fire from the UNHCR. Despite personal appeals by Sadako Ogata, 238 Haitians were forcibly returned. Brushing aside U.N. reports putting the outflow of refugees at no more than 5,000, President Bush justified the return as an attempt to avoid a "magnet" effect that would lead to a mass exodus from Haiti. In refusing to accept the majority of Haitian refugees, the United States ignored a basic tenet of a treaty on refugees to which the nation has been a party since 1968. International refugee law forbids the return of refugees in the absence of adequate assurances that they will not be persecuted [Arthur Helton, Lawyers Committee for Refugees, in *The Miami Herald*, 11/24/91]. The United States is nevertheless one of the major resettlement countries in the Western Hemisphere, with a 1991 admissions quota of 125,000 persons—an increase of 18,000 over the previous year. Former Soviet citizens were the largest group under this quota (52,000), followed by the Vietnamese.

3. Information

For the first time in its 14-year existence, the **Committee on Information (COI)** has begun to coherently address practical problems with the way the U.N. disseminates information to the press and public. No longer satisfied with the carefully balanced consensus that has character-ized its work in the last two years, COI initiated pragmatic discussions during its 1992 annual session in March and April aimed at solidifying heightened public interest in the United Nations and meeting unprece-dented demands from the media for timely and accurate information on its various activities. These discussions produced recommendations on several issues not previously considered by the Committee in a rational and orderly way, including the designation of COI as the sole subsidiary body mandated to give direction to the **U.N. Department of Public Information (DPI)**; a review of the usefulness and cost-effectiveness of U.N. publications; a study on the adequacy of working facilities for the press at U.N. Headquarters; and a program to restructure the Organiza-tion's network of information centers around the world [U.N. press release PI/765, 4/15/92]. These issues will likely form the core of a more action-oriented U.N. information strategy in the 1990s.

Developing country members of COI continued to promote the

establishment of a **"new world information and communication order"**—previously referred to by the acronym **NWICO**—in an effort to reduce disparities in the international flow of information and to assist developing countries in building modern communication infrastructures. Fierce disagreements over whether NWICO would reverse the worldwide domination of developed country media or promote press censorship prevented COI from reaching consensus for its first 12 years, but these battles passed with the confrontationalist politics of the cold war. Developed countries have recognized that disparities exist and have pledged to reduce them. Since 1990 the General Assembly has been able to adopt an annual resolution on "information in the service of humanity" without a vote, upon the consensus recommendation of COI. The 47th Session of the General Assembly is expected to do the same.

An accompanying resolution on U.N. "public information policies and activities" constitutes a "major breakthrough," both in its preparation and in its substance. In the past, COI has simply added new priorities to the previous year's resolution, producing a confusing and often contradictory set of directives for DPI that failed to articulate a clear information strategy and guarantee the most efficient use of scarce resources. In 1992 the Committee provided a shortened list of priority subjects for DPI to focus its dissemination efforts on (the major peace and security, human rights, and economic and social issues), and highlighted the four specific concerns that had been identified at the Committee's 1992 session (described above). "Micromanagement" of DPI was giving way to more effective leadership characterized by broader guidelines [U.N. press release PI/757, 3/30/92; PI/765, 4/16/92].

These measures were designed to complement the Secretary-General's wider effort to restructure the senior levels of the Secretariat—in part through the appointment of a new Under-Secretary-General for Public Information, Eugeniusz Wyzner, on February 7—and to ensure that streamlining and cost control within the various departments would be an ongoing process. In recognition of its uniquely close working relationship with DPI, COI was to be directly involved in this process. Beginning in 1991 the Committee's officers and the representatives of the regional groups in its membership were requested to stay in contact with officials in DPI, both during and between COI's annual sessions, to maintain the momentum toward reform [A/Res/46/73].

The publications review was similarly intended to encourage DPI to make the best and most efficient use of existing resources. COI would consider a report next year on costs, circulation, language versions, and target audiences, while the Secretary-General was to provide criteria for judging the timeliness, usefulness, and cost-effectiveness of all U.N. publications. Items produced at a loss would eventually have to be discontinued or, if possible, produced outside DPI by commercial publishers.

With only limited office space at Headquarters for 200 media organizations from 43 countries, there was little DPI could do within existing resources to improve the **working conditions of part-time and full-time journalists** covering the U.N. beat. But according to the Under-Secretary-General, a plan was being drafted to address the needs of the press corps in the 1990s, possibly involving major financial commitments. To defray some of these costs, DPI might consider charging rent to major news organizations, with discounts accorded to developing country media. Accommodations for journalists from the least developed countries would be free-of-charge [U.N. press release PI/764, 4/9/92]. In addition to financial aspects, the Secretary-General will also report on possibilities for greater coordination in the provision of media services, including accommodations, press releases, and accreditation. This might promote further structural reform in DPI and eliminate those journalists who purportedly occupy U.N. office space but rarely cover U.N. activities.

The Secretary-General's tentative proposal to integrate, as a cost-saving measure, about 20 of the U.N.'s 67 information centers with field offices of the U.N. Development Programme (UNDP) provoked the most heated discussion of the session. Not yet in final form, the restructuring plan would preserve the functional autonomy of the centers while facilitating the sharing of premises, telecommunications equipment, and administrative, reference, and computer services with UNDP. Several centers are already headed by UNDP officials who served concurrently as center directors.

After assurances from the Under-Secretary-General that mandated information programs would still be delivered and that no centers would be closed down, COI approved a recommendation requesting a detailed explanation of the plan. COI further suggested that the General Assembly affirm its intention to establish new centers in developed and developing countries. They pointed out that although the centers in the South were often granted premises free of charge by host countries—and therefore required less financial support than those in the North—the South would nonetheless bear the burden of the integration proposals. COI recommended that the Secretary-General investigate ways of redressing the imbalance in resource allocations.

4. Health

In response to fundamental political, social, and economic changes throughout the world, the **World Health Organization's (WHO)** Executive Board began 1992 by creating a working group to examine WHO's structure, flexibility, leadership potential, and capabilities for promoting and supporting international health work [WHO/4, 1/29/92]. Although the working group will not present its findings to the Executive Board until January 1993, **Dr. Hiroshi Nakajima, WHO's Director-General**, has outlined four components of a new **"Paradigm for Health"** [EB/89/11] to serve as the main thrust for public health action in a changing world: (1) that individuals, families, and communities take responsibility for their own health needs, while governments continue to keep in mind that their policies have a major role in determining the quality of life for their citizens and the quality of health care they receive; (2) that priority is given to assuring access to health care for all, with special support provided for the countries and population groups in greatest need; (3) that all resources, financial and human, are mobilized for health; and (4) that evaluation of the effectiveness of public health action takes place in a wider social, political, and economic context.

During its January 1992 session the Board examined the second global evaluation of the progress toward WHO's "Health for All" goal, established as the organization's working priority in 1977. This evaluation [EB/89/10], covering the years 1985–91, notes that despite substantial improvement in the world health picture, economic problems continue to widen the gap between least-developed countries and other developing countries. In the developed countries, changes in life-style and in the environment, coupled with the rapid aging of populations, has led to the growing prevalence of cancer, cardiovascular disease, diabetes, and still other chronic diseases. The populations of developing countries are beginning to face the same problems; and their burden is aggravated by the spread of HIV/AIDS and the resurgence of such diseases as malaria, tuberculosis, and cholera. The evaluation was forwarded to the **45th World Health Assembly**, WHO's premier policy organ, which met between May 4 and 15, 1992.

Despite the somewhat pessimistic picture, WHO has recently recorded significant victories in its struggle for health for all. In October 1991 members of the U.N. community celebrated the "greatest public health success story of the past decade": immunization coverage against six major childhood diseases for 80 percent of the world's children—part of a continuing global effort at universal immunization led by WHO and UNICEF's **Expanded Programme on Immunization** [press kit, Childhood immunization: a global achievement]. Encouraged by this success, a new worldwide initiative was launched in December 1991 to improve existing vaccines and develop new ones to help reduce childhood mortality by the year 2000 [WHO/UN 100, 12/18/91]. The **Childhood Vaccine Initiative** involves an even more ambitious mobilization of U.N. agencies, public and private foundations, private industry, and bilateral aid programs than in the past.

Noting progress on a variety of other fronts, WHO predicts the eradication of **guinea worm disease** by 1995, the target date [WHO/UN 26, 4/10/92]. A similar WHO-led effort wiped out **smallpox** in 1979; and the **Onchocerciasis (river blindness) Control Programme** enters its fourth and final six-year phase in which the disease is expected to be eliminated from most of West Africa, where it had once posed a major threat [WHO/ UN 15, 2/27/92]. In the fight against leprosy, which still affects an estimated 5–6 million persons worldwide, a new drug treatment has given hope to the efforts to wipe out one of mankind's oldest diseases [WHO/UN 10, 2/20/91].

No such progress has been made in the fight against **HIV/AIDS.** According to the most recent statistics, more than 1 million people have been newly infected with human immunodeficiency virus (HIV), the causative agent for AIDS, since April 1991 [WHO/UN 9, 2/12/92]. The 46th General Assembly, expressing its continued commitment to the prevention and control of AIDS, called upon WHO to intensify efforts by the U.N. system to combat the disease. (WHO workers in Geneva have gone so far as to distribute condom-containing key rings to other U.N. staffers in that city in an effort to raise AIDS awareness [*The InterDependent*, 1–2/92].) U.N. agencies, intergovernmental and nongovernmental organizations, member states, and the public and private sector were encouraged to pitch in [A/Res/46/203].

WHO continues to direct and coordinate the global response to the HIV/AIDS crisis through the **Global Programme on AIDS.** The 45th World Health Assembly considered an updated strategy to meet the growing challenge of HIV/AIDS, which proposed directing particular attention to the value of treatment and prevention programs that focus on improving women's health, education, and status; of a social environment that gives greater support to prevention programs; of publicizing the public health dangers of stigmatization and discrimination; and of increasing emphasis on care [WHO/4, 1/28/92]. Indeed, in March 1992 the **U.N. Commission on Human Rights** adopted its own resolution concerned with discrimination against people infected with HIV/AIDS. In recognition of the growing size and scope of the AIDS crisis, "Sharing the Challenge" was selected as the theme of World AIDS Day 1991 (traditionally held in December), reflecting the conviction that "a challenge of this magnitude cannot be met by any one community, country, or organization in isolation" [WHO/UN 96, 11/28/91].

Nevertheless, WHO came in for criticism at mid-year by a leading AIDS research group for its failure to provide an adequate response to the AIDS problem. The group, led by Dr. Jonathan Mann, former head of the global AIDS program at WHO, claims that the World Health Organization is "underestimating . . . the scope of the problem" [*The New York Times*, 6/4/92]. Whereas WHO predicts that the number of people infected with the HIV virus by 2000 will be "at most" 40 million, the group estimates that as many as 110 million people may be infected with HIV by this date [ibid.]. No country or community has managed to halt the HIV virus, which is spreading with "astounding rapidity" in many areas of the world [ibid.].

As the world community is becoming aware, the challenge is not only to the health sector but to the social and economic life of nations as well. This is especially true in developing countries, which will be home to an estimated 90 percent of the world's HIV/AIDS cases by the year 2000. In East and Central Africa, where a third of the sexually active adults in many urban areas are already infected, child mortality rates are reverting to their 1980 levels, canceling gains made through immunization and other child-survival programs. In addition to direct health costs of HIV/AIDS, indirect costs—in particular the loss of income and the decreased productivity of the labor force—threaten long-run economic growth [*Finance & Development*, 12/91]. **Women and children** have become increasingly vulnerable, whether as casualties or survivors. HIV-infected women have given birth to almost 1 million infected children, over half of whom died immediately or have since developed AIDS. Additional millions of children, though not infected themselves, will become orphans. It is estimated that by the year 2000 over 10 million children, mostly in sub-Saharan Africa, will lose their mothers to AIDS [WHO/UN 75, 10/15/91].

The theme of World AIDS Day 1992, **"AIDS: A Community Commitment,"** was inspired by countless community actions to contain the spread of the disease. On that day, via a series of large-scale community media events, attempts will be made to sensitize the public to the effects of HIV/AIDS and of its costs to the community at large [WHO/UN 22, 3/27/92].

Another ongoing WHO concern has been the effect on local populations of radiation from nuclear accidents. In April 1992, WHO and the governments of Belarus, the Russian Federation, and Ukraine signed a new agreement providing a legal framework for the operation of the **International Programme on the Health Effects of the Chernobyl Accident,** which was established after the 44th World Health Assembly in May 1991 [WHO/UN 28, 4/10/92]. Responding to overall health needs in the republics of the former Soviet Union, an area of the world with which it has had little to do in the past, WHO and UNICEF sponsored five fact-finding missions to the 11 republics of the Commonwealth of Independent States and to the Baltic states in February 1992. The fact-finders concluded that the international community should respond immediately to the "looming crisis" in these regions. The report of the joint WHO-UNICEF missions is part of a series of assessments that WHO and UNICEF, in conjunction with the governments of France, Japan, and the

United States, will use to develop a consolidated plan of action in 1992 [WHO/UN 20, 3/18/92].

In response to an urgent health problem on yet another continent, WHO appointed Dr. Jean-Paul Menu as its **special envoy to Cambodia,** where the large U.N. Transitional Authority (UNTAC) is monitoring a cease-fire effort after years of civil war and overseeing the rehabilitation of the country [WHO/UN 18, 2/4/92]. Since his appointment, Menu has been forced to deal with the outbreak of a form of malaria that is resistant to the usual drugs and that threatens not only the resident population but UNTAC's civilian and military personnel and the returning 360,000 Cambodian refugees as well. WHO is supporting the reestablishment of an antimalarial program, with funding from the United Kingdom, but without the assurance of sufficient supplies and personnel to ensure its success [WHO/UN 18, 3/17/92].

One of the 35 agenda items at the 45th World Health Assembly, which met May 4–15, 1992, was a discussion of the 270-page report of the **WHO Commission on Health and the Environment** [EB/89/23]—the findings of a two-year study of the links between health and environmental degradation, including the implications of rapidly expanding global population, pollution, and urbanization and the potential effects of climate change. The report, occasioned by the U.N. Conference on Environment and Development (UNCED), will be WHO's main contribution to UNCED and will become the basis of a special chapter in UNCED's final "Agenda 21" document.

Delegates at the Assembly were also asked to support WHO and UNICEF's new **"baby friendly" hospital initiative**—a global campaign to foster national action to encourage breast-feeding, as scientific studies continue to show that breast milk is not only the cheapest and best food available to infants but also immunizes and protects against early disease and infection [WHO/UN 19, 3/18/92]. In response to concerns regarding **transmission of the HIV virus through breast-feeding,** WHO and UNICEF convened an expert group to study the problem. The group recommended that in settings where infant mortality is high, "breast-feeding should remain the standard advice to pregnant women, including those who are known to be HIV-infected, because their baby's risk of becoming infected through breast-milk is likely to be lower than its risk of dying from other causes if deprived of breast-feeding" [WHO/UN 33, 5/4/92].

The Assembly also considered the **Accra Initiative on Health** adopted at the international forum on "Health: A Conditionality for Economic Development? Breaking the Cycle of Poverty and Inequity," held in Accra, Ghana, December 4–6, 1991. The declaration asserts that health must be one of the major criteria for assessing development strategies and that health should be integrated into those strategies [*WHO'S*

News, 2/92]. The theme of the Assembly's special Technical Discussions—
"Women, Health, and Development"—already recognizes such asser-
tions [WHO/UN 30, 4/21/92].

Cardiovascular disease continues to earn the appelation "public
health enemy No. 1." By adopting **"Heartbeat—The Rhythm of
Health"** as the theme for World Health Day 1992, WHO sought to alert
people to the dangers of heart attacks and strokes, which kill an estimated
12 million people a year. During the April 7 event governments were
urged to provide the financial, material, and human resources for preventive efforts, which could save 6 million lives a year [information kit, World Health
Day, 1992].

4. Drug Abuse, Production, and Trafficking

As the U.N.'s **Decade Against Drug Abuse (1991–2000)** was getting
under way, the International Narcotics Control Board (INCB) painted
only a few bright spots in an otherwise grim picture of the illicit drug
situation worldwide: There is a considerable decline in the quantity of
heroin transiting India (India assigns part of the credit to a denial of bail
to drug traffickers); the number of cocaine users in the United States
declined by 70 percent between 1985 and 1990 (mostly among young
people, it is noted, but no further explanation is supplied); Colombian
authorities have managed to incarcerate a significant number of drug
lords of the powerful Medellín cartel; some West European countries
report a leveling off or decline in the use of cannabis and heroin; most of
Europe reports a steadily increasing number of requests for drug treatment; and increasing vigilance by Africa's governments has led to a
sizable increase in the quantity of illicit drugs intercepted. These last two
might also be interpreted as having a grim flip side: The increase in
requests for treatment and in quantity intercepted could signal an increase
in drug use and trafficking. Among the avowedly disheartening drug data
offered by INCB is the fact that heroin abuse is on the increase throughout the world (most notably in the Near and Middle East and Asia, many
areas of which had been virtually free of addiction problems as late as
1980); and that trafficking—and collateral use—is rapidly growing in
Eastern Europe and the republics of the former Soviet Union, with an
upsurge of poppy cultivation now anticipated in the newly independent
states of Central Asia [*Report of the International Narcotics Control Board for 1991*, E/INCB/
1991/1].

A global consensus that activities to reduce demand are as important
as activities to reduce supply was one of the achievements of the General
Assembly's **February 1990 Special Session on Drugs.** Such a two-
pronged approach to drug control is given formal recognition in the

Global Programme of Action voted on at the session (which establishes priorities among the activities outlined by the 1987 International Conference on Drug Abuse and Illicit Trafficking) and by the **1988 Convention against Illicit Traffic in Narcotic Drugs and Psychotropic Substances.**

Asserting a need for greater efficiency, coordination, and dollar-stretching in countering the threat of drug abuse and trafficking, the General Assembly agreed in 1990 to integrate the U.N.'s three drug units into one **U.N. International Drug Control Programme (UNDCP),** effective September 1991. The INCB secretariat was one of these, but the Assembly did not alter **INCB** itself—a body of experts, created by treaty law, that monitors the legal production of drugs and their movement from source to consumer to trace illegal diversions, including the drugs, substances, and precursor chemicals covered in the 1988 convention. The Board's 1991 report noted the increase in the number of states parties to this last treaty (up 14 for a new total of 60) and to the two other drug-control treaties: the 1961 Single Convention on Narcotic Drugs, amended by the 1972 Protocol (4/133) and the 1971 Convention on Psychotropic Substances (3/106) [ibid.].

The **Commission on Narcotic Drugs (CND)**—the main policy-making organ for international drug control, reporting to ECOSOC—underwent a number of changes too. The most recent is an increase in size from 40 to 53 members (traditionally, states with a particular domestic interest in the issue). According to the decision taken at ECOSOC's resumed first regular session in June 1991 [nar./inf.lett./1992/1], the 13 new seats were earmarked for particular geographical areas (4 for the African group, 3 each for the Asian group and the Latin American and Caribbean group, 1 each for the Eastern Europe group and the Western European and Others group, and 1 to rotate between the Asian and the Latin American–Caribbean group every four years). Another ECOSOC resolution called on the Commission to give policy guidance to UNDCP itself and to review the progress being made in implementing the Global Programme of Action and the subsequent U.N. System-Wide Plan to assist the process.

Addressing the Council for the first time as **Executive Director of UNDCP, Giorgio Giacomelli** reported on the drug control programs traditionally supported by the Fund for Drug Abuse Control, one of the three bodies integrated in the new Programme. Of 20 new projects in 1990, he noted, most were in Africa and the Caribbean [nar./inf.lett./1992/1]. The Fund is now supporting 118 projects in all in 67 countries—most in Asia, where UNDCP recently established a regional center largely with Japanese money [ibid.; U.N. press release SOC/NAR/599, 3/23/92].

Among the UNDCP initiatives launched as part of the U.N. Decade Against Drug Abuse itself is a program to harmonize national drug legislation in all the countries of Central Africa, increasingly a transit route for cocaine making its way to Western Europe; and a program that offers common training to a small group of African lawyers as a means of aiding the harmonization process—and of increasing the prospects for adherence to such a body of law here and elsewhere on the continent [nar./inf.lett./1991/5]. In November 1991, Colombia gave formal agreement to two projects: one to enhance local expertise in drug testing for forensic purposes, and the other to computerize the country's judicial system, improving and speeding up legal processing [ibid.]. And in March 1992, Czechoslovakia and UNDCP signed the papers for that country's first drug project—this to establish four mobile customs-control units for border areas along the Balkan drug-trafficking route, a new regional effort. UNDCP will provide vehicles, drug-detection and radio-communications equipment, and a highly sophisticated mobile x-ray unit [U.N. press release SOC/NAR/598, 3/9/92].

UNDCP continues to support efforts at controlling the supply of drugs as well, usually working in conjunction with other U.N. agencies and with local authorities. Such efforts are usually aimed at curtailing the dependency of rural farmers on **drug-producing crops** and at improving a wide variety of social and other services rendered to farmers and the surrounding community—with a growing degree of success, say UNDCP and the U.N. Development Programme [UNDP, "Special Report: Grappling With Drugs," World Development, 5/91]. One of the newest projects, entered into on December 12, 1991, by UNDCP, the International Fund for Agricultural Development, and the Laotian government will attempt the gradual elimination of opium poppy cultivation in the country's Xieng Khouang highlands. A pilot project in Morocco will attempt to do the same with regard to cannabis cultivation [nar./inf.lett./1991/4]. And two coca crop substitution projects already well under way in Colombia have made "considerable progress," reducing illicit coca cultivation in the area by 30 percent, or 1,300 hectares. In those areas in which the project has been operational since 1985, the percentage is at least twice that. Here, new roads, agro-industrial plants, improved sanitation, water supply, and health care services, schools, houses, and shops bear additional witness to change [ibid.].

UNDCP Executive Director Giacomelli went on to advise ECO-SOC that 53 countries had contributed to the voluntary Fund in 1990—with $41.5 million in new pledges—but that just nine countries were responsible for 90 percent of the total. Italy continues as the main donor; it contributed $31.6 million in 1991 [ibid.]. Despite Washington's call for a worldwide war on drugs, notes Jeffrey Laurenti, Executive Director of Multilateral Studies at the United Nations Association of the USA, the Bush administration "will slash its contribution to the U.N. Drug Control Programme by nearly 40 percent this year" ["The U.S. Retreats in the War on Drugs," The Christian Science Monitor, 4/30/92].

Funding and the efficient use of scarce financial and personnel resources were clearly on the mind of the 46th General Assembly, which touched on such matters in four of its five resolutions on international drug control. The issue was considered most directly in Resolution 104. This resolution, "endorse[d]" not only ECOSOC's resolution 1991/38 that directed the Commission on Narcotic Drugs to monitor UNDCP activities and supply policy guidance but also "the proposal of the Secretary-General to place the **financial resources** of the existing U.N. Fund for Drug Abuse Control under the direct responsibility of the Executive Director of the U.N. International Drug Control Programme as a fund for financing operational activities, mainly in developing countries." Just how far this "policy guidance" went was the subject of lengthy and heated debate at the Commission's 35th session, which was held in Vienna, April 6–15, 1992. A number of delegates contended that the Commission should have a considerable say in allocating these voluntary funds, while major donors contended that no change was warranted in the existing practice. In the end the Commission asserted its power to set budget priorities, and it asked the Executive Director to submit with his proposed budget the general criteria that govern the utilization of all budget resources—this on "an experimental basis" [U.N. press release SOC/NAR/618, 4/20/92].

Among other themes running through the 35th Commission session was the need for locating **alternative funding sources** for the developing world's fight against the cultivation of illicit crops and drug trafficking. Each of two Commission resolutions on the subject takes a novel approach to the problem. One (an initiative of UNDCP) proposes a "debt-for-drugs" swap, whereby the official debt of producer countries is converted into local currency to be used for alternative development projects. The second proposes that member states consider allocating confiscated drug monies and other assets for UNDCP's drug-control efforts. Now, just two months before the U.N. Conference on Environment and Development, the Commission spoke of drug cultivation's **effect on the ecosystem**—through deforestation and the degradation of natural reserves, through the use of toxic chemicals on illicit crops, and through irresponsible disposal of wastes—and stressed the importance of assessing the damage [ibid.].

At the urging of the United States, the Commission added to the list of **"precursor chemicals"** banned under the 1988 U.N. Convention against Illicit Traffic in Narcotic Drugs and Psychotropic Substances ten more. The listing of these chemicals that have licit uses but are also used in the manufacture of heroin and cocaine is intended to lead to national monitoring of their production and export [ibid.].

One of the 46th General Assembly's resolutions on drugs had "reaffirmed" the necessity of ensuring that **U.N. Charter principles** are strictly respected in the course of the Organization's antidrug efforts, naming state sovereignty, territorial integrity, noninterference, and "non-use of force or the threat of force in international relations" [A/Res/ 46/101]—concerns that have attended U.S. antidrug efforts in Latin America. The Cuban representative, speaking directly to this point at the 35th Commission, recommended against "setting up . . . supranational bodies or agencies that would allow powerful countries to take unilateral action, even if it was under the aegis of international instruments" [U.N. press release SOC/NAR/606, 4/8/92].

The 46th Session also requested the Secretary-General to report to the 47th on the progress made by governments and U.N. bodies in implementing the Global Programme of Action [A/Res/46/102]. The Commission later praised the idea and suggested publicizing the positive findings [U.N. press release SOC/NAR/611, 4/13/92].

6. Other Social Issues

The Status of Women

September 3, 1991, marked the tenth anniversary of the entry into force of the **U.N. Convention on the Elimination of All Forms of Discrimination against Women.** Adopted in December 1979, three years into the U.N. Decade for Women (1976–85), the 30-article Convention affirms the civil, political, economic, and social rights of women and sets standards that states parties must meet in improving the conditions under which women live and work. Among the most recent to ratify or accede to the Convention were Burundi, Estonia, Israel, Latvia, Nepal, the Netherlands, and Seychelles (though not yet the United States) [CEDAW/C/ 1992/L.1], for a total of 114 states parties by March 31, 1992.

Monitoring the implementation of the Convention and examining the reports received from the states parties is the **Committee on Elimination of Discrimination against Women (CEDAW),** which met in New York for its 11th annual session January 20–31, 1992. Prominent on its agenda was the issue of **violence against women**—a matter not explicitly addressed in the Convention but the subject of considerable attention at the Economic and Social Council (ECOSOC) in 1991, which at the recommendation of its **Commission on the Status of Women (CSW)** identified such violence as the result of "a power imbalance between women and men" [ECOSOC resolution 1991/18] and asked a group of experts to draft a framework for an international legal instrument on the subject. Violence against women is also a topic that CEDAW has suggested for the agenda of the **World Conference on Human Rights,** to be held in June 1993. In making a case for consideration of this problem at the

World Conference, CEDAW argues that gender-based violence impairs women's enjoyment of those rights and that the failure to mention this form of violence specifically in appropriate forums and documents is to neglect an important aspect of human rights [CEDAW/C/1992/L.1/Add.15]. To this end, CEDAW has recommended that the Secretary-General make sure that just such a "gender perspective" will be adopted in all documentation prepared for the conference [CEDAW/C/1992/L.1/Add.14; U.N. press release WOM/635, 1/29/92]. CEDAW investigations into the issue of violence against women included a review of the manner in which states parties to the Convention have implemented Article 6, which deals with exploitation, trafficking, and prostitution—another sort of gender-based behavior that, the committee says, puts women at special risk of violence and abuse.

Of the 46th General Assembly's four resolutions on the subject of women, the most comprehensive dealt with implementation of the **Forward-Looking Strategies for the Advancement of Women to the Year 2000**—the declaration of the world conference in Nairobi that capped the U.N. Decade of Women. Touching upon everything from adequate support for CEDAW's activities to the need for continuing the weekly radio programs on women, the Assembly called on member states to "give priority to policies and programmes relating to employment, health and education for the empowerment of women" [A/Res/46/98]. Another resolution "requested" the Secretary-General to submit to the 47th Session a study of the "barriers to the advancement of women and an action programme for the advancement of women in the Secretariat for the period 1991–1994" [A/Res/46/100].

Speaking at a commemoration of International Women's Day, the new U.N. Secretary-General, Boutros Boutros-Ghali, noted his commitment to giving women every opportunity to serve in **senior posts,** both in the **Secretariat** and in **peacekeeping operations,** but went on to say that restructuring of the Secretariat entails eliminating a number of posts in "the top echelon" and that he did "not foresee an increase in the number of women at senior levels in the very near future" [U.N. press release SG/SM/4712/Rev. 1, 3/6/92]. (A more extensive discussion of the status of women in the Secretariat can be found in Chapter VII of this volume, Finance and Administration.)

ECOSOC's Commission on the Status of Women, which is given a major role in promoting and monitoring the implementation of the Forward-Looking Strategies, held its 36th annual session in Vienna between March 11 and 20, 1992. One of its actions was to name **China** as the host of the fourth **World Conference on Women**—the first to be held in an Asian country [U.N. press release WOM/661, 3/23/92]. The choice of date, September 4–15, 1995, just before the opening of the General Assembly, takes account of the fact that any later event could well be overshadowed by celebrations of the U.N.'s 50th anniversary [E/CN.6/1992/

3]. The General Assembly and the Commission in turn called on the U.N. Secretary-General to appoint a woman as secretary-general of the Conference by the end of 1992 [A/Res/46/98; U.N. press release WOM/661, 3/23/92].

The Commission continues to organize its discussion around the three "priority themes"—equality, development, and peace—based on the Forward-Looking Strategies. At its 36th session in 1992 it turned its attention to the need for attacking de facto discrimination even where antidiscriminatory laws are already on the books (equality), for increasing women's involvement in environmental protection and the development process (development) in anticipation of the U.N. Conference on Environment and Development (UNCED) in June 1992, and for ensuring women's participation in political decision-making (peace). One of the draft resolutions adopted by the Commission requested governments and multilateral institutions to help finance a greater role for women in environmental management programs and allow them greater access to environmentally sound technologies, particularly in developing countries. The same resolution asked governments and organizations to "ensure equitable participation of women in their delegations" at UNCED [U.N. press release WOM/661, 3/23/92].

During its eight-day session the Commission reviewed the report of the expert group that was asked to suggest a framework for an international instrument on violence against women and which recommended a declaration on the subject. The expert group draft defines its subject as "any act, omission, controlling behaviour or threat, in any sphere, that results in physical, sexual or psychological injury to women," and it encourages international organizations to foster greater "coordination within the U.N. system between human rights treaty bodies to effectively address the matter" [E/CN.6/1992/4]. The Commission recommended that ECOSOC convene an "inter-sessional working group" to refine the draft, with a view to finalizing it for subsequent consideration by ECOSOC [U.N. press release WOM 661, 3/23/92].

Another expert group had been mandated to consider the problem of integrating the needs of **elderly and aging** women into the development process and, conversely, to consider this population's potential contribution to national development. The experts noted the value of vocational training and retraining programs, of a ready supply of glasses and hearing aids, and of equal access to credit and loans to an active and productive elderly population [E/CN.6/1992/8]. The Commission's draft resolution on the subject invited the preparatory committees for the 1993 World Conference on Human Rights and the 1994 International Conference on Population and Development to include on their agendas the situation of elderly women, who face discrimination on the grounds of both age and sex [U.N. press release WOM/661, 3/23/92].

The **U.N. Department of Public Information** continues its ECO-

SOC-mandated campaign to disseminate information on women's rights and related issues to the widest possible audience in advance of the 1995 World Conference on Women. It followed up on *The World's Women, 1970–1990: Trends and Statistics*—the long-awaited collaborative effort among a variety of U.N. system bodies, published in June 1991—with its own *Women: Challenges to the Year 2000* (March 1992). This latest book, using statistics from the U.N. database, goes on to evaluate the status of women in specific areas: legislation, health, education, political participation, employment, legal literacy, and the peace movement. U.N. information centers throughout the world are encouraged to publish the text of the Convention to Eliminate All Forms of Discrimination against Women in all local languages.

DPI's 14-minute **weekly radio program, "Women/Femmes"**—the only U.N. radio program on a single theme—received a mention in the 46th General Assembly's omnibus resolution on the status of women. Here, the Secretary-General was requested to continue funding the program from the regular U.N. budget and to increase the number of languages in which it is disseminated [A/Res/46/98]. The program began in 1979 and reaches 400 radio stations around the world by shortwave. Among its recent weekly offerings have been a global survey of the status of abortion and an examination of the advantages and disadvantages for women of a united Europe.

The General Assembly traditionally reviews the work of two autonomous agencies that are attempting to raise women's social and economic status and ensure the integration of women's needs and skills in national development plans: the **International Research and Training Institute for the Advancement of Women (INSTRAW)** and the **U.N. Development Fund for Women (UNIFEM)**. INSTRAW carries out this effort through research, training, and the dissemination of information—whether on "sectoral issues" (the role of women in managing water supply and energy) or, as with 1991's special focus, on a "global issue" (the role of women in sustainable development). UNIFEM, created in 1984, is supplying the actual funds for programs that give women greater access to training, technologies, and credit, and that help them establish "viable commercial enterprises" [*Women News*, nos. 4 & 5, 1991]. New to its program in 1991 were issue-oriented undertakings—one, in cooperation with the U.N. High Commissioner for Refugees, to encourage greater attention to gender concerns in national refugee policies; the second to promote the inclusion of women's concerns in the UNCED process [A/46/439]. Despite general belt-tightening, this voluntary fund saw a 13 percent increase in contributions between 1990 and 1991 [UNIFEM press release, 3/16/92].

Because the report on the implementation of the Forward-Looking Strategies always includes a preview of the priority themes to be considered at the next session of the CSW, the 47th General Assembly will have previews of the work on the themes of "increasing awareness by women of their rights, including legal literacy," "women in extreme poverty: integration into national development planning," and "women in the peace process."

Crime

The months following the **Eighth Congress on Prevention of Crime and the Treatment of Offenders,** held in Havana in 1990, have seen a refining of the U.N.'s organizational chart in the crime prevention area—the first step in fulfilling the Congress's call for an effective crime prevention program. The General Assembly, on recommendation of the Congress, had quickly established an Intergovernmental Working Group on the Creation of an Effective International Crime and Justice Programme [A/Res/45/108], which met in Vienna the following August to elaborate proposals for carrying this out. The group's proposals were considered at a **Ministerial Meeting on the Creation of an Effective United Nations Crime Prevention Programme,** held in Versailles, France, in November 1991. Among the main proposals was one to replace the Committee on Crime Prevention and Control—the group of experts that had been developing standards and guidelines in the crime prevention and criminal justice field—with a body made up of the representatives of member states. Given a mandate by the General Assembly (the thinking went), such an intergovernmental body is more likely than a committee of independent experts to translate policy decisions and priorities into practice through practical action and concrete technical and cooperative activities. (The experts themselves had called attention to the need for the translation.) This **new Commission on Crime Prevention and Criminal Justice** would take its place as one of the functional commissions of the Economic and Social Council (ECOSOC) [A/Res/46/152, Annex].

In mid-December the General Assembly gave its unanimous approval, and on February 5, 1992, ECOSOC formally dissolved the old committee and agreed to establish the new commission [E/1992/L.12]. At this same organizational session ECOSOC elected 40 member states to take seats on the Commission—13 more than were allotted the old committee. Members will serve for three years (except for half of the present group, which will rotate off after two years, as decided by lot). Owing to budgetary constraints, the new Commission will meet once a year for a working session of no more than ten days.

The Versailles meeting's **Statement of Principles for the crime program** offered some broad directives, calling for a practically oriented effort and for strengthened operational activities, but it left more detailed priority-setting to the body itself in the interest of flexibility and pragmatism [A/Res/46/152, Annex]. As the discussion at the April 1992 inaugural session of the

Commission indicated [U.N. press release SOC/CP/75, 5/4/92], members tended to view those priorities differently, although a considerable number of the delegates stressed the importance of preventing transnational crime, especially organized crime. Of the eight draft resolutions adopted at this initial session in Vienna, most dealt with organizational matters, as might be expected, but a number of substantive issues were also discussed, among them the matter of assistance to states in countering money-laundering and related offenses.

The same Statement of Principles issued by the Versailles ministers assigns to the Commission the formulation of the programs for future crime congresses—formerly the responsibility of each congress itself—so as to assure a focused discussion and a coherent work program for the event. By limiting the topics to be discussed, the Commission intends to streamline congress procedures and avoid fruitless debate on controversial subjects. The April Commission drafted a list of **topics for the Ninth Congress**, to take place in 1995, and has asked for ECOSOC's approval of the four: "international cooperation and practical technical assistance for strengthening the rule of law; action against national and transnational economic, organized, and environmental crime; management and improvement of criminal justice systems; [and] crime prevention strategies for urban areas, and juvenile and violent criminality" [E/CN.15/1992/L.9/Rev.1]. The same resolution acknowledges a bid by Iran to host the event.

Yet to be acted on is the Statement of Principles' call for an increase in the number of staff who will aid the Commission in carrying out its mandate. The Commission inherited its predecessor's secretariat—**the Crime Prevention and Criminal Justice Branch of the Centre for Social Development and Humanitarian Affairs** in Vienna—but is hoping for enough staff to qualify for division status (a minimum of 15).

On hand to ease the transition during the opening days of the inaugural Commission session were some of the expert members of the dissolved Committee, who had served in their individual capacity and not as representatives of governments. (Several governments have already designated former committee members as their Commission delegates; and formal provision has been made for enlisting the aid of experts when the nations' political appointees consider it necessary.) A former committee member observed wryly that the Commission's advantage is that its decisions are the decisions of governments and will therefore be respected by them, whereas governments can ignore the advice of experts [U.N. press release SOC/CP/70, 4/23/92].

The 47th General Assembly will have before it a summary of expert and governmental opinion about strengthening international cooperation in combatting organized crime, as requested at both the 44th and 45th sessions [A/Res/44/71, A/Res/45/123]. Also to be considered at the upcoming session under the crime prevention and criminal justice rubric is a report by the Secretary-General on implementing the Statement of Principles that guides the reorganizational effort as well as a report on the efforts to ensure that "sufficient resources are provided to [the U.N. African] Institute [for the Prevention of Crime and the Treatment of Offenders] within the overall appropriations of the budget for the biennium 1992–1993" [A/Res/46/153].

Children and Youth

There are some encouraging signs of progress on youth fronts in the year-and-a-half since the 1989 **Convention on the Rights of the Child** entered into force [E/ICEF/1991/2 and *State of the World's Children 1992*]—a period that also saw the first **World Summit for Children**. Here, national leaders agreed to translate key children's rights into specific goals, establishing target dates of five-to-ten years for implementing them. At the opening of the 46th General Assembly in 1991, **United Nations Children's Fund (UNICEF)** Executive Director James P. Grant told an interviewer that the commitments made at the Summit had produced increased support for the Convention and had led a considerable number of states to formulate national programs of action to address children's needs, with the immediate effect of giving the WHO-UNICEF **Expanded Immunization Programme (EPI)** the boost it needed to reach a five-year goal right on target [*The New York Times*, 9/19/91].

The children's rights convention entered into force only eight months after it was opened for signature—a record for human rights treaties—and by March 1992 it had been ratified by 114 countries—another human rights record [*State of the World's Children 1992*]; at mid-year 30 more states had signaled their intent to do the same. As of the same date, the World Summit's **Declaration on the Survival, Protection and Development of Children** and Plan of Action had gathered 135 signatures.

The world leaders gathered at the Summit had pledged to formulate their own national programs of action to meet 27 agreed-upon child welfare goals by the year 2000, and to report their plans to UNICEF by the end of 1991. By May 1992, 128 had complied or were in the process of complying [interviews with *A Global Agenda: Issues Before the 47th General Assembly of the United Nations*]. Some middle-income countries, among them Mexico and Peru, had begun implementing their programs [UNICEF, *First Call for Children*, 1–3/92]. At regional conferences in the course of the year, heads of state throughout the developing world had reconfirmed their commitment to the Convention and to the Summit's goals [*State of the World's Children 1992*].

The **Committee on the Rights of the Child**—a group established by the Convention and mandated to monitor its implementation—met for the first time in October 1991 and drafted the guidelines for reports that each state party to the Convention must submit to the committee within two years of ratification and every five years thereafter. These reports will indicate the measures taken to comply with the Convention and, as decided by the committee, must be buttressed by statistics [*First Call for Children*, 1–3/92]. The committee, which elected Mrs. Hoda Badran of Egypt as Chair, asked the U.N. Secretary-General to schedule a week-long meeting to allow a committee working group to consider the first round of country reports, and asked that the committee itself be permitted two meetings a year, up from one, beginning in 1993 to permit a more than cursory review of the reports [ibid.].

The General Assembly has asked to see the committee's report as well as requesting the Secretary-General himself to report to the 47th Session on the progress that states are making in implementing the Convention [A/Res/46/112]. The same resolution "invites the Secretary-General to convene a brief meeting of the states parties to the Convention, preferably during the forty-seventh session, to determine the duration of the future meetings of the Committee . . . prior to the consideration of the question by the Assembly."

It was at the 46th General Assembly that UNICEF's Executive Director Grant and WHO's Executive Director Hiroshi Nakajima certified that the EPI had reached its goal, having succeeded in providing for the **immunization against six deadly childhood diseases of 80 percent of the world's children** under age one. Grant revealed his nervousness about ever reaching that well-publicized goal, and stated that until the September 1990 gathering of world leaders at the Summit for Children it had appeared that EPI would fall 10 percent short [*The New York Times,* 9/19/91]. Following on the success of EPI—described by one UNICEF officer as the largest international peacetime operation ever mounted—UNICEF is now pressing for **90 percent immunization** coverage and for the fulfillment of other specific Summit health goals [UNICEF Annual Report 1991]. To consolidate these gains, UNICEF, WHO, and others are cooperating to minimize future vaccine price increases and assure a stable supply of high-quality vaccines. UNICEF has introduced a Vaccine Independence Initiative in several of its country programs, and is hoping to set up a "revolving vaccine fund" to facilitate government purchases of vaccines using local currencies to ease some of the burden on poor developing countries [UNICEF/CF/EXD/1992–006].

UNICEF has provided **emergency support to Albania, Romania, Yugoslavia, and the Russian Federation**, in the form of essential drugs, medical supplies, high-protein food, and vegetable oil [E/ICEF/1992/CRP.3]. Emergency aid to drought-ridden **Sudan** and to war-ravaged **Iraq** dominated its activities in the Middle East and North Africa region, and UNICEF also took the lead in providing water supplies and sanitation facilities to refugee camps in the region [E/ICEF/1992/10].

As agreed to at the Children's Summit, many industrialized countries have been reviewing their aid programs in the light of the Plan of Action. The U.S. Congress, for example, appropriated $500 million in Fiscal Year 1992 for international follow-up to Summit commitments and a much larger sum for specific country programs. The Netherlands, granting $7.5 million in debt relief to Ecuador, Honduras, and Jamaica, stipulated that the money was to be used for children's programs. And the last year has seen similar initiatives by Germany, Switzerland, and Canada. The Development Assistance Committee of the Organization for Economic Cooperation and Development, which attempts to coordinate aid by the industrialized nations, is said to be considering ways of allocating aid in relation to Summit goals [*State of the World's Children 1992*].

Coordinating efforts on the multilateral level—to join forces where goals overlap, promote efficiency, and speed up desirable results—is the **Task Force for Child Survival and Development,** composed of WHO, UNICEF, the U.N. Development Programme, the World Bank, and the Rockefeller Foundation. Formed in 1984 to assist in accelerating global immunization efforts, it will now focus on still other Summit goals. UNESCO's efforts to fulfill these goals are targeted at education. In December 1991 it hosted in Paris the International Consultative Forum on Education for All to examine plans for, and the progress of, universal education in the year since the World Conference on Education for All, held in Jomtien, Thailand [*First Call for Children*, 1–3/92].

Concerned with the welfare of young people in the **15-to-24 age bracket** specifically is a similar group of members of the U.N. family, including WHO, UNICEF, the International Labour Organisation (ILO), the Food and Agricultural Organization (FAO), the U.N. Educational, Scientific and Cultural Organization (UNESCO), and the U.N. Development Programme's U.N. Volunteers (UNV). The Centre for Social Development and Humanitarian Affairs (CSDHA) in Vienna is the U.N. system's coordinator of youth programs and promoter of youth policies. It also administers the **U.N. Youth Fund,** which is helping to support national and regional activities for, by, and about youth.

"Many of the problems affecting young people result from the lack of adequate policies to deal with the continuous growth of the youth population," notes a recent U.N. publication [DPI/1129, 12/91]. It estimates that this group, 1 billion in 1990, will increase to 1.4 billion by 2025. **International Youth Year (IYY)** in 1985 called attention to the growing numbers and the needs of the teen-to-early adult population, and the U.N. General Assembly—itself acting as the U.N. World Conference for IYY—endorsed a series of guidelines for national youth policies and programs [A/Res/40/14]. The U.N. Secretariat has continued to promote implementation of the guidelines, as well as to promote interagency cooperation—and cooperation among and between these agencies, youth-related intergovernmental organizations, and young people themselves. But for all the initiatives, programs, and activities that have followed IYY, the Secretary-General reported to the 46th General Assembly that stronger efforts were required to achieve the objectives of the Year, including a review of the guidelines for further planning and for follow-up in the light of newly emerging youth issues and the changing international climate [communiqué from U.N. Office at Vienna (UNOV)].

The tenth anniversary of IYY in 1995 will be the occasion for launching special global activities to ensure that youth-related concerns are better integrated in national development strategies and activities. In compliance with the 45th General Assembly's Resolution 103, the Secretariat is preparing a draft **world youth program of action toward the year 2000 and beyond,** which will be submitted for the General Assembly's approval in 1995, its 50th Session.

In a related action, the Economic and Social Council decided to establish an open-ended ad hoc working group of the Commission for Social Development at the Commission's 33rd session in 1993, with a view to reviewing and appraising the progress achieved and obstacles faced in implementing the IYY objectives: Participation, Development, Peace. It is also to have a hand in drafting a calendar of activities to mark the anniversary and in preparing the draft of the world youth program of action. An Expert Group Meeting on Youth, held in Vienna from December 9 to 13, assisted the Secretariat with a preliminary draft. This draft was circulated among member states, concerned U.N. agencies, and relevant intergovernmental and nongovernmental organizations. The Secretary-General will submit a revised draft to the Commission for Social Development at its 33rd session for discussion by the working group on youth [ibid.]. The 47th Session of the General Assembly will have before it a report by the Secretary-General on "Policies and programmes involving youth."

Despite signs of increasing concern for the welfare of young people around the globe, child mortality, malnutrition, various means of exploitation, and **lack of education** continue to plague whole countries and even regions. A ten-year survey by UNESCO of over 100 developing countries reveals that government expenditure per pupil actually declined in two-thirds of those countries and that in half of them the proportion of children of school age who will actually attend primary school also declined. The children of Africa, where the total educational expenditure was cut by nearly 30 percent, were the hardest hit. At the same time, government spending in almost all developing countries is biased toward higher education for the few rather than basic education for all [*State of the World's Children 1992;* UNESCO, *The World Education Report,* 1992], and girls continue to receive short shrift [UNICEF Annual Report, 1991]. A surge in **child pornography and child prostitution** has also been noted, affecting over 1 million children, primarily in Asia—many no more than five years old. Cited among the major exploiters are tourists and the "sex tours" organized for visitors from industrialized countries [*First Call for Children,* 4/6/92].

Nor are child-welfare problems confined to developing countries. The **United States,** for example, has not kept up with other industrialized nations in assuring health care for children and their mothers. Its child mortality rate—resulting in 40,000 deaths of children under the age of one each year—is the highest in the First World; and preventable child-hood diseases, including measles, mumps, and rubella, reached epidemic proportions in 1990–91 [*The New York Times, 3/29/92*]. Indeed, such cities as Maputo, the capital of Zimbabwe, now have a higher level of child immunization than does New York City; one in five American children live in poverty; and the United States is one of the few states—and the only industrialized state—yet to sign, much less ratify, the Convention on the Rights of the Child [*The Christian Science Monitor, 2/4/92*]. UNICEF notes that conditions in some of the **states of the former Soviet Union,** formerly compared to those of developed countries, also "appear to be nearer those of lower middle-income developing countries" [U.N. press release ICEF/1738, 3/23/92]. In Albania—the worst case—approximately 20 percent of all children are malnourished, and the government's severe spending cuts have led to a doubling of infant mortality rates since 1989 [*State of the World's Children 1992*]. UNICEF's annual Executive Board meeting, in June 1992, took up the agency's response to such emergency situations, including discussion of UNICEF "intervention as a mediator for children in armed conflict" [U.N. press release ICEF/1738, 3/23/92].

Although this is not a budget year for UNICEF, which has a biennial budget cycle, finances were an important topic at the June session: Income, which not only grew steadily but exceeded projections during the 1985–90 period (with an especially large jump after the Children's Summit in 1990), dropped unexpectedly in 1991—mainly the result of a falloff in government contributions [E/ICEF/1992/AB/L.12; E/ICEF/1992/AB/L.13].

The 44th General Assembly proclaimed **1994 the International Year of the Family (IYF),** the 46th approved a program for the preparation and observance of the Year, and the 47th will monitor IYF preparations under the agenda item on social development. The theme chosen for the year is "Family: resources and responsibilities in a changing world" [communiqué from UNOV].

Aging

The U.N. General Assembly debated the question of aging as early as 1948, but it was not until 1982 that the U.N. program on aging captured world attention. In that year, the United Nations organized the **World Assembly on Aging** in Vienna, attended by 124 member states and numerous nongovernmental organizations. The World Assembly launched the **International Plan of Action on Aging** and set in train a series of U.N.-related initiatives, among them the establishment of the International Institute of Aging in Malta, the African Society of Gerontology, and the Banyan Fund Association (after a tree symbolizing longevity); the designation of **October 1 as the International Day for the Elderly;** and the launching of a global information campaign.

As the U.N. program on aging moved into top gear in 1991 to promote observance in 1992 of the tenth anniversary of the World Assembly on Aging, it coordinated a year-long series of consultations aimed at developing a practical strategy for 1992–2001 to improve the prospects for implementation of the World Assembly's Plan of Action. The 47th General Assembly will have two reports on aging—one promotional and one dealing with that ten-year strategy. "In a sense, the aging issue is really taking off," said Sylvie Bryant, Chief of the U.N. Office of Vienna (UNOV) in New York. UNOV's Centre for Social Development and Humanitarian Affairs (CSDHA) has been the lead agency in coordinating the world organization's program on aging.

CSDHA launched the **information campaign** for the 1992 anniversary with a flyer entitled "A Day, a year and a decade for aging," which suggested activities for the international, national, and local communities, with special attention to the last. CSDHA worked with "redisseminators"—chosen for their outreach to diverse constituencies around the world—to achieve maximum global coverage for its campaign at little cost. At the same time, the Federation of Organizations of the Elderly established special "1992 Committees" to promote the anniversary year at the local level among its 100 million or so members [communiqué from CSDHA/UNOV]. A second stage of the information campaign is being spearheaded by the U.N. Department of Public Information.

One important element of the 1992 campaign is the **U.N. Principles for Older Persons,** adopted by the 46th General Assembly [A/Res/46/91]. The Assembly urged the U.N. to disseminate the 18 Principles widely and called upon governments to incorporate them in their national programs. The Principles address such issues as independence for the elderly at home and in the workplace; participation of older persons in society and in policy-making; care from family, community, and society; self-fulfillment and access to cultural, spiritual, and recreational resources; and dignity, security, and freedom from exploitation or abuse.

The **strategy for the coming decade** that the 47th General Assembly will review takes the form of a set of global targets. These targets, says CSDHA, reflect a consensus of many actors in the field of aging—U.N. agencies and bodies, governments, organizations of older persons, and still other social, religious, professional, and academic organizations—on what can be achieved by combining forces in the years ahead, by building on existing structures and procedures, by adding a component on aging to existing development schemes, and by tapping the talents of older persons [communiqué from CSDHA/UNOV].

Despite the renewed attention to aging issues, **lack of funds** is likely to remain an obstacle to implementing the U.N.'s recommendations. "Those of us working on social issues think there should be far more money allocated to aging, as well as population issues, disability, and women because they are all critical to older people," said Susanne Paul, Chair of the NGO Committee on Aging and U.N. Representative of the Church World Service, which participated in developing the global targets. "Many of us want to empower older people to survive, develop, and participate. At the same time," she added, "governments have to take some responsibility for creating an environment for people to thrive."

Indeed, insufficient funding was a recurring theme in discussions about aging at the 46th General Assembly. During debate in the Third Committee, representatives of the Nordic countries, the European Community, and developing countries noted that the 1982 International Plan of Action on Aging had been poorly implemented because of funding problems [A/C.3/46/SR.20, SR.21]. Countries with "less-developed economies" expressed frustration over the financial burden of maintaining or implementing social programs of all kinds.

The General Assembly noted "with concern" the steady decline in contributions to the **U.N. Trust Fund for Aging** since 1982 [A/Res/46/94]. It also called upon the Secretary-General "to give all possible support, in the form of both regular and extrabudgetary resources, to the Aging Unit of [CSDHA] to enable it to fulfill its mandate as lead agency for the action programme on aging" [A/Res/46/91].

The U.N. Trust Fund for Aging, established in 1980 to provide technical assistance to developing countries, spent more money than it received in contributions between 1982 and 1990. In the 18-month period ending in December 1989, for example, Fund expenditures exceeded income by more than $106,000, and, according to figures provided by the UNOV, the Fund's balance had dwindled to $205,348. The private **Banyan Fund,** established in May 1991 and affiliated with the United Nations, is still in the process of raising sufficient funds from corporations, foundations, charities, and individuals for specific projects on aging, especially in developing countries.

There are signs that the downward trend in the Trust Fund's income and balance is reversing. During the 18-month period ending in June 1991, the Fund had a net income of $119,437, and its balance had increased to $323,083. This was the first time the Fund had a positive net income since 1981, although the Fund balance remained far below its 1981 level of approximately $700,000 [A/45/420].

Bryant of UNOV's New York office notes that longer life spans in developing countries will force the U.N. to make aging a priority on its agenda in the future.

Disabled Persons

The Third Committee discussion of the **U.N. Decade of Disabled Persons** (1983–92) at the 1991 General Assembly left little doubt of the delegates' eventual verdict: Attention has been drawn to the needs of disabled persons—

a primary goal—but relatively little progress has been made toward fulfilling those needs [A/C.3/46/SR.26]. The U.N. budget provides no additional financial resources for the Decade, but there had been hopes that such a Decade would spur regional and national efforts to carry out the 1982 **World Programme of Action Concerning Disabled Persons** [A/Res/37/52]. Its long-term goal is not only the rehabilitation of disabled persons and their full participation in society but also the prevention of disability itself.

To the Decade's credit, say those intimately involved in it, is a qualitative change in the perceptions of disability and a dispelling of much of the mythology surrounding handicap. For the first time in history, the issue of disability and the myriad concerns of disabled persons are appearing on the political agenda at both national and international levels, in both developed and developing countries. Disabled persons and their organizations are more apt to participate in policy formation. And factual knowledge, research, and data collection have improved significantly over the decade [communiqué from CSDHA/UNOV].

The U.N. Secretary-General's report to the 46th Session stressed the World Programme's "long-term goal" [A/46/366], and it went on to urge governments, bodies of the U.N. system, other intergovernmental organizations, and nongovernmental groups to begin developing the legislation and employment and education policies that will enable disabled persons to reach it.

The focal point for disability issues in the U.N. system is the Center for Social Development and Humanitarian Affairs (CSHDA) of the U.N. Office at Vienna (UNOV), which is developing its role as a clearinghouse for disability information and has instituted a "unique interagency mechanism" to coordinate activities among U.N. bodies and nongovernmental organizations as well [communiqué from CSDHA/UNOV]. Among the bodies regularly involved in this effort are the World Health Organization, which assesses national and local rehabilitation services; and the International Labour Organisation and the U.N. Relief and Works Agency for Palestine Refugees, which are exploring income-generating activities for disabled persons.

The shift of focus of the U.N. disability program from "awareness-raising to action" will now require a stronger emphasis on **technical cooperation activities.** A number of the developing country representatives who spoke in the Third Committee stated that worsening economic conditions had discouraged government efforts at implementing previously defined policies as well as at designing more ambitious ones [A/C.3/46/SR.26]. The Secretary-General's report to the 46th Assembly noted that the U.N. had recorded an increasing number of "urgent requests for assistance, particularly from grass-roots and national organizations in developing countries," but was restricted by the limited resources of the **Voluntary Fund for the Decade** [A/46/366]. The Fund, which was set up in 1980, has distributed $3 million in seed money to small-scale catalytic and innovative projects.

Capacity-building and institutional development are the main focus of Fund-assisted activities; most are aimed at training the trainers, leadership development, exchanges of knowledge and experience, data collection, and applied research [communiqué from CSDHA/UNOV].

The Secretary-General recommended to the 46th Assembly that the Fund continue beyond the Decade but take on a new name. The Assembly, in turn, asked the Economic and Social Council (ECOSOC) to render its opinion on the matter to the 47th Session [A/Res/46/96].

One of the U.N. disability program's ongoing priorities is the implementation of the rights of disabled persons through national disability legislation and international standard-setting activities. CSDHA/UNOV is currently drafting a **manual on national disability legislation** for developing countries. At the same time, an ad hoc open-ended working group of ECOSOC's Commission for Social Development has been elaborating **Standard Rules on the Equalization of Opportunities for Disabled Persons.** The group, composed of government experts and observers from U.N. agencies and intergovernmental and nongovernmental organizations, expects to adopt a draft text of these Standard Rules (along with a mechanism to monitor the application of the rules) at its third session, in September 1992. After the Commission has considered the text, it will be forwarded to ECOSOC, coming before the General Assembly in 1993 [communiqué from CSDHA/UNOV].

To apply these rules, however, member states will need an appropriate national infrastructure and legal and other mechanisms, now widely lacking. The General Assembly and ECOSOC called for a U.N. expert group to begin devising a long-term strategy for implementing these and other provisions of the World Programme of Action. Elements of such a strategy were discussed by an expert group in Vancouver in April 1992, at a meeting held in conjunction with "Independence 92"—an international exposition and congress celebrating the creativity of people with disabilities. A "strategy paper" will be submitted to the Commission for Social Development in 1993 and presented to the General Assembly at the 48th Session [ibid.].

Also of some urgency as the Decade comes to a close is agreement on the very **words used to express such concepts** as "impairment," "disability," "handicap," and "disabled person" in each of the official languages into which the World Programme of Action is translated, taking into account new phrasing and heightened sensitivities [interviews with *A Global Agenda: Issues Before the 47th Session of the General Assembly*]. The Secretary-General was requested to "finalize the review" of these phrases [ibid.].

The 46th General Assembly decided to mark the **conclusion of the Decade** for the Disabled with two days' worth of special plenary meetings "at the appropriate global level" during the 47th Session; October 12 and 13 have since been designated. In the delegates' hands will be the Secretary-General's report on the outcome of the Decade and on the orientation of the disability program in the future. Secretariat personnel note that the amount of time set aside for the Headquarters celebration is considerable—and that it will take considerable effort to make the world organization's own meeting rooms fully accessible to the disabled persons who take part [interviews with *Issues/47*].

Shelter and the Homeless

The Global Strategy for Shelter (GSS) to the Year 2000 [A/Res/43/181], adopted by the United Nations General Assembly in December 1988, focused global and national attention on an enormous challenge confronting all countries generally but developing countries in particular. Though calling for the mobilization of international and national cooperation in meeting this challenge, the GSS stresses that shelter goals are ultimately dependent on efforts of individual governments acting in their own social, economic, and cultural contexts.

In June 1991 the **U.N. Commission for Human Settlements,** the intergovernmental body responsible for coordinating, monitoring, and evaluating the GSS, adopted its "Second report on the implementation of the Global Strategy for Shelter to the Year 2000" [A/46/8/Add.1] at its 13th biannual session in Harare, Zimbabwe. The report provides a comprehensive evaluation of the role of governments, U.N. agencies and organizations, bilateral and multilateral institutions, and nongovernmental organizations in carrying out the GSS in 1990 and 1991. The report concluded that in general "a positive beginning has been made" but that "the condition of shelter and services, especially for the poor, in many developing and some industrialized countries has not shown marked improvement" [ibid.].

In response to the Commission's report, the 46th General Assembly commended governments that had initiated national shelter strategies, urged governments that had not already begun them to increase their efforts, and adopted the Commission's proposed **Plan of Action for 1992–93** [A/Res/46/163]. In addition, the General Assembly decided to consider at its 47th Session the Commission's request for a **U.N. conference on human settlements (HABITAT II)**, possibly in 1997. Such a conference would review trends in policies and programs in human settlements, conduct a mid-term review of the GSS, review the human settlements program in light of the U.N. Conference on Environment and Development (UNCED), and make recommendations for future action at the national and international levels [A/Res/46/164].

Within the U.N. system, the **U.N. Centre for Human Settlements (HABITAT),** located in Nairobi, provides substantive support to member states in their national efforts to implement the GSS. In addition to some 260 ongoing technical assistance projects in over 100 developing countries, HABITAT currently provides short-term advisory services to countries that have not yet envisioned far-reaching initiatives, organizes sub-regional informational and training seminars throughout the developing world, and conducts a research and development program for the GSS. In addition, in 1991, HABITAT developed a much needed set of shelter indicators for use by governments as guidelines to review progress in the formulation and implementation of national strategies [HS/C/13/4].

The promotion of women in human settlements continues to be of great concern to HABITAT, which is "focusing particularly on women in low-income households and disadvantaged communities, promoting them as agents of change and important users in the area of human settlements" [World Habitat Day 1991 Information Kit]. In this regard, HABITAT recently organized an interregional seminar to promote the participation of women in the GSS. The Commission, in turn, passed a special resolution [13/13] that urged both governments and HABITAT to take gender-sensitive steps to strengthen the role of women in shelter strategy.

In anticipation of UNCED in June 1992, the theme of World Habitat Day 1991 (the first Monday in October) was "Shelter and the Living Environment." At HABITAT's behest, human settlements will comprise a separate chapter of "Agenda 21"—the conference's final document, which is intended to guide policies and programs for sustainable development well into the 21st century. Recognizing that the issue does not exist in isolation, UNCED will also consider human settlements within several other chapters, among them those dealing with the quality and supply of freshwater resources, the protection and management of land resources, and the environmentally sound management of wastes. In the year leading up to the Conference, HABITAT's Executive Director, Arcot Ramachandran, emphasized the interrelationship among human settlements, the environment, and sustainable development, stating that "any consideration of the living environment must begin from the subject of housing and must be concerned primarily with the quality of life of the 1 billion people who are either homeless or housed in such inadequate conditions that their lives cannot be sustained. This is the world's single greatest environmental problem" [*Habitat News*, 8/91].

The Commission will meet for its 14th session from April 26 to May 7, 1993, in Nairobi. The provisional agenda includes a progress report on HABITAT activities, the GSS, and UNCED, and two special themes: improvement of municipal management; and cost-effective building materials, technologies, and transfer mechanisms for housing delivery [ibid.].

VI
Legal Issues

Although the General Assembly's activities made far fewer headlines than did the Security Council's resolutions on Libya and Iraq, the 46th Session made history of its own by repealing a controversial 1975 resolution equating Zionism with racism (with implications on several legal fronts) and by choosing to admit the two Koreas under Article 4 of the Charter. The 46th Assembly, and the numerous bodies reporting to the Assembly, made steady progress on a variety of other legal fronts, in part because the United States and the Russian Federation find themselves on the same side of many issues. But what continues to elude consensus in the post-Gulf War era is how to reconcile the ever-growing demands on the United Nations with the principle of sovereignty, especially in the light of U.N. Charter Article 2(7) proclaiming nonintervention in matters of "domestic jurisdiction." This issue, as well as continuing North-South divisions, is preventing progress in a number of areas.

1. The International Law Commission

The 46th General Assembly, pursuant to the statute of the International Law Commission (ILC), elected a new complement of 34 commission members to a five-year term, which began on January 1, 1992 [Decision 46/ 313]. The ILC, established in 1947 to assist the Assembly in codifying and progressively developing international law, consists of individuals who serve in their personal capacities, not as representatives of their governments. At the 43rd session of the ILC, April 29–July 19, 1991—the last presided over by the "old" membership—the group covered all the items on its current agenda and, perhaps by way of farewell, managed to adopt complete sets of draft articles for three of the agenda topics: final adoption of the draft on jurisdictional immunities of states and their property, and initial drafts of the law of the non-navigational uses of international watercourses and of the Code of Crimes against the Peace and Security of Mankind (which had been on the ILC agenda since 1947) [A/46/405 offers a compendium of these texts].

The ILC's **Draft Code of Crimes against the Peace and Security of Mankind** is now before governments for their comments, which are due by January 1, 1993. It completed the Code during its 43rd session by provisionally adopting a number of general articles as well as five new substantive "crimes": genocide, apartheid, systematic or mass violations of human rights, exceptionally serious war crimes, and willful and severe damage to the environment [A/46/10]. At previous sessions the ILC had identified seven others: aggression; threat of aggression; intervention; colonial domination and other forms of alien domination; international terrorism; the recruitment, use, financing, and training of mercenaries; and illicit traffic in narcotic drugs [see *A Global Agenda: Issues Before the 46th General Assembly of the United Nations*, pp. 236–38; and *Issues/45*, pp. 193–95]. The new draft Code no longer distinguishes between "crimes against peace," "war crimes," and "crimes against humanity" [compare the conclusion of the ILC's 42nd session that drug trafficking is a "crime against humanity"; see *Issues/46*, pp. 237–38].

Article 19 on **genocide** is based entirely on Article II of the Convention on the Prevention and Punishment of the Crime of Genocide adopted by the General Assembly in 1948. Genocide is simply defined as

> any of the following acts committed with intent to destroy, in whole or in part, a national, ethnic, racial or religious group as such: (a) killing members of the group; (b) causing serious bodily or mental harm to members of the group; (c) deliberately inflicting on the group conditions of life calculated to bring about its physical destruction in whole or in part; (d) imposing measures intended to prevent births within the group; and (e) forcibly transferring children of the group to another group [A/46/10, p. 261].

The list is intended to be exhaustive, not illustrative. It includes physical or biological destruction but does not extend to "cultural" genocide, that is, the destruction of the linguistic, religious, cultural, or other identity of a group.

The crime of **apartheid** in Article 20, based on Article II of the International Convention on the Suppression and Punishment of the Crime of Apartheid adopted by the General Assembly in 1973, provides a description of the courses of conduct constituting the crime but, because the intention was to cover a variety of possible cases, does not provide specific examples, such as the case of South Africa. The crime is defined as "acts based on policies and practices of racial segregation and discrimination committed for the purpose of establishing or maintaining domination by one racial group over any other racial group and systematically oppressing it." The prohibited courses of conduct include denial of the right to life and liberty; imposition of physically destructive living conditions; legislative measures calculated to deny participation in the political, social, economic, and cultural life of the country; racial segregation; forced labor; and persecution of organizations and persons who oppose apartheid [ibid., p. 263]. On the theory that only those who wield state authority are guilty of this crime, Article 20 targets "leaders" and "organizers."

Article 21 on the **systematic or mass violations of human rights** identifies as crimes the acts of murder, torture, establishing or maintaining the status of slavery, servitude, or forced labor, and persecution on social, political, racial, religious, or cultural grounds if these are committed in a systematic or massive way; and it goes on to include deportation or forcible transfer of a population, which necessarily entails a mass-scale element [ibid., p. 265]. The list of human rights here is based on a 1954 ILC draft code but broadened to reflect more recent developments in human rights, including subsequent multilateral conventions. The list is now exhaustive, not merely illustrative; and the crime is not confined to state officials but could conceivably extend to private groups that engage in the identified practices. According to the commentary, some members of the ILC were opposed to including "persecution" because of the absence of a universally accepted definition of the term [ibid., p. 268].

An **exceptionally serious war crime** under Article 22 is defined as an "exceptionally serious violation" of the principles and rules of international law applicable in armed conflicts, consisting of any of the following: acts of inhumanity, cruelty, or barbarity; settlement of occupied territory or changes to the demographic composition of such territory; use of unlawful weapons; use of weapons of warfare that can be expected to cause or are intended to cause widespread, long-term, and severe damage to the environment; large-scale destruction of civilian property; and "willful" attacks on property of "exceptional religious, historical, or cultural value" [ibid., p. 269]. According to the commentary, this provision is an obvious compromise between those who wanted a general definition of war crimes and those who sought an extensive, detailed list of the war crimes covered [ibid.]. What constitutes the "most serious among the most serious" of war crimes has primarily to do with the seriousness of the effects of the violation. The list does not necessarily duplicate the list of "grave" breaches under relevant multilateral conventions of humanitarian law [ibid., pp. 270-71]. Article 22 extends both to international armed conflicts (within Article 1[4] of Protocol I Additional to the Geneva Conventions) and to non-international conflicts (covered by Article 3, common to all four 1949 Geneva Conventions). The Article's language is intentionally vague on occasion (as in the case of "unlawful weapons") to permit "progressive development" (such as, for example, a future expansion of the list of banned weapons [ibid., p. 271]). Not all elements of Article 22 drew unanimous agreement even within the ILC; and at least one state filed a formal reservation respecting war crimes that cause harm to the environment [ibid., p. 273].

The direct source of Article 26, which brands as criminal **willful and severe damage to the environment**, is Article 55(1) of Protocol I Additional to the 1949 Geneva Conventions. Article 26 goes beyond Protocol I by making such harm to the environment criminal, whether or not it occurs in the course of an armed conflict. Three elements define this crime: (1) "widespread, long-term and severe damage" (2) to the "natural" environment (3) that has been brought about by "wilful," not merely negligent, behavior. The term willful is intended to exclude deliberate violation of regulations forbidding or restricting the use of certain substances or techniques "if the express aim or specific intention was not to cause damage to the environment"—a limitation that, as might be expected, was severely criticized by some members of the ILC, who argued that this limitation was not consistent with the definition of environmental war crimes in Article 22 [ibid., p. 276].

Other aspects of the substantive crimes now included in the Draft Code of Crimes against the Peace and Security of Mankind were criticized during discussions in the General Assembly's Sixth Committee [see, e.g., comments by Papua New Guinea on the omission of the concerns of indigenous peoples and on the state-actor limitations in connection with terrorism, A/C.6/46/SR.31]. Some states held sharply opposing views about the scope of the crimes covered by the Code. Guatemala, at one extreme, suggested that the list of Code crimes remain open and even expanded to encompass the confiscation of property acquired illegally [A/C.6/46/SR.33]; the Netherlands, at the other, argued that the Code already covered far too many crimes and should extend only to aggression, genocide, and certain violations of human rights [A/C.6/46/SR.26].

The general provisions of the Code adopted by the ILC proved on the whole even more controversial than did the provisions on particular crimes [see, e.g., discussion in the Sixth Committee, A/C.6/46/SR.22, pp. 7–8]. Article 3—which states that individuals may be found criminally liable and that this liability may be extended to those who aid, abet, or provide the means for the commission of the crime as well as to those who merely attempt the crime—proved particulary contentious. The fact that Article 3 leaves open the possibility of widening the scope of the Code (or of particular crimes within it) to include criminal liability for sovereign states found both partisans and detractors [A/46/10, p. 251; see also draft Article 5, ibid., p. 255, which also leaves open the possibility of state responsibility]. (Contrary to the preference of some states, however, Article 3 does not extend liability to those who become "accessories after the fact" by, for example, giving shelter to those who commit genocide [see ibid., p. 253].) Member states also noted that the article fails to resolve whether liability for attempt should apply to all Code crimes or only to some [see ibid., pp. 253–54]. Similarly, Article 14, relating to defenses and extenuating circumstances, might be described as an agreement to disagree, since, as currently drafted, it merely states that competent courts shall permit defenses "under the general principles of law, in the light of the character of each crime." It also states that the competent courts, in passing sentence, shall take into account "extenuating circumstances" [ibid., p. 257]. The vagueness of this provision reflects differences among states with respect to the propriety of such defenses as self-defense, coercion, necessity, *force majeure,* and error [ibid., p. 258]. Likewise unresolved is the question of appropriate penalties. Some states are decidedly opposed to imposing the death penalty, and there are at least three schools of thought on the subject of penalties in general: leave the issue to domestic law, provide a single scale of penalties applicable to all crimes, or accompany each definition of the particular crime with the corresponding penalty [ibid., pp. 260, 200–213]. Resolution of the question of applicable penalties was left to the second reading of the Code. Less controversial were provisions to exclude as a defense the "motive" of the accused (Article 4) [ibid., p. 254] or the fact that the person was merely "following orders" (Article 11) [p. 256]. As in prior years, critics charge that the ILC appeared more inclined to release a complete draft text, however inadequate, than to achieve the precision many states believe is essential for a criminal code [see, e.g., S. McCaffrey, "The 43rd Session of the International Law Commission," 85 *American Journal of International Law* 703 (1991), p. 707; note also comments by Israel, A/C.6/46/SR.31, and Turkey, A/C.6/46/SR.34].

During a review of the ninth report of its special rapporteur, the ILC discussed the related issue of the **jurisdiction of an international criminal court.** It has been examining the possibility of establishing such a court pursuant to a request by the General Assembly [see *Issues/46,* pp. 239–41]. At the 43rd session the discussion centered on the rapporteur's draft provisions for the jurisdiction of the court—in his view, extending to charges against individuals but not against states and covering all or some of the crimes in the ILC's own Draft Code of Crimes against the Peace and Security of Mankind [A/46/10, pp. 214–15].

As at the ILC's prior session, Commission members embraced the idea of an international criminal court with varying degrees of enthusiasm, and at least some expressed the view that further work on the matter should await a clear and specific mandate from the General Assembly [ibid., p. 217]. Similar doubts about the usefulness and viability of an international criminal court were expressed in the Assembly's Sixth Committee by states as various as the United States and Cuba [see A/C.6/46/SR.31]. As in prior sessions of the ILC, members differed about whether the court should be an appellate body with the power to review decisions rendered by national courts or whether it ought to have exclusive jurisdiction; about whether the court should have jurisdiction over only a small number of the most serious Code crimes or over international "crimes" not covered by the Code; and about whether sovereign consent to jurisdiction ought to be required. There was also no consensus with respect to the rapporteur's suggestion that states be able to institute proceedings in the court but that, in the cases of aggression or threat of aggression, such proceedings would be subject to a prior determination by the Security Council [A/46/10, pp. 218–35]. In its resolution on the ILC's report, the General Assembly requested that the ILC continue to examine issues with respect to establishment of an international criminal court [A/Res/46/54].

The **Jurisdictional Immunities of States and Their Property** has been on the ILC's agenda since 1978, and during its 43rd session in late spring 1991, the ILC adopted a final text of a set of draft articles [see *Issues/46*, pp. 244–45, for a summary of these; for text of articles and commentary, see A/46/10, pp. 11–151]. The 22 draft articles avoid irreconcilable doctrinal issues in favor of a series of pragmatic compromises in specific, enumerated areas in which sovereigns cannot invoke immunity in the courts of another state. Significant changes were made between the ILC's first and second readings of these articles, including a considerable expansion of the "commercial transactions" (formerly "commercial contracts") that fall outside the scope of immunity, and the deletion of a provision that had allowed for no immunity in "fiscal matters" [see A/46/10, pp. 69, 75, for a discussion of proposed Article 10]. Further, the ILC did not include in the text submitted to the General Assembly provisions on the settlement of disputes, indicating that this issue should be determined at an international conference of plenipotentiaries that the General Assembly would convene for the express purpose of examining the draft articles and concluding a multilateral convention on the subject [ibid., p. 10]. When the Sixth Committee sat down to discuss the Commission's report at the 46th Assembly, not all saw the wisdom of convening the ILC-recommended conference. Along with specific reservations about particular articles (including proposed distinctions for states within a federated state and between state governments and state-owned commercial enterprises), many states had general reservations about whether there was sufficient international consensus to warrant a conference at this time [see, e.g., comments by Argentina, Colombia, Australia, and the United States, A/C.6/46/SR.35,23,24, and 27]. In the end, the Assembly opted to have states submit written comments on the draft articles on jurisdictional immunities by July 1, 1992, and to establish an open-ended working group of the Sixth Committee to examine, in light of the comments filed, the articles and the question of convening an international conference in 1994 or thereafter [A/Res/46/55].

During its 43rd session the ILC also approved, on first reading, a set of 32 draft articles concerning the **Law of the Navigational Uses of International Watercourses**. The text, with the exception of provisions concerning private remedies and dispute settlement that were drafted by the special rapporteur, is being sent to governments for comments, which are due on January 1, 1993 [A/Res/46/54]. The ILC had made substantial progress since its 1990 session, when it provisionally adopted six articles to join the 21 others it had so approved previously [see *Issues/46*, p. 245]; the topic has been an agenda item since 1971. The most significant break-through at the 43rd session is to be found in Article 2, where an "international watercourse" is now defined as, among other things, "a system of surface and underground waters constituting by virtue of their physical relationship a unitary whole and flowing into a common terminus" [A/46/10, p. 162; see also S. McCaffrey, "The 43rd Session of the International Law Commission," 85 *American Journal of International Law* 703 (1991), p. 705]. This approach to the topic, which sees a watercourse as a "system" in constant motion, had been resisted by some states out of fear that it would subject too great a portion of their freshwater resources to the emerging regime; but the effect of the definition is to make possible the "full implementation of the principle of equitable and reasonable utilization of a watercourse" [A/46/10, p. 157]. The five other new provisions are Articles 10 (relationship between uses), 26 (management), 27 (regulation), 28 (installations), 29 (international watercourses and installations in time of armed conflict), and 32 (nondiscrimination). The degree of importance that some states, particularly developing states, attach to international watercourses was clear in the Sixth Committee, where a number of delegates stressed the need to give priority to the conclusion of this topic [see, e.g., comments by Pakistan, A/C.6/46/SR.34, and Bangladesh, A/C.6/46/SR.26]. Indeed, in submitting the ILC's report, the Chair noted that the topic had acquired urgency with the increasing frequency of disputes between the two or more states that share the world's 214 basins of international watercourses on which 40 percent of the world's population depends [A/C.6/46/SR.22, p. 6]. Nonetheless, delegates at the Sixth Committee expressed a variety of views on such issues as whether underground waters should be included in the concept of watercourses, whether the draft was too constraining for a framework agreement, and whether the current provisions gave too much weight to protecting ecosystems and too little to the need for economic development [compare comments by Turkey, Brazil, and Argentina, A/C.6/46/SR.26,34, and 35].

The ILC's work on **International Liability for Injurious Consequences Arising Out of Acts Not Prohibited by International Law,** on its agenda since 1978, received a mixed reception in both the 43rd session of the Commission and the Sixth Committee, and not a single article on the subject has received even provisional acceptance. The topic remains more or less where it was during the ILC's 42nd session, when the Commission addressed the rapporteur's panoramic report canvassing 33 proposed articles [see *Issues/46*, pp. 242–43]. At the 43rd session, the ILC discussed the rapporteur's seventh report, which sought to assess the topic from a broader perspective, and Commission members were asked to address basic issues, such as the title of the topic, prevention of and liability for transboundary harm, and harm to the "global commons" [A/ 46/10, p. 279]. Whether the ILC (having at least momentarily cleared its agenda of three major items) will be devoting major resources to this topic remains to be seen. Although some states argue that it ought to be given priority, there are difficulties with the topic as presently conceived. These difficulties are suggested by the general discussion in the ILC, during which a number of members stated bluntly that the time devoted to the topic was out of all proportion to the progress achieved. Divisions reemerged between those in favor of going forward with adoption of ten articles under discussion since 1988 and those who question how "the Commission could even begin drafting an instrument without having some firm idea of its content and structure" [ibid., p. 280]. For some, the topic involved progressive development of principles not yet present in current substantive law, involving such areas as nuclear accidents, protection of the ozone layer, hazardous wastes, and industrial accidents with transboundary impact, where no precise rules for reparation or liability existed in the relevant existing multilateral treaties [ibid., p. 282]. Others saw the task as essentially one of codification, involving the selection of existing international legal principles relating to the environment rather than the invention of new law [ibid., pp. 280–81]. Still others expressed doubt that such an instrument would pay sufficient attention to the needs and limitations of developing countries and asserted that it would be inequitable to apply the same standards of liability to developing and developed countries [ibid., pp. 282–83].

The very nature of the instrument was another source of difference: Should it be an "umbrella" framework convention, a hortatory code of conduct, a treaty with a flexible rule on liability yet binding rules on preventive obligations, or a mix of some or all of these? There was also the question of whether the instrument should deal with harm to the "global commons"—another crucial issue—with some members insisting on inclusion but others suggesting that this falls outside the ILC mandate, viz. to address the harm that emanates from one state and affects the territory of another [ibid., pp. 302–4; see *Issues/45*, pp. 196–97]. Similar contradictory positions on basic issues emerged when the topic was raised in the Sixth Committee [compare, e.g., comments by Israel and Egypt, A/C.6/46/SR.34; and Yugoslavia, Greece, India, and Uruguay, A/C.6/46/SR.35]. The United States, for its part, suggested that the topic was "not proving amenable to codification" and that the ILC should clarify the relationship between this topic and the topic of state responsibility [A/C.6/46/SR.35].

The ILC's concern with **Relations between States and International Organizations,** dealing with the privileges and immunities of international organizations, including their property, premises, and personnel, has been intermittent [see, e.g., *Issues/46*, pp. 145–46]. The ILC has in the past given the topic relatively low priority, reflecting a perception that it is already covered extensively in existing conventions. In addition, the ILC's last effort on the first part of this topic—its 1975 Vienna Convention on the Representation of States in Their Relations with International Organizations [see *Issues/45*, p. 199]—has not been adopted by most of the states that are host to international organizations. At its 43rd session, the ILC considered the special rapporteur's sixth and seventh reports, which contained draft articles on archives, publications and communications, and fiscal immunities and exemptions; subject to members' comments, all of these were referred to the drafting committee [A/46/10, pp. 307–22]. Relatively few member-state delegates addressed the topic in detail in the Sixth Committee during the 46th General Assembly.

Due to lack of time, the 43rd ILC session did not consider its special rapporteur's third report on **state responsibility**—an agenda topic since 1975 [see *Issues/46*, pp. 241–42]. This topic will probably receive greater attention in the future, as will some of the potential new agenda items identified in the ILC's report on its long-term program of work: the law of confined international ground waters, extraterritorial application of national legislation, the law concerning international migrations, extradition and judicial assistance, the legal effects of resolutions of the United Nations, international legal regulations on foreign indebtedness, the legal conditions of capital investment and agreements pertaining thereto, institutional arrangements concerning trade in commodities, legal aspects of the protection of the environment of areas not subject to national jurisdiction (global commons), rights of national minorities, international commissions of inquiry (fact-finding), and the legal aspects of disarmament [A/46/10, p. 334]. Discussion of this list in the Sixth Committee did not reveal a clear consensus with respect to the ILC's future agenda, and some states suggested that the ILC should complete its current tasks before taking on new ones [see, e.g., comments by the United States, A/C.6/46/SR.35]. There was, nonetheless, considerable support for some of these new topics, particularly international ground waters, the legal effects of U.N. resolutions, and the global commons.

The Sixth Committee also considered, at the recommendation of the General Assembly, the ILC's draft articles on **most-favored-nation clauses** [A/33/10; discussion at A/C.6/46/SR.4]. The 46th Assembly, following the Sixth Committee's recommendation, then agreed to bring these articles to the attention of states and intergovernmental organizations for their consideration [Decision 46/416].

The 46th General Assembly was unable to break the stalemate over the question of convening a plenipotentiary conference to seek adoption of the ILC's **Draft Articles and Draft Optional Protocols One and Two on the Status of the Diplomatic Courier and Diplomatic Bag Not Accompanied by Diplomatic Courier** [see *Issues/45*, pp. 192–93, and *Issues/46*, p.

246]. Informal consultations had resumed at the 46th, with attention focusing on articles concerning protection of the diplomatic bag, inviolability of temporary accommodation, and immunity from jurisdiction. Alternative proposals for these articles were circulated, but no consensus was reached on the issues involved or on the larger question of whether a new convention was necessary, given existing texts on point and the relative absence of serious difficulties over the treatment of the diplomatic courier and bag [see, e.g., comments by Canada, A/C.6/46/SR.40, pp. 3–6]. Accordingly, the Assembly decided to resume these informal consultations during its 47th Session [A/Res/46/57].

2. Peace and Security

The U.N. Security Council, which took center stage when it came to imposing the terms of the peace on Iraq in the Gulf War, has devoted considerable attention to the implementation of **resolutions stemming from the conclusion of hostilities** in that war [for background see *Issues/46*, pp. 246–48].

Two 1991 resolutions—the most complex set of decisions ever taken by the Council—established the framework for its subsequent decisions concerning Iraq. The first of these, **Security Council Resolution 686**, makes numerous demands on Iraq to "be assured of Iraq's peaceful intentions" and to restore "international peace and security in the region." Among other things, it demands that Iraq rescind legal measures purporting to annex Kuwait; accept financial liability for any loss, damage, or injury resulting from the invasion and illegal occupation of Kuwait; release all Kuwaiti and third-country nationals; and return all Kuwaiti property seized. **Security Council Resolution 687** of April 1, 1991, citing Chapter VII of the Charter and the same general purposes, imposes additional conditions on Iraq—among them the requirement that the Iraqi government respect international boundaries established in a 1963 agreement it signed with Kuwait; that it agree to further boundary demarcation conducted under the auspices of the U.N. Secretary-General; that it agree to the presence of a U.N. observer unit to monitor the Khor Abdullah waterway and a demilitarized zone; that it ratify the Convention on the Prohibition of the Development, Production and Stockpiling of Bacteriological (Biological) and Toxic Weapons and on Their Destruction; that it systematically destroy, under international supervision, all chemical and biological weapons and certain ballistic missiles in its possession; that it forgo development of these same weapons as well as of nuclear weapons; that it agree to on-site international inspection of nuclear facilities; and that it renounce all acts of international terrorism.

Resolution 687 also confirms Iraq's liability for "any direct loss, damage, including environmental damage and the depletion of natural resources, or injury to foreign Governments, nationals and corporations, as a result of Iraq's unlawful invasion and occupation of Kuwait"; and it directs the Secretary-General to devise a mechanism to adjudicate Iraq's financial liabilities. One result was the Council decision of May 20, 1991, to establish a **Compensation Fund,** a claims **Commission,** and a **Governing Council** to process claims against Iraq [S/Res/692]. On August 15, 1991, the Security Council decided that "compensation to be paid by Iraq . . . shall not exceed 30 per cent of the annual value of the exports of petroleum and petroleum products from Iraq" [S/Res/705]. It also authorized states purchasing oil products from Iraq to pay directly into a U.N. escrow account administered by the Secretary-General, which would be used to meet Iraq's financial obligations. Among the financial obligations named were not only the claims indicated in Resolution 687 but also the costs incurred by the International Atomic Energy Agency (IAEA) in carrying out its weapons inspection and half the expenses of the Iraq-Kuwait Boundary Demarcation Commission [S/Res/706]. Resolution 712 of September 19, 1991, indicates that the oil products subject to Resolution 706 are under Iraqi title but are nonetheless immune from legal proceedings, attachments, or execution and that all states should take measures to protect the proceeds from diversion. Resolution 712 also confirms that the escrow account enjoys the privileges and immunities of the United Nations. Still other resolutions give effect to various other aspects of Resolutions 686 and 687 (see, e.g., S/Res/688 condemning repression of Iraqi civilians, especially the Kurds; S/Res/689 confirming that the U.N. Iraq-Kuwaiti Observation Mission can be terminated only by Council decision; S/Res/699 concerning weapons destruction and inspection programs; S/Res/707 condemning Iraq for violations of its obligations to cooperate with the IAEA; and S/Res/715 approving the IAEA's plan for ongoing monitoring and verification).

The extensive nature of the Security Council's actions with respect to Iraq has led commentators to suggest that Iraqi sovereignty has been put in "receivership." Most of the Council's actions are unprecedented; certainly on no previous occasion has an international organization simply told a sovereign state what its borders are, what proportion of its export earnings it is entitled to keep, what kinds of observers and inspectors it must admit into its territory, what types of weapons it may possess, and what treaties it must ratify. Whether these actions are consistent with international law or the Charter or basic principles of fairness is a matter of some controversy. Certainly, Iraq "accepted" these terms only because it "had no choice"; and before doing so, it asserted that Resolution 687 contained "iniquitous provisions" constituting "an unprecedented assault on the sovereignty, and the rights that stem

therefrom, embodied in the Charter and in international law and prac-
tice" [letter from Iraqi Minister for Foreign Affairs, 4/6/91, S/22456]. In particular, Iraq
claimed that, according to international law, boundary demarcations can
be imposed only with sovereign consent. The resolution's provision on
this subject, it said, as well as provisions relating to possession of weapons
and adherence to weapons treaties, interfere with Iraq's internal affairs,
threaten its national security, and impose dangerously uneven requirements for different members of the international community, since no
such burdens are being put on other states, notably Israel [ibid.]. Iraq
charged further that the Security Council's determination that only Iraq
is financially liable for the horrific consequences of the Gulf War is
unfair, ignoring as it does Iraq's own claims for redress with regard to
civilian casualties and damage to the country's infrastructure. Baghdad
contended that the financial-liability provisions "partake of a desire to
exact vengeance and cause harm, not to give effect to the relevant
provisions of international law" [ibid.], and concluded that Resolution 687
was adopted for purely "political" purposes "which bear no relation to
the Charter or to international law" [ibid.].

Defenders of the Security Council's decisions argue that the United
Nations' extraordinary measures are justified by the extraordinary legal
violations to which it was reacting—among them naked aggression and
pervasive violations of humanitarian law—and are well within the terms
of Chapter VII's Articles 39 and 41. Border demarcation, weapons
limitations, and related prohibitions are designed to reduce the threat to
international peace posed by aggressor states; and financial liability is
"reasonably related to the establishment of a just peace" [see, e.g., O. Schachter,
"United Nations Law in the Gulf Conflict," 85 *American Journal of International Law* 452 (1991)].

Yet, even some of those who defend the Council's actions assert that
aggressor states do retain their entitlements under the Charter with
respect to sovereign equality, political independence, and territorial
integrity [ibid.]. The extent to which these and other Charter principles
limit Security Council action—for example, its ability to demand the
ouster of Saddam Hussein—and what entity is able to impose such limits,
remains unclear. The Security Council actions to implement the peace
are therefore likely to generate as many legal controversies as did the
original authorization of economic sanctions and then of force to drive
Iraq out of Kuwait [compare *Issues/46*, pp. 247–48].

The conduct of the Gulf War is also having a spillover effect on the
discussion of emerging environmental regimes. Thus, at recent meetings
of the Sixth Committee, speakers have disagreed over the need for new
legal instruments on **exploitation of the environment as a weapon in
times of war.** Some, such as the representative of Kuwait, argue that
priority should be given not to the elaboration of new norms but to
compliance with existing conventions [see U.N. press release GA/L/2709, 10/24/91].

The 46th General Assembly directed that an item entitled "Protection of the environment in times of armed conflict" be placed on the provisional agenda of the 47th [Decision 46/417].

There were equally sharp differences of opinion about the well-publicized Security Council action regarding Libya, which followed by two months the indictment of two Libyan intelligence agents by a U.S. district court in connection with the bombing of **Pan American flight 103,** which exploded over Lockerbie, Scotland, on December 21, 1988. The November 14, 1991, indictment had charged that the two agents, acting with other conspirators, placed a suitcase containing a portable radio cassette player with a plastic bomb and detonating device on a flight from Malta to Frankfurt, to be routed aboard a Pan Am flight bound for London and then transferred to flight 103 [A/46/831, Annex]. On the same date, the Lord Advocate of Scotland announced that warrants had been issued for the arrest of the same two Libyan nationals on charges of conspiracy, murder, and contravention of the Aviation Security Act of 1982; and he supplied the same details contained in the U.S. indictment [A/46/826, Annex I]. The two indictments, which culminated what was said to have been a three-year, $30 million international probe involving interviews with some 14,000 people in 40 countries, came just two weeks after French authorities had announced criminal charges against four other Libyans in connection with the 1989 bombing of a French airliner, **Union de transports aériens flight 772** [see, e.g., *The Christian Science Monitor*, 11/18/91]. Both the U.S. and British governments immediately called on the Libyan government to surrender for trial the persons charged, accept "complete responsibility" for the actions of Libyan officials, disclose all relevant details, and pay "appropriate compensation" [A/46/826, Annex II]. The British, French, and U.S. governments then issued a joint declaration requiring, in addition, that Libya commit itself "concretely and definitively to cease all forms of terrorist action and all assistance to terrorist groups" [A/46/828, Annex]. The Libyan government denied any involvement in such actions and refused to comply with requests to extradite its nationals [see, e.g., *The New York Times*, 1/22/92].

On January 21, 1992, the Security Council, acting on a text initiated by France, the United Kingdom, and the United States, unanimously approved **Resolution 731,** which implied that the issue raised Chapter VII concerns by expressing the Council's "deep" distress at

> all illegal activities directed against international civil aviation, and affirming the right of all States, in accordance with the Charter of the United Nations and relevant principles of international law, to protect their nationals from acts of international terrorism that constitute threats to international peace and security.

Among other things, the resolution "strongly deplore[d]" Libyan government refusal to participate in the "requests to cooperate fully in establishing responsibility for the terrorists' acts . . . against Pan American flight 103 and Union de transports aériens flight 772" and urged Libya to respond to the "requests to cooperate" by France, the United Kingdom, and the United States [S/Res/731]. The Libyan authorities, for their part, stated that the accusations were based on "false premises and assumptions" and indicated that the Security Council had no right to demand the extradition of Libyan nationals, since this was not required by international law [see, e.g., U.N. press release SC/5348, 1/21/92]. According to Libya, the dispute concerned the proper interpretation of the 1971 Montreal Convention for the Suppression of Unlawful Acts against the Safety of Civil Aviation [24 UST 568, TIAS 7570] and thus should be resolved in accordance with the Convention's provisions for dispute settlement, that is, arbitration and thereafter referral to the International Court of Justice (ICJ) [SC/5348; see Convention, ibid. at Article 14]. The United Kingdom and United States responded that the issue did not involve the Montreal Convention, since the present case involved state-sponsored terrorism; that the Security Council was not dealing with a legal dispute under the Convention but with a threat to international peace and security under the terms of the Charter; and that because there "can be no confidence in the impartiality of the Libyan courts" and there is no international tribunal with criminal jurisdiction, the criminal trials should be conducted either in Scotland or in the United States [see, e.g., U.K. press release, 1/21/92; and U.N. press release SC/5348, 1/21/92]. These countries went on to argue that swift and effective action was required for effective deterrence. Furthermore, they said, there was no intention of establishing a broad precedent against the "domestic" rules of many countries barring the extradition of nationals; the issue here involved the exceptional case of government involvement in terrorism [U.K. press release, 1/21/92].

In the weeks following adoption of this resolution, various attempts were made to resolve the impasse, notably by the Secretary-General and the Arab League. The Secretary-General's reports to the Council traced an "evolution" in the Libyan government's response to Resolution 731. He relayed the information that Colonel Qaddafi was willing to try the suspects in Libya, provided the necessary evidence was supplied by the British and U.S. governments; and that Qaddafi had suggested that these governments send their own judges and that representatives from the Arab League, the Organization of African Unity, and the Islamic Conference observe the proceedings [U.N. press release SC/5388, 3/31/92]. A later report of the Secretary-General indicated that Libya was "ready to comply" with Resolution 731, subject to conditions. Furthermore, despite Libya's claim that "constitutional" obstructions prevented the extradition of Libyan nationals and that the issue of compensation was "premature," it had offered to make the subjects available for questioning through the Secretary-General and to provide the requested information, and had agreed to condemn terrorism outright [S/23672; see also SC/5388]. Letters from Libyan officials offered still other alternatives to extradition, including the establishment of a U.N. legal committee of neutral judges for a comprehensive inquiry in Libya, with the possibility of a later trial in a neutral third country, should this appear justified [SC/5388]. At the same time, Libya filed applications in the International Court of Justice directed at "enjoining " further action by the United States and the United Kingdom [see further discussion in section 8, "International Court of Justice," below].

A decision on Libya's request for provisional measures was pending in the World Court when, on March 31, 1992, the Security Council, by a vote of 10–0, with 5 abstentions (China, Cape Verde, India, Morocco, and Zimbabwe), decided to give Libya until April 15, 1992, to comply with the extradition request or face Chapter VII sanctions. **Security Council Resolution 748** (strongly reminiscent of some of the early decisions directed against Iraq) stated that the "suppression of acts of international terrorism . . . is essential for the maintenance of international peace and security." Under its terms, by April 15 all states were required to: cut air links with Libya (except those based on humanitarian needs); prohibit the provision of arms-related material, advice, or assistance; reduce the level of Libyan diplomatic representation in their territory (including, subject to consultation with the relevant international organization, Libyan representation at international organizations); prevent the operation of all Libyan Arab Airlines offices; and deny entry to or expel Libyan nationals who had been expelled from or denied entry to other states because of involvement in terrorism. At the same time, the Council established a Committee to examine the states' reports on implementation and provided that the Council would review these measures as well as possible violations every 120 days. Not included among the sanctions prescribed in Resolution 748, however, is an oil embargo—the measure, short of force, most likely to have an impact on Libya. Though this sanction was apparently discussed, the idea was dropped, allegedly because of Europe and Japan's heavy reliance on Libyan oil [see, e.g., *The Christian Science Monitor*, 4/2/92].

Adoption of the Libyan sanctions, which went into effect as scheduled, brought reactions that ranged from outrage to disappointment that the Council had acted too hastily, without even waiting for a decision from the ICJ (this was the stand taken by China and Cape Verde, both of which had abstained from the voting). Libya and Iraq condemned the action as itself a "form of terrorism" and an "act of vengeance" that threatened the peace and would "affect the credibility of the United Nations as an international instrument for peace and stability" [U.N. press release SC/5388]. Qaddafi attacked the resolution as the product of a "Western Christian crusade" against the Muslim world [see, e.g., Agence France Presse, 4/4/92]. Others, such as Zimbabwe, Jordan, and additional members of the

Arab League, suggested that Libya had moved significantly toward compliance with Resolution 731 and that the Council had not exhausted diplomatic efforts, as set forth in Article 33 of the Charter, but had opted for a confrontational approach that would only aggravate the situation [see, e.g., U.N. press release SC/5388, 3/31/92; see also the Council of Arab States' resolution of 3/22/92, S/23745]. Yet other U.N. members, such as Mauritania, argued that the sanctions would punish the Libyan people for "an act for which the responsibility had not been established" [SC/5388]. The main proponents of the Libyan sanctions, the United States and Britain, however, defended the action as "appropriate . . . , measured, precise and limited, a nonviolent response to violent and brutal acts" tailored to "fit the offense" and undertaken only after all peaceful efforts to gain compliance had failed [ibid.].

These differing reactions are likely to be reflected in the conflicting views of academics, some of whom applaud the United Nations' new-found powers while others speak of the "perversion" of the Charter by a Security Council they see as acting on an agenda that is tailored to the needs of the West [compare the views of Anthony D'Amato (letter to *The New York Times*, 3/3/1992) to those of Marc Weller (op-ed, ibid., 2/15/92)]. Some of these U.N. critics are not likely to be mollified by the relatively brief ICJ decision dismissing Libya's requests for relief on the day prior to the one on which the Security Council sanctions were to go into effect [see section 8 below]. For other observers, the starkness of the choices available to the Security Council—do nothing, sanctions, or outright war—suggests the need for an international criminal court [see, e.g., op-ed by Jonathan Power, *Los Angeles Times*, 4/5/92; see also *Issues/46*, pp. 239–41].

In action reminiscent of Security Council Resolution 662 (1990), which had called for the restoration of the "legitimate" government of Kuwait, the General Assembly reacted to the September 1991 **ouster of the elected government of President Jean-Bertrand Aristide in Haiti** by strongly condemning the "attempted illegal replacement of the Constitutional President of Haiti" and affirming as "unacceptable any entity resulting from that illegal situation" [A/Res/46/7]. The Assembly demanded that President Aristide be restored to power and requested that members and the Secretary-General support efforts by the Organization of American States (OAS) to this end [ibid.]. The Secretary-General was asked to report on the situation at the 47th Session.

The Assembly expressed similar concern for the **situation in Afghanistan,** adopting a consensus resolution that expressed support for the principle of self-determination and for the Agreements on the Settlement of the Situation Relating to Afghanistan ("Geneva Agreements"), which had been negotiated under U.N. auspices [A/Res/46/23; see also Chapter I, "Making and Keeping the Peace"—Afghanistan, in the present volume]. In an indirect reference to the Soviet invasion of Afghanistan, the resolution cast the situation as the result of "the violation of the principles of the Charter . . . and of the recognized norms of inter-State conduct." It also noted the need to preserve the "sovereignty, territorial integrity, political independence and non-aligned and Islamic character of Afghanistan . . ." and asked the Secretary-General to report on the issue to both the Security Council and the General Assembly [A/Res/46/23; see also discussion of A/ Res/46/130 and 137 in section 9, "Other Legal Issues," below].

The most publicized action by the General Assembly over the past year, with implications for human rights, the legitimacy of the State of Israel, and the search for peace in the Middle East, was the **repeal of its own Resolution 3379 (XXX)** of November 10, 1975, which equated Zionism with racism. By a vote of 111–25–13, the Assembly "revoke[d]" the resolution without comment or preamble [A/Res/46/86]; the Islamic and Middle East countries formed the majority of those opposed. "Revocation" of a General Assembly resolution (all of which are intended purely as recommendations) is virtually unprecedented, but the original continued to elicit strong emotions in the United States as well as in Israel, and repeal had long been a goal of the United States. (Israel, whether as a reaction to the 1975 rebuff or out of disdain for the world organization, had expressed little interest in pursuing the matter [Josh Friedman, "Zionism = Racism Resolution Repealed," *The InterDependent*, 1-2/92].) Washington saw Resolution 3379 not only in symbolic terms but also as an action that called into question the United Nations' claims of impartiality when it came to the work of eliminating racism—and particularly so in the case of such U.N. bodies as the Committee on the Exercise of the Inalienable Rights of the Palestinian People. The "Zionism is racism" resolution, in fact, had led the United States to withhold the portions of assessed U.N. contributions that it believed were allocated to the tainted activities [see, e.g., the U.S. Foreign Relations Authorization Act, Fiscal Years 1986 and 1987, Pub. L. No. 99-93]. It is unclear whether the revocation will change U.S. practice on these withholdings.

In action on still another front, the 46th General Assembly voted to encourage amendment (through a conference to this end) of the **Treaty Banning Nuclear Weapon Tests in the Atmosphere, in Outer Space and under Water** directed at turning that agreement into a "comprehensive test-ban treaty" [A/Res/46/28]; dissenting votes were cast by the United Kingdom and the United States, and 35 members abstained. By separate action, the Assembly also voted (France and the United States dissenting) to ask the Conference on Disarmament to report to the 47th Session on progress toward the achievement of a comprehensive nuclear test-ban treaty [A/Res/46/29; see also A/Res/46/32]. The Assembly also encouraged states that have not yet done so to adhere to the **Convention on Prohibitions or Restrictions on the Use of Certain Conventional Weapons Which May Be Deemed to Be Excessively Injurious or to Have Indiscriminate Effects,** as well as related protocols [A/Res/46/40].

The Assembly was able to adopt by consensus a resolution calling for **respect for the principles enshrined in the Charter of the United Nations and international law in the fight against drug abuse and illicit trafficking** [A/Res/46/101]. This resolution, no doubt intended by many states as a reference to the U.S. invasion of Panama and the capture of Manuel Noriega, affirms that:

> the international fight against drug trafficking should not in any way justify violation of the principles enshrined in the Charter of the United Nations and international law, particularly the right of all peoples freely to determine, without external interference, their political status and to pursue their economic, social and cultural development, and that every State has the duty to respect this right in accordance with the provisions of the Charter [ibid.].

Just how this resolution comports with the International Law Commission's ongoing efforts to define drug trafficking as an international crime [see section 1, "International Law Commission"] is not clear. The resolution calls for continued consideration of this issue at the 47th Session under the heading "narcotic drugs."

The Assembly expressed concern for the **protection and security of small states,** especially from the action of mercenaries, terrorists, and drug traffickers, and expressed hope that this concern could be alleviated by strengthening regional security arrangements as well as by continued monitoring on the part of the Secretary–General [A/Res/46/43]. The issue will be revisited at the Assembly's 49th Session in 1994. The 46th Session also adopted a resolution affirming that **"good–neighborliness"** is fostered by each state's respect for the rule of law in the conduct of international relations [A/Res/46/62].

The Assembly decided to defer until the 47th Session consideration of an item asserting the **"necessity of ending the economic, commercial and financial embargo imposed by the United States of America against Cuba"** [A/Res/46/407].

3. International Criminal Law

As it had done most recently at its 44th Session, the Assembly "unequivocally" condemned "as criminal and unjustifiable, all acts, methods, and practices of **terrorism** wherever and by whoever committed" [A/Res/46/51]. This resolution enumerated the many multilateral conventions on point and called on states to

> fulfill their obligations under international law to refrain from organizing, instigating, assisting or participating in terrorist acts in other

States, or acquiescing in or encouraging activities within their territory directed towards the commission of such acts.

It went on to request that the Secretary-General continue to seek the views of members about convening an international conference on international terrorism.

In fact, the 46th Assembly's condemnation of terrorism is not as "unequivocal" as it purports to be, since it does not clarify how the outlaw "terrorist" is to be distinguished from the "freedom fighter" engaged in activities that advance the cause of national liberation. Instead, the resolution includes the now-standard disclaimer that nothing in the "present resolution could in any way prejudice the right to self-determination, freedom and independence . . ." [See *Issues/45*, pp. 200–201]. The hedged language made possible the consensus behind the resolution, but the fragility of that consensus was clear in the discussions of the Sixth Committee. Here were signs of the traditional division between those favoring an international conference that would define "terrorism" in such way as to differentiate it from the struggle of peoples for "self-determination" (e.g., Papua New Guinea, Kuwait, Ghana, Uganda, Madagascar, and many other "non-aligned" countries) and those opposed to any suggestion that individual acts of terrorism might be justified in some cases and who foresee little real progress toward a general definition at such a conference (e.g., the United States, members of the European Community [EC], New Zealand, Nepal, South Korea, Canada, Australia, Hungary, Israel, Singapore, and the Nordic countries) [see, e.g., A/C.6/46/SR.12, 13, and 17]. The latter states suggested that for now it was best to focus on existing instruments and that implementing these ought to be a priority; but at least some of the states in the former category had a different priority—that of expanding the terms of the terrorism debate, and they saw an international conference as a means of accomplishing this. The representative of Papua New Guinea, for example, suggested the need to expand "terrorism" to include economic coercion by foreign multinationals, discriminatory licensing arrangements in the fishing industry that are calculated to perpetuate economic dependency, and the deprivation of indigenous peoples' property, resources, and culture—arguments that were reiterated by the delegate of Libya [see A/C.6/46/SR.13, pp. 4–6]. Terrorism will appear on the agenda of the 48th Assembly in 1993.

Responding to the 45th Assembly's call for an assessment of the United Nations' efforts with respect to **crime prevention and criminal justice** [see *Issues/46*, p. 251], the Secretary-General recommended that the Committee on Crime Prevention and Control be dissolved and that a **Commission on Crime Prevention and Criminal Justice** be established as a new functional commission of ECOSOC [A/Conf.156/3]. The Assembly recommended, in turn, that ECOSOC take this step at its next session in 1992 [A/Res/46/152]. The resolution also contains a statement of principles, a program of action (including details about goals, scope, and priorities), and an outline of the structure and management of the new Commission, among whose duties is to provide policy guidance to the United Nations in the crime prevention and criminal justice field. The Commission will be funded by the U.N. regular budget; and voluntary contributions will supplement the budget for technical assistance projects [ibid.; see also Chapter V: "Other Social Issues"—Crime].

More controversial, presumably because of the fiscal consequences, was the Assembly's call for appropriations to support the work of the U.N. African Institute for the Prevention of Crime and the Treatment of Offenders; 37 states, predominantly Eastern European and Western industrialized countries, abstained [A/Res/46/153]. A report of the Secretary-General on this and other U.N. regional institutes that offer technical programs to assist the administration of justice had concluded that these institutes were handicapped by limited resources, and particularly so in the case of those operating in developing countries [A/46/524].

In a related action, the Subcommission on Prevention of Discrimination and Protection of Minorities of the Commission of Human Rights released a report, prepared by Louis Joinet, on **the independence of the judiciary and the protection of practicing lawyers** [E/CN.4/Sub.2/1991/30]. The report surveys existing practices (whether constitutional, regulatory, or legislative) that help to protect lawyers and judges as they fulfill their respective duties, as well as the effectiveness of international activities to promote these protections. It concluded, with respect to the latter, that

> advisory services were pointless when rendered to States that did not satisfy the conditions of minimal respect for human rights: infrastructure, a clearly and regularly affirmed political will, and so on. Quite apart from questions of ethics, such a minimum is indispensable if such services are to be effective [ibid., para. 290].

The Assembly formally adopted and promulgated for wide dissemination the **principles for the protection of persons with mental illness and for the improvement of mental health care** that had been drafted by a working group of the Commission on Human Rights [A/Res/46/119, Annex]. The principles seek to incorporate such persons into the system of protections contained in other human rights instruments, but they go beyond existing instruments in many respects. The principles contain, for example, procedural guarantees (such as the right to legal counsel and to a fair hearing by independent tribunal) with respect to decisions on legal capacity and the appointment of personal representatives; a definition of "informed consent"; and restrictions on standards of care, including bans on involuntary psychosurgery and sterilization. The principles join an ever-growing body of similar provisions elaborating on the human rights entitlements of those who are subject to the **administration of justice** [see *Issues/46*, pp. 249–52]. The 46th General Assembly encouraged wider dissemination of these numerous international standards [A/Res/46/120; Report of the Working Group on Detention, Commission of Human Rights, E/CN.4/Sub.2/1990/32, reviews these standards in the context of persons under detention]. Efforts to implement these standards will be examined at the 48th Assembly Session.

4. Effectiveness of the Organization

The end of the cold war has raised expectations of momentous changes in the United Nations—not least in the Organization's approach to preventive diplomacy and peacekeeping. What some of those changes might be could well become clearer after July 1, 1992, when the new U.N. Secretary-General, Boutros Boutros-Ghali, makes his recommendations for strengthening the Organization, as requested by the heads of state who gathered at the unprecedented Security Council "Summit" in January 1992. Some of the changes broached recently, such as the admission of new permanent members to the Security Council, would require an amendment of the U.N. Charter. Among the proposals in the peace and security area is the idea—warmly embraced by France at the January Summit—of a U.N. rapid-deployment force capable of taking on urgent peacekeeping operations [for a general discussion, see *The InterDependent*, Spring 1992].

In a wide-ranging annual **Report on the Work of the Organization** in 1991—the last of his term in office—Secretary-General Javier Pérez de Cuéllar addressed a number of issues relating to the future of international law and the U.N. Charter [A/46/1]. Contrasting the climate of the U.N. at the time of his first annual report in 1982 with the climate today, he stressed the Organization's "renaissance" and its role in developing the principles of the Charter and international law. The Secretary-General also drew attention to U.N. activities that were not "foreseen in its original design," including Secretariat involvement in tasks far removed from the traditional peacekeeping, especially those related to the implementation of Security Council decisions on Iraq-Kuwait [see section 2, "Peace and Security," above]. According to the Secretary-General, the Secretariat's role in demarcating the boundary between Iraq and Kuwait, in helping to eliminate Iraq's "mass destruction capability" through joint efforts with the IAEA, and in arranging the return of Kuwaiti property seized by Iraq, among other "onerous tasks" deriving from Security Council action, is "breaking new ground in international experience and the responsibilities of the Secretariat." At the same time, Pérez de Cuéllar noted, the enforcement action against Iraq could not be "carried out exactly in the form foreseen by Articles 42 *et sequentia* of Chapter VII," due to "the costs imposed and the capabilities demanded by modern warfare" [see *Issues/46*, pp. 246–48]. These considerations led the Secretary-General to enumerate areas requiring "collective reflection" for the future.

Specifically, the Secretary-General suggested that **enforcement action under the Charter** "requires a discipline all its own," and that the Security Council, when acting under Chapter VII, needs mechanisms to help it ensure observance of the rule of proportionality in deploying armed force, assist third-party states disadvantaged by the imposition of economic sanctions, and calculate the human effect of sanctions on the population of targeted states. Pérez de Cuéllar also labeled the Gulf War a "startling failure" of collective "preventive diplomacy" and argued that the scheme foreseen in Article 99 of the Charter, whereby the Secretary-General focuses attention on situations likely to threaten the international peace, is hampered by his lack of access to information, particularly of the sort derived from space-based and other technical surveillance systems. Access to such information would enable the United Nations to maintain "an impartial and effective global watch over situations of potential or incipient conflict" without having to rely on particular states to place the item formally on the agenda of the Security Council. The Secretary-General also suggested that there must be a fundamental shift in the perception of the role the United Nations plays with respect to conflicts—away from the view that the Organization is a place for "litigation that is likely to result in a negative verdict for one or the other party" and toward a view of the Organization as an instrument of "mediation that can help reconcile legitimate claims and interests and achieve just and honorable settlements."

With respect to the protection of **human rights,** the Secretary-General asserted that this has now become "one of the keystones in the arch of peace" and, further, that Article 2(7) (noninterference in essential domestic jurisdiction) is no longer regarded as a protective barrier behind which states can engage in massive or systematic violations of human rights. He added (perhaps referring to the recent Security Council decisions concerning the protection of the Kurds in Iraq) that it "seems beyond question that violations of human rights imperil peace," but went on to say that the "maximum caution needs to be exercised lest the defence of human rights becomes a platform for encroaching on the essential domestic jurisdiction of States and eroding their sovereignty." With this in mind, Pérez de Cuéllar suggested that three principles guide the U.N. in carrying out its mandate to protect human rights: even-handed, not selective, enforcement in similar cases; adherence to multilateral action sanctioned by the Charter, not unilateral action; and proportional reaction relative to the wrong committed.

With respect to **arms limitation and disarmament,** the Secretary-General supported "the idea of promoting transparency in the arms trade through a United Nations-based scheme for registration and disclosure" that would be "conducive to voluntary restraint." (At its 46th Session, the General Assembly had endorsed a "standardized reporting system" and voted to include discussion of the issue at its 48th Session [A/Res/46/25].) The Secretary-General also noted new challenges with respect to the **environment** and expressed the hope that the first world summit conference on environment and development mandated by the General Assembly would result in the evolution of respected and enforceable international law on point [A/46/1]. Regarding the **internationalization of crime and drug trafficking** [see, for example, *Issues/46*, pp. 237–38, 249–52], he praised the attempt to formulate more coherent and integrated anti-crime strategies through the U.N. International Drug Control Programme as well as through efforts to confront the "social institutions" and "social discrimination" that help create these problems. In support of these efforts, the Secretary-General directed attention to, among other things, the need for rules respecting gender equality and the rights of the disabled and the aged.

Finally, Pérez de Cuéllar argued that progress on all these fronts requires that the Secretary-General be given latitude to manage the Secretariat without overly "detailed or rigid" legislative regulations imposed by the General Assembly and that the Organization be provided the financial resources to which it is legally entitled. On this last point, Pérez de Cuéllar noted that the Organization still faced a financial crisis; at the time he was writing, only 49 members were fully current on their annual contributions and over $809 million in assessed contributions were outstanding. (This was quite apart from the $486 million owed to the United Nations for peacekeeping expenses.)

The Secretary-General closed his report with a plea for "balance" between the U.N.'s principal organs (presumably referring to the Security Council and the General Assembly), as envisioned in the Charter, to prevent the "divisive" perception that the world body serves only the interests and outlook of one group of nations. He called for balance in the principles of Charter interpretation as well, recognizing that Charter principles "are by no means frozen," since "their scope and the manner of their application [are] determined by changing global conditions," but urging that evolution of such principles proceed on the basis of "shared understandings" and a "genuine consensus."

The **financial shortfalls in the peacekeeping area** noted in the Secretary-General's report were clear throughout the Assembly resolutions dealing with the various missions [see A/Res/46/192–98]. This problem prompted the Assembly to call for a continued **comprehensive review of the whole question of peacekeeping operations in all their aspects,** which has been under study by a Special Committee [A/Res/46/48].

Some of the issues raised by Pérez de Cuéllar's final Report on the Work of the Organization were also raised during the sessions of the **Special Committee on the Charter of the United Nations and on the Strengthening of the Role of the Organization** that were held in November 1990 and February 1991. Discussing the Security Council's voting procedures during the Committee's general debate, one government representative expressed the view that Article 27 of the Charter, read literally, requires the "affirmative" votes of all permanent members to render a valid decision, while another representative argued that 40 years of institutional practice indicate that only the absence of a negative vote by a permanent member is required for binding action [A/46/33, p. 4]. Delegates also differed on the merits of a proposal submitted by Libya that expressed concern about the "adverse consequences" for the maintenance of international peace and security of the application of the principle of "consensus" among the permanent members. Libya proposed a definition of "procedural matters" in which the use of the veto would be suspended or restricted, and proposed a study of other fields in which the "principle of consensus" would not apply. One delegate suggested that these proposals were ill timed, since the Security Council has been functioning effectively [ibid., pp. 5–6].

The Special Committee on the Charter also completed its work on the **Draft Declaration on Fact-Finding by the United Nations in the Field of the Maintenance of International Peace and Security**—a hortatory guide intended to encourage the use of fact-finding by the Security Council, the General Assembly, and the Secretary-General to defuse situations likely to lead to breaches of or threats to international peace and security [ibid., pp. 7–11; for background and summary, see *Issues/46*, pp. 252–53]. Although some delegations indicated their preference for a provision expressly stating that all fact-finding activities of a mission must cease should a state withdraw its consent to the continued presence of such a mission, no such provision was included; these states indicated, however, that such was their understanding of the Declaration [A/46/33, p. 11; see also comments by Venezuela in the Sixth Committee, A/C.6/46/SR.9, p. 16]. Pursuant to the recommendation of the Sixth Committee, the General Assembly approved the Declaration and urged its dissemination [A/Res/46/59 and Annex]. Among other things, the Declaration states that fact-finding should be comprehensive, impartial, and timely; it also affirms that the sending of a fact-finding mission to the territory of any state requires that state's prior consent.

The Special Committee on the Charter also examined the Secretary-General's final progress report on the preparation of the **Draft Hand-**

book on the Peaceful Settlement of Disputes Between States [A/46/33, pp. 19–21; report at A/AC.182/L.68]. That report summarized the final meeting of the Consultative Group on the Handbook, which had been chaired by the Legal Counsel of the United Nations. The nearly 200-page Handbook [text in A/46/33, Annex] is designed to help increase compliance with international law by providing information on established procedures for dispute settlement between different subjects of international law [see *Issues/46*, p. 253, for background and summary]. Some delegations expressed the view that the Handbook would prove useful in the drafting of a universal convention on the peaceful settlement of disputes [A/46/33, p. 19]. The Assembly followed the Special Committee's recommendation and requested that the Handbook be published and disseminated widely in all the official languages of the United Nations [A/Res/46/58].

The Special Committee on the Charter also continued to examine a working paper submitted by the then Soviet Union entitled **"New issues for consideration in the Special Committee"** [A/46/33, pp. 12–18; working paper at A/AC.182/L.65]. The working paper identifies new subjects for the Committee's agenda, including (1) strengthening cooperation between the Organization and regional organizations with respect to international peace and security; (2) broadening the peacemaking efforts of the Secretary-General; (3) elaborating a general convention on the peaceful settlement of disputes; and (4) studying the best means of implementing Charter norms through provisional measures or other enforcement action [see *Issues/45*, p. 205]. Much of the discussion focused on ways to improve the Charter's mechanisms for collective security, with the representative of the Russian Federation now proposing study of, among other things, the roles of military observers, peacemaking and peacekeeping efforts, demilitarized zones, truces, cease-fires, and civilian experts [A/46/33, p. 13]. The Soviet/Russian paper drew generally favorable comments, but one representative suggested that it ought to have called as well for a reexamination not only of the role of the General Assembly in the maintenance of international peace but also of the possibilities of eliminating the permanent members' Security Council veto and of expanding the composition of the Security Council to "better reflect the composition of the Organization" [ibid., p. 14; see comments by Colombia in the Sixth Committee, A/C.6/46/SR.9, pp. 11–13]. Others saw a link between the Soviet/Russian proposals and the possibility of drafting a set of guidelines for "sanction management," that is, for resolving issues arising from recent Security Council decisions, such as the granting of exceptions to sanctions for humanitarian reasons, the recognition of the economic impact of sanctions upon states that are not the target of such sanctions, and enforcement action against states that fail to comply with Council sanctions [A/46/33, p. 15]. Discussion of the Special Committee's report in the Sixth Committee also prompted general discussion of the possibility of Charter amendment, with Germany urging elimination of the "enemy-state" clauses in Articles 53 and 107 [A/C.6/46/SR.9, p. 2], and Ukraine suggesting that the Organization "adapt itself to the new conditions of international life" by, among other things, eliminating some of its "outmoded bodies" [ibid., p. 9].

During the Special Committee's 1991 sessions, Russia submitted a second working document providing greater specifics on how to enhance the cooperation between the Organization and regional organizations. It proposes, for example, that regional efforts to maintain international peace and security be given priority and that local disputes be considered by the Security Council only after the parties have exhausted regional efforts. It also proposes regular meetings between the Secretary-General and the leaders of regional organizations to exchange information on situations that may threaten the peace and to consider joint initiatives toward the settlement of regional disputes [A/46/33, pp. 16–18; working paper at A/ AC.182/L.72]. The Special Committee resolved to resume discussion of the Russian proposals at its next session before deciding which of them to put on the future agenda. For its part, the General Assembly urged the Special Committee to give priority to, among other things, the question of the maintenance of international peace and security, including proposals for cooperation with regional organizations [A/Res/46/58]. The latter was accorded priority at the start of the Special Charter Committee's session in February 1992 [U.N. press release L/2631, 2/3/92], which resumed discussion of many of these issues, including the implementation of Security Council sanctions [see working paper on assistance to third states affected by the application of Security Council sanctions, A/AC.182/L.73 and Rev.1] and the possibility of advisory ICJ opinions at the request of the Secretary-General [U.N. press release L/2643, 2/10/ 92].

Many of the themes taken up in the report of Secretary-General Pérez de Cuéllar and in the report of the Special Committee on the Charter were echoed in an October 23, 1991, letter to the Secretary-General from the Nordic countries [A/46/591]. The letter expresses the support of these countries for, among other things, preventive diplomacy by the Security Council and Secretary-General, registration and monitoring of international arms transfers, routinized fact-finding missions in accordance with the Declaration on Fact-Finding, enhancement of the Organization's ability to respond to requests for electoral assistance, adequate financing for the Secretary-General's dispute-settlement and U.N. peacekeeping operations, and clarification of the modalities for Council enforcement action.

Pursuant to the request of the 45th Session of the Assembly [see *Issues/ 46*, pp. 253–54], the Secretary-General circulated for comment **draft conciliation rules of the United Nations** and reported the replies [A/46/383]. Several of the comments were substantive; the U.N. Commission on International Trade Law (UNCITRAL), for example, expressed concern about the differences between these rules and UNCITRAL's own conciliation rules and suggested that the United Nations' rules were at various points too rigid or complicated [see, e.g., A/46/383, pp. 15–17; see also comments by the Netherlands in the Sixth Committee, A/C.6/46/SR.9, p. 4].

5. International Organizations and Host Country Relations

Pursuant to the General Assembly's requests in 1987 and in 1990 that all states report to the Secretary-General their views on **measures needed to enhance the protection, security, and safety of diplomatic and consular missions and representatives** [see *Issues/46*, pp. 254–55], the Secretary-General filed a report on the subject in September 1991 [A/INF/46/4]. It reveals that states reported 35 cases of violations of international law governing diplomatic and consular premises between November 1990 and the end of September 1991, compared to 16 and 40 cases, respectively, reported in the two previous years [ibid., p. 5]. The reports filed with the Secretary-General cover a wide range of incidents of varying seriousness, from an alleged violation of diplomatic premises to acts of violence against diplomatic and consular missions to bombings and even murder.

The General Assembly voted to hold informal consultants during the 47th Session for the purpose of examining the possibility of an **additional protocol on consular functions to the Vienna Convention on Consular Relations** [A/Res/46/61]. The 45th Assembly had raised the issue and asked the Secretary-General to seek the views of governments on the matter [see *Issues/46*, p. 255]. The Secretary-General reported to the 46th Session that some states supported the idea of an additional protocol while others indicated the enormous difficulty of formulating applicable rules [A/46/348 and Add.1,2; A/C.6/46/SR.41]. The proposal for such a protocol, supported by Austria and Czechoslovakia, is driven by the concern that the Vienna Convention on Consular Relations of 1963, which focuses on consular privileges and immunities, lacks precise rules regarding consular functions and thus leads to bilateral arrangements to fill the lacunae. The Netherlands, speaking at the Sixth Committee on behalf of the 12 states of the EC, countered that bilateralization of the issues was not necessarily bad, since this approach permitted states to tailor their consular treaties to their specific circumstances [A/C.6/46/SR.41, p. 4].

The **Committee on Relations with the Host Country,** established in 1971 to deal with the security of missions and the safety of mission personnel, held five meetings during the 46th Session [A/46/26]. Among the issues discussed were complaints by the Cuban Mission that the host state was permitting demonstrations near the Mission's premises, resulting in acts of intimidation and vandalism against the Mission and its personnel. The United States responded that it was doing all it could to prevent such acts, including round-the-clock uniformed police coverage, that no illegal or prosecutable offense had occurred in the presence of law enforcement personnel, and that the Cuban Mission had declined to cooperate in providing witnesses to any criminal act [A/46/26, pp. 6–7].

The ongoing controversy over U.S. travel restrictions on members of missions and U.N. personnel from certain member states [see *Issues/45*, pp. 206–7; *Issues/46*, p. 255] lessened somewhat with the lifting of restrictions for the Mongolian, Albanian, and Bulgarian Missions, but some travel restrictions continued, drawing complaints from Iraq and Libya [A/46/26, pp. 8, 16]. The Committee also heard complaints from Iraq relating to the freezing of that Mission's bank accounts in the United States. Iraq contended that such action was discriminatory and that the funds would not be used for purposes covered by the relevant Security Council resolutions [see section 2, "Peace and Security," above]. The United States responded that its actions were consistent with paragraph 4 of Security Council Resolution 661 (1990) and paragraph 9 of Security Council Resolution 670 (1990); and it added that the unfreezing of these accounts was beyond the scope of the Host Country Committee. Furthermore, it noted, the Iraqi Mission's checking account had not been frozen, and Iraq could replenish that account with funds from outside the United States and use these to carry out the Mission's official functions [A/46/26, pp. 9–10].

The Host Country Committee also discussed the indebtedness problem faced by many missions—a consequence of political and economic changes at home that have left overseas installations at least temporarily strapped for funds. A working group had proposed that the Organization provide assistance when urgent, but it received a response from the Secretary-General stating that the United Nations could not recognize any legal liability to missions and suggesting that, at least as a preliminary matter, there were a number of practical and legal difficulties with the suggestion [ibid., pp. 11–13, and Annexes I and II]. As an alternative, the working group was exploring the possibility of assistance from the business community in New York. In response to a complaint from Costa Rica about traffic citations, the United States responded that although diplomats were not required to appear at judicial proceedings, this did not imply that the United States was obliged to continue to grant the privilege of operating a motor vehicle to those who abused that privilege [ibid., p. 15]. Among the other issues raised before the Host Committee was the possibility of extending an invitation to the head of the U.S. Office of Foreign Missions to meet with the Committee [ibid., pp. 16–17]. At the 46th General Assembly, the Sixth Committee spent only a short time discussing the Host Country Committee's report. It focused on the issues raised by that report but took up some new concerns as well, including complaints from Romania about travel restrictions and a plea from Ecuador that the Committee expand its membership to include wider geographic representation [A/C.6/46/SR.44]. As usual, the General Assembly endorsed the report of the Committee and its recommendations [A/Res/46/60].

At later meetings of the Host Country Committee in 1992, Libya challenged the U.S. request that it reduce by three the number of staff at its U.N. Mission. The United States and France responded that this request was required by Security Council Resolution 748 (1992), which prevailed over the Headquarters Agreement between the United States and the United Nations [U.N. press release HQ/523, 4/23/92; see also section 2, "Peace and Security," above]. In the course of the April meeting the United States announced that it was lifting its ceilings on the number of staff at the Permanent Missions of the Russian Federation, Ukraine, and Belarus [ibid.].

One of the few remaining **membership issues** was resolved when the General Assembly, acting by consensus on September 17, 1991, voted to admit to membership both the Democratic People's Republic of Korea and the Republic of Korea, pursuant to the recommendation of the Security Council [A/Res/46/1]. Thanks in part to the end of the cold war and the fall of the Berlin Wall, there were a considerable number of additional membership applications to consider. Successful in their bids were Armenia, Azerbaijan, Bosnia, and Herzegovina, Croatia, Estonia, Federated States of Micronesia, Kazakhstan, Kyrgyzstan, Latvia, Lithuania, Marshall Islands, Moldova, San Marino, Slovenia, Tajikistan, Turkmenistan, and Uzbekistan, bringing U.N. membership to 178 as of spring 1992 [U.N. press release ORG/1144, 5/22/92].

The status of the island of **Mayotte,** subject to competing claims by France and the Federal Republic of Comoros, remains unresolved, however. The Assembly, by a vote of 115–1–34 (France), affirmed the "sovereignty, unity and territorial integrity" of the Comoro Archipelago and the sovereignty of the Islamic Republic of the Comoros over Mayotte, invited France to "honor the commitments entered into prior to the referendum on the self-determination of the Comoro Archipelago of 22 December 1974," urged France to accelerate negotiations to ensure the "prompt return" of Mayotte to the Comoros, and requested the Secretary-General to maintain contacts with the Organization of African Unity in the interests of reaching a peaceful negotiated solution [A/Res/46/9]. The Assembly directed the Secretary-General to report on the issue at the 47th Session and put the item on the agenda for that session. The Assembly also granted observer status to the Caribbean Community [A/Res/46/8].

6. Economic Relations

Reiterating its support for the "promotion of entrepreneurship," "private sector development," and "market-oriented approaches," the 46th General Assembly passed by consensus an **"entrepreneurship"** resolution not unlike the one it had passed by a vote at its 45th Session [A/Res/46/166; see *Issues/46*, p. 257]. This resolution requests that U.N. organs and bodies undertake activities to promote entrepreneurship and that the Secretary-General submit to the 48th Session in 1993 his recommendations for U.N. action to this effect—these to "include the role of women in entrepreneurship, the environmental aspects of private sector activities and the impact of the international economic environment" [A/Res/46/166]. In related action, the Assembly took note of the initial report of the Secretary-General, prepared at the request of the 45th Session, concerning institutional developments intended to **strengthen international organizations in the area of multilateral trade,** and it scheduled a review of the Secretary-General's further report for the 47th Session [A/Res/46/207]. The Secretary-General's initial report on the subject consists of a note prepared by the U.N. Centre for Trade and Development (UNCTAD) secretariat providing a historical survey of international organizations' efforts on point, starting with the Havana Charter proposals for an International Trade Organization, former and current General Agreement on Tariffs and Trade (GATT) initiatives, former and current initiatives within UNCTAD and ECOSOC, and not overlooking proposals from academics [A/46/565, Annex]. Although UNCTAD's note stresses the "need and opportunity" for institutional reform relating to multilateral trade (given the increasing interdependence of national economies and the "virtually universal acceptance of the merits of an open, competitive and non-discriminatory international trading system"), it identifies many contested issues that would have to be addressed in connection with institutional reform, including procedures for implementation, surveillance, and systematic monitoring across a range of interrelated issues [ibid., pp. 14–17].

More controversial and reflective of persisting North-South divisions were a range of activities involving aspects of the New International Economic Order. Thus, by a vote of 117–10–27, with developed countries dissenting, the General Assembly approved a resolution originally introduced by Cuba in the Sixth Committee that creates a working group of the Committee to "develop the principles and norms of international law relating to the **new international economic order**" [A/Res/46/52; for prior efforts, see, e.g., *Issues/45*, p. 208]. States and international organizations were requested to give comments on priorities to this working group, which is to report to the 48th General Assembly. The resolution was needed, said Cuba, because the imbalances and dislocations of international economic relations had made for an "unequal order" and ignored the "aspirations of the developing world." The United States, opposing the resolution, called it an "anachronism"—a return to the days of "sterile confrontation" [U.N. press release GA/L/2731, 11/22/91].

A North-South split was also evident in the Assembly's affirmation, by a vote of 123–2–34, that the **"right of development** is an inalienable human right and that equality of development opportunities is a prerogative both of nations and of individuals within nations" [A/Res/46/117]. Nearly all of the Western industrialized states and many East European states abstained; the United States and Israel were the sole dissenters. In a related action, the Assembly requested that the Secretary-General submit to the Commission on Human Rights concrete proposals for implementing and promoting the "right to development" [A/Res/46/123; see also the Secretary-General's report on the issue, E/CN.4/1991/12].

The Secretary-General of UNCTAD, having responded to the 45th Session's call for intensive consultations aimed at the adoption of the long-stalled **Code of Conduct on the Transfer of Technology** [see *Issues/46*, p. 258], reported on these consultations at the 46th Session [A/46/564, Annex]. His report indicates that the April 1991 consultations, though well attended, were inconclusive. Despite "general agreement" to relaunch negotiations on the Code by taking a "fresh approach" (according to which an intergovernmental group of experts, working under UNCTAD auspices, would be given clear terms of reference to prepare for new formal negotiations), there was no avoiding some of the long-standing divisions between developed and developing countries when it came to the issue of instructing the experts. Developing countries proposed broad terms of reference, while developed countries favored providing specific guidance with respect to two major issues that have yet to be resolved: the evaluation of restrictive practices and applicable law. Developed countries continued to insist on the exclusive application of competition law principles to regulate restrictive licensing practices, without regard to the effect on economic development; and they sought to affirm the right to contract freely as well as the right to choose applicable law and the dispute settlement forum. The 46th General Assembly voted merely to transmit the UNCTAD report to the eighth session of UNCTAD [A/Res/46/214]—which will be debating the terms of references for the experts—and to take up the item again at its 47th Session.

The 46th Session also voted to convene a joint U.N.-International Maritime Organization (IMO) Conference of Plenipotentiaries on a **Draft Convention on Maritime Liens and Mortgages** prepared by UNCTAD and the IMO, which have indicated the need for international uniformity on the subject. The conference will be held in Geneva during the first half of 1993 [A/Res/46/213].

UNCITRAL, established in 1966 and with a present membership of 36, representing the various geographic areas and the principal legal and economic systems of the world, is charged with the progressive harmonization and unification of international trade law. The 46th General Assembly reaffirmed UNCITRAL's mandate as the "core legal body within the United Nations system in the field of international trade law" and, expressing concern about the relatively low level of participation by experts from developing countries, it requested that the Fifth (Administrative and Budgetary) Committee consider granting travel assistance to facilitate such participation [A/Res/46/56; see the report of the Secretary-General on the same issue, A/46/349]. The Assembly had words of praise for UNCITRAL's May 1992 Congress on International Trade Law—a contribution to the U.N. Decade of International Law, 1990–99.

By tradition, the Assembly also considered UNCITRAL's report of its previous session [A/46/17]—in this case its 24th, held June 10–28, 1991— where one topic of discussion was the **Draft Model Law on International Credit Transfers** that had been adopted in 1991 by the Commission's Working Group on International Payments [see *Issues/46*, pp. 259–60] and sent to all governments and to interested international organizations for comment. At the UNCITRAL session the Commission had before it reports of the Working Group on the Model Law [see A/CN.9/344, reporting on the Working Group's 22nd session], the Secretary-General's report on comments received pertaining to the Model Law [A/CN.9/347 and Add.1], and a commentary on the Model Law prepared by the UNCITRAL secretariat [A/CN.9/346; each briefly discussed in the UNCITRAL Report, A/46/17, p. 5]. The commentary on the Model Law, among other things, compares the Model Law to provisions in Article 4A of the Uniform Commerical Code of the United States. Article 4A governs the kinds of credit transfers that the draft Model Law governs (Article 4A deals with both domestic and international credit transfers). As noted in the commentary, Article 4A is singled out because it is the only legislative text in existence that provides a basic legal structure for credit transfers; in all other countries the relevant law is derived from a multitude of sources. This 38-section Article has been fruitful as a source of ideas for the Working Group [A/CN.9/346, p. 4].

The Commission reviewed the text of Articles 1-15 of the Model Law on International Credit Transfers, which would apply to credit transfers between sending and receiving banks located in different nations [see *Issues/46*, pp. 259–60]. These articles, inter alia, define the law's sphere of application, contain relevant definitions (e.g., of "credit transfer," "payment order," "originator," and "beneficiary"), provide for variation by agreement, and spell out the obligations of sender and receiving bank. Among the issues raised were the possible difficulties of having two different bodies of law, one for domestic credit transfers and another, the Model Law, applicable to international credit transfers; the suggestion (ultimately rejected) that the Model Law be applicable only to electronic transfers; and the compatibility of the Model Law with attempts to prevent money laundering [A/46/17, pp. 6–7, 68]. The United States has expressed the hope that care will be taken to prevent adverse effects on existing high-speed, high-volume, electronic credit systems and on the future development of such systems [see, e.g., A/CN.9/347/Add.1, p. 9].

UNCITRAL's Working Group on the New International Economic Order, meeting in New York for its 13th session (July 1991) and in Vienna for its 14th (December 1991), continued consideration of a draft **Model Law on Procurement** [reports at A/CN.9/356 and A/CN.9/359, respectively]. The Model Law, on the Commission's agenda since 1986, is designed to assist states in restructuring or improving their rules governing transactions involving governmental agencies—transactions that now constitute a significant portion of the trade between developing and developed states [see *Issues/46*, p. 260]. At the close of the Working Group's 12th session, the Group had requested that the secretariat revise Articles 1–27 of the law in accord with comments made. The 13th session of the Working Group considered draft Articles 28–42 on the examination, evaluation, and comparison of tenders; rejection of all tenders; negotiations with contractors and suppliers; acceptance of tender and entry into force of procurement contract; record of tendering proceedings; competitive-negotiation proceedings; and single-source procurement [A/CN.9/356]. The Working Group requested that the secretariat revise these articles in accord with comments made at that session, and it reaffirmed its earlier decision that the Model Law would include a commentary [ibid.]. At its 14th session, the Working Group again reviewed the first 27 articles of the Model Law, made the preliminary decision to aim the commentary at legislatures (providing them with guidance on enactment of the law), and expressed its intention to complete the Model Law at its next session [A/CN.9/359]. The 15th session of the Working Group was scheduled for June 22–July 2, 1992 in New York.

UNCITRAL's Working Group on International Contract Practices has been at work on a **Uniform Law on Guarantees and Stand-by Letters of Credit** since 1989, with the aim of supplying a basic framework for such guarantees to fill gaps in national law and contractual practice [see *Issues/46*, pp. 260–61]. At the Working Group's 15th session, in 1991, it examined two notes by the secretariat discussing fraud and other objections to payment, injunctions and other court measures, and conflict of laws and jurisdiction; discussed such issues as whether the guarantor should have a "reasonable time" in which to examine a claim under a guarantee to decide whether to pay or whether to provide a fixed number of days for this purpose; and considered whether the Uniform Law should contain provisions creating a duty to notify a principal of a claim, obliging the guarantor to give notice of rejection to the beneficiary, and imposing further duties of notification on financial institutions [A/CN.9/345]. On these and other issues, much of the discussion centered on whether the Uniform Law should replicate relevant provisions in the International Chamber of Commerce's Draft Uniform Rules for Demand

Guarantees. The Working Group resumed discussion of proposed Articles 1–13 of the Uniform Law at its 16th session, in November 1991 [report at A/CN.9/358].

Also ongoing is UNCITRAL's project for a **Legal Guide on Drawing Up International Countertrade Contracts** (that is, trade that consists of the direct exchange or barter of goods without the use of currency). This is a topic with priority for many countries, especially those in the developing countries that often resort to countertrade because of shortages of hard currency [see *Issues/46*, p. 259]. To date the Commission has examined several sample chapters of the Guide prepared by the secretariat, and has generally agreed on the approach, structure, and substance of those provisions [A/46/17, p. 71]. The Working Group on International Payments examined additional draft chapters of the Guide at its 23rd session in New York in September 1991 [report at A/CN.9/357].

The Working Group on International Payments has also been examining the legal problems of **electronic data exchange**—a topic that emerged from UNCITRAL's request to the secretariat that it prepare a preliminary study on the need for uniform legal principles to guide the formation of international commercial contracts by electronic means [see *Issues/46*, p. 261]. UNCITRAL has now received various reports on the subject. One of the most recent—a 1991 Report by the Secretary-General on "Electronic Data Interchange" (EDI)—describes the relevant current activities in various organizations and surveys the contents of a number of standard interchange agreements already in use or being developed [A/CN.9/350]. The EDI report notes that such documents vary considerably, according to the different needs of different users, and that the wide variety of contractual arrangements may hinder the development of a satisfactory legal framework for use in business. It concludes that various standardization efforts are under way, but that no one concerned with worldwide harmonization of the legal rules has even begun to work on a standard communications agreement. It therefore suggests that such an agreement might prove useful to promote this type of contracting [ibid., p. 29].

Despite general support for such a project by the members of UNCITRAL, there was no agreement on its priority. The prevailing view was that the Commission should continue monitoring developments in other organizations while the Working Group on International Payments identifies the legal issues involved, especially with regard to the feasibility of a standard communications agreement [A/46/17, p. 75]. At the Working Group's 24th session in 1992, it decided to recommend the preparation of legal norms and rules on the use of EDI in international trade to provide guidance to users, national legislators, and regulatory authorities [A/CN.9/360, p. 34], but it made no formal recommendation of the form in which these rules would be expressed. The Working Group agreed that, for the moment at least, it was not necessary to develop a standard communications agreement [ibid.].

The U.N. Secretary-General will report to the 25th session of UNCITRAL on current activities of international organizations related to **harmonization and unification of international trade law** [see *Issues/46*, pp. 261–62 for summary of last report]. His report will have a different focus than is usual, since it will canvass multilateral and bilateral development organizations about the extent to which they have been involved in activities to help modernize domestic commercial laws within developing countries [for an interim progress report, see A/CN.9/352].

The **U.N. Convention on the Carriage of Goods by Sea (the "Hamburg Rules")**, adopted on March 31, 1978, by a diplomatic conference convened by the General Assembly at Hamburg, Germany, will come into force on November 1, 1992. Zambia, which deposited its instrument of accession in October 1991, supplied the crucial 20th instrument necessary to bring the rules into effect [U.N. press release L/T/4294, 10/17/91]. The impetus for developing the Hamburg Rules was dissatisfaction with the earlier legal regime based on the "Hague Rules." The new convention governs the rights and obligations of shippers, carriers, and consignees under a contract of carriage of goods. The central, but by no means exclusive, focus is on the liability of a carrier for loss of, or damage to, the goods and for delay in delivery.

7. Space Law

The 46th General Assembly endorsed the 1991 Report of the **Committee on the Peaceful Uses of Outer Space** [A/46/20], which included the Legal Subcommittee's report of its 30th session and the progress made on its ongoing threefold agenda: elaboration of draft principles on the use of nuclear power sources in outer space, the definition and delimitation of outer space and the character and utilization of the geostationary orbit, and the legal ramifications of the principle that exploration and utilization should be for the benefit of all states, especially developing countries [A/Res/46/45].

Regarding the **use of nuclear power sources in outer space,** a Working Group of the Legal Subcommittee is continuing to work on draft principles and has already reached consensus on a number of them. In 1990 it agreed on Principle 3, containing "guidelines and criteria for safe use" [see *Issues/45*, pp. 211–12]; and at the end of its 30th session, in 1991, the Working Group reached consensus on Principle 8, concerning state responsibility for national activities in outer space involving nuclear power sources [see *Issues/46*, pp. 262–63], and Principle 9, which addresses "liability and compensation" [A/46/20, pp. 18–19]. This last principle tracks the provisions in the 1967 Treaty on Principles Governing the Activities of States in the Exploration and Use of Outer Space, including the Moon and Other Celestial Bodies, as well as the Convention on International Liability for Damage Caused by Space Objects. It establishes the basis for an assessment of international liability on any "State from whose territory or facility a space object is launched" in accordance with international law and the principles of "justice and equity"; and it announces that the compensation is intended to make the injured party whole and will include reimbursement for substantiated expenses for search, recovery, clean-up operations, and for assistance received from third parties [ibid., p. 19]. A representative of the IAEA participated in the discussions, and it is likely that the agency's expert advice will be sought in the future. Participants acknowledged that even the principles accepted to date will be reexamined once the full set of principles is completed. Some delegates stated that the complete set of principles must include clear provisions for safety standards, notification procedures, and definition of responsibility in case of accidents [ibid., p. 20]. Much of the work of the Legal Subcommittee in the immediate future is likely to focus on completing these principles, with attention to a possible overlap between its approach to the issue and the Scientific and Technical Subcommittee's approach to the same issue [see, e.g., U.N. press release OS/1555, 3/30/92].

Discussion of the **definition and delimitation of outer space** consisted of reiterations of positions taken at prior sessions [see *Issues/46*, p. 263], and there is no indication that some form of agreement can be reached between those who advocate a conventionally defined boundary between air and outer space and those who argue that such delimitation is unnecessary and should be removed from the agenda [A/46/20, p. 21]. Discussion of the **character and utilization of the geostationary orbit** led to a similar stalemate, as in prior years [see *Issues/46*, pp. 263–64]. Again, while some delegations stated that the geostationary orbit is part of outer space and governed by the legal regime of the 1967 Treaty, other delegates, prominently those of the developing countries and the equatorial countries, advocated a special legal regime to assure equal access and regulate utilization. There was similar disagreement over the proper role of the International Telecommunications Union (ITU) on this question, with some delegations recommending that the ITU have exclusive jurisdiction over the issue and others contending that the work of the ITU in this area merely complements the work of the Outer Space Committee [A/46/20, pp. 21–22].

The Legal Subcommittee's consideration of the application of the principle that the **exploration and utilization of outer space** should be carried out for the benefit and in the interests of all states, put on its agenda by the General Assembly in 1989, also remained at a stalemate. The developing countries continued to view the topic as an opportunity for elaborating a "new international legal framework" that will ensure equal access to and benefit from outer space activities. The developed states have tended to view the subject as calling for an exchange of views and nothing more [ibid., p. 23; see *Issues/46*, p. 264]. At its meetings in 1992 the Legal Subcommittee had before it a working paper submitted by a group of developing countries containing a set of detailed "principles regarding international cooperation in the exploration and utilization of outer space for peaceful purposes" [A/AC.105/C.2/L.182].

The 46th General Assembly's resolution regarding the operations of the Committee on the Peaceful Uses of Outer Space also noted and endorsed the extensive agenda of the **Scientific and Technical Subcommittee** [A/Res/46/45; see also "Global Resource Management" section on International Space Year in the present volume], whose work, as noted above, may occasionally overlap with that of the Legal Subcommittee. And as in prior sessions, the Assembly passed, by a vote of 155–0–1 (the United States), a resolution encouraging bilateral and multilateral negotiations to prevent an **arms race in outer space;** and it placed the same item on the agenda of the 47th Session [A/Res/46/33; see *Issues/46*, p. 265].

8. International Court of Justice

On August 14, 1991, the Deputy Registrar of the International Court of Justice (ICJ) informed the Secretary-General of the death of Judge Taslim Olawale Elias of Nigeria and of the resulting vacancy on the Court. Pursuant to the Statute of the Court, the vacancy was filled by the same method as that laid down for regular election: The U.N. Secretary-General issued invitations for nominations and the Security Council and General Assembly proceeded to elect Bola Ajibola, also of Nigeria, to the Court [Decision 46/315]. Judge Ajibola will complete Judge Elias's term, which expires on February 5, 1994.

Perhaps the most publicized recent action by the Court was its prompt dismissal on April 14, 1992, one day prior to the effective date of Security Council sanctions against Libya [see section 2, "Peace and Security" above], of **Libya's applications to the Court** against the United States and Britain, respectively. Libya had filed these applications on March 3, requesting interpretation or application of the Montreal Convention for the Suppression of Unlawful Acts against the Safety of Civil Aviation, and its claims grew out of the Security Council's consideration of alleged involvement by Libyan nationals in international terrorism and the U.S. and British requests that Libya extradite those allegedly responsible. Libya alleged that the Court's jurisdiction was based on Article 36(1) of the Statute of the Court and Article 14(1) of the Montreal Convention.

Libya contended that its dispute with Britain and the United States dealt with an offense covered by Article 1 of the Montreal Convention (i.e., the alleged destruction of an aircraft); that under Article 5 of that Convention, Libya is entitled to exercise criminal jurisdiction over persons charged with such an offense; and that under Articles 7 and 8, Libya is obliged either to prosecute such offenders (which it was trying to do) or to extradite them, if allowed to do so by local law (which Libyan law did not) [Libyan Application against the United Kingdom, 3/3/92]. Libya further contended that Britain and the United States were not operating within the framework provided under the Montreal Convention and were, instead, intent on compelling the surrender of the accused in violation of the Convention; and it also asserted that the two countries were refusing to assist Libya in its prosecution of the suspects in violation of Article 11(1) of the Convention. Libya was therefore requesting of the Court a declaration that it had complied fully with its obligations under the Montreal Convention, that the United Kingdom and the United States were in breach of their legal obligations under this Convention, and that these two states were

> under a legal obligation immediately to cease and desist from such breaches and from the use of any and all force or threats against Libya, including the threat of force against Libya, and from all violations of the sovereignty, territorial integrity, and the political independence of Libya [see, e.g., ibid., pp. 9–10].

By two separate requests to the Court on the same day, Libya also sought the indication of provisional measures. It requested that the Court "enjoin the United Kingdom and the United States" from "taking any action against Libya calculated to coerce or compel Libya to surrender the accused individuals to any jurisdiction outside of Libya" and that it "ensure that no steps are taken that would prejudice in any way the rights of Libya with respect to the legal proceedings that are the subject of Libya's Applications" [U.N. press release ICJ/515, 3/10/92]. Since no Libyan national is currently a member of the Court, Libya was permitted to appoint Judge ad hoc Ahmed Sadek El-Kosheri to sit in these cases.

Libya's requests for provisional relief were the only subject of the Court's resulting brief order in the Case Concerning Questions of Interpretation and Application of the 1971 Montreal Convention Arising from the Aerial Incident at Lockerbie [ICJ Reports, 1992, Order of April 14, 1991]. The Court's order, which drew the votes of 11 of the 16 judges, came after a three-day oral hearing and did not address many of the arguments raised by either Libya or the United States. Although the United States argued that Libya had not presented a *prima facie* case for jurisdiction under the Montreal Convention—which, it argued, failed in any case to extend to the rights Libya claimed—and that Libya had not demonstrated the risk of imminent injury required for provisional relief, the Court focused solely on one other argument for rejecting Libya's applications: that the Security Council was appropriately seized of the matter and had rendered a binding decision on the issue. Thus, the Court majority stated that Libya had a "Charter-based duty to accept and carry out" Security Council Resolution 748, as did the United States, in "accordance with Article 25 of the Charter" [ibid., p. 14]. Further, said the Court, it "considers that *prima facie* this obligation extends to the decision contained in resolution 748 . . . whereas, in accordance with Article 103 of the Charter, the obligations of the Parties in that respect prevail over their obligations under any other international agreement, including the Montreal Convention" [ibid.]. The Court was careful to note that since this was a request for indication of provisional measures, it was not making "definitive findings of fact or of law on the issues relating to the merits," or even making a finding that it has jurisdiction [ibid., pp. 14–15]. Indeed, said the Court, its ruling was limited to determining that whatever rights Libya had under the Montreal Convention, if any, "cannot now be regarded as appropriate for protection by the indication of provisional measures" [ibid., p. 15]. The decision leaves open the possibility that Libya will pursue its claims under the Montreal Convention in future action on the merits before the Court.

Despite the limited nature of the Court's order in the Libya case, its immediate significance was apparent: It strengthened the hand of the Security Council and undermined the claim that the Council should wait for the Court to act before imposing sanctions. It is unclear whether the ruling will have a wider impact—by, for example, giving rise to the notion that the Court is either unwilling or unable to make a finding that a U.N. organ (or specifically the Security Council) is acting *ultra vires*. Certainly the Court did not appear to make such a broad ruling, and it has not hesitated to review the legality of action by U.N. organs in other contexts in the past. The case did raise the prospect of a conflict between the Security Council and the Court for the first time; that conflict has been averted, at least temporarily.

On November 12, 1991, the full Court, with Judges Hubert Thierry and Keba Mbaye sitting as judges ad hoc, rendered its decision in the case concerning the **Arbitral Award of 31 July 1989 (Guinea-Bissau v. Senegal)** [31 ILM 32 (1992)]. The Court upheld the validity of the arbitral award, which had been rendered in the course of a maritime dispute between the parties. The Court had previously dismissed a request for indication of provisional measures pending an outcome in the case [see *Issues/45*, p. 218; 29 ILM 624 (1990)]. Guinea-Bissau, acting on the basis of its 1989 acceptance of the Court's 36(2) jurisdiction as well as Senegal's acceptance of that jurisdiction, had sought to have the arbitral award declared "inexistent" or "null and void" [see *Issues/46*, p. 268]. The Court unanimously rejected Guinea-Bissau's claim that the arbitral award was "inexistent" and, by a vote of 11–4, rejected the plea of nullity. By a further vote of 12–3, it found that Senegal was justified in seeking the application of the "valid and binding" award.

The arbitral award under challenge in this case had partially delimited the maritime boundaries in dispute between Senegal and Guinea-Bissau, since a majority of the arbitrators had concluded that a 1960 agreement between France and Portugal, applicable to Guinea-Bissau and Senegal, delimited those maritime spaces in existence as of 1960—namely, the territorial sea, the contiguous zone, and the continental shelf—but not those that did not then exist, such as the exclusive economic zone [see Judgment, para. 16]. Guinea-Bissau's challenge to this arbitral award led the Court, through the majority opinion and the various concurring and dissenting opinions issued, to canvass, as the Court's Judge Christopher Gregory Weeramantry (Sri Lanka) put it in his dissent, a "fascinating range of legal issues," including basic questions concerning the extent the Court should be an "appellate" body sitting in review of supposedly final arbitral awards, the rules governing interpretation of agreements to submit to arbitration, and the types of procedural or other defects in an arbitral award that may give rise to a finding of nullity.

With respect to jurisdiction, the ICJ interpreted Senegal's reservations to its consent to 36(2) jurisdiction (made on December 2, 1985) to mean that the parties here had consented to have the Court consider only the question of the validity of the arbitral award, not the substantive merits of that award. The Court thereby avoided suggestions that it was inappropriately sitting in "appellate" review over the merits of a "final" arbitration [Judgment, paras. 23–24; see also Declaration of Judge ad hoc Mbaye]. The majority thereupon rejected Guinea-Bissau's complaints that the award was defective because one of the arbitrators was physically absent from the meeting at which the award was pronounced, because the separate opinion rendered by one of the arbitrators (Mr. Barberis) cast doubt on the degree of agreement supporting the award, and because the arbitrators had failed to answer one of the questions posed to them and had failed to append to their award a map indicating the maritime delimitation. The Court stated that its mandate was to "ascertain whether by rendering the disputed Award the Tribunal acted in manifest breach of the competence conferred on it by the Arbitration Agreement, either by deciding in excess of, or by failing to exercise, its jurisdiction" [Judgment, para. 47]. It proceeded to interpret the parties' arbitration agreement in "accordance with the general rules of international law governing the interpretation of treaties . . . reflected in Articles 31 and 32 of the Vienna Convention on the Law of Treaties, which may in many respects be considered as a codification of existing customary international law on point" [Judgment, para. 48]. The Court concluded that the arbitrators' "partial delimitation" was within their mandate and therefore binding, despite flaws in the award and the way it was rendered.

Although the Court upheld the award, the majority and separate opinions contain numerous criticisms of the way Senegal and Guinea-Bissau drafted their initial agreement to arbitrate, the way the arbitrators interpreted and carried out their mandate, and even the decision of the parties to submit this dispute to the Court. These criticisms may prove enlightening to other states contemplating the peaceful settlement of a dispute. In the end, neither the arbitral award upheld in this case nor the ICJ's judgment settled all the maritime boundary issues in dispute between Guinea-Bissau and Senegal. Indeed, as is noted in the Court's judgment [para. 67], on March 12, 1991, Guinea-Bissau filed a second application concerning these further delimitations. It thus appears that, should the parties fail to reach agreement on the outstanding maritime boundary questions and the Court affirm jursidiction over this second application, the Court will deal with the actual merits of this dispute.

Portugal's proceeding against Australia, filed on February 22, 1991, concerning **certain activities of Australia with respect to East Timor** remains at the pleading stage, with Australia's countermemorial due on June 1, 1992. Portugal claims that the people of East Timor and Portugal suffered serious "legal and moral damage" as a result of an agreement between Australia and Indonesia relating to the exploration and exploitation of certain areas in the continental shelf [see *Issues/46*, p. 269].

Also at the pleading stage is the dispute between Finland and Denmark concerning **passage through the Great Belt** (the Store Baelt, one of the three straits linking the Baltic to the Kattegat and the North Sea)—a case that is expected to define further the nature and limits of the right of free passage within international straits. This proceeding, instituted by an application from Finland on May 17, 1991, is based on both states' acceptance of the Court's 36(2) jurisdiction. Finland complains that Denmark's planned construction of a high-level bridge would exclude the passage of vessels, such as drill ships and oil rigs, with a height greater than 65 meters, calling this a violation of its right to free passage through the Great Belt—a strait whose use for international navigation is acknowledged by both states. Finland had also filed, on May 23, 1991, a request for provisional measures that would include, among other things, a Court order directing Denmark to refrain from constructing the planned bridge pending the outcome of this case. Judges ad hoc were appointed by both parties and, in July 1991, at six public sittings, the Court heard oral observations from both parties concerning the request for provisional measures [A/46/4, p. 18]. On July 29, 1991, the Court, relying on assurances from Denmark that "no physical obstruction of the East Channel will occur before the end of 1994" [Order of July 29, 1991; *ICJ Reports 1991*, para. 27], unanimously rejected Finland's request for provisional

relief, concluding "that the circumstances as they now present themselves
. . . are not such as to require the exercise of its power under Article 41
of the Statute . . ." [*ICJ Reports 1991*, para. 38]. By separate order the Court set
the case on an expedited schedule, requesting Finland's memorial on the
merits by December 30, 1991, and the countermemorial by Denmark by
June 1, 1992 [Order of July 29, 1991].

Libya's territorial dispute with Chad, arising from separate notifi-
cations to the Court by each of the states in 1990 [see *Issues/46*, p. 268; A/46/4, p.
13], remains at the pleading stage. Both parties filed their initial memorials
within the August 26, 1991, time limit; and both countermemorials were
due by March 27, 1992 [Order of August 26, 1991]. Also at the pleading stage is
Iran's claim against the United States for compensation growing out of
the destruction of Iran Air Airbus A-300B, flight 655, **Aerial Incident of
3 July 1988 (Islamic Republic of Iran v. United States)** [see *Issues/46*, p. 267].
Iran requested and received an extension for filing its response to the
United States' preliminary objections to jurisdiction; June 9, 1992, was
the new date supplied [Order of December 18, 1991].

The Court is also handling a July 1991 application by **Qatar
instituting proceedings against Bahrain** "in respect of certain existing
disputes between them relating to sovereignty over the Hawar islands,
sovereign rights over the shoals of Dibal and Qit'at Jaradah, and the
delimitation of the maritime areas of the two states" [A/46/4, p. 18]. Qatar
claims that its sovereignty over the Hawar islands is firmly established
under customary international law as well as under local practices and
customs. It rejects the legality of a British declaration of 1939 that the
islands belong to Bahrain; it similarly rejects a British demarcation
decision in 1947 purporting to set seabed boundaries and giving Bahrain
sovereign rights to the disputed shoals. Bahrain has claimed in the past
that Dibal and Qit'at Jaradah are part of its territory, and that these are
islands with territorial waters, not shoals. Jurisdiction is claimed on the
basis of Article 36(1) of the Court's statute, based on commitments said
to have been made by the two states in the context of mediation by King
Fahd of Saudi Arabia. Besides a declaration establishing its sovereignty
over the Hawar islands, Dibal, and Qit'at Jaradah, Qatar is asking the
Court to "draw in accordance with international law a single maritime
boundary between the maritime areas of sea-bed, subsoil and superjacent
waters appertaining respectively to the State of Qatar and the State of
Bahrain" [A/46/4, p. 19]. By letter to the Registrar of the Court, Bahrain has
contested the basis of jurisdiction, and the Court has ordered the parties
to address this question initially by written pleadings. Qatar's memorial
was due on February 10, 1992, and Bahrain's countermemorial on June
11, 1992 [Order of October 11, 1991; U.N. press release ICJ/509, 11/15/91].

Nicaragua's claim to reparations against the United States growing
out of **Military and Paramilitary Activities In and Against Nicaragua**

[see *Issues/44*, p. 218] ended when, on September 12, 1991, the agent of Nicaragua informed the Court that, owing to agreements between his government and the United States "aimed at enhancing Nicaragua's economic, commercial and technical development to the maximum extent possible," his government "had decided to renounce all further right of action based on the case . . . and, hence, does not wish to go on with the proceedings" [31 ILM 105]. In response, the President of the Court gave the United States until September 25, 1991, to respond; and on that date, the United States wrote that it "welcomes" the Nicaraguan request for discontinuance [31 ILM 106]. An order discontinuing the case was thereupon issued on September 26, 1991 [*ICJ Reports 1991*, p. 47; 31 ILM 103]. Thanks to an agreement to an out-of-Court settlement between Nicaragua and Honduras, the Court discontinued the related pending case, **Border and Transborder Armed Actions (Nicaragua v. Honduras)** [ICJ press release, 5/27/92].

Between November and December 1991, the Court heard the parties' oral arguments in the case instituted by Nauru against Australia concerning **certain phosphate lands in Nauru.** Australia had made preliminary objections to the jurisdiction of the Court and the admissibility of Nauru's application. Accordingly, proceedings on the merits had been suspended pending the Court's consideration of these issues [see *Issues/46*, p. 268]. The oral proceedings were confined to the issues of jurisdiction and admissibility [U.N. press release ICJ/510, 11/15/91].

Also pending are decisions on the merits in two other contentious cases: **Maritime Delimitation in the Area between Greenland and Jan Mayen (Denmark v. Norway)** and a Chamber's decision in the **Land, Island and Maritime Frontier Dispute (El Salvador/Honduras; Nicaragua Intervening)** [see *Issues/46*, pp. 265–68].

According to the report of the ICJ to the General Assembly [A/46/4, p. 3], 53 states have now made declarations (albeit many with reservations) recognizing the Court's "compulsory" jurisdiction under Article 36(2) of the Statute of the Court. Two additional treaties providing for the jurisdiction of the Court in contentious cases were deposited with the Secretariat of the United Nations: the Convention on the Marking of Plastic Explosives for the Purpose of Detection [see *Issues/46*, p. 252] and the Franco-Libyan Treaty of Friendship and Good Neighborliness. During the plenary meeting of the General Assembly that considered the ICJ's report, Secretary-General Javier Pérez de Cuéllar availed himself of the opportunity to note that the Court, through its advisory opinions, has assisted the political organs of the United Nations in settling disputes that threaten to erupt into crises, and he asked that the General Assembly now consider authorizing the

> Secretary-General to request, *with the consent of the parties to the dispute*, Advisory Opinions from the Court. The request would come

from the Secretary-General and the opinion given by the Court would be for his use. The political contents of the case would be de-emphasized and the parties would be able to detach themselves from the request and the proceedings. This would leave the Secretary-General the flexibility to find the best way to use the Advisory Opinion in the search for a solution to the dispute [ICJ press release, 11/8/91; emphasis in original].

The Secretary-General repeated this suggestion in his last annual Report on the Work of the Organization, indicating that this would strengthen the role of the Secretary-General and be "wholly in accord with the complementary relationship between the [Security Council, the General Assembly, and the International Court of Justice] which has grown fruitfully over the years" [A/41/1, p. 4]. During discussion of the Secretary-General's suggestion in the Special Committee on the Charter of the United Nations and on the Strengthening of the Role of the Organization, as well as in the Sixth Committee, a number of delegates expressed doubt about the wisdom and feasibility of the idea [see A/46/33, p. 14; A/C.6/46/SR.9].

9. Other Legal Developments

As was the case at the 45th Session of the Assembly, the debate on the proper role of the United Nations in the facilitation or promotion of democracy generated more heat than light, and it led once again to the adoption of two contrary resolutions supported by two very different groups of states [compare *Issues/46*, pp. 271–72]. In one, the 46th Assembly reaffirmed, by a vote of 134–3–13 (Cuba, North Korea, and Kenya in dissent), its previously stated commitment [A/Res/45/150] to **enhancing the effectiveness of the principle of periodic and genuine elections,** and it asked the Secretary-General to report on guidelines for U.N. electoral involvement at the 47th Session [A/Res/46/137]. Aware of the possibilities for conflict between U.N. involvement in promoting democracy and Article 2(7) of the U.N. Charter prohibiting the Organization from interfering in any state's "domestic jurisdiction," the resolution seeks to assure nervous governments that there is "no single political system or electoral method that is equally suited to all nations" and that international efforts "should not call into question each State's sovereign right . . . to choose and develop its political, social, economic and cultural systems, whether or not they conform to the preferences of other States." (It also asserts that U.N. electoral verification should remain an "exceptional activity" to be undertaken in "well-defined circumstances, *inter alia,* primarily in situations with a clear international dimension.") The conflicting resolution—on **respect for the principles of national sovereignty and non-interference in the internal affairs of States in their electoral processes**

[A/Res/46/130, passed by a vote of 102-40-13]—takes these reservations and runs with them. It not only reaffirms the Article 2(7) non-intervention principle and the 1990 Assembly's Resolution 151 [see *Issues/46*, p. 272] but goes on to state that "there is no universal need for the United Nations to provide electoral assistance to Member States." On the contrary,

> any activities that attempt, directly or indirectly, to interfere in the free development of national electoral processes, in particular in the developing countries, or that intend to sway the results of such processes, violate the spirit and letter of the principles established in the Charter and in the Declaration on Principles of International Law concerning Friendly Relations and Cooperation among States in accordance with the Charter of the United Nations [ibid.].

In a related action, the Assembly endorsed the Secretary-General's efforts to organize and supervise, with the assistance of the Organization of African Unity (OAU), a referendum for self-determination for the people of **Western Sahara** [A/Res/46/67].

A resolution on the **U.N. Decade of International Law 1990–99** [A/Res/46/53] expresses appreciation for the Secretary-General's progress report on implementation of the U.N. Decade program and requests future annual reports [for more on the Decade, see *Issues/45*, p. 219; *Issues/46*, pp. 269–71]. The Secretary-General's report contains an analysis of the activities relating to the goals of the Decade undertaken by the 13 governments and approximately 40 international organizations that responded to the inquiry [A/46/372]. The report reveals that several states see the Decade of International Law as an opportunity to review their policies with respect to accession to treaties and to consider the possibility of withdrawing treaty reservations made in the past. It also canvasses the various forms of assistance and technical advice being offered by international organizations to facilitate treaty accession; surveys ways to encourage treaty implementation and to promote peaceful settlement of disputes; summarizes the means that regional and other organizations have used to encourage the progressive development or codification of international law; notes the methods states have used to encourage the study of international law at all levels as well as the topics covered in seminars and international symposia; surveys national approaches to recording relevant state practice; and summarizes the practice of international organizations with respect to publication of relevant treaties. The report concludes with a survey of the relevant legal activities engaged in by U.N. bodies (most of which are surveyed in this chapter).

The Secretary-General's report, as well as the objectives of the Decade, were also the subject of discussion in the Sixth Committee, where various speakers called for the commemoration of the Decade through greater respect for human rights, accession to multilateral treaties, and acceptance of the compulsory jurisdiction of the ICJ [see, e.g., A.C.6/46/SR.37; see also Report of Working Group of Sixth Committee, A/C.6/46/L.8].

The 46th General Assembly's Resolution 50, on the U.N. Programme of Assistance in the **Teaching, Study, Dissemination and Wider Appreciation of International Law,** endorses recommendations made by the Secretary-General [A/46/610], as well as the diverse efforts of, among other groups, the Codification Division of the Office of Legal Affairs, the U.N. Institute for Training and Research, UNESCO, and the Hague Academy of International Law. The Assembly also voted to appoint 25 states (six from Africa, five from Asia, three from Eastern Europe, five from Latin America and the Caribbean, and six from Western Europe and other regions) as members of an Advisory Committee for this program for four years [A/Res/46/50].

The Assembly appealed to parties to the Convention on the Elimination of Racial Discrimination to fulfill their financial obligations to the **Committee on the Elimination of Racial Discrimination.** The Committee is charged with implementing the Convention, and the financial arrears impair its ability to meet regularly [A/Res/46/83]. The Assembly also urged states to submit the periodic reports on implementing measures called for by the Convention and asked that the Secretary-General report to the 47th Session on the problems encountered [ibid.]. The Assembly expressed similar concerns with respect to other financial or reporting obligations under other human rights instruments [see A/Res/46/111, A/Res/46/112, A/Res/46/113]. It also called on states to ratify the 1990 **International Convention on the Protection of the Rights of All Migrant Workers and Members of Their Families** [A/Res/46/114].

Under the rubric of the status of the **International Convention on the Suppression and Punishment of the Crime of Apartheid,** the 46th Assembly called on states to ratify the Convention, and called on all states whose transnational corporations continue to do business with South Africa to terminate such dealings [A/Res/46/84]; the vote was 118–1–39 (the United States). The same resolution requested the Commission on Human Rights to intensify its efforts to identify lists of individuals, organizations, and representatives of states who are responsible for crimes under the Convention, as well as those against whom legal proceedings have been undertaken.

At its resumed 46th Session in 1992, the Assembly decided to convene a **World Conference on Human Rights** in June 1993 in Vienna [U.N. press release GA/8317, 5/6/92].

VII
Finance and Administration

1. The Fifth Committee's Agenda in 1992

At the beginning of its 46th Session, the General Assembly allocated 25 items to the Fifth (Administrative and Budgetary) Committee. Three other items were added as the session progressed. While some items did not call for lengthy discussion, others—such as the Secretary-General's program budget proposals and the scale of assessments—were highly complex or politically sensitive. Quite clearly, such a large number of items cannot all be discussed properly during the 50 to 60 meetings the Fifth Committee can hold during an Assembly session. Furthermore, it is generally agreed that several items do not need to be considered every year.

In an attempt to rationalize its work, the Fifth Committee decided that certain items will henceforth be considered in even-numbered years and others in odd-numbered years. Because 1992 is an even year, the Fifth Committee's agenda at the forthcoming session will include a review of the efficiency of the administrative and financial functioning of the United Nations, program planning, and personnel questions along with the related items of the U.N. common system and pension system. The Committee's agenda will also include several items that will continue to be considered annually, among them the current financial crisis and financial emergency of the United Nations, the budgets of U.N. peace-keeping operations, and the review of the current biennial program budget of the Organization. In 1992 the Fifth Committee will also once again return to the scale of assessments, an item that, the Assembly decided, should be considered twice in three years [A/Res/46/220].

2. U.N. Finances

The Financial Crisis Continues

In his last report to the General Assembly on the Work of the Organization, Secretary-General Javier Pérez de Cuéllar did not mince words in speaking of the financial crisis confronting the United Nations:

. . . it is hardly comprehensible that Governments impose far-reaching and costly responsibilities on the organization, as they judge they must, but are themselves unwilling to fulfil corresponding financial obligations. Voluntary contributions, however welcome and generous they may be, cannot reliably fill the gap. This places the Secretary-General in an often intolerable situation. . . . Under the Charter, it is a legal duty of Member States to pay their assessed contributions . . . payment must be made on time and in full if the Secretariat is to retain the capability of responding, on behalf of the membership as a whole, to the pressing tasks required of it . . ." [A/46/1].

At the end of 1990 unpaid contributions to the regular budget, for all years up to and including 1990, totaled $403 million. The corresponding figure at the end of 1991 was $439.4 million, an increase of 9 percent.

There were a few bright spots in an overall dismal picture. In particular, **the United States,** while remaining the major debtor, reduced its arrears of contributions to the regular budget from $296.2 million at the end of 1990 to $266.4 million a year later, i.e., by $29.8 million, or just over 10 percent. But this favorable development was more than offset by increased indebtedness by members of the **Commonwealth of Independent States (CIS),** which stood at $53.3 million on December 31, 1991, as against $3.8 million a year earlier. The amount owed by South Africa, another major debtor, increased by more than $4 million, to $45 million. The number of countries that had paid their annual assessments for the year in full by December 31, 1991, and had no arrears remained disappointingly low—74 out of the then membership of 159.

The program budget for the biennium 1992–93 was approved by the General Assembly on December 20, 1991. Rule 105.6 of the Financial Regulations and Rules of the United Nations provides that no later than 30 days after the adoption by the Assembly of the relevant resolution, the Secretary-General must request member states to remit their contributions. Regulation 5.4 is unambiguous as to when those contributions are due; it reads in part: "contributions . . . shall be considered as due and payable *in full* [emphasis added] within thirty days of the receipt of the communication of the Secretary-General. . . ."

The rate of compliance in 1992 with Regulation 5.4 has been low. Only 15 member states (Australia, Botswana, Canada, Denmark, Finland, France, Ghana, Iceland, Ireland, Kuwait, Liechtenstein, Netherlands, New Zealand, Norway, and Sweden) paid their 1992 regular-budget assessments in full by the end of January. Eleven others (Bahrain, Belgium, Brunei Darussalam, Cyprus, Ethiopia, Luxembourg, Malta, the Federated States of Micronesia, Portugal, Spain, and Sri Lanka) fulfilled their obligations by the end of February, and 13 (Austria, Colombia, Czechoslovakia, Fiji, Greece, Italy, Jordan, Malaysia, Myanmar, Namibia, Singapore, United Arab Emirates, and the United Kingdom) in

March and April. Twenty-six member states made partial payments toward their 1992 assessments by the end of April; the rest paid nothing.

Of the five permanent members of the Security Council only two (France and the United Kingdom) paid their 1992 assessments in full by April 30 and one (China) made a partial payment. Neither the United States nor the Russian Federation paid anything on account of their 1992 assessments, though both were among the member states that made payments in 1992 toward their arrears.

As of April 30, 1992, 15 member states (South Africa and 14 developing countries, of which 11 are in Africa, one in Asia, and two in Latin America) were at least two years in arrears and **could thus lose their votes in the General Assembly** under Article 19 of the U.N. Charter. The total amount of unpaid contributions to the regular budget as of April 30, 1992, stood at nearly $1.1 billion. As the Secretary-General points out in his latest report on the financial situation of the United Nations, the amount outstanding is equivalent to 105 percent of the regular-budget assessment for 1992 [A/46/600/Add.2, para. 3].

The Organization's financial difficulties have been exacerbated by the large amounts of unpaid contributions for peacekeeping operations financed by assessments. As of October 31, 1991, outstanding contributions to the nine such operations in existence at the time totaled $463.5 million, of which $141 million was owed by the United States and $126.8 million by the former USSR [A/46/600/Add.1]. Since then three additional peacekeeping operations have been authorized: two in the closing months of 1991 and one in February 1992, namely, the **U.N. Advance Mission in Cambodia (UNAMIC), the U.N. Transitional Authority in Cambodia (UNTAC) and the U.N. Protection Force in Yugoslavia (UN-PROFOR).** The amounts appropriated by the General Assembly for these missions were $14 million net for UNAMIC for the period to April 30, 1992; $200 million for UNTAC "to meet the initial, unavoidable requirements"; and $250 million for UNPROFOR for requirements until October 1992.

As of April 30, 1992, unpaid assessed contributions to peacekeeping operations totaled $805 million, of which $787 million related to ongoing operations and $18 million to three completed operations: the U.N. Iran-Iraq Military Observer Group (UNIIMOG), the U.N. Transitional Assistance Group (UNTAG) in Namibia, and the U.N. Observer Group in Central America (ONUCA). Of the $805 million owed by member states for peacekeeping, $557 million was owed by the five permanent members of the Security Council, as follows:

United States	$308.3 million	
Russian Federation	203.2	"
France	25.1	"

United Kingdom	17.5	"
China	3.0	"
	$557.1 million	

On average, only 36.3 percent of the first assessment for newly established peacekeeping operations is paid at the end of three months, and only 56.8 percent is paid at the end of six months. Such a pattern, if repeated for the most recent operations and those that may be established in the future, could place them in serious jeopardy [A/46/600/Add.2, para.8].

As of April 30, 1992, member states owed a total of nearly $1.9 billion in assessed contributions, as follows:

Regular budget: arrears	$ 416.0 million	
1992 assessments	677.4	"
	$1,093.4 million	
Peacekeeping operations:	805.3	"
	$1,898.7 million	

Thus, the total amount of unpaid assessed contributions has virtually doubled since the end of October 1991, when it stood at $988 million [A/46/600/Add.1, para. 1].

Of the $1.9 billion outstanding at the end of April 1992, 45 percent ($863.4 million) is owed by the United States. Three other member states owe more than $100 million each, namely, the Russian Federation ($341.3 million), Japan ($158 million), and Germany ($103 million). Only nine member states (Austria, Botswana, Denmark, Finland, Ghana, Liechtenstein, Namibia, New Zealand, and Sweden) had paid in full their assessed contributions to both the regular budget and the peacekeeping operations; unfortunately for the financial health of the United Nations, these nine states account for only 3.36 percent of the scale of assessments.

In his latest report on the financial situation, the new Secretary-General, Boutros Boutros-Ghali, stated that over the previous few months the situation worsened, owing in particular to the initiation or expansion of complex tasks in the areas of peacekeeping and conflict resolution. The Secretary-General warned that unless member states acted promptly and decisively to provide the resources required to meet the expanded responsibilities they have entrusted to the United Nations, it may not be possible to maintain the Organization's operations [A/46/600/Add.2, paras. 10 and 11]. Thus, unless in the interim period there proves to be a substantial improvement in the collection rate for both the regular budget and assessed peacekeeping operations, the financial crisis confronting the 47th General Assembly will be worse than that of one year ago. At that time the Assembly's agenda included not one but two items on the financial problems of the Organization: "the current financial crisis of the U.N." and "the financial emergency of the U.N."

In his 1991 report on the subject, issued on U.N. Day (October 24), Secretary-General Pérez de Cuéllar pointed out that, having completely exhausted the **Working Capital Fund** and the **Special Account** which, between them, constituted the cash reserves of the Organization, he was obliged—in order to meet current operating requirements under the regular budget and for new peacekeeping operations—to borrow from the few peacekeeping funds that held cash in excess of their immediate requirements. Unless substantial contributions were received shortly, the Organization would be insolvent [A/46/600].

In an addendum to his report, the Secretary-General, while once again appealing to member states to meet their financial obligations, also submitted a set of specific proposals:

(a) to charge interest on the amounts of assessed contributions that are not paid on time;

(b) to suspend the Financial Regulations of the United Nations to permit the retention of budgetary surpluses;

(c) to increase the Working Capital Fund to a level of $250 million (from $100 million) as of January 1, 1992;

(d) to establish a temporary peacekeeping reserve fund, at a level of $50 million, as from the same date;

(e) to authorize the Secretary-General to borrow commercially;

(f) to establish a Humanitarian Revolving Fund of $50 million, through a one-time assessment on member states; and

(g) to establish a U.N. Peace Endowment Fund, with an initial target level of $1 billion, to be created by a combination of assessed and voluntary contributions [A/46/600/Add.1].

To underline the importance he was attaching to the problem, the Secretary-General personally introduced his proposals in the plenary of the General Assembly rather than in the Fifth Committee.

The attitude of the **Advisory Committee on Administrative and Budgetary Questions (ACABQ)** to the Secretary-General's proposals was unenthusiastic [A/46/765]. The Fifth Committee took up the two agenda items jointly on Friday, December 13, 1991, virtually on the eve of the date originally set for the completion of the Assembly's business. Only a dozen delegations spoke to the agenda items. The informal consultations, conducted over a period of a week, failed to produce consensus. It was proposed that the Committee revert to the subject at the resumed 46th Session of the Assembly in 1992, but this was not done, and the matter has now been deferred to the 47th Session.

A feature of the Secretary-General's proposals last year was that they would increase the burden on those member states that have been meticulous in complying with their financial obligations. Not surprisingly, those states were not enthusiastic. However, the Secretary-General's proposals are still on the table and the situation will have to be addressed sooner or later.

There are two distinct aspects to the U.N. financial crisis: the existence of enormous unpaid assessments both to the regular budget and for peacekeeping operations, and the need for the Organization to have a cash reserve so as to be able to respond immediately when new peacekeeping or humanitarian operations are authorized. It would be unrealistic, for domestic political and economic reasons, to expect member states to address both aspects of the financial crisis simultaneously.

While the United States does not bear sole responsibility for the financial crisis, it has greatly aggravated it and, because it is the major debtor, it is within its power to alleviate the situation. According to U.N. figures, the contribution arrears owed by the United States as of April 30, 1992, amounted to $555 million for the regular budget, and $308 million for peacekeeping operations, for a total of $863 million. As regards the regular-budget arrears, there is a difference between the U.N. figures and the figures as calculated by the United States. This is attributable to the fact that, while the United Nations does not recognize the right of a member state unilaterally to refuse to pay its share of expenses in the regular budget to which it objects, the United States—following the example of other member states, notably the former Soviet Union—has been withholding its share of the cost of a few activities. For instance, the United States withheld nearly $12 million of its $271 million assessment for 1991, consisting of $6 million relating to the construction of a U.N. conference center at Addis Ababa, Ethiopia; $5.3 million attributable to a dispute between the United States and the United Nations over reimbursement from the Tax Equalization Fund of U.S. federal, state, and local taxes levied on the U.N. emoluments of staff of U.S. nationality; $740,000 relating to the activities of the Committee on the Inalienable Rights of the Palestinian People and of the related Secretariat unit; and $375,000 for the Preparatory Commission of the Sea-bed Authority [*Washington Weekly Report*, XVIII-1].

To understand the situation with regard to the amounts owed by the United States with respect to regular-budget assessment arrears, it is also necessary to note that when a contribution is received by the Organization, it is set off—in accordance with the Financial Regulations—against the oldest indebtedness. Thus, payments that the United States may consider as having been made toward a particular year's assessments may appear on the books of the United Nations as extinguishing older arrears, including amounts that the United States has indicated it does not intend to pay for political reasons.

Of the amounts that the United States considers as constituting arrears and that, in accordance with an approved plan, are to be paid off in five installments, two have already been approved by Congress, but only one has been paid. The payment of $259 million by the United States for its share of the U.N. regular budget for 1991 was made pursuant to the Fiscal Years 1992–93 Foreign Relations Authorization Act and the Fiscal Year 1992 State Department appropriations legislation, both of which were signed by President Bush at the end of October 1991. The appropriation legislation also provided a total of $145.6 million for assessed contributions to U.N. peacekeeping operations (including a portion of the related arrearages).

The FY 1992–93 Foreign Relations Authorization Act, which sets the upper limit on U.S. assessed contributions to international organizations during those years, also contains a revised Kassebaum-Solomon amendment, which grants the President the discretion to withhold 20 percent of funds appropriated for assessed contributions in the event that U.N. consensus-based budgeting procedures begin to falter [ibid., XVII-36]. Such a provision is, of course, inconsistent with the obligations of member states under the Charter. In this connection it may be noted that the United States waited for the General Assembly to adopt what is deemed to be a zero-growth program budget for 1992–93 before it released the balance of what it considered to be its share of the 1991 assessments.

As regards the U.S. share of assessments for peacekeeping operations, the administration introduced an important initiative in Congress in January 1992 when, in the budget request for Fiscal Year 1993, it sought $700 million for a "peacekeeping contingency fund"—$350 million by way of supplemental appropriations for Fiscal Year 1992 and the balance for Fiscal Year 1993—thereby recognizing both the importance to the United States of peacekeeping operations and their unpredictability, and hence the need to make contingency provisions for them [ibid., XVIII-2, XVIII-3]. The continuing appropriations resolution for foreign aid, approved by Congress and signed into law by the President in March 1992, contains $270 million out of the $350 million requested by the President for supplemental contributions to U.N. peacekeeping in Fiscal Year 1992 [ibid., XVIII-11]. The administration's budget request for Fiscal Year 1993 also includes full funding for the U.S. contribution to the U.N. regular budget (excluding, of course, the items to which the United States has been objecting).

The forecast for the immediate future is that the United Nations will continue to lead a hand-to-mouth existence. The fact that the United States pays its regular-budget assessments late in the year rather than at the beginning, as stipulated in the Financial Regulations of the United Nations, adds to the Organization's cash flow problems. The continuing financial difficulties of the Russian Federation and the other states of the former Soviet Union will also have an adverse impact on the financial situation of the world body.

Financial difficulties may already have contributed to delays in launching new peacekeeping operations and may have limited their size. If the United States sets up a meaningful peacekeeping operations contingency fund and if other major contributors make comparable arrangements, so that funds for start-up costs are speedily made available to the Secretary-General, there will be less need for special funds for that purpose under U.N. authority. National arrangements may be more attractive for member states, especially for those that have domestic budgetary shortfalls that they must fill by borrowing.

It is possible that at the 47th Session the member states will be able to engage in thorough and result-oriented discussions of the problems of the financial crisis of the United Nations, something that they failed to do in 1991.

A New Scale of Assessments

Article 17, paragraph 2 of the U.N. Charter states that "the expenses of the Organization shall be borne by the Members as apportioned by the General Assembly." To help it with the task of apportioning those expenses, the Assembly has a **Committee on Contributions,** which currently consists of 18 members. The Committee carries out a technical analysis of the data on the basis of which it assesses each member's "capacity to pay" and, accordingly, the share of the budget to be borne by that state. "Capacity to pay" has been the fundamental criterion since the early days of the Organization; over the years, the Assembly added several other criteria by which the Committee on Contributions must be guided in carrying out its work. Not surprisingly, those criteria and the manner in which they should be applied gave rise to protracted discussions at various sessions of the General Assembly. At its 45th Session in 1990, after once again debating the issues, the Assembly gave the Committee detailed guidance on how it should go about constructing a new scale for 1992 and—it was hoped—also for the following two years [A/Res/ 45/256].

The Committee duly submitted such a scale to the Assembly at its 46th Session [A/46/11]. Despite the fact that most speakers on the subject acknowledged that, with possibly one exception, the Committee had faithfully followed the Assembly's directives, there was widespread dissatisfaction with the results. Forty-three speakers took part in the debate; as several of them spoke on behalf of groups of states, the debate reflected the views of 62 states, which testifies to the interest member states attach to how much they would be called upon to contribute toward the "expenses of the Organization." One speaker went so far as to say that the report of the Committee on Contributions was "possibly the most important" item on the Fifth Committee's agenda. It should be borne in mind in this connection that the scale of assessments recommended by the Committee on Contributions applies to only one part of the "expenses of the Organization," namely, the so-called regular program budget, which accounts for approximately 30 percent of U.N. expenses. A different scale (derived from the regular-budget scale) has been used since 1973, each time "as an ad hoc arrangement," to apportion the expenses of peacekeeping operations authorized by the Security Council. Finally, technical cooperation and certain other activities carried out by the United Nations have traditionally been financed from voluntary contributions.

After prolonged discussion in the Fifth Committee and protracted informal consultations, the scale proposed by the Committee on Contributions was approved by consensus for the years 1992–94 "unless a new scale is approved earlier by the General Assembly on the recommendation of the Committee on Contributions . . . on the basis of substantial changes in relative capacity to pay, taking into account, as appropriate, representations made by Member States and/or its ongoing work on methodology . . ." [A/Res/46/221 A]. To assist the Committee in that ongoing work, the Assembly, in part B of the same resolution, listed the various points to be studied further by the Committee. Not surprisingly, those were the very points raised by delegations in their statements at the Assembly's 46th Session. Since the Committee on Contributions has been requested to report back to the 1992 (47th) session of the Assembly, last year's debate is likely to be repeated this year.

When considering the various points at issue, one should bear in mind that over half the U.N. members are assessed at the floor rate of 0.01 percent. Furthermore, since the shares in their totality must add up to 100 per cent, every reduction in the share of a particular member state assessed at more than the floor rate necessarily requires a corresponding increase in the share or shares of other states.

In Resolution 221 B, the 46th General Assembly reaffirms that "the capacity of Member States to pay is the fundamental criterion for determining the scale of assessments." But how is this capacity to be measured? The first step, on which there is no disagreement, is to **calculate each country's national income in national currency.** For countries with market economies the calculation involves adding net income from the rest of the world to the country's gross domestic product and then subtracting the consumption of fixed capital; for centrally planned economy countries the calculations are more complex. In each case, the data used are those provided by the government concerned. But are those data reliable and comparable? Several delegations expressed doubts on this score. A further complicating factor is the length of the base period. Should it continue to be ten years, because a long statistical base period tends to even out the fluctuations resulting from abrupt or short-lived economic changes? Or should the base period be shortened so as to better reflect member states' capacity to pay at the time of payment? Member states with declining economies tend to favor a shorter base, those with growing economies a longer one.

In its report to the 46th Session of the General Assembly [A/46/11], the Committee on Contributions included a table which showed that, for most member states, a scale using a three-year base (1987–89) paralleled very closely the ten-year base scale (1980–89). The assessments of 117 member states would be the same under a three-year base scale as under a ten-year one; 27 states would benefit from the use of a three-year base, and 15 states would see their assessments increased. But of the 27 benefiting states, 13 would have their assessments reduced by only one point (i.e., 0.01 percent); of the four states that would benefit most from the use of the three-year base, only one would be a developing country. As for those that would be assessed at higher rates if a three-year base were used, the majority would be developed countries. It should be pointed out in this connection that if different three-year and ten-year base periods were used, different results would, in all likelihood, be obtained. The length of the base period is one of the criteria that the Committees on Contributions has been asked to study further.

The next step in developing the scale of assessments involves **converting the local currency amounts into U.S. dollars.** In the case of freely convertible currencies this presents no problem. But the membership also includes states with artificial exchange rates—sometimes several rates being in force at one and the same time, depending on the kind of transaction involved. Special problems arise when a state maintains the exchange rate despite high inflation in terms of its national currency. Faced with such problems the Committee, in a few instances, used a "price-adjusted" rate of exchange (PARE), but that approach did not meet with universal approval at the 46th Session of the Assembly. The choice of appropriate rates of exchange is another issue on which the Committee on Contributions will be reporting to the Assembly in 1992.

The national income figures expressed in U.S. dollars yield the so-called "machine scale." In implementation of decisions taken over the years by the General Assembly, the Committee on Contributions adjusts the "machine scale" to take account, in that order, of (a) the foreign debt burden of individual countries, (b) low per capita income, (c) floor and ceiling rates of assessment, (d) the "scheme of limits," and (e) ad hoc adjustments. According to the data provided by the Committee on Contributions in its report [A/46/11, annex IB], adjustments for foreign indebtedness transferred a total of 71 points (0.71 percent) from 36 states (including two members of the EC) to 17 states, one of which was a developing country. In the course of the debate in the Fifth Committee, the question was raised whether the states that had made sacrifices to pay off or reduce their foreign debts deserved relief equally with states whose foreign indebtedness did not decline. The granting of debt adjustment to two EC members was also questioned.

The adjustments for low per capita income acounted for the biggest shift in the assessment burden: a total of 827 points (8.27 percent). The concept underlying this adjustment is that of two countries having the same national income, the one with the smaller population (who are consequently richer per capita) has a greater capacity to pay. The Committee on Contributions recommended that countries with a per capita income of less than $2,600 a year should benefit from the adjustment ($2,600 being approximately the average annual per capita income for the world as a whole). The recommendation was accepted despite the fact that some member states argued for a higher figure ($2,800 or even $3,000), while others pointed out that the IMF and the World Bank did not regard countries with a per capita income above $2,000 as having a low per capita income.

The adjustments attributable to the existence of a "floor" rate of 0.01 percent and a "ceiling" of 25 percent result from the fact that, had the scale been constructed solely on the basis of capacity to pay with the adjustments discussed in the preceding two paragraphs, 51 states would have been assessed at rates lower than the current "floor" and one state (the United States) at a rate higher than the current "ceiling" of 25 percent.

The "scheme of limits," which accounted for the transfer of 382 points, had been designed to prevent excessive fluctuations in assessment rates between one scale and the next. The scheme was criticized in the debate in the Fifth Committee on the grounds that a ten-year base period already adequately addressed the problem, and in the 46th Assembly's Resolution 221 B the Committee on Contributions has been requested to recommend a method for phasing out the scheme over two three-year scale periods.

The ad hoc adjustments are introduced into the scale to mitigate the adverse effects of disasters (both natural and man-made) or other developments (such as the collapse of the price of a commodity on which a given state is particularly dependent) on a state's capacity to pay. These adjustments depend on the willingness of other states to take over the additional assessment burden. The total number of points offered for ad hoc adjustments when the current scale was being prepared was 50; they were offered by one state (Japan) and 28 states benefited from them.

Although Resolution 46/221 was adopted without a vote, 17 speakers representing 30 member states spoke in explanation of position after the adoption of the resolution. This shows the extent to which the views of member states continue to diverge. Consideration of the question of the scale of assesssments at the 47th Session of the General Assembly is thus likely to be contentious. In this connection one should also bear in mind that some members of the Committee on Contributions expressed the view that assessment rates need not be based exclusively on the principle of capacity to pay, and that other factors, such as membership in the Security Council, participation in the Secretariat, etc., should also be taken into account. Those views were also voiced in the Fifth Committee in 1991. Although they were opposed by most speakers and found no reflection in Resolution 46/221, the states being called upon to contribute more and more to "paying the piper" feel that they should also have a greater say in "calling the tune"—something that is certain to be a factor in the consideration of this agenda item at the 47th General Assembly.

As has already been said, the scale of assessments used for apportioning the expenses of peacekeeping operations is not identical with the scale used for the regular program budget, the main difference being that the permanent members of the Security Council are assessed at higher rates (for example, the U.S. assessment is 30.4 percent as against 25 percent under the regular scale). The special scale has been in use—each time as "an *ad hoc* arrangement"—since the adoption of Assembly Resolution 3101 (XXVIII) of December 11, 1973. The appropriateness of the special scale has been questioned on Capitol Hill; and on the occasion of the approval of the appropriations for the latest peacekeeping operation in Yugoslavia (UNPROFOR), the U.S. delegation expressed concern and stated that the matter was under review in Washington [A/C.5/46/SR.62].

How to apportion the mounting costs of peacekeeping operations is a question that is bound to be discussed, at least informally, at the 47th General Assembly. Japan is already emerging as a major contributor to the operations in Cambodia. Should the European states, and especially the EC, shoulder more of the costs of the operation in Yugoslavia? Chapter VIII of the Charter makes provision for regional arrangements for the maintenance of international peace and security. But if the main burden of financing at least some peacekeeping operations is to be shifted from the U.N. membership as a whole to the states members of regional organizations, such organizations will naturally seek to exercise control over the operations and their outcome. The question that the permanent members of the Security Council will have to ask themselves is whether being "penny wise" might not ultimately turn out to be "pound foolish."

3. The Program Budget for 1992–93

On December 20, 1991, the General Assembly adopted without a vote a program budget for the biennium 1992–93 (the "regular budget") in the amount of $1,940 million net (an expenditure budget of $2,389 million, less income estimates of $449 million). The corresponding final net requirements for 1990–91 having amounted to $1,767 million (expenditure of $2,168 million less income of $401 million), the nominal increase was of the order of 9.8 percent. Provision for inflation in 1992–93 accounted for most of that increase.

How much "real growth" there was in the program budget was a matter of considerable concern to both ACABQ and the Fifth Committee at the 46th Session of the Assembly. In his initial estimates the Secretary-General had calculated "real growth" at 0.9 percent, but that calculation, in keeping with approved methodology, excluded the so-called "non-recurrent" items (e.g., construction costs and the costs of special conferences). The methodology was questioned by several delegations on the ground that "non-recurrent" items in fact occur in each biennium. Some delegations felt that the rate of "real growth" was, in actual fact, higher than the Secretary-General had indicated.

The Secretary-General's initial estimates, the estimates as recommended by ACABQ (which were the basis for the "first reading" of the program budget in the Fifth Committee), and the approved program budget (which includes the add-ons attributable to decisions taken in the course of the Assembly) are summarized in the following table:

	Initial estimates	ACABQ recommendations	Approved appropriations
	$ million	$ million	$ million
Expenditure	2,363	2,320	2,389
Income	−402	−402	−449
Net amount	1,961	1,918	1,940

The program budget for 1992–93 covers the first biennium of the medium-term plan for 1992–97. The five broad priority areas identified by the General Assembly in that plan were maintenance of international peace and security, the economic development of developing countries, the economic recovery and development of Africa, the environment, and international drug control [A/Res/45/253, section I, para. 12].

The extent to which the program budget proposals reflected those priorities was questioned by some delegations. For instance, the representative of India drew attention to the high rates of real growth proposed for human rights and humanitarian affairs, which was not one of the five priority areas, whereas negative rates of growth were proposed for Science and Technology for Development and for Trade and Development [A/C.5/46/SR.13, para. 22].

The U.S. representative argued that:

it was important that the medium term plan should not act as a straight jacket. . . . Careful consideration should be given to granting the Secretary-General new authorities that would enable him to take a more selective approach and to clarify priorities. The fact that budgets had to be approved by the General Assembly meant that the Secretary-General's use of such new authorities would be subject to review by Member States. As a rule, resources should be concentrated in areas in which the U.N. had a comparative advantage and could achieve results. Member States should also play a more active role in the priority-setting process. The Secretary-General's priorities and programme and funding options should be presented in a way that allowed Member States to take an active part in the allocation of resources [A/C.5/46/ SR.13, paras. 44 and 45].

Developing-country delegations were cool to the idea of granting the Secretary-General more flexibility in the transfer of resources. The Kenya delegation, for instance, could not agree to resources being redeployed away from activities deemed obsolete to areas where they would have maximum impact without the necessary legislative mandate, because intergovernmental bodies were in the best position to identify which activities were unnecessary [A/C.5/46/SR.14, para. 20].

In point of fact, as was stated by both the Committee for **Programme and Coordination (CPC)** and ACABQ in its first report on the program budget proposals for 1992–93, several sections of the program budget were prepared by the Secretary-General without the competent intergovernmental bodies having reviewed their programs of work. ACABQ was of the view that the **Regulations Governing Programme Planning, the Programme Aspects of the Budget, the Monitoring of Implementation, and the Methods of Evaluation** annexed to Resolution 37/234 called for greater involvement of the specialized bodies in the planning and programming process [A/46/7, paras. 63 and 64]. CPC, for its part, considered that intergovernmental bodies should review the program of work covered by most sections of the program budget and make recommendations on the proposed activities and priorities; they should also fulfill their role during the implementation of the program budget [A/46/ 16, para. 30]. In Resolution 189, section II, the 46th General Assembly requested the Secretary-General to institutionalize the consultative process with member states on the medium-term plan, or its revisions, and to include the program of work in his program budget proposals.

In Resolution 255 of December 21, 1990, the 45th General Assembly had decided on a proposed program budget outline for the biennium 1992–93 in an amount of $2,006.2 million at the initial 1990–91 rates; at 1992–93 rates the outline estimate amounted to $2,366.3 million. Thus the Secretary-General's initial estimates for 1992–93 were within the outline estimate; the approved expenditure budget exceeded the outline amount by less than 1 percent.

Several delegations addressed the relationship between the outline and the program budget proposals, and in particular whether the zero growth premise in the outline was binding. The Nordic delegations did not think that a zero growth rate for the budget should be the aim at a time when new tasks were constantly being entrusted to the Organization; for them, it was extremely important that the United Nations should be able to respond to changing political needs and circumstances [A/C.5/46/SR.9, para. 45]. The Kenyan delegation was of the same opinion [A/C.5/46/SR.14, para. 19]. The Mexican delegation warned against excessive rigidity, which could virtually immobilize the Organization [A/C.5/46/SR.10, para. 7]. The representative of Ghana stated that the main purpose of the outline was to serve as an indicator of resource requirements and of real growth; he agreed with the Chairman of ACABQ that the outline was neither a ceiling nor a directive to be followed to the letter [A/C.5/46/SR.11, para. 25]. A similar view was expressed by the Chinese delegation [ibid., para. 36].

The 12 states of the European Community, on the other hand, stressed that as the main purpose of the outline was to involve member states in the budget process at an earlier stage, it was important to maintain confidence in the process and to respect the level established in the outline [ibid., para. 5]. The delegations of Australia, Canada, and New Zealand recalled that the outline provided for zero growth and said that resources from obsolete and ineffective programs should be transferred to new and higher priority activities [ibid., para. 88]. The representative of the Russian Federation said that his delegation was adamant that the budget not exceed the level set in the outline, which represented an absolute ceiling for proposed expenditures; it could not agree to any real growth [A/C.5/46/SR.14, para. 2]. The representative of Japan described the outline as a dynamic instrument for facilitating dialogue between the Secretary-General and member states on the total level of resources as well as for identifying new priorities; the outline did not impose a rigid framework on the activities of the Organization; the point of departure for program budget proposals should be the outline and not the revised estimates for the previous biennium [A/C.5/46/SR.11, para. 46].

There was no unanimity concerning the role of extrabudgetary resources (voluntary contributions) in financing U.N. activities. The Secretary-General estimated those resources at $3,084 million in 1992–93, including $2,672 million for operational projects. Some delegations, such as those of Austria and the Nordic countries, warned against increased reliance on voluntary contributions for activities and programs mandated by the General Assembly, because assessed contributions were a more reliable source of funding than voluntary ones (a somewhat questionable assumption given the large volume of assessed contributions that remains uncollected). For that reason the Nordic countries supported the Secretary-General's proposal that two posts in the Office of the U.N. High Commissioner for Refugees (UNHCR) and several posts in the U.N. Relief and Works Agency for Palestine Refugees (UNRWA) be transferred from extrabudgetary funding to the regular budget. ACABQ had questioned the propriety of the proposed transfers in the light of earlier General Assembly decisions and of recommendation 62 of the **Group of High-Level Intergovernmental Experts to Review the Efficiency of the Administrative and Financial Functioning of the United Nations** (adopted by the 41st General Assembly in Resolution 213) that "a serious effort should be made by the Secretary-General to discourage the present practice of transferring extrabudgetary posts to the regular budget." The General Assembly decided that the posts in question should not be transferred to the regular budget. On the other hand, the Assembly approved subventions from the regular budget to several institutes, all of which were supposed to be financed from voluntary contributions. Several delegations joined in the consensus regarding those subventions somewhat reluctantly. For instance, the U.S. representative said that his delegation remained convinced that programs that could not attract sufficient voluntary contributions should be reduced or canceled [A/C.5/SR.36, para. 50]. The strength of the opposition to such subventions from the regular budget can also be gauged by the fact that a proposal in the Second Committee that a $2 million grant be made to the U.N. Institute for Training and Reseach (UNITAR) was not acted upon.

Notwithstanding the differences of opinion such as those referred to above, the programing and budgeting procedures introduced since the 41st Session of the Assembly worked reasonably well and facilitated the adoption of the program budget for 1992–93 without a vote. In particular, the add-ons attributable to decisions taken during the Assembly session totaling $2.8 million could be accommodated easily within the contingency fund of $18 million approved for the 1992–93 biennium. Still, some member states continue to feel that there is need for further improvement in the programing and budgeting process. The U.S. delegation, for instance, did not believe that the collective interests and needs of member states were served by the process as it had evolved over the preceding two decades. The delegation called for action to improve the process, including the creation of an **independent office of U.N. Inspector General** [A/C.5/46/SR.13, paras. 46 and 47]. It should be recalled in this connection that the U.N. system already has a Joint Inspection Unit, and that the Organization has its own Internal Audit Division, in addition to the Board of External Auditors. The functioning and reports of the Joint Inspection Unit are to be considered in depth at the 47th Session of the General Assembly.

The 12 members of the European Community called for a budget document that would be drafted as a policy document, as opposed to the current strictly administrative document, which provided a tremendous amount of detail but not enough information on the objectives of programs and the resources required to achieve them. They were also concerned by the fact that the approved budget was not necessarily implemented along the lines of the proposal [A/C.5/46/SR.11, para. 19]. Reference was also made in the discussion to the lack of clarity in the relationship between the regular budget and extrabudgetary resources.

The General Assembly endorsed the CPC recommendation that the Secretary-General should submit to the General Assembly at its 47th Session the prototype of a new budget format [A/Res/46/185 B, section VIII, para. 2]. An ad hoc technical seminar to review the methodology used for the preparation of the program budget, which had been recommended by CPC and endorsed by the Assembly, met in April 1992. The conclusions of the seminar were not available at the time of writing.

The 47th General Assembly will also consider revisions to the program budget for the current biennium, 1992–93. In particular, the reorganization announced by the new Secretary-General at the beginning of 1992 will have an impact on the structure of the program budget in view of the disappearance of some organizational units (such as the Office of the Director-General for Development and International Economic Cooperation) and the merging of some programs.

As has already been said, Third World delegations at the 46th Session were cool to the idea that the Secretary-General be granted greater flexibility in reallocating approved resources. Their reticence in this regard reflected their concern that the Secretary-General might be influenced by the major contributors, especially the United States, to divert resources away from programs to which the developing countries have traditionally attached importance. The apparent downgrading of those programs, such as Science and Technology for Development, in this year's restructuring is likely to strengthen the Third World's disquiet, and that may well affect the discussion in the Fifth Committee of the revised program budget for the current biennium.

In response to specific requests by the 46th Assembly in Resolution 185, the Secretary-General will also be submitting in 1992 several reports on matters that may have an impact on the regular budget of the Organization. Perhaps the most complex issue to be covered by these reports, with possibly far-reaching consequences, is the development of procedures and norms, including workload analyses, to justify the creation, suppression, reclassification, conversion, and redeployment of posts. The question of how many posts are needed to carry out the work program, and at what levels, has for years bedeviled the work of ACABQ and the Fifth Committee. As a rule, ACABQ has tended to reduce the number of new posts and upgradings requested by the Secretary-General.

Some of those reductions are subsequently restored in the Fifth Committee, usually on the initiative of delegations whose nationals were to be appointed or promoted. Regardless of the justification in support of the proposals, the outcome of the discussion in the Fifth Committee usually hinges on how much political support a particular activity enjoys among member states. It has been generally, though tacitly, recognized that requests for the reclassification of posts are sometimes made in order to secure promotion for the incumbents. It remains to be seen whether delegations will agree to become less involved in the process of post creation and classification in the future.

Other matters on which the Secretary-General will be reporting in the context of the revisions to the 1992–93 program budget include the honoraria payable to members of organs and subsidiary organs; the amount of representation allowances for Under-Secretaries-General and Assistant Secretaries-General; the impact of the so-called "successor arrangements" for the payment of support costs for UNDP-funded projects by UNDP to the agencies executing them; the organization of editorial services in New York and of language services at Addis Ababa and Nairobi; the level of resources to be made available to the multinational programming and operational centers (MULPOCs); the funding of Staff Union activities; the program of technological innovations (in this connection the Assembly has called for an independent expert study of the integrated management information system—IMIS—project, which has been experiencing costly delays); and the workload of certain commissions and committees. This last-named item is a euphemism for pressures on the part of the membership of certain bodies that tend to hold long sessions (such as ACABQ) to secure for themselves the payment of honoraria or other benefits by the United Nations (they already receive an allowance, usually at 40 percent above standard rate, for each day of attendance away from their normal place of residence). While the financial implications of some of the above items may not be very great, the personal involvement of delegation members in certain issues may lead to controversy.

4. Staffing and Administration

Composition of the Secretariat: Geographical Distribution, Recruitment, and Career Development

Because 1991 was a "budget year," i.e., a year when the Fifth Committee had to consider and approve a new biennial budget, the assumption was that personnel questions would not be considered in great detail. Several factors, however, were responsible for a prolonged discussion of this item. One of them was the submission by the Secretary-General, in response to the 45th Assembly's Resolution 239, section III, of a report on alternative options for desirable ranges for the geographical distribution of staff in the Professional and higher category [A/C.5/46/2]. Another factor was secondment from government service, a question that assumed greater importance following the developments in Eastern Europe and the former Soviet Union and the resultant changes in the attitude of the governments concerned toward their nationals' being granted permanent appointments. Both these factors influence the recruitment policies and practices of the Organization, but they also have an impact on the career development of staff, including such matters as the improvement of the status of women in the Secretariat and movements from the General Service to the Professional category.

Article 101, paragraph 3, of the U.N. Charter states that

> The paramount consideration in the employment of the staff and in the determination of the conditions of service shall be the necessity of securing the highest standards of efficiency, competence and integrity. Due regard shall be paid to the importance of recruiting the staff on as wide a geographical basis as possible.

The relative importance of the two desiderata in that Article, and how to apply what became known as "the principle of equitable geographical distribution," has been the subject of prolonged and occasionally bitter debate at session after session of the General Assembly. The debate led to the introduction of so-called "desirable ranges" of representation of member states in the Secretariat. In this connection it should be borne in mind that certain groups of staff are not counted when "desirable ranges" are calculated. These groups include staff in the General Service and other locally recruited categories; staff with special language qualifications; the staff of the Voluntary Programmes (such as UNDP, UNICEF, UNRWA, UNHCR), which are not considered part of the Secretariat proper because they have the authority to appoint their own staff, and which are financed wholly or largely from voluntary contributions; and staff on short-term appointments (i.e., serving on contracts for less than one year). In practice, therefore, the "desirable ranges" apply to a minority of staff—2,600 out of 29,246 as of June 30, 1991—who serve in what are known as "posts subject to geographical distribution."

The "desirable range" for each member state is calculated on the basis of a complex formula, which takes account of three factors: U.N. membership, population, and contribution rate as reflected in the scale of assessments. The weight to be attached to each factor has been—and continues to be—the subject of disagreement among member states. For each weighting combination the three factors yield a number deemed to be the midpoint of the desirable range for each member state. The range itself is determined by applying a 15 percent flexibility factor upward and downward from the midpoint.

It is obvious that the "desirable range" of a member state will be affected by the relative weight to be attached to each of the three factors. Thus, greater emphasis on the membership factor would allocate more posts to the states at the floor or the low end of the scale of assessments; conversely, enhancing the importance of the contribution factor would work to the disadvantage of those states, whereas the major contributors would benefit; raising the weighting of the population factor would clearly lead to more posts being allocated to the more populous member states.

Originally, the contribution rate was the determinant factor, but pressures from the smaller—and numerically more numerous—member states gradually eroded its importance. At present the "desirable ranges" are calculated using this formula: membership = 40 percent, contribution = 55 percent, population = 5 percent. In his report the Secretary-General shows the impact of ten alternative formulae in which the membership factor accounts for between 40 and 47 percent, the contribution factor between 47 and 54 percent, and the population factor between 5 and 7.2 percent of the total.

What would be the practical impact of changing the formula now used to calculate the desirable ranges? The tables annexed to the Secretary-General's report (based on 2,700 posts subject to geographical distribution and the then U.N. membership of 159) show that for a small country assessed at the floor level of 0.01 percent, seven of the alternatives yield a range of 2–14 posts (which corresponds to the current range) and three alternatives a range of 3–14 posts—hardly a momentous change. At the other extreme, namely, for the United States, a change in the formula could have significant consequences: The current desirable range for the United States is 327–442 posts; all the alternative formulae yield lower ranges, the most extreme being 283–383 posts.

Not surprisingly, member states expressed preference for the alternatives that benefited them most. Thus, the representatives of Bangladesh, Brazil, China, India, Indonesia, Iran, Nigeria, and Pakistan called for increasing the weighting of the population factor, whereas Hungary felt that that factor should be given limited weight. Several delegations (Bulgaria, China, Congo, Cuba, Egypt, Nepal, and Senegal) expressed preference for the alternative that gave equal weight to the factors of membership and contribution. The representatives of the United States and Japan argued that there was no need to change the current formula; parity of membership and contribution was unacceptable to Japan. Some delegations also advocated increasing the number of posts subject to geographical distribution. The differences of opinion could not be reconciled in the informal consultations, and the question of desirable ranges has been deferred de facto to the 47th General Assembly, at which personnel questions are to be discussed in depth. The increase in the membership of the United Nations in 1991 and 1992—to 178—after the Secretary-General's report was prepared will have an appreciable impact on the desirable ranges of all member states that are assessed at a rate higher than the floor.

Agreement on the formula for calculating "desirable ranges" will not in itself ensure "equitable geographical distribution" in the Secretariat. Of crucial importance in this respect are the recruitment policies and practices as well as the existence of vacancies. In recent years the number of vacant posts subject to geographical distribution has been limited because of the recruitment freeze imposed partly because of financial difficulties and partly in order to bring about the **15 percent reduction in the size of the Secretariat** mandated by the member states on the recommendation of the **Committee of Eighteen.**

In his report on the composition of the Secretariat submitted to the 46th General Assembly describing the situation as of June 30, 1991 [A/46/370], the Secretary-General indicated that out of the then total membership of 159, two-thirds (103 states) were within their desirable ranges. Nine states were unrepresented, 24 states were underrepresented (i.e., the number of their nationals in posts subject to geographical distribution was below the low end of the desirable range), and 23 states were overrepresented.

The nine unrepresented member states were Albania, Bahrain, Brunei Darussalam, Kuwait, Liechtenstein, Maldives, São Tomé and Principe, Solomon Islands, and Vanuatu. This list illustrates the difficulties in attaining full membership representation in the Secretariat. One of the nine unrepresented states (Liechtenstein) had been newly admitted to the world body; another (Albania) could be regarded as sui generis because of the consistently isolationist policies pursued over the years by its former leadership; in two others (Bahrain and Kuwait) local remuneration levels were too high to make U.N. employment attractive for their nationals; and all the others had very small populations. The Secretary-General's report to be submitted to the 47th General Assembly will show a higher number of unrepresented states because of the admission of new members in 1991 and 1992.

Of the 23 overrepresented states, nine were in Africa, six in Asia and the Pacific, three each in North America and the Caribbean (regarded as one region) and in Latin America, and two in the Middle East. All were Third World countries.

As was to be expected, speakers representing countries below the lower end—or even the midpoint—of the desirable range urged the Secretary-General to redouble his efforts to improve geographical representation. Other speakers laid stress on being unrepresented at senior levels. Several representatives called for greater developing-country representation at those levels, despite the fact that, as of June 30, 1991, nearly half the staff in posts at levels D-1 and above (181 out of 371) were nationals of developing countries.

Reference has already been made to the small number of appointments that could be made to posts subject to geographical distribution and to the inhibiting effect of that situation on efforts to improve geographical representation. In the 12 months up to June 30, 1991, there were 170 such appointments, a quarter of which were "replacements" of departing staff members from China, Eastern Europe, and the former Soviet Union. The number of appointments in respect of which the Secretary-General had a more or less free hand thus amounted to not more than 120.

Several speakers repeated the oft-heard argument that there would be greater staff turnover—and thus greater opportunities for improving geographical distribution—if there were fewer staff holding permanent contracts. Some delegations were in favor of half the staff in posts subject to geographical distribution being on fixed-term contracts. One delegation advocated shorter periods of service for staff in senior posts to allow for the periodic rotation of heads of Secretariat departments and offices and the more equitable redistribution of such posts; and the 12 states of the European Community asked that urgent consideration be given to the introduction of a ten-year limit on the employment of officials at the Under-Secretary-General and Assistant Secretary-General levels.

The representatives of several East European countries expressed dismay at the fact that, following Administrative Tribunal Judgement No. 482, many of their nationals serving on fixed-term contracts had been granted permanent appointments in keeping with Resolution 37/126 of December 17, 1982, which requires that staff members be given every reasonable consideration for a career appointment after five years of continuing good service. It was pointed out by them that the granting of such contracts on the basis of merely "satisfactory" service would dilute the requirement in the Charter for "the highest standards" of efficiency, competence, and integrity. The granting of permanent contracts to officials initially appointed at the behest of former Communist governments interfered with the ability of the new governments to nominate "fresh blood." They therefore favored the continuation of the practice whereby departing staff were "replaced" by others having the same nationality in accordance with section I of Resolution 35/210 of December 1, 1980, in which the Secretary-General was requested "to continue to permit replacement by candidates of the same nationality" as an exception to the general rule that no post should be considered the exclusive preserve of any member state, provided that such an exception was necessary to ensure that the representation of member states concerned was not adversely affected. They said that they intended to continue the policy of seconding their nationals to the Secretariat.

The General Assembly having affirmed in Resolution 45/239 A, section II, of December 21, 1990, that secondment from government service was not in conflict with the Charter, the Secretary-General submitted a draft resolution in which he suggested that the Staff Regulations be amended to lay down conditions for a valid secondment that would be consistent with Administrative Tribunal Judgement No. 482. While no delegation objected to the Secretary-General's proposal, no action was taken on the draft in view of the de facto decision of the Fifth Committee to defer further consideration of personnel questions until the 47th Session.

The practice of filling **junior Professional posts** (P-1 and P-2) through competitive examinations held in underrepresented countries and regions was supported in the debate. Several delegations, however, drew attention to the very long delays between the holding of an examination and the offer of appointment to successful candidates. The fact that the first competitive examinations to fill vacancies at the P-3 level were held in 1991 was welcomed by several speakers. It was suggested that all staff, particularly senior officials whose performance directly affects the quality of work of all those under their authority, be recruited by competition. The Committee was informed that one reason for the delay in offering appointments to successful candidates was that several posts had been filled under a policy aimed inter alia at improving the representation of women.

The **percentage of women** in posts subject to geographical distribution increased slightly between June 30, 1990, and June 30, 1991: from 28.3 percent (725 out of 2,561) to 29.2 percent (759 out of 2,600). At the most senior levels (D-2 and above) the percentage of women rose from 8.8 percent (10 out of 113) to 9.3 percent (12 out of 129). The delegations that referred to the advancement of women in the Secretariat deemed that improvement to have been too modest and urged the Secretary-General to redouble his efforts; at the current rate, the Assembly target of 25 percent women in posts at levels D-1 and above set in Resolution 45/239 C and the target of 35 percent women in Professional posts by 1995 would not be met. At the same time, it was pointed out that appointing women should not be allowed to have an adverse effect on equitable geographical distribution or the quality of the staff. According to the Russian Federation representative, women should be given priority, all other things being equal and to the extent possible; any other approach would have great repercussions on the overall personnel situation in the Secretariat [A/C.5/46/SR.24, para. 52]. Overall, the advancement of women in the Secretariat aroused only modest interest among delegations at the 46th General Assembly.

While there can be no question that there must be no discrimination against women on the basis of sex in appointments and promotions (Article 8 of the Charter precludes it), the Secretary-General's ability to effect rapid improvements is limited. Staff turnover is greatest among nationals of member states that traditionally have been opposed to permanent contracts; yet the persons nominated by those states to replace their departing nationals have been predominantly male. For example, during the 12-month period to June 30, 1991, only two out of the 24 Soviet nationals (as they were then) appointed to posts subject to geographical distribution were women (both at the P-3 level); the corresponding number for China was one out of six; there were no women among the nationals of Bulgaria, Czechoslovakia, or Poland appointed to such posts. Only Hungary, with two women out of three appointments, broke the pattern. The granting of permanent appointments to the nationals of countries that had required them to serve on fixed-term contracts, most of whom are men, has created a new obstacle in the way of increasing the representation of women in posts subject to geographical distribution.

The highest proportion of women in those posts is to be found among nationals of member states that have always favored permanent contracts for U.N. staff. Since it is difficult and indeed undesirable in a career service to parachute too many persons into senior posts over the heads of serving staff, the number of women in senior posts can increase only gradually. Not surprisingly, the percentage of women in senior posts is highest in such areas as the language services and in those parts of the administration in which there have been, for decades, large numbers of women in Professional posts; there has thus been enough time for them to get promoted to senior posts. But in departments that in the past had few women Professionals, progress is bound to be slower than might appear desirable. As for the top echelon, where the Secretary-General normally appoints persons nominated by member states, the remedy lies as much in the hands of those states as with the Secretary-General.

The improvement of the status of women in the Secretariat is part of the **broader question of the career development of staff.** Despite the plea by the President of the New York Staff Committee for a genuine system of career development in the United Nations, only Australia, Canada, and New Zealand drew attention in their joint statement to the importance of career planning and staff training. This lack of interest was perhaps attributable to the fact that the Secretary-General had not submitted a report on this aspect of personnel policies to the 46th Session. A report on the formulation of a comprehensive career development plan is to be submitted to the General Assembly at its 47th Session.

According to the President of the New York Staff Committee, the lack of career prospects and opportunities for promotion had a particularly demoralizing effect on staff in the **General Service and related categories** [A/C.5/46/SR.18, para. 9]. The General Assembly has traditionally paid little attention to those categories except, occasionally, with regard to their salary levels or when a delegation called for the extension of the principle of equitable geographical distribution to the Principal level of the General Service category. For a number of years there have been pressures among staff in the General Service and other locally recruited categories for the abolition of the division of the Secretariat staff into categories and in favor of a "unified Secretariat." Several practical considerations stand in the way of that objective. First, whereas the salary scale for the Professional and higher category is approved by the General Assembly for worldwide application and is expressed in U.S. dollars, there is a different General Service salary scale for each duty station; these scales are determined by the Secretary-General by reference to the best prevailing local conditions and they are expressed in local currency. The top of such a local scale may be well below the bottom of the Professional scale, or there may be considerable overlap between the two (as is the case, for example, in Geneva). Secondly, as has already been said, the General Service and other locally recruited categories are not counted for purposes of geographical distribution. Thirdly, locally recruited staff are not liable for transfer to other duty stations.

A purely formal abolition of categories, retaining all the existing differences, would serve no useful purpose, nor would it improve the upward mobility of the staff in the General Service and other locally recruited categories—though it may perhaps give the impression that their career prospects have become better. What is in the interest of both the staff and the Organization is to ensure that locally recruited staff with the necessary qualifications and potential for professional growth are not prevented from transferring to the Professional category. The barrier between the categories has never been watertight, and scores if not hundreds of staff who began their careers in the General Service category were subsequently promoted to the Professional category; many former and current staff who were so promoted served or serve in grades P-5, D-1, and D-2; one staff member who began her career as a G-2 retired as an Assistant Secretary-General. In the past there were no set criteria for promotion to the Professional category; the determination was made in the course of the annual review and the beneficiaries were very often staff at or near the end of their careers. Now promotion to the Professional category is predicated on success in competitive examinations (the so-called "G-to-P exams"). While the current system has worked to the disadvantage of otherwise competent staff who are bad at examinations, it has enabled younger General Service staff to move to the Professional category earlier in their careers than had been the practice in the past.

The main problem with the current system is that the number of P-1 and P-2 posts available for successful candidates is very limited—partly because of the decline over the years in the number of posts at those levels, and partly because of the need to reserve posts for direct entry into the Professional category via, for example, the special competitive examinations referred to above. The fact that the bulk of General Service staff tend to be nationals of the countries in which the main U.N. offices are located also militates against increasing the number of posts available for G-to-P examinations, because those countries already tend to be at the upper limit or above their desirable range.

Taking the floor in the debate on personnel questions, the representative of Barbados stressed the fruitlessness of the Fifth Committee's "annual ritual consideration of personnel questions."

> The ritual began with a statement from the Assistant Secretary-General for Human Resources Management in which selective reference was made to provisions of previous General Assembly resolutions, explanations were offered as to why various mandates could not be fulfilled, and the implementation of imaginative new programmes was promised. Representatives, on the other hand, bemoaned the fact that the list of unrepresented and under-represented Member States remained the same or had grown, referred to actions by the Secretariat that had affected them positively or negatively, and requested studies on proposals that would be to their advantage. The ritual ended with the adoption of resolutions that rehashed all previous resolutions, incorporated shopping lists from all interested parties and guaranteed a resumption of the ritual at the succeeding session of the General Assembly [A/C.5/46/SR.32, para. 13].

The discussion of personnel questions at the 46th Session followed the "ritual" described by the representative of Barbados except that, as has already been said, it proved impossible to reach agreement on any resolution on personnel questions.

Respect for the Privileges and Immunities of International Officials

The Fifth Committee had before it a report by the Secretary-General that contained a consolidated list, as of June 30, 1991, of staff members under arrest and detention or missing and with respect to whom the United Nations and the specialized agencies and related organizations have been unable to exercise fully their right to protection. The list contained 78 names; some of the persons concerned had been missing or in detention for years (since 1980 in two cases). Forty-three of the 78 were cases that occurred during the preceeding 12-month period; all the persons concerned were **UNRWA staff detained by the Israeli authorities** in the occupied West Bank or Gaza. The total number of UNRWA staff who were arrested or detained during that period was 160; 110 of them were subsequently released without charge or trial, and seven were sentenced to various terms of imprisonment. The report also contained particulars of incidents involving five UNICEF staff members who were arrested during the 12-month period and subsequently released in two African countries; one was then rearrested (in Ethiopia). One International Telecommunication Union (ITU) staff member was briefly detained in a European country. Other violations of the privileges and immunities of international organizations and their staff reported by the Secretary-General included the imposition by the Sudanese authorities of a tax payable by international officials of Sudanese nationality when they renewed their passports, and various levies imposed by the Israeli authorities on U.N. Truce Supervision Organization (UNTSO) goods and staff.

The Assistant Secretary-General for Human Resources Management told the Fifth Committee that violence in several areas over the past 12 months had led the Secretary-General to take measures to ensure the safety and security of staff and their families. However, the United Nations also had to consider the political ramifications of such decisions and their effect on programs; the Organization needed to avoid appearing to lead an exodus from a country [A/C.5/46/SR.15, para. 64].

Several delegations expressed concern over the violations of privileges and immunities, but the references to this problem often tended to be pro forma. The representatives of Ethiopia and Israel disputed the information in the Secretary-General's report and pointed out that staff members had an obligation to refrain from abusing their status by engaging in activities that threaten the national interests of member states or in acts of violence. The representative of Senegal also referred to the need for international officials to refrain from abusing their privileges and immunities. The statement by the representative of Israel that it was the practice of his country's authorities to inform the heads of UNRWA's offices in the administered areas, upon their request, as to the circumstances of the detention of UNRWA staff members, as well as the details of trials and judgments, elicited a rebuttal by UNRWA, which Legal Counsel described as "lengthy and very blunt" [A/C.5/46/SR.37, para. 39]. The Sudanese representative said that "contributing the small sum of money involved when renewing their passports" was an "honor" for Sudanese nationals, and that the contribution was "voluntary" [A/C.5/46/SR.24, para. 58]. The U.N. position, as explained by Legal Counsel, was that because the payments were levied on the basis of income, they constituted a tax on the salaries of U.N. officials [A/C.5/46/SR.37, para. 38].

Remuneration of Staff in the Professional and Higher Category

This is a question to which the General Assembly devoted much time and effort in recent years. The comprehensive review of the conditions of service of the Professional staff was completed by the **International Civil Service Commission (ICSC)** in 1990, and the results of that review were considered by the General Assembly at its 45th Session that year [see *A Global Agenda: Issues Before the 46th General Assembly of the United Nations*].

At the 46th session the Assembly dealt with the question of whether Professional salaries should continue to be adjusted automatically for future cost-of-living increases. The problem had its genesis in the decision taken by the General Assembly in 1985 to the effect that the margin by which the net remuneration of U.N. officials in the Professional and higher category serving in New York could exceed that of officials in comparable positions in the U.S. federal civil service (the "comparator") should be 10 to 20 percent [A/Res/40/244, section I]. Four years later the Assembly tightened the arrangement when it requested the ICSC to monitor the annual net remuneration margin over the five-year period beginning in calendar year 1990 with a view to ensuring, to the extent possible, that by the end of that period the average of the successive annual margins was around the "desirable mid point," i.e., 15 percent above the level of net U.S. federal civil service salaries [A/Res/44/198, section I].

In 1990, the first year of the five-year period referred to above, the ICSC calculated the margin to have been 17.4 percent; in the second year of the quinquennium it was 18.9 percent (because the dates on which U.S. and U.N. salaries are adjusted do not coincide, the ICSC calculates the annual margin by averaging the differences over the 12 months of the calendar year). Consequently, if an average 15 percent margin is to be achieved in 1990–94, the margins in 1992, 1993, and 1994 will have to be below 15 percent. That would require freezing U.N. salaries for a period of time. The problem had been discussed at the 45th Session of the General Assembly, at which time the Commission was requested to monitor the evolution of the margin and to study the impact of potential changes in the U.S. federal civil service pay levels, and to submit recommendations to the Assembly at its following session, with a view to avoiding a prolonged freeze of the emoluments of U.N. Professional staff.

The reason the U.S./U.N. margin was so wide in 1990 and 1991 was that U.S. federal civil service pay had not kept pace with the cost of living. The fact that U.S. federal civil servants were underpaid was recognized in the Federal Employees Pay Comparability Act (FEPCA) of 1990, which was enacted by Congress on the basis of findings of the Office of Personnel Management. The pay-setting process under FEPCA begins as of January 1994. It provides for a national adjustment of pay scales equal to the movement of the employment cost index (ECI) for 1992 and 1993. Thereafter the national adjustment will be equal to ECI less 0.5 percent, but there will also be local adjustments for high-wage parts of the country. In the meantime, the United States has also introduced pay systems outside the framework of the General Schedule; these pay systems cover the staff of some U.S. government agencies that had previously applied the General Schedule, as well as the staff of some newly established agencies.

Bearing in mind that, over the years, FEPCA would tend to reduce the U.S./U.N. margin, the organizations in the U.N. system of salaries and allowances argued against freezing U.N. Professional salary scales (freezing salaries in New York would have repercussions at all other duty stations, because the U.N. Professional salary structure aims at ensuring equality of purchasing power throughout the world). The ICSC calculated that with the full implementation of FEPCA, the U.S./U.N. margin would decline to about 15 percent (i.e., to the midpoint of the range) by 1994 and to around 10 percent by 1996. For that reason, and also because of the adverse impact a freeze would have on the recruitment competitiveness of U.N. organizations and on staff morale, the Commission unanimously decided to request the General Assembly to rescind the decision it had taken in Resolution 44/198, section I [A/46/30, paras. 103–5].

When the ICSC recommendations were discussed in the Fifth Committee, differing views were expressed, and the 46th Assembly's decision reflected a compromise: Instead of rescinding the decision on five-year averaging in Resolution 44/198, as the Commission had recommended, the Assembly decided—without saying it in so many words—not to apply that decision during the five-year period 1990–94. It also decided that such post adjustment increases (cost-of-living adjustments) as might become due between then and 1994 could be implemented only to the extent that they were compatible with the upper limit of the margin (thereby agreeing with the ICSC recommendation on this point). The Commission was requested to submit a report to the General Assembly in 1994 in order to enable the Assembly to address the issue of the average margin over a five-year period [A/Res/46/191, section IV].

One of the differences between the U.S. and the U.N. systems of remuneration is that the take-home pay of the U.N. Professional staff comprises a salary element, which is uniform at all duty stations for each grade and step, and a post adjustment, which varies from duty station to duty station so as to ensure that U.N. emoluments have equal purchasing power everywhere. In section I.H of Resolution 198 the 44th General Assembly approved the establishment of a floor net salary scale for U.N. staff, effective July 1, 1990. The reference point for that scale was the corresponding base net salary levels of officials in comparable positions serving at the base city of the comparator civil service (namely, Washington, D.C.). In section I.E of the same resolution the Assembly approved the introduction of mobility and hardship allowances, the amounts of which were to be calculated by reference to the floor net salary scale. In Resolution 191, the 46th Assembly approved an 8.6 percent increase in the U.N. floor net scale, with a corresponding reduction in post adjustment, effective March 1, 1992, as recommended by the ICSC [A/46/30, para. 125]. While the Commission's recommendation was generally supported, several delegations questioned the need to increase the mobility and hardship allowances simultaneously. The General Assembly requested ICSC to include in its report to the 1992 session a cost-benefit analysis of the operation of the mobility/hardship allowance, as well as an assessment of the personnel management benefits and details of savings achieved in other administrative costs with the introduction of the current arrangements [A/Res/46/191, section V].

In the preamble to section VI of Resolution 191, the 46th General Assembly reaffirmed that the "Noblemaire principle" should continue to serve as the basis for comparing U.N. common system emoluments with those of the highest paid civil service. The erosion of the purchasing power of U.S. federal civil service pay and the weakness of the U.S. dollar in relation to other major currencies has led some delegations in recent years to question whether the U.S. federal civil service was still the highest paid national civil service and should be used as a comparator under the "Noblemaire principle" to determine the levels of U.N. salaries.

In Resolution 198, section I.B, the 44th General Assembly had requested the Commission to propose a methodology to the Assembly at its 46th Session for carrying out checks every five years to determine which is the highest paid civil service. The discussion of the question in the Commission brought out the complexity of defining, measuring, and comparing the remuneration systems of national civil services. The Commission recommended, and the Assembly agreed to, a two-phase approach to the problem. Once phase I has been completed—and the Assembly has not set a deadline for that exercise—the Commission is to seek further guidance from the General Assembly [A/Res/46/191, section VI].

The question of the remuneration of staff in the Professional and higher category will again be addressed by the General Assembly at its 47th Session in 1992. In particular, the Assembly decided to defer until the 47th Session a decision on the recommendations of the Commission regarding the conditions of service of staff at the Under-Secretary-General, Assistant Secretary-General, and equivalent levels [A/Res/46/191, section VII]. The Commission had carried out a review of those conditions at the request of the 45th General Assembly in Resolution 241, section V, which had been partly motivated by uneasiness over the supplementary payments by governments to their nationals serving in senior posts in the U.N. Secretariat. The Commission's recommendations had included an increase in net remuneration in a range of 7–11 percent and more generous rent subsidies [A/46/30, para. 173].

Remuneration of Staff in the General Service and Related Categories

Unlike the situation in 1990, when the General Assembly was faced with a disagreement between the ICSC and the Secretary-General over General Service salaries in New York [see *Issues/46*], the conditions of service of the General Service and related categories did not figure prominently in the Fifth Committee discussions at the Assembly's 46th Session. The Commission reported that it had carried out two surveys of best prevailing conditions: in Geneva and in Vienna. The former, which resulted in a recommendation to increase salaries and dependency allowances, was accepted by the organizations concerned and implemented as of January 1, 1991. The latter resulted in a somewhat lower salary scale, coupled with increases in dependency allowances and transitional measures to prevent temporary reductions in pay.

The ICSC also reported on the progress it had made on the review of the methodologies of the best-prevailing-conditions surveys, which had been requested in Resolution 45/241, section XIII. The 46th General Assembly noted the results of the Geneva and Vienna surveys and the related financial implications, and requested the ICSC to conclude speedily the review of the survey methodology and the study of the relativities between the terms and conditions of service of staff in the Professional and higher category and those in other categories, as well as the broader question of the recruitment and retention of staff that had been requested in section XIV. The Commission's report on these issues is to be submitted to the Assembly at its 1992 session [A/Res/46/191, section X].

The Assembly approved a new scale of **staff assessment** (the U.N. equivalent of national income taxes) for the General Service and related categories; this action had no effect on the take-home pay of the staff [A/Res/46/191, section III].

The Integrity of the U.N. Common System, and the Role and Function of the ICSC

During the year covered by its report to the 46th General Assembly, the ICSC was faced with decisions of the International Labour Organisation (ILO) and the International Telecommunication Union (ITU) to grant special benefits to their staff, which threatened to undermine the unity and cohesiveness of the common system. The two organizations had not consulted the Commission in advance.

The ILO decision was to proceed with the establishment of a voluntary thrift benefit fund, as a complement to the participation of ILO staff in the U.N. Joint Staff Pension Fund (see below). The ITU had taken two decisions: One, taken by the Administrative Council of the Union, was to set up a pension purchasing power protection insurance plan; the other, taken by the ITU Secretary-General, was to grant a special post allowance to headquarters staff at the Professional and Director levels. The Commission was informed by the ITU that the special post allowance fell under article 3.8 (b) of the Union's staff regulations, which applied when additional responsibilities were temporarily given to staff members. The implementation of the recommendations of a high-level committee, which had considered basic changes in the functioning of the ITU, imposed such additional responsibilities. The Commission was not convinced by the argument adduced by the ITU, and concluded that the Union's decision to grant special post allowances to its Professional and Director staff was incompatible with the concept of the common system [A/46/30, paras. 33–44].

In Resolution 268 on the decisions taken by the ILO and the ITU, the 45th General Assembly had already expressed concern about the potential impact of those decisions on the U.N. common system and pension system. When the question was discussed again at the 46th Session, there was unanimous support for the integrity of the common system. Several delegations went so far as to advocate sanctions against organizations belonging to the common system that did not adhere to its rules and regulations. In Resolution 191, section II, the 46th General Assembly was strongly critical of the decisions taken by the ILO and ITU. It also requested the Coordination Committee of the World Intellectual Property Organization (WIPO), which had established a working group on Professional remuneration, to seek the views of the competent common system bodies and to transmit those views to the WIPO Governing Body. The Assembly reiterated its appeal to common system organizations to refrain from seeking to establish additional entitlements and benefits for their staff, and it urged the governing bodies of those organizations to fully respect the decisions taken by the General Assembly, on the recommendation of the Commission and the Pension Board, in respect to the conditions of service of the staff.

The intergovernmental bodies and the executive heads of the specialized agencies have traditionally been jealous of their independence. They have therefore been resentful of attempts by the General Assembly to impose its primacy in matters of conditions of service and of the role assigned to the ICSC. This resentment found its expression in criticism of various aspects of the functioning of the Commission. The **interagency Administrative Committee on Coordination (ACC)**, which, though chaired by the Secretary-General of the United Nations, often tends to reflect the feelings of the specialized agencies, prepared a report in which it was critical of the alleged increasing politicization of the Commission, a lack of appreciation for the differences between the organizations in the common system, and an overburdened work program accompanied by an increasingly regulatory approach to personnel policy issues. The ACC submitted a series of recommendations relating to the selection process for appointment to the Commission, the staggering of such appointments, and the work program of the Commission and its secretariat. The ACC also felt that its comments should be available to the General Assembly when the latter considered the ICSC report [A/46/275].

The Commission has also been under fire from the staff unions and associations that have been pressing for a joint negotiating body to determine the conditions of employment and that had also put forward the idea that the ICSC should be replaced by a tripartite body, like the Pension Board. (The Board consists of representatives of the General Assembly and the governing bodies of the other member organizations of the Fund, of the executive heads, and of the participants.) The staff bodies have been critical of decisions being taken at executive meetings of the Commission, from which they were excluded.

While it would be difficult to deny that political considerations have played a part in the selection of candidates for appointment to the Commission or that competent members failed to be reelected because of the unpopularity in the Fifth Committee of policies pursued by the countries of which they happened to be nationals, the ACC cannot claim to be blameless. In particular, the ACC has not sought out qualified candidates sufficiently early to have had an impact on the choice of candidates by regional groups; it has been reluctant (for understandable reasons) to express views on the relative qualifications of the candidates; and it has tended to favor candidates who are more likely to be "friendly."

In its report to the General Assembly, the ICSC firmly rejected all allegations of politicization. It endorsed the recommendation of the ACC that the Assembly should have available to it the ACC comments when it considers the Commission's reports. It agreed that its program of work was overburdened, but pointed out that the organizations and the staff were partly to blame for that state of affairs. As for the other ACC recommendations, the ICSC either did not see any merit in them or indicated that action along the lines advocated was already being taken by the Commission itself [A/46/30, vol. II].

In Resolution 191, section I, the 46th General Assembly indicated that it was satisfied with the way the ICSC had been discharging its mandate. While acknowledging the importance of maintaining the fullest possible participation of organizations and staff in the work of the

Commission, the Assembly at the same time reaffirmed the right of the Commission to hold executive meetings.

Pension Matters

The three main points that the General Assembly considered at its 46th Session under the agenda item "U.N. pension system" were:

- the pensionable remuneration and consequent pensions of staff in the General Service and related categories;
- the pension adjustment system; and
- the methodology for determining the pensionable remuneration of ungraded officials.

Both the Pension Board and the ICSC reported to the Assembly on the first and third items. These two items will be discussed further at the Assembly's 1992 session.

The **pensionable remuneration** of staff in the General Service and related categories is determined in a manner that differs from the approach taken for the Professional and higher category. In the case of the latter, the scale of pensionable remuneration is approved for each grade and step by the General Assembly itself; the scale is expressed in U.S. dollars and is applied worldwide. By contrast, there is no worldwide scale of pensionable remuneration for the General Service and related categories; instead, there is a separate gross salary scale for each duty station. This is due to the fact that the salaries of staff in those categories are set by reference to the best prevailing conditions in the locality; the comparisons are made on a net (after-tax) basis and the salaries are expressed in local currency. To determine the corresponding pensionable remuneration, the net salary is converted into U.S. dollars at the applicable U.N. operational rate and grossed up using a scale of staff assessment (the U.N. equivalent of income tax), which is approved by the General Assembly for worldwide application. The staff assessment rates are progressive, and the bands are expressed in dollars. Certain allowances that are considered pensionable are then added to the gross salary. Since the parities of the various currencies are not constant, the pensionable remuneration of staff in the General Service and related categories varies, sometimes monthly, upwards or downwards, at all duty stations except those where the local currency is the U.S. dollar or is tied to the dollar.

It will be readily seen from the foregoing that changes in the parity of the local currency and the rates of staff assessment have a major impact on the pensionable remuneration and, consequently, on the pensions of staff in the General Service and related categories. The heavier the "taxation" through staff assessment, the higher the pensionable remuneration, especially for the more highly paid staff (because of the progressivity in the scale). A weakening of the dollar also raises pensionable remuneration. Sometimes there are aberrant results, as for instance when the U.N. operational rate of exchange is not adjusted immediately upon the devaluation of the local currency and local salary rates become inflated: An extreme case occurred a few years ago in a Latin American country where, for a couple of months until the U.N. operational rate was adjusted, the pensionable remuneration of senior-level local General Service staff was higher than that of officials at the Under-Secretary-General and comparable levels. But even if one disregards such situations, the fact remains that in high-wage countries with strong currencies (such as most West European countries), there exists an overlap between the pensionable remuneration of staff in locally recruited categories and in the Professional category. Since part of Professional pay is nonpensionable, the consequence of the overlap is that a retired Professional staff member may get a smaller pension than does a former General Service staff member with the same length of service whose take-home pay had been lower than his own. This situation has given rise to concern in the General Assembly.

Both the Pension Board and the ICSC have given detailed consideration to the question whether the methodology described above should be changed and, if so, how that should be done. In the Board no agreement could be reached on whether to retain the existing methodology (the course favored by the staff associations and, at least for the time being, by the Executive Heads) or to replace it by an alternative approach such as establishing pensionable remuneration (or pensions, or both) by reference to local practice, by using the "income replacement" method already applicable to Professional staff, or by using local tax rates instead of the staff assessment for grossing up local salaries. The opinions in the ICSC were also divided. Both bodies recognized the complexity of the problem and the potential magnitude of the impact of an eventual decision on the pensions of large numbers of staff (staff in the General Service and related categories account for well over half the total staff of the organizations in the U.N. system); indeed, a solution advantageous to the staff at some duty stations might adversely affect staff at other duty stations.

In the circumstances, only limited action was taken by the General Assembly at its 46th Session. As has already been noted, the Assembly approved a new scale of staff assessment; this scale raised somewhat the gross salary of staff with incomes of up to $20,000 while reducing the gross salary of staff with incomes above that amount. The new scale will be applied at each duty station as of the date of the next adjustment of the local salary scale, subject to transitional arrangements that protect the current levels of pensionable remuneration [A/Res/46/191, section III]. The Assembly having concurred with the conclusions of the Commission and the Board that further studies were required, the related recommendations are to be submitted to the Assembly's 47th Session. At the same time, the 46th Assembly appeared to rule out retention of the current methodology by noting in the preamble to Resolution 192, section II, "the positions in the Commission that the current arrangements have given rise to inconsistencies and anomalies and that therefore retention of the current methodology without change is not a viable option."

The basic pension paid by the U.N. Pension Fund is denominated in U.S. dollars; after award the benefit is periodically adjusted to compensate for cost-of-living increases in the U.S. But only a portion of the staff of the organizations in the U.N. system retire in the United States or in countries whose currency is linked to the dollar. When the value of the U.S. dollar in terms of other major currencies declined precipitously in the 1970s following the collapse of the system of fixed parities, which dated back to the Bretton Woods agreement, pensioners living in many non-dollar countries experienced large losses in the purchasing power of their pensions.

Remedial measures were taken by the General Assembly on the recommendation of the Pension Board. Over the years, the **pension adjustment system** grew in complexity. The main characteristics of the system as it gradually evolved are: (a) the calculation of two initial amounts for each benefit, one in U.S. dollars (the "dollar track") and the other in the currency of the retired individual's country of residence (the "local track"), with the initial local currency amount calculated using a 36-month average exchange rate at the time of retirement; and (b) when calculating the local track, the addition to the initial dollar pension of an amount that varies from country to country and that is payable only to retirees who reside in high-cost countries (this addition is referred to as the "Washington formula" because the related agreement was hammered out at a meeting of the Pension Board held in Washington, D.C.). The Washington formula as originally approved did not apply in countries where the cost of living measured in U.S. dollars was less than 22 percent higher than in New York; in the countries where the formula was applied, the extra benefit was calculated by reference not to the entire average pensionable remuneration of a participant but to an amount not exceeding the pensionable remuneration for the top step of grade P-2. The pension on the dollar track is adjusted for cost-of-living increases in the United States; the adjustments on the local-currency track reflect cost-of-living increases in the country of residence. The pensioner is entitled to the larger of the two amounts, subject to a limitation: When the adjusted dollar pension is higher, the amount payable cannot exceed the adjusted local currency amount by more than 20 percent. This system is known as the two-track system with a 20 percent cap.

Because the system was deliberately designed, for cost reasons, to provide only partial compensation for inflation and currency fluctuations, pensioners living in high-cost strong-currency countries saw the purchasing power of their pensions decline, sometimes by substantial amounts. The continued weakness of the U.S. dollar since the mid-1980s led the Pension Board to recommend, and the General Assembly to approve, a number of additional temporary measures, adding to the complexity of the pension adjustment system.

For staff in the Professional and higher category, the scale of pensionable remuneration has been calculated in such a way as to ensure for pensioners retiring in New York a so-called income replacement level of 50 percent after 25 years of contributory service (as the comparison is made between a pre-tax pension and a post-tax take-home pay, the true income replacement level is below 50 percent). In high-cost strong-currency countries the "income replacement level" has been lower than in New York, and this situation gave rise to great dissatisfaction, especially among staff who had served in Europe and retired in European countries. It was that dissatisfaction with the level of benefits payable by the U.N. Pension Fund that led the Administrative Council of the ITU to set up a pension purchasing power protection insurance plan and played a role in the decision of the ILO to set up a voluntary thrift benefit fund (see above).

After struggling with these complex issues for two years, the Pension Board submitted to the General Assembly, and the Assembly approved, a liberalized Washington formula for participants in the Professional and higher category, which lowered the threshold of applicability and increased the amount to be added in calculating the initial local currency pension. For separations after March 31, 1992, the add-on is calculated by reference to the pensionable remuneration for the top step of grade P-4 (instead of P-2), and the "formula" is applied in all countries where the cost of living expressed in U.S. dollars exceeds that in New York by 5 percent (instead of 22 percent). In countries where the Washington formula, as adjusted, is applied, the percentage increase in the pension attributable to the cost-of-living difference is approximately 3 percentage points lower than that difference. Thus, while the principle that there should not be full compensation for cost-of-living differences between retirees' countries of residence has been maintained, the gap between high-cost strong-currency countries and New York has been greatly narrowed, and the income replacement level in the former countries has been raised to close to the New York level. In the circumstances, the ITU will not implement its proposed pension purchasing power protection insurance plan.

While the General Assembly approved the changes in the pension adjustment system recommended by the Pension Board, it was uneasy about the potential cost implications. The Assembly endorsed the views of the ACABQ that the Board, on the basis of experience with actual costs, should determine whether any fine tuning of the modification was warranted in order to limit costs; the Assembly asked the Board to ensure that changes in the pension adjustment system do not require increases in the financial liabilities of member states. The Board was requested to continue at its next regular session (to be held in June 1992) to search for economy measures, including in particular a change in the "cap" provision. This provision has been criticized in the Fifth Committee on the ground that it can provide adjustments that are larger than what is needed to maintain the purchasing power of pensions [A/Res/46/192, section IV].

Except for the Secretary-General of the United Nations and the executive heads of the International Civil Aviation Organization and the Universal Postal Union (the latter is not a member of the U.N. Pension Fund), all the executive heads of the organizations in the U.N. system and all other **ungraded officials** are participants in the U.N. Pension Fund. In the past there was one level of pensionable remuneration for the executive heads of the "major" agencies (such as ILO or FAO), for the Administrator of UNDP, and for the Director-General for Development and International Economic Cooperation (a post abolished in the 1992 reorganization of the top echelon of the U.N. Secretariat), and—with a few exceptions—another level for the executive heads of the smaller agencies. In 1984 the General Assembly reduced the pensionable remuneration of the ungraded officials in the United Nations itself and its associated programs, and imposed an upper limit on the amount of a pension for other than ungraded officials; the pensionable remuneration of the Administrator and the Director-General was also reduced on the initiative of the Secretary-General. Not all the specialized agencies followed the General Assembly's lead. When, subsequently, the Regulations of the Pension Fund were amended to incorporate a schedule of pensionable remuneration for the Professional and higher category, that schedule extended only up to and including the Under-Secretary-General level. The pensionable remuneration of the Administrator and the Director-General has been determined since April 1987 by reference to the pensionable remuneration for the top step of level D-2. Currently, there are major differences in the pensionable remuneration of the executive heads of the specialized agencies.

At the request of the 45th General Assembly in Resolution 242, section II, both the ICSC and the Pension Board have considered this departure from the common system. The Pension Board could not reach a consensus on the issues involved. The Commission's recommendation was that all ungraded officials (whether appointed or elected) who are participants in the U.N. Pension Fund should have their pensionable remuneration determined in accordance with the procedure used by the United Nations. At the same time, the Commission recognized that the governing bodies of the various agencies are free to make pension arrangements for their ungraded officials outside the U.N. Pension Fund.

The General Assembly endorsed the Commission's approach. It urged the governing bodies of the member organizations of the Fund, while taking into account the need to protect acquired rights derived from their earlier decisions, to review the levels of the pensionable remuneration of their ungraded officials who are currently participants in the Fund with a view to eliminating the divergencies from the levels established on the basis of the methodology recommended by the ICSC, which those governing bodies were urged to adopt. The General Assembly agreed that in the event a governing body decides that its elected officials should not be participants in the Fund, the alternative pension arrangements to be determined by that governing body should take into account the desirability of establishing some comparability in the pension arrangements applicable to such officials [A/Res/46/192, section III].

The question of the pensionable remuneration of executive heads is likely to be considered again at the 47th General Assembly, because in Resolution 192 the 46th Assembly requested the ICSC to submit recommendations regarding guidelines for determining the pension arrangements for ungraded officials who do not become participants in the Fund, as well as appropriate monitoring procedures. The Pension Board has been requested by the Assembly to recommend amendments to the Fund's Regulations that would incorporate provisions governing the pensionable remuneration of ungraded officials, and to extend the provisions that place a limit on the highest levels of pension to cover all participants in the Fund, including ungraded officials.

Index